LIBRARY SCIENCE ANNUAL

VOLUME 2

1986

LIBRARY SCIENCE ANNUAL

VOLUME 2

1986

Bohdan S. Wynar EDITOR

Heather Cameron ASSOCIATE EDITOR

ASSISTANT EDITORS
Anna Grace Patterson
Hannah L. Kelminson

1986   **LIBRARIES UNLIMITED**
LITTLETON, COLORADO

NORFOLK, VIRGINIA

*Ref
Z
666
.L45
1986
v.2*

Copyright © 1986 Libraries Unlimited, Inc.
All Rights Reserved
Printed in the United States of America

No part of this publication may be reproduced, stored in a
retrieval system, or transmitted, in any form or by any means,
electronic, mechanical, photocopying, recording, or otherwise,
without the prior written permission of the publisher.

LIBRARIES UNLIMITED, INC.
P.O. Box 263
Littleton, Colorado 80160-0263

ISBN 0-87287-541-5
ISSN 8755-2108

Library Science Annual is a companion volume to *American Reference Books Annual.*

Libraries Unlimited books are bound with Type II nonwoven material that meets and exceeds National Association of State Textbook Administrators' Type II nonwoven material specifications Class A through E.

LYMAN BEECHER BROOKS LIBRARY
NORFOLK, VIRGINIA

Contents

NOV 0 8 1986

Part III
REVIEWS OF PERIODICALS

Part IV
ABSTRACTS OF LIBRARY SCIENCE
DISSERTATIONS
by Gail A. Schlachter

Publications Cited

FORM OF CITATION	PUBLICATION TITLE
AL	American Libraries
ARBA	American Reference Books Annual
BL	Booklist
BR	Book Report
C&RL	College & Research Libraries
CLJ	Canadian Library Journal
EL	Emergency Librarian
JAL	Journal of Academic Librarianship
LJ	Library Journal
RBB	Reference Books Bulletin
RQ	RQ
SLJ	School Library Journal
SLMQ	School Library Media Quarterly
TN	Top of the News
VOYA	Voice of Youth Advocates
WLB	Wilson Library Bulletin

Introduction

In their follow-up study to Chen and Galvin's landmark 1975 report, "Reviewing the Literature of Librarianship" (*ARBA* 75), Webreck and Weedman have concluded that the status of the professional library review literature had not changed much between 1975 and 1983 (see pp. 3-12). Specifically, their analysis of the reviewing mechanisms of the professional library literature for 1983 found that even though "more monographs are published each year ... a smaller percentage of the total are reviewed in the professional media. The reviews that do appear are concentrated on a minority of the titles published, and there are a core number of journals which tend to duplicate the coverage of these titles.... The recommendations for these titles are usually positive" (p. 12).

These findings parallel the assertions about the professional library review literature made by the editors of *Library Science Annual* in last year's inaugural volume. Accordingly, *LSA* volume 2 has retained the same broad objectives and scope of that first effort:

1. To review all English-language monographs and reference books in library science published in a year, not just selected or recommended titles. Volume 1 reviewed 253 titles, principally U.S., a few Canadian imprints, and some other imprints distributed in the United States. Volume 2, extending coverage to Canadian imprints, reviews 305 titles.

2. To evaluate systematically all English-language library science periodicals and indexing services. Each year, the editors of *LSA* will select titles for review. Forty-two periodicals published in the United States and Canada were reviewed in volume 1, including some of national or regional interest and some that are subject-oriented. Volume 2 reviews 22 titles and begins coverage of library science databases with reviews of LIBRARY LITERATURE (WILSONLINE) and LIBRARY & INFORMATION SCIENCE ABSTRACTS (LISA).

3. To highlight research trends in library science by providing abstracts of the most significant doctoral dissertations produced in a year. For volume 1, Gail A. Schlachter contributed abstracts of 32 dissertations. For volume 2, Schlachter has expanded coverage to 50 abstracts.

4. To report on the production and distribution of knowledge in library science through essays by prominent library educators, practitioners, and publishers. Specific areas will be emphasized in each volume. For example, volume 1 included several essays on library science publishing. Volume 2 features several important articles on reviewing. Sue Webreck and Judith Weedman's revealing analysis of the professional library review literature, cited earlier, is followed by thoughtful essays on reference book reviewing by Jim Rettig, on children's and young adult book reviewing by Claire England and Adele Fasick, and on book reviewing in Canada by Gwynneth Evans. Next come two interesting surveys: one on library ephemera by Norman Stevens and one on library science histories by Laurel Grotzinger.

Completing part 1 is Director of Publishing Services at ALA Gary Facente's tribute to ALA's publishing division. It is appropriate that ALA's substantial contribution to library science publishing be lauded in this, its 100th anniversary year.

Articles in volume 3 of *LSA* will focus on collection development, and several prominent library science publishers will be invited to contribute profiles of their firms.

5. To attempt, over time, a permanent record of the intellectual activity in librarianship and to impose bibliographic control over the literature.

Certain categories of materials are not covered in *LSA*. Those include specific periodical articles, publications of vanity presses, and certain inhouse publications which are institution-specific. For the time being, limited distribution research reports, audiovisual materials, and some continuing education "kits" produced by ALA divisions or affiliates will not be covered.

REVIEWING POLICY

The editors of *Library Science Annual* have applied the same rigorous reviewing standards that *American Reference Books Annual* is noted for. The *LSA* staff keeps an up-to-date list of well-qualified library educators and practitioners so that books may be assigned for review appropriately. This year *LSA* has used the services of over 154 librarians and scholars at libraries and universities throughout the United States and Canada; their names are listed following this introduction. Reviews in *LSA* are signed as a matter of editorial policy.

Standard instructions for *LSA* reviewers, prepared by the editorial staff, are briefly summarized here: Reviewers should discuss the work and then provide well-documented critical comments, positive or negative. Such things as the usefulness of the given work; organization, execution, and pertinence of contents; prose style; format; availability of supplementary materials (e.g., indexes, appendices); and similarity to other works and/or previous editions are normally discussed. Reviewers are encouraged to note intended audience and/or level, but the review need not conclude with specific recommendations for purchase.

All the materials reviewed are given full bibliographic description, and citations to other review sources are given for books.

ARRANGEMENT

LSA is arranged in four parts. Part 1 contains 7 essays contributed by authors well known in Canada and the United States, treating various library science publishing areas. Part 2, comprising reviews of 305 books, is arranged into subjects, including such areas as acquisitions, cataloging, comparative and international librarianship, management, school library media centers, and special libraries and collections. Reviews of 22 periodicals, arranged under the headings National, Subject-oriented, Regional, and Databases, compose part 3. The fourth and final part has abstracts of 50 dissertations listed alphabetically by title.

AUDIENCE

We hope that all professional librarians will benefit from *Library Science Annual*. It has been created with the needs of students and researchers, practitioners and library educators in mind. We believe that publishers and other information professionals will also find much of interest. We urge librarians to contribute their suggestions for improvement, and to support our efforts to create an outstanding annual review for librarians in the United States and internationally.

ACKNOWLEDGMENTS

In closing, we wish to express our gratitude to the many contributors without whose support this second volume of *LSA* could not have been compiled. We would also like to thank the members of our staff who were instrumental in the preparation of *LSA*: assistant editors Hannah L. Kelminson and Anna Grace Patterson; as well as Judy Gay Matthews, Kay Minnis, and Gloria Powell. Special recognition should be given to Mary Ann Goff, who compiled the author/title index and proofread this volume, and to Debbie Burnham-Kidwell, who compiled the subject index.

Editorial Staff

Bohdan S. Wynar, Editor-in-Chief
Heather Cameron, Associate Editor
Anna Grace Patterson and Hannah L. Kelminson, Assistant Editors

Contributors

Donald C. Adcock, Director of Library Services, Glen Ellyn District 41, Ill.

Ann Allan, Assoc. Professor, School of Library Science, Kent State Univ., Ohio.

Mohammed M. Aman, Dean, School of Library Science, Univ. of Wisconsin, Milwaukee.

Frank J. Anderson, Librarian Emeritus, Sandor Teszler Library, Wofford College, Spartanburg, S.C.

James D. Anderson, Assoc. Professor, Graduate School of Library and Information Studies, Rutgers Univ., New Brunswick, N.J.

Margaret Anderson, Assoc. Professor, Faculty of Library and Information Science, Univ. of Toronto.

Theodora Andrews, Pharmacy Librarian and Professor of Library Science, Purdue Univ., West Lafayette, Ind.

Gary D. Barber, Coordinator of Reference Services, Daniel A. Reed Library, State Univ. of New York, Fredonia.

Ruth E. Bauner, Morris Library, Southern Illinois Univ., Carbondale.

Carol Willsey Bell, Investigator, Occupational and Physical Therapy Board of Ohio, Columbus.

Mary K. Biagini, Asst. Professor, School of Library Science, Kent State Univ., Ohio.

Ron Blazek, Professor, School of Library Science, Florida State Univ., Tallahassee.

Marjorie E. Bloss, Asst. Director, Technical Services and Automation, Illinois Institute of Technology, Chicago.

George S. Bobinski, Dean, School of Information and Library Studies, State Univ. of New York at Buffalo, N.Y.

Barbara E. Brown, Head, General Cataloging Section, Library of Parliament, Ottawa.

Robert H. Burger, Assoc. Professor of Library Administration, Univ. of Illinois, Urbana-Champaign.

Lois Buttlar, Asst. Director, Instructional Resources Center, and Asst. Professor, Dept. of Educational Psychology, Administration, Technology, and Foundations, Kent State Univ., Ohio.

Greg Byerly, Coordinator of Library Automation, Kent State Libraries, Kent State Univ., Ohio.

Heather Cameron, Staff, Libraries Unlimited.

Esther Jane Carrier, Reference Librarian, Lock Haven Univ. of Pennsylvania, Lock Haven.

Jefferson D. Caskey, Professor of Library Science and Instructional Media, Western Kentucky Univ., Bowling Green.

Joseph H. Cataio, Chicago.

Larry Chasen, Manager, General Electric Space Systems Division Library, Philadelphia, Pa.

Frances Neel Cheney, Professor Emeritus, Dept. of Library Science, George Peabody College for Teachers, Vanderbilt Univ., Nashville, Tenn.

Boyd Childress, Social Sciences Reference Librarian, Auburn Univ., Ala.

Margaret E. Chisholm, Director, School of Librarianship, Univ. of Washington, Seattle.

John W. Collins III, Librarian of the Graduate School of Education, Gutman Library, Harvard Univ., Cambridge, Mass.

C. Donald Cook, Professor, Faculty of Library and Information Science, Univ. of Toronto.

Judith Ann Copler, Head, Interlibrary Services, Indiana Univ., Bloomington.

Bill J. Corbin, Lecturer in Library and Information Science, Vanderbilt Univ., Nashville, Tenn.

Emmett Corry, OSF, Assoc. Professor, Library and Information Science, St. John's Univ., Jamaica, N.Y.

Betty Costa, Library Media Consultant, Think Small Computers, Inc., Hayden, Colo.

Camille Côté, Assoc. Professor, Graduate School of Library Science, McGill Univ., Montreal.

Brenda Coven, Reference Librarian, State Univ. of New York at Stony Brook.

Richard J. Cox, Head, Governmental Records Div., Alabama Dept. of Archives and History, Montgomery.

Milton H. Crouch, Asst. Director for Reader Services, Bailey/Howe Library, Univ. of Vermont, Burlington.

William J. Dane, Supervising Art and Music Librarian, Newark Public Library, N.J.

Donald G. Davis, Jr., Assoc. Professor, Graduate School of Library and Information Science, Univ. of Texas, Austin.

Carol A. Doll, Asst. Professor, Davis College, Univ. of South Carolina, Columbia.

G. Kim Dority, formerly Staff, Libraries Unlimited.

Thomas Wm. Downen, Assoc. Professor, Dept. of Instructional Technology, Univ. of Georgia, Athens.

Judy Dyki, Library Director, Cranbrook Academy of Art, Bloomfield Hills, Mich.

Michael B. Eisenberg, Asst. Professor, School of Information Studies, Syracuse Univ., N.Y.

Claire England, Assoc. Professor, Faculty of Library Science, Univ. of Toronto.

G. Edward Evans, Librarian of Tozzer Library, Harvard Univ., Cambridge, Mass.

Gwynneth Evans, Executive Secretary, National Library of Canada, Ottawa.

Gary Facente, Assoc. Executive Director for Publishing Services, American Library Association, Chicago.

Joyce Duncan Falk, Data Services Coordinator and Reference Librarian, Library of Univ. of California, Irvine.

Evan Ira Farber, Librarian, Earlham College, Richmond, Ind.

Adele M. Fasick, Professor, Faculty of Library and Information Science, Univ. of Toronto.

Susan J. Freiband, Consultant, Library and Information Services, Washington, D.C.

Elizabeth Frick, Assoc. Professor, School of Library Service, Dalhousie Univ., Halifax.

Mary Ardeth Gaylord, Reference Librarian, Kent State Univ., Ohio.

Ray Gerke, Sterling C. Evans Library, Texas A&M Univ., College Station.

Edwin S. Gleaves, Chair, Dept. of Library Science, George Peabody College, Vanderbilt Univ., Nashville, Tenn.

Allie Wise Goudy, Assoc. Professor and Music Librarian, Western Illinois Univ., Macomb.

Frank Wm. Goudy, Assoc. Professor, Univ. Libraries, Western Illinois Univ., Macomb.

Suzanne K. Gray, formerly Coordinator of Science, Boston Public Library, Mass.

Laurel Grotzinger, Dean and Chief Research Officer, Western Michigan Univ., Kalamazoo.

Leonard Grundt, Professor, Library Dept., Nassau Community College, Garden City, N.Y.

Mark Y. Herring, Director, E. W. King Memorial Library, King College, Bristol, Tenn.

Joe A. Hewitt, Assoc. Univ. Librarian for Technical Services, Univ. of North Carolina, Chapel Hill.

Sally Holmes Holtze, Editor, *Fifth Book of Junior Authors & Illustrators.*

Helen Howard, Director and Assoc. Professor, Graduate School of Library & Information Studies, McGill Univ., Montreal.

Janet R. Ivey, Head of Support Services, Boynton Beach City Library, Fla.

E. B. Jackson, Professor Emeritus, Graduate School of Library and Information Science, Univ. of Texas, Austin.

Thomas A. Karel, Asst. Director for Public Services, Shadek-Fackenthal Library, Franklin and Marshall College, Lancaster, Pa.

Linda S. Keir, Reference Librarian, Univ. of Dayton, Ohio.

Dean H. Keller, Assoc. Director of Public Service and Collection Development, Kent State Libraries, Kent State Univ., Ohio.

Thomas G. Kirk, College Librarian, Berea College, Ky.

Susan Beverly Kuklin, Director of Santa Clara County Law Library, San Jose, Calif.

Shirley Lambert, Staff, Libraries Unlimited.

Mary Larsgaard, Asst. Director, Special Collections, Arthur Lakes Library, Colorado School of Mines, Golden.

Hwa-Wei Lee, Director of Libraries and Professor, Ohio Univ., Athens.

Norma J. Livo, Professor, College of Education, Univ. of Colorado, Denver.

Sara R. Mack, Professor Emeritus, Kutztown Univ., Pa.

Kathleen McCullough, Bibliographer, School of Humanities, Social Science and Education, and Assoc. Professor of Library Science, Purdue Univ., West Lafayette, Ind.

Margaret McKinley, Head, Serials Dept., Univ. Library, Univ. of California, Los Angeles.

Edward P. Miller, Consultant, Denver, Colo.

Marilyn L. Miller, Assoc. Professor, School of Library Science, Univ. of North Carolina, Chapel Hill.

Paula Montgomery, Chief, School Library Media Services, Maryland State Dept. of Education, Baltimore.

P. Grady Morein, Univ. Librarian, Univ. of Evansville, Ind.

Mary Lee Morris, Catalog Librarian and Instructor in Library Science, Golden Library, Eastern New Mexico Univ., Portales.

Mary Lou Mosley, Instructional Designer, Educational Development, Maricopa Community Colleges, Phoenix, Ariz.

K. Mulliner, Assistant to the Director of Libraries, Ohio Univ. Library, Athens.

James M. Murray, Law Librarian and Asst. Professor, Gonzaga Univ. Law Library, Spokane, Wash.

Danuta A. Nitecki, Assoc. Director for Public Services, Univ. of Maryland Libraries, College Park.

O. Gene Norman, Head, Reference Dept., Indiana State Univ. Library, Terre Haute.

Judith E. H. Odiorne, Library Consultant, Oxford, Conn.

Jeanne Osborn, formerly Professor, School of Library Science, Univ. of Iowa, Iowa City.

Berniece M. Owen, Catalog Librarian, School of Law Library, Gonzaga Univ., Spokane, Wash.

Joseph W. Palmer, Assoc. Professor, School of Information and Library Studies, State Univ. of New York, Buffalo.

Jane Pearlmutter, Program Coordinator, Library and Information Studies, Communication Programs, Univ. of Wisconsin, Madison.

Daniel F. Phelan, Media Library, Ryerson Polytechnical Institute, Toronto.

Edwin D. Posey, Engineering Librarian, Purdue Univ. Libraries, West Lafayette, Ind.

Gloria Palmeri Powell, Staff, Libraries Unlimited.

Ann E. Prentice, Director, Graduate School of Library and Information Science, Univ. of Tennessee, Knoxville.

Gary R. Purcell, Professor, Graduate School of Library and Information Science, Univ. of Tennessee, Knoxville.

Richard H. Quay, Social Science Librarian, Miami Univ., Oxford, Ohio.

Hannelore B. Rader, Director, Library/Learning Center, Univ. of Wisconsin-Parkside.

Kristin Ramsdell, Asst. Librarian, Meyer Library, Stanford Univ., Palo Alto, Calif.

James Rettig, Reference Librarian, Univ. of Illinois, Chicago.

James Rice, Assoc. Professor, School of Library and Information Science, Univ. of Iowa, Iowa City.

Philip R. Rider, Instructor of English, Northern Illinois Univ., DeKalb.

Jane Robbins-Carter, Director and Professor, School of Library and Information Studies, Univ. of Wisconsin, Madison.

Ilene F. Rockman, Assoc. Librarian, California Polytechnic State Univ., San Luis Obispo.

Antonio Rodriguez-Buckingham, Professor, School of Library Service, Univ. of Southern Mississippi, Hattiesburg.

A. Robert Rogers, Dean (deceased 1985), School of Library Science, Kent State Univ., Ohio.

JoAnn V. Rogers, Assoc. Professor, College of Library Science, Univ. of Kentucky, Lexington.

Samuel Rothstein, Professor, Univ. of British Columbia, Vancouver.

Michael Rogers Rubin, Attorney, United States Dept. of Commerce, Washington, D.C.

Rhea Joyce Rubin, Library Consultant, Oakland, Calif.

Edmund F. SantaVicca, Humanities Reference Bibliographer, Cleveland State Univ. Libraries, Ohio.

Pat R. Scales, Librarian, Greenville Middle School and Adjunct Instructor, Furman Univ., Greenville, S.C.

Gail A. Schlachter, President, Reference Services Press, Los Angeles.

Isabel Schon, Professor, College of Education, Arizona State Univ., Tempe.

Anthony C. Schulzetenberg, Professor, Center for Information Media, St. Cloud Univ., Minn.

Eleanor Elving Schwartz, Coordinator, Library/Media Program, and Assoc. Professor, Kean College of New Jersey, Union.

LeRoy C. Schwarzkopf, formerly Government Documents Librarian, Univ. of Maryland, College Park.

Gerald R. Shields, Asst. Dean, School of Information and Library Studies, State Univ. of New York, Buffalo.

Bruce A. Shuman, Reference Librarian, Johnson Free Public Library, Hackensack, N.J.

Wesley Simonton, formerly Director, Library School, Univ. of Minnesota, Minneapolis.

Tom Smith, Serials Librarian, Himmelfarb Health Sciences Library, George Washington Univ. Medical Center, Washington, D.C.

Jeanne Somers, Asst. Director for Technical Services, Kent State Univ. Libraries, Kent State Univ., Ohio.

Natalia Sonevytsky, Head, Reference Dept., Barnard College Library, New York, N.Y.

Barbara Sproat, Librarian, Denver Public Libraries, Colo.

Normal D. Stevens, Univ. Librarian, Univ. of Connecticut, Storrs.

Leon J. Stout, Univ. Archivist, Pennsylvania State Univ. Libraries, University Park.

Robert D. Stueart, Dean, Graduate School of Library and Information Science, Simmons College, Boston, Mass.

James H. Sweetland, Asst. Professor, School of Library and Information Science, Univ. of Wisconsin, Milwaukee.

Rebecca L. Thomas, Elementary School Library/Media Specialist, Onaway Elementary School, Shaker Heights, Ohio.

Lawrence S. Thompson, Professor of Classics, Univ. of Kentucky, Lexington.

Andrew G. Torok, Assoc. Professor, Northern Illinois Univ., DeKalb.

Dean Tudor, Professor, School of Journalism, Ryerson Polytechnical Institute, Toronto.

Phyllis J. Van Orden, Professor and Assoc. Dean, School of Library and Information Studies, Florida State Univ., Tallahassee.

Carol J. Veitch, Director, Currituck County Library, Barco, N.C.

Kathleen J. Voigt, Reference Librarian, Univ. of Toledo, Ohio.

Susan J. Webreck, School of Library Science, Univ. of Michigan, Ann Arbor.

Judith Weedman, School of Library Science, Univ. of Michigan, Ann Arbor.

Jean Weihs, Course Director, Library Techniques, Seneca College of Applied Arts & Technology, North York, Ont.

Darlene E. Weingand, Asst. Professor, Univ. of Wisconsin, Madison.

Lucille Whalen, Assoc. Dean and Professor, School of Library and Information Science, State Univ. of New York, Albany.

Wayne E. Wiegand, Assoc. Professor, Library Science, Univ. of Kentucky, Lexington.

Constance D. Williams, formerly Staff, Libraries Unlimited.

Robert V. Williams, Assoc. Professor, College of Librarianship and Information Science, Univ. of South Carolina, Columbia.

Wiley J. Williams, Professor, School of Library Science, Kent State Univ., Ohio.

Glenn R. Wittig, Asst. Professor, School of Library Science, Univ. of Southern Mississippi, Hattiesburg.

Hensley C. Woodbridge, Professor, Dept. of Foreign Languages, Southern Illinois Univ., Carbondale.

Lubomyr R. Wynar, Professor, School of Library Science, and Director, Program for the Study of Ethnic Publications in the United States, Kent State Univ., Ohio.

Virginia E. Yagello, Head, Chemistry Library, Ohio State Univ., Columbus.

A. Neil Yerkey, Asst. Professor, School of Information and Library Studies, State Univ. of New York, Buffalo.

Arthur P. Young, Dean of Libraries, Univ. of Rhode Island, Kingston.

Marie Zuk, Language Arts Coordinator, Carman-Ainsworth School District, Flint, Mich.

Anita Zutis, Librarian, Brooklyn Public Library, N.Y.

Part I
ESSAYS

Professional Library Literature:
An Analysis of the Review Literature*

Book reviews are a critical component in the professional and scholarly literature of a field. They perform a number of functions which are vital to the communication process. This study examines factors which influence how well these functions are performed by the review media for the professional and scholarly literature in the field of library science.

Reviews serve to alert readers of the journals in which they appear to the existence of new works. For many professionals, this may be the only systematic way of learning about newly published books in the field which might be of value to them. For individuals selecting books for library collections, reviews also serve as notification of materials which should be considered for purchase.

Book reviews are generally considered to be evaluative in purpose. They serve a gatekeeping function in the channels of formal, published communication; no reader or selector can—or probably should—acquire everything which is published, and reviews provide a tool for deciding which books are worth expenditure of time and money.

In addition, reviews add to the general knowledge of the individuals who read them. Reviews provide an awareness of what subjects are currently of professional concern to practitioners and scholars, some summary of the opinions and facts which constitute the books, and the reviewer's judgment of the value and accuracy of that content.

Reviews provide the first and in many cases the only public feedback to the author of a book. Individual reactions may or may not be communicated by colleagues on a personal basis; an evaluative review provides a public statement of the reception of a work by the profession. While each review expresses only one reader's opinion, if a book receives multiple reviews, they collectively provide some assessment of the work's perceived value to the audience for which it was written. Since the communication of an author's ideas to others is the implicit purpose of publication, even one review holds significance for the author as an indication of the success of that communication. Although authors may feel for various reasons that reviews do not provide trustworthy information for them, the reviews still have significance as the public, formalized statement of response to the book.

Reviews may also contribute to (or detract from) an author's professional standing, as they assess both the contribution of the work and in some cases the reputation of the author.

Reviews thus serve as intermediaries between an author and other professionals and scholars in the field, providing information to each about the other. In 1975, Ching-Chih Chen and Thomas J. Galvin reported on the state of the art of reviewing in the profession of librarianship.[1] After an examination of the reviews of monographs published in 1971, they concluded that improvement was needed in the reviewing process. The object of this report is to assess the situation twelve years later, examining the reviewing of monographs published in 1983.

*The authors wish to acknowledge with thanks the assistance of Mark Patrick in collection of data.

Since 1971, there has been a 42 percent increase in the number of monographs published per year and a 45 percent increase in the average cost per book.[2,3] This increase is reflected in the professional literature of library science, with a 31 percent change from 1971 to 1983 (see table 1).

Table 1.

	1971	1983
New books published in U.S.	24,288	42,236
New library science books published in U.S.	222	321
Average cost per book	$13.25	$24.22

Those involved in collection development in library science or who wish to select monographs for their own reading are faced with difficult choices regarding which works to include and which to exclude. The results of a study such as this can be useful in assessing the value of reviews for this decision-making process.

The findings and conclusions of the Chen-Galvin study are summarized in the first section of this report in order to provide information which will be used for comparative analyses. The second section outlines the method used by the current investigators, and reports the findings of this study. Results of the Chen-Galvin study are highlighted in conjunction with the reporting of the current findings, to provide the perspective of change over time.

THE CHEN-GALVIN STUDY

Scope of the Study

The purpose of the Chen-Galvin study was "to describe the present state of reviewing of current English language monographs in the field of library science, as reflected in American and Canadian journals."[4] The imprint year chosen for the investigation was 1971; works surveyed were English-language monographs in the field of library science published in North America or available in North America through normal distribution channels. The total number of such titles for 1971 was 222; 164 of those titles were reviewed in at least one professional periodical. A total of 372 reviews were located and examined; those reviews were found in twenty-two periodical publications. The following areas were addressed by the study:

1. The portion of the literature which could be identified through the primary announcement media.

2. The existence of reviews for this literature in selected American and Canadian professional library periodicals.

3. The works receiving the greatest number of reviews.

4. The relative comprehensiveness of the various review media.

5. The timeliness of the review media.

6. The depth of the reviews.

7. The extent to which the reviews evaluated rather than simply described the works.

8. The frequency of negative reviews.

9. The number of reviewers involved and their affiliations.

Methodology of the Chen-Galvin Study

As the first stage of the study, the investigators compiled a list of monographs meeting the selection criteria through a search of classes 020 through 029 in *Book Publishing Record*, *Publishers Weekly*'s "Weekly Record," *Forthcoming Books*, and the actual review media. A thirty-month period was used, from January 1971 through June 1973.

The second stage of the study identified and examined a list of twenty-nine "high yield" professional periodicals published in the United States and Canada. These journals were the ones expected by the investigators to be the most important review media for library science monographs. They were thought to review a significant number of professional titles, to provide more than simple descriptive information, to be addressed to a national audience, and to be published at least semiannually.[5] Seven journals were subsequently omitted from the study because they did not meet these conditions during the time period in question, resulting in a total of twenty-two journals considered to be high-yield review media.

All issues of each journal were systematically searched for reviews, and those reviews were recorded. Short, unsigned, exclusively descriptive announcements were omitted. The following data were gathered: title of the work reviewed, author, source and date of the review, name of the reviewer, length of review, and the reviewer's evaluation of the work.

Results of the Chen-Galvin Study

Seventy-five percent of the monographs were announced through the standard media, and thus readily accessible to selectors in search of professional library science publications. Twenty-five percent of those titles, however, never appeared in the announcement media; for them, the only access was through the reviews which eventually appeared. This group included titles from North American trade publishers, university presses, and professional organizations; only thirteen (23.6 percent of the non-announced titles) were published outside North America.

Of the 222 new titles identified with 1971 imprints, 164 (74 percent) were reviewed in the twenty-two high-yield journals. The highest number of library science titles reviewed in any single medium was 87, 39 percent of all titles identified; the periodical was *Library Journal*. Second highest was 74, or 33 percent, in *Canadian Library Journal*. The percentage dropped steeply at that point to 14 percent in *College and Research Libraries*.

Significant duplication existed in review coverage of the titles. Forty-three percent of all titles identified were reviewed in more than one journal. Of these 95 titles, 76 percent were reviewed in *Library Journal*. Chen and Galvin estimate that using only the five highest-yield journals, selectors of library science monographs would have access to more than four-fifths of the new titles in the field being reviewed by the major journals.

Chen and Galvin also examined length of time between date of publication for a monograph and the appearance of a review. Precise publication dates could be determined for 109 of the monographs. The average time lag for these was found to be 8.46 months. When only those journals reviewing twenty or more of the monographs were considered, the average was 8.1 months. The lowest average time lag was for *Wilson Library Bulletin* (5.4 months); the highest was *College and Research Libraries* with a 12.1 month lag.

The most extensive reviews were found in *Library Quarterly* (an average of 875 words in length) and *Library Journal* (408 words).

By far the largest number of reviews were positive in character. Chen and Galvin found 70.9 percent of the reviews to be favorable. An additional 10.2 percent were not evaluative in character.

Chen and Galvin conclude that "the reviewing process is of limited value with regard to the 'selection' function, and that in the fields of library and information science, the 'peer appraisal' aspect of book reviewing might more correctly be termed 'peer congratulation.' The results of our study suggest a need for the professional journals to broaden review coverage of new works in library and information science, to strive to expedite the reviewing process, and to seek a higher critical level in appraising the output of the library press."[6]

SCOPE AND METHODOLOGY

In the present study, the investigators sought to address those questions that were also examined in the Chen-Galvin project: What portion of the current monographic literature of library science that is published in North America or available through the normal distribution channels of the American book trade can be identified through primary announcement media and cumulative publication sources—*American Book Publishing Record* (*BPR*) and *Books in Print* (*BIP*)? What portion of this literature is reviewed in selected American and Canadian professional periodicals? Which of these periodicals are most comprehensive in their coverage of the monographic literature? Which publications are reviewed most extensively? What is the average length of these reviews? What is the frequency of negative reviews? In addition, this study examined the similarities and differences in the findings of the two projects and noted the changes that were evident since the earlier study.

This study was concerned with the quantity of English-language monographs in library science with 1983 imprint dates, and the ways in which these monographs were identified—through the announcement media, cumulated publication sources, or professional periodical reviews. The year 1983 was chosen in order to allow a systematic review of the selected periodicals for a thirty-month period, and to present timely results.

A list of the publications was compiled through a search of classes 020 through 029 in the 1983-1984 cumulation of *BPR*, supplemented by a search of *BIP* for 1983 and 1984. *Publishers Weekly* (*PW*) and *Forthcoming Books* (*FB*) had been searched by Chen and Galvin. Since that time, *Publishers Weekly* has discontinued the "Weekly Record." *BIP*, which is the index to *Publishers Trade List Annual*, was used in order to obtain additional data about the English-language monographs published in 1983.

Thirty-two professional journals believed to contain reviews of the literature were examined for the thirty-month period. Included among these were the journals identified by Chen and Galvin, and relevant titles which began publication after the 1975 study. The periodicals selected for inclusion in this study met certain specified criteria. They were selected on the basis of being published in the United States or Canada with a predominantly national audience, including evaluative reviews, and appearing on at least a semiannual basis. Data recorded for each review included author, title, and publisher of the monograph reviewed, source and date of publication of the review, name of the review, and evaluative comment of the reviewer.

THE ANNOUNCEMENT MEDIA

The search of *BPR* and *BIP* resulted in the identification of 204 English-language monographs published in 1983 in the field of library science. Titles were included from the 020-029 class of *BPR* and an online search of *BIP*.

A search of the thirty-two periodicals uncovered 117 additional titles that had not been cited in either *BPR* or *BIP*. This indicates that approximately 36 percent of the total monographic literature of librarianship with an imprint date of 1983 was not identified in the major announcement and cumulative listing media.

These findings differ from those of Chen and Galvin (see table 2).

Table 2.

	1971	1983
Titles cited in announcement media	167 (75%)	204 (64%)
Additional titles cited in review literature	55 (24%)	117 (36%)

It is interesting to note that the absolute number of titles (204) cited in the announcement media in this study increased 18 percent while the percentage of titles cited decreased by 11 percent. These differences could be attributed in part to the fact that the "Weekly Record" section of *PW*, which had yielded additional titles for Chen and Galvin, was not available for 1983; however, a search of *BIP* produced additional titles that were not available in *BPR*. In addition, the differences could be explained by the increase in the number of titles published and the inability of the announcement media to keep pace with this influx of new titles.

THE REVIEW MEDIA

Since 1971, there have been changes in the professional journals in the field of library science. Some have ceased publication or changed in format while others have entered the market. Thirty-two American and Canadian periodicals were initially selected for study. These included twenty-one journals used by Chen and Galvin, and eleven others thought to yield reviews of the professional literature. Upon examination of these journals for the thirty-month period (January 1983-June 1985), eleven titles were eliminated because they did not contain reviews of 1983 English-language monographs, or they contained brief, unsigned descriptions of new books. Five journals which had been used by Chen and Galvin were eliminated for these reasons (*Choice, Drexel Library Quarterly, Kirkus Reviews, Law Library Journal*, and *Library Resources and Technical Services*). The other titles eliminated in this study that had not been used in the previous study included: *American Libraries, Journal of* the American Society for Information Science, Electronic Libraries, and *Journal of Library Administration*.

Seven journals were used for the first time in this study. These included: *Information Technology and Libraries, Journal of Academic Librarianship, Library Acquisitions: Theory and Practice, Library and Information Science Research, Library Hi Tech, Library Software Review*, and *Online Review*. Two of these periodicals (*Journal of Academic Librarianship*

and *Library Hi Tech*) yielded more than thirty-five reviews each for a total of 18 percent of all the reviews.

The twenty-two journals reviewed a total of 214 English-language library science monographs with 1983 imprint dates. This represented 67 percent of the library and information science titles published in that year. The information in table 3 indicates how these results compare to those of the 1971 study.

Table 3.

	1971	1983
Titles reviewed	164 (74%)	214 (67%)
Titles cited in announcement media, but not reviewed	58 (45%)	103 (51%)
Titles cited in announcement media and reviewed	NA	99 (49%)

There was a 6 percent increase in the number of titles that were identified in the announcement media but were not reviewed in the professional literature. This confirms one of the conclusions in the previous study that the citing of a title "in the chief announcement medium is not, in itself, any guarantee of a book's receiving attention in the primary review journals."[7] Furthermore, the increase in the percentage of titles not reviewed implies that the review coverage has not kept pace with the increase in the number of monographs published.

Review coverage of titles with a 1983 imprint ranges from a high of seventy reviews

(*Library Journal*) to a low of one review (*Catholic Library World* and *School Librarian*). The number of 1983 imprints in library science which were reviewed in one of the twenty-two periodicals is listed in table 4. The data indicate that no single review source covers even one quarter of the new monographs in the field. The reviews in *LJ* represented 32 percent of all the titles reviewed and 22 percent of the titles identified for the year. *Library Journal* also yielded the highest number of reviews of monographs with a 1971 imprint date; however, the percentage of reviews in *LJ* during the previous study was higher.

Table 4.
Quantitative Coverage and Length of Reviews in Journals

Journal	Total Number of Reviews	Average Number of Words Per Review
Booklist	50	276
Canadian Library Journal	64	211
Catholic Library World	1	250
College and Research Libraries	25	595
Information Technology & Libraries	17	720
Journal of Academic Librarianship	53	249
Journal of Library History	8	1157
Library Acquisitions: Theory and Practice	9	489
Library and Information Science Research	5	540
Library Hi Tech	37	594
Library Journal	70	214
Library Quarterly	45	778
Library Software Review	4	115
Medical Library Association Bulletin	21	545
Microform Review	3	400
Online Review	7	878
RQ	42	195
School Librarian	1	140
School Library Journal	14	321
School Library Media Quarterly	3	683
Special Libraries	6	783
Wilson Library Bulletin	27	80

The number of reviews for the seven journals with the greatest yield was higher in this study than in the previous one, but the percentage of coverage of titles was lower in this study.

The information in table 5 compares those journals that had the highest yield of reviews in 1971 and 1983.

Table 5.

Journal	1971 Number (Rank)	1983 Number (Rank)
Library Journal	87 (1)	70 (1)
Canadian Library Journal	74 (2)	64 (2)
College and Research Libraries	36 (3)	25 (9)
Library Quarterly	31 (4)	45 (5)
Wilson Library Bulletin	26 (5)	27 (8)
Booklist	21 (6)	51 (4)
RQ	21 (6)	42 (6)
Journal of Academic Librarianship	-	53 (3)
Library Hi Tech	-	37 (7)

DUPLICATION OF COVERAGE

Similar patterns of coverage were discovered in this study as had been found in the Chen-Galvin project; however, only 29 percent of the titles known to have been published in 1983 received more than one review in the professional literature compared with 43 percent of the monographs published in 1971. The five highest-yield review media — *Booklist, Canadian Library Journal, Journal of Academic Librarianship, Library Journal,* and *Library Quarterly* — contained a large portion of the reviews of those monographs that received one or more reviews. Twenty-one titles (9 percent of all titles reviewed) received 30 percent of all the reviews, and these reviews appeared most often in the five highest-yield review journals.

The duplication patterns of the reviews are recorded in table 6. The data indicate that *Library Journal* contained 54 percent of the titles that received more than one review in the professional literature. The *Journal of Academic Librarianship* contained the third highest yield of reviews; the *JAL* "Guide to Professional Literature" section was not included. This section contains summaries and citations for critical reviews from selected library and education periodicals. An examination of the March 1983 issue revealed that approximately 143 titles were included in the "Guide," and that 75 appeared for the first time. The *JAL* review section and the "Guide to Professional Literature" identify a significant portion of the new titles in the field.

Table 6.
Duplication Patterns and Five Highest-Yield Review Journals.

Number of Reviews Per Title	Number of Titles	Number of Titles Appeared in				
		Booklist	Canadian Library Journal	Journal of Academic Librarianship	Library Journal	Library Quarterly
9	6	5	5	3	6	3
8	3	3	2	3	3	1
7	5	2	4	5	3	3
6	7	5	6	3	3	3
5	13	7	8	8	11	4
4	15	5	7	6	11	5
3	20	7	6	6	7	0
2	27	6	7	5	8	6
Subtotal	96	40	45	39	50	24
1	118	10	19	14	20	21
Grand Total	214	50	64	53	70	45

TIME LAG IN REVIEWING

The data indicate that there were ten periodicals which reviewed twenty or more publications with 1983 imprint dates. Table 7 depicts the number of reviews which appeared in the thirty-month period under investigation:

Table 7.

Journal	1983	1984	1985
Booklist (50)	20	30	0
Canadian Library Journal (64)	6	55	3
College and Research Libaries (25)	7	6	12
Journal of Academic Librarianship (53)	13	32	8
Library Hi Tech (37)	12	24	1
Library Journal (70)	39	28	3
Library Quarterly (45)	3	28	14
Medical Library Association Bulletin (21)	0	16	5
RQ (42)	23	19	0
Wilson Library Bulletin (27)	21	6	0

The five highest-yield review journals for 1983 publications contained the majority of the reviews between fall 1983 and spring 1984. The majority of reviews from those journals which covered fewer than twenty monographs appeared during or after spring 1984. This indicates that in addition to carrying the most reviews, the highest-yield review media are also the most timely.

LENGTH OF REVIEWS

The findings generated from the analysis of these reviews confirmed those of Chen and Galvin. They found that a large portion of each review tended to be descriptive, and that the more abbreviated reviews tended to be less evaluative, especially less negative.

The average length of reviews for monographs published in 1971 was 389 words while the average length of reviews for monographs with a 1983 imprint date was 462—an increase of 16 percent. The reviews from the highest-yield category of journals in this study averaged 346 words per review while the five highest-yield journals in the original study produced reviews which averaged 484 words. Although this indicates a decrease of 29 percent, it must be

noted that the journals in this study contained 10 percent more reviews than did those in the earlier study. See table 4 for data on the average number of words per review in the twenty-two journals used in the present study.

REVIEWERS

The 512 reviews examined in this study were written by a total of 376 individuals. Thirty-seven percent of the reviewers wrote two or more reviews while 63 percent of the individuals wrote one review. The majority of reviews in *Booklist* and 96 percent of the reviews in *Wilson Library Bulletin* were written by one individual. Table 8 depicts the number of reviews written by individual reviewers.

Table 8.

Number of individuals	Number of reviews by each individual	Total
1	36	36
1	26	26
1	8	8
1	5	5
3	4	12
7	3	21
42	2	84
320	1	320
Total = 376		Total = 512

POSITIVE AND NEGATIVE REVIEWS

The overall orientation of the reviews was positive; only 9 percent of all reviews provided negative appraisals. Thirty-three percent of the negative reviews were written by individuals who each wrote two or more reviews. The original study found that 81 percent of the

reviews for monographs published in 1971 provided favorable evaluations. On the basis of these findings it appears that in addition to the increase in the number of books published in 1983 there was also an increase in the number of recommendations for purchase. Consumers are not only faced with more selections, but also with more recommendations for more expensive additions to their collections.

SUMMARY

The objective of this study has been to describe the reviewing mechanisms of the professional library literature for 1983. This has been accomplished by analyzing the primary announcement media, cumulated publication sources, and professional library periodical reviews. Additionally, the findings of the Chen-Galvin project which appraised the reviews of the English-language monographs of library science for 1971 were compared with the results of this study.

The findings indicate that the number of reviews which appeared in the selected journals has increased over the past twelve years, but that this increase is not proportionate to the increase in the number of titles published. This suggests that the reviewing media have not been able to keep pace with the growth of the professional materials. The outcome is indeed unfortunate for the budget-conscious members of the profession who are faced with the task of selecting relevant items from a large field.

The problem is exacerbated by the fact that many titles of potential interest cannot be located through either the announcement media or the review sources. Over one-half of the publications (103) with a 1983 imprint date that were cited in *BPR* or *BIP* were not reviewed in any of the major periodicals selected for analysis. Furthermore, more than one-third (117) of the titles which were reviewed did not appear in the primary announcement media or cumulated publication sources. These findings suggest that comprehensive coverage is achieved only through examination of both the announcement media and review sources.

The journals which produced the greatest number of reviews tended to review the same titles. Twenty-one titles received 30 percent of all the reviews, while 118 titles (55 percent of all titles reviewed) received only one review each. *Library Journal* and *Canadian Library Journal* carried the most reviews of monographs published in 1971 and 1983. The journal which had the third highest number of reviews in 1971 (*College and Research Libraries*) dropped to ninth place in 1983. *C&RL* was supplanted by the *Journal of Academic Librarianship* which reviewed 25 percent of all the titles which received reviews.

The vast majority (91 percent) of all titles reviewed received positive or neutral evaluations. This phenomenon could be due to the desire of the journal editors to publish only positive reviews instead of using the limited amount of space for negative evaluations, the inability of the reviewers to criticize the work of their colleagues, or the excellence of all the monographs published in 1983 and reviewed. It seems likely that there is truth to each of the above premises; however, it does not solve the dilemma of those who must make wise selection decisions.

The state of reviewing the literature of librarianship is similar now to what it was in 1971. The exceptions are that more monographs are published each year, and a smaller percentage of the total are reviewed in the professional media. The reviews that do appear are concentrated on a minority of the titles published, and there are a core number of journals which tend to duplicate the coverage of these titles. Furthermore, the recommendations for these titles are usually positive. The results of this study echo those of Chen and Galvin which appear to have gone unheeded in the past dozen years. The professional review journals should strive to diversify the coverage of new titles and should aim for a critical evaluation of the cited works.

NOTES

[1]Ching-Chih Chen and Thomas J. Galvin, "Reviewing the Literature of Librarianship: A State of the Art Report," in *American Reference Books Annual 1975*, ed. Bohdan S. Wynar (Littleton, Colo.: Libraries Unlimited, 1975).

[2]*Bowker Annual of Library and Book Trade Information* (New York: R. R. Bowker, 1972), 176, 183.

[3]*Bowker Annual of Library and Book Trade Information* (New York: R. R. Bowker, 1985), 460-61, 465.

[4]Chen and Galvin, xxxi.

[5]Chen and Galvin, xxxiii.

[6]Chen and Galvin, xl.

[7]Chen and Galvin, xxxiv.

Susan J. Webreck and Judith Weedman

Reference Book Reviewing Media:
A Critical Analysis

Total sales of all reference books during 1984 exceeded $465.2 million.[1] Although that figure represents only about 5 percent of all book sales during the year, it is still a large amount of money, especially from librarians' perspective.

Unlike most trade books, reference works are created principally for libraries. Libraries are a very important market; for publishers specializing in reference works, libraries are almost the only market. Publishers attempt to reach this market through a variety of means: reviews, direct mail, sales calls, and promotions at library conferences. A survey commissioned by the Association of American Publishers and conducted by the Center for Book Research at the University of Scranton concluded that librarians rank "reviews and expert recommendations" as the most important sources of information in making acquisitions decisions.[2] (Next in importance are publishers' promotional materials.) Thus the quality of reviews in library periodicals is of paramount importance both to librarians involved in book selection and to publishers.

The point of this article is to assess the state of reference book reviewing today. The 1985 issue of *American Reference Books Annual* (*ARBA*), published in April 1985 and covering books published in 1984 and the last days of 1983, was selected as a means of defining the universe of reference book publishing for 1984 since *ARBA* strives to review every reference book published in English in the United States each year. It also reviews annuals on a three- or five-year cycle.

Furthermore, *ARBA* cites reviews in all of the other reference review media discussed in this article. This feature has simplified comparison of review media by identifying titles reviewed by more than one.

This limited study essay answers several questions: How much unanimity of judgment is there among the reviewing media? How well collectively do the review media cover the output of American reference book publishers? How frequently do the review media, both collectively and individually, make positive judgments, negative judgments, and mixed judgments? Do there seem to be any correlations between quality of reviews and some other attribute(s)? How well do reviewers spot and exploit opportunities to compare a title under review with existing works of similar purpose or nature? It also invites further study to confirm these tentative answers. The broad, multifaceted topic of the range and quality of reference book reviewing would make an ideal dissertation topic.

ASSESSMENT OF REVIEWS

As a first step in judging the range of reference book publishing and the response to this output by the individual reviewing sources, a count was made of the number of titles reviewed in the six major sources—*ARBA*, *Choice*, *Library Journal*, *Reference Books Bulletin*, *RQ*, and the *Wilson Library Bulletin*—during calendar year 1984. These counts are listed in table 1.

The wide difference between the most voluminous source, *ARBA*, and the second most voluminous, *Choice*, can probably be explained by differences in audience. *Choice* limits its coverage to books appropriate for academic libraries, concentrating on those suitable for

Table 1.
Number of Titles Reviewed during Calendar Year 1984.

ARBA	1,659[a]
Choice	595
LJ	249
RBB	509
RQ	104
WLB	242

[a]Excludes seventy-nine entries: numbers 399-401 and 426-35 in "Travel," numbers 587-616 in "Military Studies," and thirty-seven entries on individual authors since in the other review media these categories are generally excluded from reference. The 1985 *ARBA* (volume 16) carried entries number 1 through 1,734, each entry number being assigned to a distinct title; the total number of titles reviewed is actually 1,659 since entries 73a, 73b, 662a, and 991a are interfiled.

undergraduates in all types of college-level institutions: junior colleges, four-year colleges, and universities. *ARBA* reviews sources for all types of libraries. It also includes reviews of ongoing annuals on a regular cycle.

As a second step, every *ARBA* entry was examined to identify those titles which, according to the citations included in *ARBA* entries, were reviewed in *ARBA* and at least two other sources. Of the 1,659 possibilities, 142 were reviewed in three or more sources. These titles were checked in the *Book Review Index* cover-ing 1984 and early 1985 to add citations which *ARBA* missed in the other five sources. The review citation record was enriched for only about one in ten of these. A systematic check of every fifth entry in *ARBA* against *Book Review Index* showed approximately the same enrichment ratio. The lag time of *BRI* is not known. If this consideration is laid aside, one can conclude that *ARBA* misses only about a tenth of the reviews in other sources. Table 2 shows how many titles were reviewed in three, four, or five sources.

Table 2.
Number of Multiply Reviewed Titles.

Reviewed in all six sources	3	>1.0%
Reviewed in five sources	16	1.0%
Reviewed in four sources	38	2.2%
Reviewed in three sources	85	5.1%
TOTAL	142	8.5%

The number of titles reviewed in at least three sources, only 8.5 percent of the 1,659 possible titles, is very small.[3] In 1964 Goggin and Seaberg complained of the inadequate number of reference book reviews; in comparing titles reviewed in *Library Journal, College and Research Libraries*, and the *Wilson Library Bulletin*, they found

> little duplication among the reference books in the three sources. In 1952, 92.5 percent of the titles were

on only one of the lists; by 1957, this had decreased to 83 percent, while the figure dropped to 80 percent in 1962. While by 1962, 4.7 percent of the titles appeared on all three lists as opposed to a 1.1 percentage in 1952, it is quite obvious that librarians need to use all three sources to keep abreast of new reference titles, even "selected" reference books.[4]

The situation has improved since the early 1960s. Since then *Choice* began publication, in 1964; *ARBA* appeared on the scene in 1970; and by 1968 *RQ* had developed its Salmagundi column, a feature in *RQ*'s first issue in November 1960, into its regular review section. With more reviewing sources operating, more reference titles are reviewed, especially thanks to *ARBA*'s review-all policy. Yet the duplication of coverage of titles in the various review media has not increased greatly.

That a high percentage of titles are reviewed in only one or two sources can be viewed as a healthy state of affairs for both publishers and their librarian customers in that more books get reviewed this way than if there were greater duplication of effort among the review media. Librarians who follow Goggin and Seaberg's advice to follow all of the review sources will, thanks to the wide dispersal of titles among the review media, have the opportunity to read expert evaluations of a greater number of titles. On the other hand, it can be argued that this is *not* good because reviewers' opinions may differ or range across a wide spectrum. Perhaps some opinions about a particular book will even stand

in polar opposition to one another. Given these possibilities, this line of argument continues, it is desirable for book selectors to have multiple opinions of a book before making a purchase decision for or against. At this point, however, this argument loses some of its force in the face of a practical consideration. Unless a librarian is willing to compile a labor-intensive file of reviews to see if the later services supply additional opinions after early reviews are published, it is better for selectors to have a wide dispersal of titles among the media. It is surely better from the publishers' point of view for the titles to be dispersed if duplication of coverage would mean (as surely it would given journals' space limitations for reviews) fewer of their books would be reviewed. As is substantiated below, most reviews are positive and very few are strongly negative.

An examination of the reviews of the nineteen titles reviewed in five or in all six of the sources shows that the dispersal of titles among the media is probably a desirable thing. Table 3 lists the sixteen works reviewed in five of the six sources.

Table 3.
Titles Reviewed in Five Sources.

Title[a]	ARBA	Choice	LJ	RBB	RQ	WLB
Almanac of American History (451)	X	X	X	X		X
American Writers before 1800 (1059)	X	X	X	X		X
Broadway Bound (1272)	X	X		X	X	X
Business Publications Index and Abstracts (179/180)	X	X		X	X	X
Cultural Atlas of China (92)	X	X	X	X		X
Dictionary of Historic Nicknames (489)	X	X	X	X		X
Dictionary of Historical Terms (484)	X	X	X	X		X
European Writers (998)	X		X	X	X	X
Facts on File Dictionary of Religions (1284)	X	X	X		X	X
Find That Tune (1206)	X	X	X	X		X
Frankenstein Catalog (1047)	X	X	X	X		X
Indians of North America (364)	X	X		X	X	X
McGraw-Hill Concise Encyclopedia of Science and Technology (1331)	X	X	X	X		X
Musicals! (1266)	X	X	X	X		X
Who's Who in Frontier Science and Technology (1329)	X	X	X	X		X
Who's Who in Television and Cable (791)	X	X	X	X		X

[a]Number in parentheses following title is the 1985 *ARBA* entry number.

Table 4 analyzes in detail the reviews of the three titles covered by all six sources.

Table 4.
Analysis of three titles.

Tice, Terrence N., and Thomas P. Slavens. **Research Guide to Philosophy**. Chicago: American Library Association, 1983. 608p. (Sources of Information in the Humanities, No. 3). $40. LC 83-11834. ISBN 0-8389-033-9.

	Descriptive	Comparative	Evaluative[a]	Audience	Recommendation[b]	Specifics	Length
ARBA (1985, entry 1275)	X	X	I		+/-	X	427
Choice (June 1984)	X		M		+		141
LJ (1 April 1984)	X		M	X	+	X	105
RBB (1 September 1984)	X	X	M		+	X	290
RQ (Summer 1984)	X	X	M		+		285
WLB (April 1984)	X		R		+/-		122

[a]Evaluative column key: I = Intensive, M = Moderate, R = Limited to recommendation statement.

[b]Recommendation column key: + = Positive, - = Negative, +/- = Mixed.

Note: The terms used in table 4 need to be explained. "Descriptive" means that the reviewer describes the purpose and/or organization of the work under review. "Comparative" means that the reviewer compares the work under review to one or more works with a similar or related purpose. "Evaluative" means that the reviewer evaluates the work under review. Within this category, "Intensive" means that the review includes evaluative remarks throughout its length. "Moderate" means that evaluative remarks are included in some part of the review other than the recommendation statement. "Limited to recommendation statement" means that evaluative remarks are confined to the review's recommendation statement. Although not necessarily the final sentence of a review, the recommendation statement usually comes in this position. "Audience" means that the review identifies the audience for which the work under review is intended or for which it is appropriate. This is frequently, although not always, expressed in terms of a type and/or size of library. Within the "Recommendation" category, a review can give a positive recommendation, or a negative recommendation, a mixed or qualified recommendation; or the review can make a noncommittal statement which cannot be construed as any sort of recommendation to the reader. "Specifics" means that the review cites specific examples from the work under review. "Length" is a measurement of the length of a review in number of words.

Table 4.—*Continued*

The American Presidency: A Historical Bibliography. Santa Barbara, Calif.: ABC-Clio, 1984. 376p. (Clio Bibliography Series, No. 15). $60. LC 83-12245. ISBN 0-87436-370-5.

	Descriptive	Comparative	Evaluative[a]	Audience	Recommendation[b]	Specifics	Length
ARBA (1985, entry 642)	X		R	X	+/-		151
Choice (July/August 1984)	X		M		+		193
LJ (15 May 1984)	X		M		+	X	88
RBB (1 September 1984)	X		M	X	+		256
RQ (Summer 1984)	X	X	M	X	+		496
WLB (May 1984)	X		R	X	+		114

Crawford, Anne, and others, eds. **The Europa Biographical Dictionary of British Women: Over 1000 Notable Women from Britain's Past.** London, Europa Publications; distr., Detroit: Gale, 1983. 436p. $55. ISBN 0-8103-1789-3.

	Descriptive	Comparative	Evaluative[a]	Audience	Recommendation[b]	Specifics	Length
ARBA (1985, entry 763)	X		I		-		214
Choice (July/August 1984)	X	X	I		+		247
LJ (1 June 1984)	X		R		+	X	109
RBB (1 December 1984)	X		M		+/-		251
RQ (Summer 1984)	X		M	X	+	X	304
WLB (June 1984)	X		R		+/-	X	128

Table 5 is a cumulation and comparison of the six sources' treatment of the nineteen titles reviewed in five of the six sources or in all six sources.

Table 5.
Comparison of Review Media Cumulative Treatment of
Titles Reviewed in Five or Six Sources.[a]

	ARBA	Choice	LJ	RBB	RQ	WLB	Total
Number of Titles	19	18	16	18	8	19	98
Percentage of universe of 19	100.	94.7	84.2	94.7	42.1	100.	100.
Descriptive	19	18	16	18	8	19	98
Percentage of that source's titles	100.	100.	100.	100.	100.	100.	100.
Comparative	7	9	8	6	6	6	42
Percentage	36.8	50.0	50.0	33.3	75.0	31.5	42.8
Evaluative							
Intensive	8	6	0	2	4	1	21
Percentage	42.1	33.3	0.0	11.1	50.0	5.0	21.4
Moderate	7	9	8	5	4	7	40
Percentage	36.8	50.0	50.0	27.7	50.0	36.8	40.8
Recommendation statement	4	3	7	9	0	11	34
Percentage	21.0	16.6	43.7	50.0	0.0	57.8	34.6
None	0	0	1	2	0	0	3
Percentage	0.0	0.0	6.0	11.1	0.0	0.0	3.0
Audience Identification	5	11	5	12	4	10	47
Percentage	26.3	61.1	31.2	66.6	50.0	52.6	47.9
Recommendation							
Positive	12	12	11	12	5	14	66
Percentage	63.1	66.6	68.7	66.6	62.5	73.6	67.3
Negative	1	1	0	0	0	0	2
Percentage	5.2	5.5	0.0	0.0	0.0	0.0	2.0
Mixed	5	5	3	5	3	5	26
Percentage	26.3	27.7	18.7	27.7	37.5	26.3	26.5
Noncommital	1	0	2	1	0	0	4
Percentage	5.0	0.0	12.5	5.0	0.0	0.0	4.0
Specifics	10	10	1	5	3	7	36
Percentage	52.6	55.5	6.0	27.7	37.5	36.8	36.7
Average Length	279.1	224.7	108.8	236.8	353.8	149.9	-

[a]For explanation of terms, see note to table 4.

The data in table 5 confirm that most reviews are positive. Of the ninety-eight reviews, sixty-six (67.3 percent) are positive, a percentage very close to the 70 percent "favorable" Covey found approximately fifteen years ago in the only in-depth study of reference book reviewing published to date.[5] Similarly, Covey found 2.3 percent of reviews passed "unfavorable" judgments; 2.0 percent in this study's universe hand down negative verdicts.[6]

Librarians sometimes complain about reviews' "lack of useful content."[7] Goggin and Seaberg reported that in her unpublished study, Catherine Glennon concluded that " 'the merely informative reviews are of little help' to the librarian."[8]

All ninety-eight of the reviews are descriptive, or in Glennon's terminology, "informative." The depth of description of the books' contents and purpose varies, just as does the intensiveness of evaluation. While depth of description was not studied, intensiveness of evaluation was. Half of the reviews in *ARBA* and half of the reviews in *RQ* engage in intensive evaluation. A third of those in *Choice* engage in intensive evaluation. In contrast, the majority of *WLB* reviews and approximately half of those in *LJ* confine their evaluation to the recommendation statement. There is a strong correlation between length of review and intensity of evaluation. The longest reviews are in *RQ* and *ARBA*, the two sources that engage in the most intense evaluation. The shortest reviews — those in *LJ* and *WLB* — depend most heavily upon their recommendation statements to carry the weight of evaluation. (As a result of the *Wilson Library Bulletin*'s format enlargement in September 1984, reference book reviews have lengthened and since that time show a greater intensity of evaluation. This is discussed in greater detail below.)

The reviews in *RBB*, although approximately the same average length as those in *Choice*, display the most variety of degrees of evaluation intensity, half depending upon the recommendation statement. *RBB* also has the largest number which are strictly descriptive rather than evaluative. One may speculate on the reasons for this; the most likely explanation seems to be contained in a statement in the *RBB* editorial board's manual, explaining the difference between a "review" and a "note." During 1984 *RBB* published three types of reviews. "Reviews" are very detailed and lengthy evaluative treatments of reference works, especially of English-language dictionaries and of general purpose, multivolume encyclopedias. "Notes" are shorter and less detailed than "reviews." In a practice now abandoned but adopted to reduce reviews' lag time, *RBB* used to publish "News Notes," very brief signed notices of new reference works. Of *RBB*'s eighteen reviews in the study group, one is a review, fifteen are notes, and two are news notes. The manual states that "a note, unlike a review, does not contain a statement that a book is 'recommended' or 'not recommended.' However, even the briefest note should leave no doubt as to the Board's opinion of a work's overall quality and of the likelihood of its proving useful in particular reference situations."[9] The fact that this statement is an explanation of the function of the "Summary Paragraph and Final Evaluation"[10] may explain why the recommendation statements — statements which should "leave no doubt" although their language is not prescribed — play such an important role in *RBB* notes.

The evidence regarding the use of specific examples from the work under review does not fall into a neat pattern, but does suggest that the use of specific examples contributes to increasing the intensity of evaluation. The data confirm the commonsense conclusion that short reviews do not accommodate many examples.

It is evident from the above that in order to evaluate a reference work carefully, a reviewer needs more than 100 or 150 words. Editorial policies dictate length. *RBB* "News Notes" sharply curtailed length, just as do *LJ* review assignments. Although *RBB* has officially dropped its "News Notes" genre and its recent reviews are somewhat longer than those eighteen reflected in table 5, it remains heavily dependent upon recommendation statements for evaluation. This issue is discussed in greater detail below. *LJ* reviews are not likely to become more evaluative unless there is a change in editorial policy allowing at least a doubling in length of its reviews.

All but 4.0 percent of the ninety-eight reviews are to some degree evaluative reviews. Table 6 shows how reviewer's judgments clustered around each of the nineteen titles reviewed.

Table 6.
Indicator of Unanimity of Reviewers' Recommendations.

Number of Reviews Fitting Distribution	Distribution of Recommendations			
	Positive	Negative	Mixed	Noncommital
3	5	0	0	0
5	4	0	1	0
1[a]	4	0	2	0
4	3	0	2	0
1[a]	3	0	3	0
1[a]	3	1	2	0
1	3	1	1	0
1	3	0	0	2
1	1	0	4	0
1	2	0	1	2

[a]Indicates titles reviewed in all six sources.

The data in table 6 show that there is considerable unanimity among reviewers when a number of them examine and pass judgment on the same book. This supports the argument that, given the great number of reference titles now published, lack of overlapping coverage among the review sources is a healthy thing. It appears that greater overlap would simply confirm many of the judgments reached by individual reviewers working independently of one another.

In addition to the unanimity of judgment among the reviewers, an examination of their unanimity of approach is another significant way of determining the value of overlap in reference book reviewing. Of the ninety-eight reviews, forty-two, or 42.8 percent, compare the work under review with one or more similar or related works. At least one of the six sources compared the work under review in sixteen of the nineteen possible cases. Table 7 shows the incidence of comparison and how comparisons cluster.

Table 7.
Indicator of Reviewers' Unanimity in Making Comparisons.

Number of Reviews Fitting Distribution	Comparative	Not Comparative
5	3	2
4	4	1
3	0	5
3	2	3
2[a]	1	5
1	1	4
1[a]	3	3

[a]Indicates titles reviewed in all six sources.

The data show that, overall, the review sources are fairly well agreed on when to make comparisons. In four cases, four of the five sources which reviewed a work made comparisons and in three cases, all five sources which reviewed a work found no other work with which to compare it. However in five cases, three of the five sources reviewing a work did make comparisons while two did not. *RQ* has the strongest record for making comparisons; when making assignments, its editor strongly stresses the importance of comparisons. With the longest average length reviews, *RQ*'s reviewers obviously have the greatest opportunity to make comparisons. Clearly, the review sources should make more comparisons and make them more consistently. More comparisons to existing reference works with which librarians are already familiar (or with which they ought to be familiar) would give readers a frame of reference in which to place the reviewer's statements and thus would enhance the reviews' value to book selectors. Like intensity of evaluation or use of specific examples, frequency and depth of comparison are partially functions of review length.

Audience identification is not a significant factor in the reviews. The source which most consistently makes recommendations in terms of audience as defined by type of library is *Choice*. The reason for this is that the instructions sent to reviewers very explicitly call for this. If a review describes and evaluates a reference work well, the reader using that review to select books for his or her library ought to have enough information on which to base a decision about whether or not the book reviewed is appropriate for that library's collection and clientele.

The data analyzed above dates from 1984, much of it from early 1984. To judge whether or not there has been significant change since then in any of the six review sources, approximately forty reviews from the most recent issues of each source were examined. There have been changes which indicate the possibility of change in quality in several of the sources. For example, *RBB* has a new editor and a new committee chair, factors which even in late 1985 and early 1986 may not yet have had an effect in the published reviews, given *RBB*'s long lag time. *Choice* appointed a new editor in 1984 and, as has been noted, in September 1984, the *Wilson Library Bulletin*'s change in format permitted longer reference book reviews. In at least one of these cases, there has clearly been an effect on the quality of reviews.

Table 8 summarizes overall performance of *ARBA 1985* and the recent performance of each of the other five review sources. Because all ninety-eight of the reviews of the nineteen most reviewed titles were descriptive, this attribute was not studied in the recent reviews. It is assumed that a very large percentage of all reviews are descriptive. With the exception of the substitution of "Typical Length" for "Average Length," all of the terms used in table 8 employ the same definitions used in table 5.

Table 8.
Recent Performance of the Six Review Media.[a]

	ARBA	Choice	LJ	RBB	RQ	WLB	Total
Number of Titles	42	43	39	46	47	41	258
Comparative	12	14	12	9	30	12	89
Percentage	28.5	32.5	30.7	19.5	63.8	29.2	34.4
Evaluative							
Intensive	12	9	2	3	11	5	37
Percentage	28.5	20.9	5.1	6.5	23.4	12.1	14.3
Moderate	14	19	17	14	27	25	116
Percentage	33.3	44.1	43.5	30.4	57.4	60.9	44.9
Recommendation statement	13	15	19	22	9	11	89
Percentage	30.9	34.8	48.7	47.8	19.1	28.8	34.4
None	3	0	1	7	0	0	11
Percentage	7.1	0.0	2.5	15.2	0.0	0.0	4.2
Audience Identification	13	25	14	9	16	13	90
Percentage	30.9	58.1	35.8	19.5	34.0	31.7	34.8
Recommendation							
Positive	28	31	30	25	35	26	162
Percentage	66.6	72.0	76.9	54.3	74.4	63.4	62.7
Negative	1	2	2	2	2	2	11
Percentage	2.3	4.6	5.1	4.3	4.2	4.8	4.2
Mixed	9	10	7	12	10	13	61
Percentage	21.4	23.2	17.9	26.0	21.2	31.7	23.6
Noncommital	4	0	0	7	0	0	11
Percentage	9.5	0.0	0.0	15.2	0.0	0.0	4.2
Specifics	13	10	7	9	17	20	76
Percentage	30.9	23.2	19.9	19.5	36.1	48.7	29.4
Typical Length[a]	279.1	216.6	120.0	201.3	328.3	241.0	

[a]Reviews analyzed in this table were published in the following issues of the sources: *ARBA 1985* (the nineteen reviews in table 5 plus twenty-three others picked at a regular interval throughout the volume, less those sections excluded in table 1); *Choice*, Dec. 1985; *LJ*, Dec. 1985, 15 Nov. 1985, 1 Nov. 1985, 15 Oct. 1985; *RBB*, 1 Jan. 1986, 15 Dec. 1985; *RQ*, Winter 1985, Summer 1985; *WLB*, Jan. 1986, Dec. 1985.

[b]With the exception of *ARBA*, "Typical Length" was derived by averaging the length of three representative reviews from each of the sources. Length for *ARBA* was derived from the reviews of the nineteen titles reviewed in five or six sources.

HOW BOOKS ARE CHOSEN FOR REVIEW

The ways in which reference books are distributed and obtained for review and the ways in which those books reviewed are selected from among those distributed is of interest. Not every reference book sent out for review is sent to all of the reference review media. Some publishers economize by sending a title to only some of the media. Some publishers rotate distribution of titles among the reference review media. Thus some books are not even candidates for multiple reviews. In some cases this is because the title in question is an expensive multivolume set and the publisher limits the number of review copies.

Attempting, however, to discern these publishers' reasons for offering a review copy to one publication but refusing it to another is impossible. If all publishers were more conscientious and more thorough in distributing review copies, if they assigned responsibility for this task to someone with a good working knowledge of the library press and the library world, there would almost certainly be more overlap of coverage among the review sources. In some publishing houses responsibility for the feeding of review copies to the review media is carefully supervised by a senior person in the promotion department. These people typically make it their business to meet and talk to the review editors to make sure they are supplying the right kinds of books to each. In other houses the responsibility is given to a very junior person who has little opportunity to meet with editors. In such cases everyone loses. The publisher loses opportunities for publicity; the review editors cannot select from as many books; and librarians are deprived of judgments on those books.

Furthermore, some small publishers just entering the reference field have no idea how to go about having their books reviewed. They sometimes stumble upon or are referred by a librarian to one of the review media. When this happens, practices vary. Some review editors will simply tell the publisher to send them a review copy; they may or may not review the book after it is received. Others will go a step further and initiate the publisher into the library reference reviewing world, supplying names, addresses, and phone numbers of the other review editors. (This is the exception rather than the rule. There is no forum for any regular exchange among the editors of the six reference review sources.)

Undoubtedly the publisher which does the poorest job in making its products known is the United States Government Printing Office. It sends out press releases on selected new publications of popular interest. However, the processes of identifying the proper person at GPO from whom to solicit a review copy and then actually securing a review copy are more challenging than dealing with any other publisher, even the largest private publishers.

Very little is known about how the review media select the books to be reviewed. In only one case is this clear; *ARBA* reviews every English-language reference book it can. All of the others work within space constraints and so must be selective. Only *Choice* is aimed at a particular audience. Thus it eliminates reference books which are not suitable for academic libraries. Beyond these clear signs, one may speculate on reasons why books are selected or rejected for review.

The availability in the reviewer pool of a reviewer who has the requisite knowledge of the book's subject may be a factor. If the editor cannot call upon a reviewer with specialized knowledge to review a book, it is likely to be passed over. Some small number of books are selected and assigned for review, but reviews are never published since the person assigned to write the review fails to produce it. Ironically, just as the distribution practices of publishers who limit review copies guarantees that some books will be reviewed in only one or two sources, the practices of others who are quite free with their review copies also contributes to this situation. No review editor wants to appear to be an extension of any publisher's promotion department. So, if a publisher floods a review editor's mail with half a dozen new books in a single month and that editor can review only twenty-five or thirty books each month, the editor will be very reluctant to devote 20 or 25 percent of the month's review space to that one publisher's products.

Editors try to pick those books for review which they perceive will be of greatest interest to their audiences. They attempt to achieve a balance and variety of genres, publishers, and perhaps audience levels among the books reviewed in a given issue of their journal. Many editors feel an obligation to review especially costly works on the assumption that their readers will be particularly keen on having guidance in making purchase decisions about these. However, beyond these loose criteria, some works may be selected for review simply because they strike the editor's fancy or relate to his or her personal interests more strongly than do others.

Unquestionably a good number of books worthy of review do not get reviewed by multiple media or are reviewed by only two or three of the six. A reason for this is that editors are also concerned about the currentness of their reviews. Lag time of reviews, an issue discussed in greater detail below, is an inevitable but never welcome factor in reference book reviewing. After the books to be reviewed for a particular issue have been selected, some very worthy books remaining on the shelf receive no further consideration simply because they are getting "old." "Old" may mean that the book's publication date is approaching within a week or two or has just passed. Rather than review these "old" books, the editors pass over them in favor of the newer books arriving in their mail boxes.

Another factor explaining why some of the review sources review a particular book and others do not is the review editors' tenacity and thoroughness in soliciting review copies from publishers. This varies among these editors.

Choice and *Library Journal* have an advantage over the other services in that their reference review sections are part of general purpose book review services. Thus they receive all types of books, including books from publishers who very rarely produce a reference work. After the books are received, the editors at *LJ* and *Choice* can sort them and pick out the reference books. Through a relationship with the *Booklist* staff, *RBB*'s editor has opportunities to learn about new reference books which have been sent to *Booklist* but not to *RBB*. Some publishers pay very careful attention to the review media and study the purpose and scope of each one, including the scope and purpose of various sections within each of the reviewing media which are the responsibility of different people at different addresses. Other publishers are absolutely indifferent to these matters. The review editors of *ARBA, RQ,* and *WLB* have difficulty securing review copies from these publishers. The problem is especially acute for the *RQ* and *WLB* editors since neither works out of the journal's editorial office and for both editors their reference reviewing activity is a sideline, albeit a very serious sideline, to careers in reference publishing and librarianship respectively.

COMMENTS ON THE
REVIEW MEDIA

A comparison of the data on *ARBA*'s overall performance and its treatment of the nineteen titles reviewed in five or six of the sources previously discussed, reveals few significant differences. The most significant is the decline from 42.1 percent to 28.5 percent in the proportion of reviews which engage in intensive evaluation. This occurred along with an increase in the percentage of reviews relying upon the recommendation statement and an increase

from no reviews to 7.1 percent of reviews which are not at all evaluative. Nevertheless, *ARBA* boasts the highest percentage of intensively evaluative reviews. *ARBA*'s guidelines state that "reviewers are encouraged to discuss intended audience and/or level, but the review need not conclude with specific recommendations for purchase. An adequate description and evaluation of a reference book will speak for itself."[11] Along with the decrease in the degree of evaluation intensity, perhaps coincident with, perhaps inseparable from that decrease, there is also a decline in the percentage of reviews using specific examples. *ARBA*'s chief drawback is its very long but unavoidable lag time. Even if it does not lend itself to use as a current acquisitions tool, it can be used each spring to learn about and make selections of the many titles not covered in the other sources. Each year *ARBA* publishes the largest body of evaluative reference book reviews; librarians should not neglect it.

Comparing *Choice*'s recent performance with its treatment of the eighteen titles it reviewed in the group of nineteen one finds a definite migration away from intensely evaluative reviews to a greater dependence upon the recommendation statement. To compound coincidence, there is in *Choice* an even greater decline in percentage of reviews citing specific examples. Since the degree of intensity of evaluation in *RQ* declined but the percentage of reviews citing specifics remained stable, it may be too much to claim a cause-and-effect relationship between the presence of specific examples and intensity of evaluation. Examples can be used in a purely descriptive manner. In the case of *Choice*, the decline in the percentage of reviews that engage in comparison is probably a more significant correlate to the decline in intensity of evaluation. *Choice*'s guidelines for reviews of reference books are not sufficiently differentiated from its guidelines for reviews of other types of books to attribute any of the characteristics (except one) of *Choice* reference reviews to editorial policy. That one exception, as has been noted above, is the strong tendency of *Choice* reference reviews to specify type of academic library or level of student for which a book is appropriate. This is a minor consideration. As the *ARBA* guidelines state, "an adequate description and evaluation of a reference book will speak for itself." Given such a description and evaluation, a book selector can judge whether or not a given book is appropriate for his or her collection and clientele. This is not a judgment a reviewer can make for each and every library. In general, the *Choice* guidelines call upon reviewers to describe, evaluate, and, where appropriate, compare the book under review. In general, the reviews succeed in doing these things. The reviewers' subject expertise is frequently evident, adding credibility to the reviews. Because it is issued eleven times per year and does a good job of evaluating and comparing reference works, *Choice* is an important tool for reference book selectors.

Of the six sources, *Library Journal* has the lowest percentage of intensely evaluative reviews and displays the greatest reliance upon the recommendation statement. It also has the highest percentage of books given a positive recommendation. Often the recommendation and the recommendation statement are both conveyed in the single word "recommended" tacked on to the end of a review. There is little qualification to these statements except when they are cast in terms of type of library. It is impossible to say what the intent of the editors of *Library Journal* reference book reviews is; unlike all of the other review editors, the editor of *LJ*'s book review section did not reply to this author's request for copies of policies and guidelines. With few exceptions, the strongest thing that can be said in favor of *LJ*'s reference book reviews is that they generally come out ahead of the other sources' reviews of the same book. Ironically, this is also sometimes a flaw in them. A review of a reference work done from galleys or proofs and stating that the index was not examined is not a trustworthy review. The index is an essential part of most reference works; it is irresponsible to assign a reference work for review before it has been indexed. *Library Journal* reference book reviews are early, but most lack substance. A reader does not learn enough from them to make well informed purchase decisions. These reviews are simply too short to be truly useful.

Writing about the *Reference Books Bulletin* under one of its earlier names, Goggin and Seaberg said that the "quality of reviewing in *Subscription Books Bulletin* remains the finest, setting standards for others to follow."[12] In a survey of reference review sources in 1970, Whitmore noted that "the quality of these reviews is usually considered among the most reliable to be found."[13] More recently, in the fourth edition to his standard reference textbook, Bill Katz called these reviews "the best available."[14] And once they were, but no longer. This committee's reviews have always been roundly criticized for their tardiness. As explained above, during 1983 and 1984 and into part of 1985 the committee attempted to ameliorate this situation by developing the genre of signed "News Notes." The data in tables 5 and 8 indicate that it was an unfortunate decision. The result was short *LJ*-like reviews very

superficial in character and overly dependent upon the recommendation statement to convey their message. Once known as the source of very detailed reviews basing judgments on numerous specific examples drawn from the works under review, *RBB* has lost its once firm sense of identity. Its decision in 1985 to discontinue news notes is a hopeful sign. Unfortunately many of the reviews published in *RBB* in January 1986 and December 1985 the latest issues available for consideration in this study, were drafted as news notes. They were not revised extensively for publication. It remains to be seen if *RBB*'s reviews will increase in intensity of evaluation, make more comparisons, and in general convey more useful information. *RBB* remains the principal source of reviews of new general purpose English-language encyclopedias. These reviews remain true to the committee's tradition of detailed analysis. *RBB* also publishes a useful annual encyclopedia roundup.

When reference book reviewers for *RQ* receive an assignment from the *RQ* review editor, they receive a sheet of instructions telling them that "The review should be 200-250 words."[15] Clearly, they regularly ignore this directive; many *RQ* reviews run more than 300 words. The result of taking this liberty is the reviewers' success in fulfilling the other instructions to "emphasize: 1) a description of the arrangement, scope, special features of the sources, etc.; 2) its strengths and weaknesses; and 3) its value/contribution to the field, *especially in comparison to other, similar publications (if they exist)*."[16] Overall, *RQ* carries the highest percentage of reviews which engage in a high degree of evaluation. None of the other sources compares works under review to other works with the great frequency of *RQ*. Clearly, the editor's explicit instructions are heeded carefully.

RQ's reviews can be faulted on two points. First, there are far too few of them and those are issued too infrequently. There is some small hope that *RQ*'s frequency will increase from four to six issues per year. Assuming each of those is the same size as present issues, *RQ* will still be the most selective of the review sources, covering perhaps 155 titles per year. *RQ* reviewed only 42.1 percent of the titles reviewed in five or six of the sources. The second point is that not all of the comparisons are valuable. While most are apt and useful, some seem forced and contribute nothing. For example, in the summer 1985 issue, the review of the *Directory of Foreign Document Collections* compares it to the *Directory of Government Document Collections and Librarians* even though "the amount of information about foreign documents holdings in that directory is slight and in no way compares with the depth of information in the work reviewed here."[17] Such lapses are rare. While this reviewer wishes the laurel could be awarded to the Current Reference Books column of the *Wilson Library Bulletin*, the evidence forces him to say that *RQ*'s reference book reviews are the class act of today.[18]

In the 1984 set of nineteen titles reviewed in five or six of the sources, the *Wilson Library Bulletin* was distinguished in two categories, one to its credit, the other not. First, it is the only source other than *ARBA* which reviewed all nineteen. Second, it is the source which depended most heavily upon the recommendation statement, a woeful 57.8 percent of the time. As has been noted, the increase in size of *WLB*'s format with the September 1984 issue allowed a lengthening of the reviews. The increase from an average length of 149.9 words per review to a typical length of 241 words per review is a 62.2 percent increase. That increase has had a definite, positive effect on the quality and usefulness of the reviews.

WLB's recent reviews show a considerable increase in intensity of evaluation. Whereas only 41.9 percent were "intensive" or "moderate," now 72 percent fall into these categories. *WLB* reviews feature far more specific examples than do any of the other sources' reviews. Both *ARBA* and *Choice* used fewer specific examples and their intensity of evaluation declined; *WLB* used more and its intensity increased. The value of examples in evaluating a reference work cannot be discounted.

Because all of *WLB*'s reference reviews are written by one person, there is no need for that person to have and follow a set of written guidelines. "Mental" guidelines exist, of course, and, were they transferred to paper, would closely resemble the guidelines of *ARBA, Choice,* and *RQ*. The purpose of the Current Reference Books column is to describe, evaluate, and compare new reference works in such a way that librarians can make informed decisions about whether or not to purchase them for their reference collections. For reasons already apparent to the avid reader of endnotes [see note 18], it would hardly be appropriate for the author of this article to comment on how well *WLB* meets its reviewing goals.

Since 1984 there has been a new entrant into the reference book reviewing field. It is too new at its task to be evaluated, but merits description here. In the spring 1985 issue of *Reference Services Review*, Recent Reference Books debuted. This first appearance of what is intended to be a regular column listed and annotated 109 reference works arranged by subject. A one- to five-star rating system as well as short recommendation statements in the brief

annotations carry the burden of evaluation. Codes indicate type of library or libraries for which a work is appropriate. The column is the work of C. Edward Wall, publisher of *RSR* and former director of the library at the University of Michigan-Dearborn.

ISSUES STILL TO BE MET

All of the sources examined above concentrate their energies on reviewing hard copy codex reference tools. Occasionally they will review a microform tool. *RQ* has a separate database review column and *RBB* occasionally includes a database review. Specialized journals such as *Database* and *Online* do a better job of covering databases. Overall, however, nontraditional formats are not covered well. Reference books will not disappear and the need for useful reviews of new ones will continue. However, if in their day-to-day provision of information service, librarians are to meet the challenges of integrating hard copy, microform, online, and CD/ROM-based information tools, they will need reviews of these nontraditional tools as well. Thus far the producers of databases have not been as forthcoming as reference book publishers in making their products available for review. Through their associations and personal contacts with database vendors and producers of other nontraditional reference tools, librarians should press these vendors to make their wares available for review through both the existing review sources and new specialized sources.

A point touched on but not yet discussed at length is the question of reviews' timeliness. In 1976, a program at the American Library Association conference in Chicago asked the questions "Where are the reviews a librarian needs when a publisher's advance catalog comes in? And how can a journal editor get 50 to 5,000 well chosen words in print timed close to a book's release?"[19] Librarians have always been concerned about these questions. The answer to the first question seems to be that, at best, the reviews are either being written or have been written and are at some stage in the editorial and production processes. Although it has been the subject of much sound and fury, the time lag issue is really a non-issue hardly worth a whimper in that hardly anything can be done about it. Yet because timeliness has been the major preoccupation of the small body of literature on reference book reviewing, the issue has to be dealt with at some length to demonstrate its non-issue status.

There has been only one major study of reference book reviewing, a book-length study by Alma A. Covey.[20] Published in 1972, it compared the lag time—the elapsed time between a book's publication date and the appearance of its reviews—in the day's major reference book reviewing media. Covey found that individual journals' average lag time ranged from 1.6 weeks to 35.8 weeks; most journals exceeded ten weeks.[21] The finding substantiates the calls for greater timeliness made in the few other studies of reference book publishing. In 1954 Pryce examined only four titles, but found reviews of two of them published a year and *five years* respectively after their publications dates.[22] In 1964 Goggin and Seaberg said that "the reviewing of reference books is highly inadequate as far as their existence and the rapidity of their appearance are concerned."[23] However, time lag will not decrease unless several things change, ideally simultaneously.

Time lag results mostly from the editorial policies and practices of the various reference review media. The two major factors are, first, the journals' policies governing which state(s) of a book it will accept for review and, second, the journals' publication schedules.

The day a finished book is shipped for review, *Library Journal* probably has already made a decision whether or not to review it and possibly has a review in hand, perhaps has already published a review. The reason is that *LJ*'s practice is to review from pre-publication states such as galleys, uncorrected proofs, or unbound signatures. It is not uncommon for an *LJ* review to note that the reviewer was not able to examine illustrations because he or she worked from one of these very early states of the book. *LJ*'s twice-a-month publication schedule will further accelerate the review's appearances. This practice accounts for the early appearance of *Library Journal*'s reviews compared to reviews of the same book in other sources.

RQ reference reviews tend to be late; its review editor, Gail Schlachter, cites a lag of fourteen weeks as typical.[24] *RQ* generally reviews from the completed book. *RQ*'s time lag is largely a by-product of its quarterly publication schedule. For some time *RQ*'s publisher, the Reference and Adult Services Division of the American Library Association, has had hopes of increasing *RQ*'s frequency from four to six issues per year. If this happens, time lag of *RQ*'s reference book reviews will shorten.

If it were studied carefully based on publication dates announced in the *Weekly Record*, the reference reviewing medium with the longest average time lag would surely be *ARBA*. As an annual, *ARBA* inherently has a long time lag. Some *ARBA* reviews will inevitably have a time lag of more than a year. At best, the review of a book published in November and included in

the *ARBA* volume covering that calendar year will have a time lag of five months by the time *ARBA* is published the following April.

The *Reference Books Bulletin*, the product of the members and selected alumni of its editorial board (which is in turn a subcommittee of the Publishing Committee of the American Library Association), employs procedures unique in the reference reviewing world. Although published within the pages of *Booklist*, the *Reference Books Bulletin* is a distinct entity. *RBB* reviews from various states of the book, a practice it has adopted only in recent years mostly in hopes of reducing the lag time of its reviews. Although like *LJ*, *Booklist* is issued twice a month, *RBB*'s procedures account for most of its considerable lag time. After a book is assigned to a reviewer and the review has been drafted and returned to the editorial office, the review is duplicated and sent to members of the *RBB* editorial board for comment. After these comments have been received and the editor and the board's chairperson have synthesized them, the editor revises the draft. The review then goes into production and generally appears six to nine months after the book was received. The editor, Sandy Whiteley, "would like to shorten this to four months," the minimum possible considering *Booklist*'s present production schedule.[25]

In the monthly *Choice* the typical lag between publication of a reference book and publication of the review is about eighteen weeks. A slight majority of its reviews appear within this period.[26] Its editor has stated that "improvement of the currency of reviews is an editorial objective at *Choice*."[27]

The *Wilson Library Bulletin*'s reference book review column, Current Reference Books, differs from all of the others in that it is the work of one person, James Rettig, head of the reference department of the Main Library at the University of Illinois at Chicago [and author of this article]. Because it is the work of only one person working without clerical help to support the reviewing operation, books are usually reviewed only in their finished state rather than in a pre-publication state. Exceptions are sometimes made, but usually only for unbound signatures. It would be too confusing to deal with galleys or proofs of as many as twenty-five different books each month; the risk of confusing sheets from one book with sheets from another is too great. The production cycle of approximately seven weeks dictates the deadline by which the Current Reference Books copy must be received at the *WLB* office. Because the column is written throughout the four weeks prior to that, time lag generally ranges from approximately twelve weeks down to eight weeks. Time lag of reviews in the September and October issues is greater, these columns being prepared over a longer period since *WLB* does not publish in July or August. Similar situations prevail at other journals; for example, one issue of *RBB* is pre-empted by the annual *Booklist* index; *LJ* publishes only one issue several months of the year; and *Choice* publishes a combined July/August issue.

Very little can be done to reduce the time any of these production or editorial practices take. If they were as insistent as it appears *LJ* is about reviewing from pre-publication states of a book, the other review media could reduce their lag time. If journals were to pay the cost for reviewers to transmit review copy over electronic communication networks, lag time could be reduced. *Reference Services Review* hopes to distribute its Recent Reference Books on floppy disk and eventually online by dial-access. This would eliminate the production time. The *Reference Books Bulletin* hopes to experiment with receiving copy from its members via ALANET. Because subscription to electronically published journals, most of which are in the sciences, has not yet caught on in libraries, it seems very unlikely that libraries would be willing to pay the cost for reference book reviews published online.

Lag time, then, is a given in reference book reviews. By some sources, more is given than by others. But in all sources, it is a given. Only if a book is reviewed the day it is received and then the review is published electronically that same day would lag time be eliminated. For this state of affairs to prevail, the review media editors would have to make major procedural changes and the economics of electronic journal publishing targeted at the library market would have to become attractive to both publishers and libraries. The fact is that librarians are not likely any time soon to have the number of reviews they would like to have coinciding with a book's publication date or receipt of a publisher's promotional brochure in the mail or a copy of the book itself in an approval shipment. If reviews are to offer librarians useful guidance in selecting reference books, the reviews' quality is more important than their timeliness provided that the review editors continue their efforts to bring reviews out as soon as they reasonably can.

The *Wilson Library Bulletin*'s positive experience and the *Reference Books Bulletin*'s negative experience illustrate that editorial policy changes can have a strong effect on the quality and usefulness of reference book reviews. The high percentage of positive recommendations is fairly meaningless. As was noted above, each book selector must place the description and evaluation contained in a review into the context of his or her collection and clientele and then make a purchase decision yea or nay.

What is needed most is greater intensity of evaluation in reviews. The overall recent rate for the six sources combined can be improved. For *LJ* and *RBB* improvement can be facilitated through editorial changes. It appears that these are well underway at *RBB*; only their effect remains to be seen and judged. The other sources can improve their performance through the technique which has made *RQ* the best source for comparative reviews — editorial leadership. If editors demand more quality of their reviewers, they will get more. Then everyone — publishers, reference book authors, review editors, librarians — will have more.

NOTES

[1] The Association of American Publishers estimated that "subscription reference," a category not defined in the *Publishers Weekly* article reporting book publishing industry statistics ("Estimated Book Publishing Industry Sales," *Publishers Weekly* 227 [28 June 1985]: 21) accounted for $465.2 million in sales in 1984. Since many reference books are *not* sold on subscription, one can assume that the total sales of all reference books during 1984 exceeded $465.2 million.

[2] "Librarians Are Key to Buying, Survey Finds," *Publishers Weekly* 228 (25 October 1985): 14.

[3] An exhaustive study of this subject would require checking at least a sample of titles from each of the other sources to determine how many titles *ARBA*, despite its wide sweep, misses. The number of titles reviewed in at least three sources is surely greater than this, but how much greater is completely unknown. To determine how much greater would require such sampling as well as checking the 1,517 titles in *ARBA* which list no citations to the other six sources or a citation of a review in only one of these sources. As was noted, it is unknown what time lag *Book Review Index* experiences and how this in turn affects a search for reviews in other sources.

[4] Margaret Knox Goggin and Lillian M. Seaberg, "The Publishing and Reviewing of Reference Books," *Library Trends* 12 (January 1964): 440.

[5]Alma A. Covey, *Reviewing of Reference Books* (Metuchen, N.J.: Scarecrow Press, 1972), 82.

[6]Ibid.

[7]M[ary] J[ane] M[cKinven], "Program on Reviews Dares to Ask: 'Who Needs Them?,' " *American Libraries* 7 (September 1976): 515.

[8]Goggin and Seaberg, 440.

[9]*"Reference Books Bulletin" Editorial Board Manual* (Chicago: American Library Association, 1985), 36. This statement also appeared in the board's earlier manual under which it operated during 1984.

[10]Ibid.

[11]Bohdan S. Wynar, ed., *American Reference Books Annual 1985* (Littleton, Colo.: Libraries Unlimited, 1985), xiv.

[12]Goggin and Seaberg, 452.

[13]Harry E. Whitmore, "Reference Book Reviewing," *RQ* 9 (Spring 1970): 224.

[14]William A. Katz, *Introduction to Reference Work*, 4th ed. (New York: McGraw-Hill, 1982), 1:53.

[15]Gail A. Schlachter, letter to author, 13 December 1985.

[16]Ibid. [Italics in original.]

[17]Gary R. Purcell, review of *Directory of Foreign Documents Collections, RQ* 24 (Summer 1985): 497.

[18]The author of this article is the editor of *WLB*'s Current Reference Books column.

[19]M[cKinven], 515.

[20]Covey, *Reviewing of Reference Books.*

[21]Ibid., 76.

[22]F. T. Pryce, "Better Reviewing Wanted," *Bookseller*, No. 2523 (1 May 1954): 1324-25.

[23]Goggin and Seaberg, 447.

[24]Gail A. Schlachter, telephone conversation with author, 12 December 1985.

[25]Sandy Whiteley, letter to author, 16 October 1985.

[26]P[atricia] E. S[abosik], "Currency of Choice Reviews," *Choice* 22 (March 1985): 935.

[27]Ibid.

James Rettig

Reviewing for a Young Audience

Ten thousand is a conservative estimate of the annual number of reviews of children's and young adults' books which have a good potential for being seen by librarians. Recent statistics credit the major book reviewing publications used by librarians with totals nearing the nine thousand mark.[1] Librarians read, write, reject, applaud, appreciate, and certainly use these reviews. Although using and preparing reviews is an important aspect of library work with the young patron, little has been written about the organization and conceptual framework of book reviewing for children and young adults. It is, therefore, useful, in an article such as this, to step back and survey the environment of reviewing as reflected in book selection and journal reviews, the reviews themselves, the underlying issues, and the research.

BOOK SELECTION AND THE SOURCES FOR REVIEWS

Although in the past many large library systems and school boards attempted to examine all children's books being considered for purchase, the shortage of trained personnel and of budget has forced librarians to re-examine that process. Having books reviewed by staff members, holding book selection meetings, and maintaining examination centers require time and money which many libraries can no longer afford. As long ago as 1978, in an *Encyclopedia of Library and Information Science* article, Priscilla Moulton wrote:

> While all library educators and practicing librarians agree that there is no substitute for actually handling and reading a children's

book as a basis for selection, in fact this desiderata seldom exists. A library purchase generally results from what reviewers say about a book, despite the limitations of this mode of acquisition.[2]

The years since then have escalated the average cost of juvenile titles and further eroded the spending power of children's librarians with a resulting increase in the dependency on reviews for selection. Most children's librarians try to keep abreast of the publication of books by subscribing to one or more of the journals which review children's and young adults' materials for librarians. By regularly reading these journals, librarians learn about the books which are considered the most likely candidates for purchase.

Reviews are supplemented by looking at publishers' catalogs, by talking with publishers' representatives, by visits to conference exhibits and to bookstores or wholesalers. It is reviews, however, which usually form the basis for decisions to purchase materials. Some libraries have a policy of requiring the citation of two or more reviews as justification for purchase of a book which is to be cataloged for the children's collection. While there are many selection aids and professional journals which are widely consulted and which carry review columns or bibliographical essays, there are five particularly influential reviewing journals in children's library service.

Booklist (1905-) is advertised as the flagship of the reviewing journals published by the American Library Association. It reviews materials for both adults and children, and notes in its prefatory statement a goal of providing a guide to current print and nonprint materials for public and school libraries. Reviews are done by staff, with some field reviewers, and the reviews are for recommended materials, excepting those done for the "Reference Books Bulletin" insertion. A symbol indicates a book, judged by the reviewer, to be a good example within a genre. Celebrating an eightieth anniversary in 1985, *Booklist* could look back on the longest history of reviewing children's books in a "heritage of quality individualized by care and concern"[3] for book, child and librarian.

The Bulletin of the Center for Children's Books (1945-), from the University of Chicago Graduate Library School, contains reviews only. Its short annotations are prepared by the editors aided by discussion within a small advisory group. Aware of the librarian's desire for summarized information, it uses codes for reading level, potential for curricular use, or developmental value. Inclusion does not mean recommendation, and books are labelled as recommended, not recommended, or marginal. Subscribers can scan the slim issues and appreciate the efficiency with which they are introduced to some of the new titles for children and young people.

The Horn Book Magazine (1924-), published by The Horn Book, Inc., contains both articles and reviews that are longer than those in other reviewing journals; it seeks "to review intelligently and reflectively those books [the editors] believe to be an important contribution."[4] Therefore, books which are reviewed are recommended, and a symbol may be used to indicate a book that is an outstanding example of an author's work, a genre, or a publishing season. Remarks on the appropriate age or grade level of a book and on its use with children are scant. Reviewers are regular, local contributors who emphasize literary or other aesthetic qualities in their reviews, and who meet to choose books for review and exchange opinion. Occasionally books may be reviewed from galleys, but reviews can appear well after publication since a report on current publishing is second to an appreciation of the book. This journal functions to keep the tone and discussion of children's literature elevated on the premise that "nothing can be too good for children."[5] Without intending to lose that tone, *The Horn Book* is being renovated. From its beginning, Randolph Caldecott's huntsmen blew their horns on the cover in a symbolic hunt for good books until a recent design featured a horn alone. This design preceded colored covers, a different one proposed for each volume year, and each one featuring a work from a well-known children's illustrator. The transition is heralded by a Maurice Sendak cover, based on a Caldecott drawing, as a centennial (1986) tribute to Caldecott. The horn remains as colophon and symbol, but the new covers underline *The Horn Book*'s commitment to a contemporary critical outlook.

Kirkus Reviews (1933-), recently bought by James and Hope Kobak, offers staff-written reviews of children's and adults' books. It uses a symbol to indicate books that are of uncommon merit, interest, or appeal; it established its reputation as a pre-publication review journal alerting its readers to good, bad, or mediocre books. Children's coverage has been revised to give "more timely, representative" reviews;[6] these recent changes suggest that *Kirkus* is a reviewing aid to watch for an interpretation of the meaning of "representative" to new management.

The School Library Journal (1954-), published by R. R. Bowker, includes articles and reviews. With the largest circulation of the major reviewing journals for children's, young adult and school librarians, and reviewing the most books, *SLJ* claims a place as the most complete source of reviews of new general trade children's books. Reviews, typically attentive to librarian's needs, are contributed by some 380 reviewers (librarians or specialists in children's literature) across the country. An editorial prerogative stars particular books which the reviewers recommend as having literary or artistic merit, reader appeal, or potential for library use. The annual policy statement in September's issue repeats a goal of providing subscribers with short critical reviews of virtually the entire annual production of hardcover general trade children's books from established publishers plus coverage of original paperbacks and worthwhile titles from small presses.

Between 1983 and 1985, editors for four of these journals changed. Anita Silvey took over *The Horn Book* from Ethel Heins. Trevelyn E. Jones became the children's book review editor at *SLJ* which continues under the general editorship of Lillian Gerhardt. Zena Sutherland retired from the *Bulletin of the Center for Children's Books*. She was replaced by Betsy Hearne, who moved over from *Booklist* which continues with the editorial services of Barbara Elleman in books for children. After thirty-two years with *Booklist*, Barbara Duree, editor in charge of books for young adults, resigned in 1986. While it is true that all of these reviewing aids change in response to readers' needs, new editors often make substantive changes which may affect the policy and scope of these journals in the next few years.

Although the major selection aids vary in their emphasis and extent of coverage, their general aims and evaluative principles are similar. Other journals are more specialized and try to fill perceived gaps in the reviewing of children's books. One such gap has been in science materials, and two journals, *Appraisal* and *Science Books & Films*, have made this area their specialty.

Appraisal: Science Books for Young People (1967-), published by the Children's Science Book Committee, Department of Science and Mathematics Education of Boston University and the New England Round Table of Children's Librarians, is well-known in its special field. Each item reviewed is evaluated by both a science specialist and a librarian who rate the item on a scale from poor to excellent. The science specialist, usually a teacher, evaluates the accuracy and clarity of the material, while the librarian concentrates on the appeal to children and on the comparison to other works. The dual approach (an appraisal of scientific fact plus an account of literary quality and attractive format) makes this journal very useful to book selectors.

Science Books & Films (1965-), published by the American Association for the Advancement of Science, covers more items than *Appraisal*, including different forms of material for all ages. Short reviews by science specialists evaluate each item, and recommended or highly recommended materials are starred.

In contrast to filling gaps in the coverage of particular subject matter like science, some journals attempt coverage from a particular perspective. Religious magazines are an example, and their reviews may be very influential among their readers.

The *Interracial Books for Children Bulletin* (1967-), from the Council on Interracial Books for Children (CIBC), is a well-known general professional journal with consciousness-raising articles and ideological reviews. The *Bulletin*'s goal is a regular analysis of learning materials for stereotypes and other forms of bias, along with recommendations of new books and alternative resources. This emphasis has led to evaluations of individual books that sometimes differ sharply from those of other journals.

CIBC reviewers are aware of the sensitivities of ethnic and racial groups, are concerned with the needs of the mentally and physically disabled, and are conscious of individuals outside the mainstream of life as it is generally portrayed in the media. Despite disagreements over evaluations of particular titles, the *IBC Bulletin* alerts librarians to issues which are sometimes overlooked. Many of the attitudes first expressed in this journal have later been adopted by other professional sources.

While librarians rely chiefly on professional reviewing journals, many adults learn about children's books from newspapers and general magazines. Magazines, like *Time* or *Newsweek*, occasionally feature an article on children's books, often timed for the Christmas buying season. The *New York Times Book Review*, like the *Times Literary Supplement*, reviews books for children, and a former *NYTBR* children's book editor noted the contribution of a newspaper in purveying reviews for general, rather than professional readers: "We do not consciously attempt to influence their buying habits."[7] Local newspapers also may carry reviews of children's books, sometimes featuring regional writers or topics. Because press coverage frequently results in requests to the library for particular titles or generates information on the regional scene, librarians usually try to read the reviews in local and national newspapers or magazines.

THE BOOKS
AND THE REVIEWERS

During the 1980s, approximately three thousand books for children have been published in the United States each year. Which of these books are likely to be reviewed? Table 1 indicates the reviewing activity of major selection aids in juvenile and children's publishing related to the publishing output in those areas. Some books not reviewed in any of the major aids may yet be covered in other journals, but librarians who depend heavily on reviews for book selection should also be aware that some books will not be reviewed at all.

Table 1.
Juvenile Books Reviewed by Leading Journals.[a]

Juvenile Book Publishing Activity (reported as a Calendar Year)				
	1981	1982	1983	1984
Number of Juvenile Books[b]	3,102	3,049	3,197	3,128

Juvenile Book Reviewing Activity (reported September to August)[c]								
	1981-82		1982-83		1983-84		1984-85	
	Number of Reviews	Percent Juvenile Books	Number of Reviews	Percent Juvenile Books	Number of Reviews	Percent Juvenile Books	Number of Reviews	Percent Juvenile Books
Booklist	1,540	50	1,546	51	1,476	46	1,468	47
Bulletin of the Center for Children's Books	490	16	439	14	445	14	450	14
The Horn Book	318	10	284	9	290	9	278	9
Kirkus	869	28	600	20	600	19	not available	not available
SLJ	2,295	74	2,357	77	2,525	79	2,419	77

[a]Figures are derived from information reported each year in *Bowker Annual* on publishing statistics and book media reviewing. Table 1 above compares reviewing activity in a twelve-month period (September to August) to publishing activity during a previous twelve month period (January to December).

[b]Publishing activity figures include both hardbound and paperbound books.

[c]Figures are those which the reviewing aids classify as juvenile. Figures for young adult books are not included. Because the aids vary in their method of classifying books, some titles considered juvenile by one reviewing source might be put under young adult by another. The figures for the various journals are not, therefore, strictly comparable.

It is difficult to identify which books are not reviewed. Virginia Witucke, using books chosen for the American Library Association's "Notable Children's Books" as her sample, showed that these "notables" are widely reviewed.[8] Is it the wide coverage which leads to a winning of awards, or is it merit which leads to a recognition in reviews?

Books written by award-winning or popular authors are usually reviewed in several journals. In adult book reviewing, this so-called "pack reviewing" has sometimes been criticized as encouraging duplication in review sources and artificially inflating the merit of a title. Yet, many readers of book reviews look forward to hearing about new books by popular favorites. These same books often receive more advertising than books by less well-known authors. While this attention is a natural response to the market, it can mean that new authors and illustrators may be neglected and their work not brought to the attention of potential buyers. In the long run, libraries and their patrons will be the poorer if new talent is not encouraged.

THE ENVIRONMENT OF CHILDREN'S BOOK REVIEWING

Many aspects of the book trade, reviewing, and library evaluation of books apply equally to both children's and adults' books. But at least three unique factors are at work in reviewing for a young audience, and these factors give rise to a number of issues that occur only, or primarily, in connection with children.

In managing library collections for adults, there are plans for automatic purchase of some materials and pressures to select particular books in response to patron demand; such acquisition is independent of any reviewing. This type of acquisition occurs less frequently in library collections for children although genre or, series titles, popular authors, or books on topical subjects are often bought without recourse to reviews. For much collection building, children's librarians can wait for reviews and have come to depend heavily on them as a means to develop permanent collections. Linked with a tendency to want evaluation to support selection decisions, this practice of habitually waiting for reviews before purchase means that reviews assume a greater importance in the development of children's than of adults' collections.

Another differentiating factor is the division of children's reviewers into distinctive disciplines. At the post-secondary level of education, English departments now accept children's literature as a legitimate study, while both education and library science departments have traditionally taught children's literature. A survey of readings for course work within the disciplines indicates that all three stress fiction rather than genre books and nonfiction.[9] The three disciplines approach their material in different ways which, while not always articulated, are often implicit in the reviews. English departments emphasize the history of children's literature, while library science and education departments stress learning theory, child development, and response to literature. Class lists from education and library science tend to include individual titles and award-winning books (the Newbery and Caldecott winners); English departments more often use anthologies and classics. A reviewer's background in one or more of these disciplines undoubtedly influences the way in which book reviewing for the young audience is undertaken and the criteria which are used in assessing the book.

In the past, reviewing books for children has generally meant reviewing them for librarians and teachers. Until about 1980, over 80 percent of children's books were purchased by schools and libraries, but the real purchasing power of institutions has declined in recent years. At a session on children's publishing at the American Library Association annual conference in 1985, publishers estimated that almost half of the books now published are purchased by individuals rather than by institutions.

These changes in the economic realities of publishing for the young have led to changes in the content and design of books for children. Trevelyn Jones, children's book review editor at *SLJ*, observed that while sales in quality trade books are up in the increasingly selective, but still substantial, library market, publishers are producing greater quantities of mass market books for stores and libraries.[10] Parents tend to buy books based on familiar characters—often those from television shows—or books in formats suitable for popular and medium-priced markets. Fragile formats, such as pop-up books and book-toys, are becoming increasingly popular; B. Dalton stores report a 500 percent increase in this format over the past ten years. The demand for full-color picture books has grown, as indicated by the fact that presently 75 percent of the picture books produced are in full color, as compared with 25 percent only ten years ago. Some librarians believe that this emphasis on color has reduced the appeal of older standard picture books of merit. Librarians are now making decisions about whether or not to purchase all of these kinds of books aimed at the home market. They present particular problems for reviewers who are writing for the library or school book selector.

Another change has been that many of the older titles which librarians have been replacing for years are now going out-of-print. Reviewers must be aware that children's librarians are ordering more new titles rather than keeping the standard books in stock. Selecting a new title requires evaluation of many possible choices, so that librarians must now spend more time in book selection.

A final, well-recognized factor distinguishing children's book reviewing from adult book reviewing is the mediation by adults of the entire procedure of publishing and selecting books for children. Adults write the books for children and decide which manuscripts to publish. Adults review the books and decide which will be available to children. Until children are of school age, they rarely can purchase books and, even then, their choices are still within the bounds of materials which have been preselected by adults. That adults tastes do not always coincide with those of children has been demonstrated by Betty Carter and Karen

Harris.[11] In comparing books chosen as favorites by children in grades six to eight with the reviews of these books in *SLJ* and *Booklist*, it was found that only three of the children's choices appeared among the lists of best books as selected by the editors. Of twenty-four books chosen by children, only eleven in *SLJ* and fifteen in *Booklist* received favorable reviews.

The discrepancy between children's and adults' choices surprises no one. The difference between choices reflects the natural concern of adults that children be given books that enrich their reading experience while children themselves are concerned with books that entertain.

In summary, these three factors—the inclination to wait for reviews, the tendency to assess from a particular, professional standpoint, and the ability to mediate reading for the audience of readers—lead to a number of issues which do not occur with the same intensity in the world of adult reviewing.

ISSUES

Appropriate Literary Standards

Most reviewing of adult books is done on the basis of generally accepted literary standards. While the potential popularity of a book may be mentioned or the psychological impact of the material noted, these are seldom used as relevant bases for evaluating the literary work. Some reviewers of children's books seek to apply similar standards to children's books. Lillian Smith in *The Unreluctant Years*, her influential text on children's literature, stated that "the qualities which are basic in good writing are literary values; that is, they do not concern the subject matter so much as how it is presented."[12] That traditional view is supported by much writing on children's literature which endorses a knowledge of the literature and a conception of literary standards as final judgment and authority for any appraisal.

Too strict an adherence to that view is at considerable variance with other objectives for children's books. Because many reviewers, as well as the readers of reviews, are eager to encourage children to read, and because the mastery of reading is essential for a child, the popular appeal of a book is a much more important factor in reviewing for children than for adults. A reviewer with the belief that reading is a valuable exercise, regardless of the trivial nature of the book, will evaluate series books and other ephemeral titles far differently than will a reviewer who is looking for high literary standards. The tension between popularity and

literary value is an ongoing theme in the reviewing of books for children.

Series books (romances, mysteries, participation books, etc.) are often criticized as a waste of children's time. Although many librarians agree that individual titles within a fiction series can have merit, it appears difficult for any series book, including nonfiction series books, to break into the circle of consistent, serious reviewing. Most journals relegate reviews of series books to notices, brief descriptions, or categorization as subliterary. Roger Sutton, recently writing about librarians "trying to do the right thing" by paperback romances for young readers, discusses the reviewing of these series books.[13] The implied conclusion is that effort spent in reviewing these items or arguing over their merits in libraries is time better spent on other, more important tasks of reviewing for collection building.

Extra-Literary Standards

In addition to the standards that can be applied to the literary merit of a book, there are other standards that are brought to bear in reviewing for children. Occasionally, the potential for causing physical harm to a child may require assessment. An example is the question of safety in books on scientific experiments, cooking, crafts, and sports. A reviewer who is evaluating books for young children must decide whether the activities suggested are safe and appropriate for children of the age for which the book is written. Reviewers warn against books which encourage young children to use matches, sharp instruments, or kitchen appliances without the supervision of an adult.

Many of the differences between reviewing for adults and reviewing for children occur because adult book reviewers are reviewing for their peers. They take neither a didactic orientation to the value of the material nor a protective stance to the determination of any physical hurt that could result from some materials. An extension of the desire to protect children from traumas or undesirable influences often leads adults to question the content in children's books. Most reviewers of children's books do take into account the probable impact of content on children. They try to determine whether the language, theme, or particular scenes are likely to be objectionable to parents, to other adults, or to the children themselves. Reviewers are aware that their readers want to be alerted to books which might be objectionable to some segments of the population.

Among the books which can cause problems are those dealing with the occult, politics, creationism and evolution, and sex and teenagers' sexuality, as well as those using language that might be offensive. Despite the growing permissiveness in language and the sexual explicitness in television and other mass media, the measure for children's books continues to be conservative. Even books which seem mild by today's media standards continue to be attacked, especially in school libraries.[14]

Following the American Library Association's suggestion for countering censorship attempts, many children's departments keep a file containing reviews of potentially controversial titles and the reasons for purchasing such titles. In case of query, this file serves as a demonstration that the material has been well received by reviewers, and that it was considered carefully before purchase. Librarians often prefer reviews which deal candidly with the possibility of objections to a particular title and, unlike reviews for adult items, reviews of children's books frequently include such comments. There is difficulty in predicting controversial items, because standards and reactions vary greatly between communities and across the country. Objections to many long-held Halloween books for their depictions of witches caught librarians and reviewers by surprise. Some reviewers decry the preference for indication of controversial material, because they fear that timid librarians will simply refuse to purchase any title which might cause trouble.

Although not a particularly controversial group of books, picture books are difficult to review well because of their visual and aural qualities. Reviews of picture books and stories for the young child often overlook these two major elements. In 1980, John Stewig examined the ways in which picture books are reviewed in the four largest book review journals.[15] He found that relatively little space was devoted to the visual aspects of these books; 43 percent of the reviews had less than a fifth and 37 percent had less than a third of the review on this aspect. He suggests that reviewers of picture books ought to pay more attention to the visual content of picture books.

A study establishing the attention paid to the euphony in reviews of books for a young child has yet to be done. It does not seem that many reviews of picture books and stories for an early age regard the sound of the text as important; yet, it must be obvious that books which will be both shown and read to young children require comment on sight and sound.

These issues of literary and extra literary standards for children's book reviewing continue to be pertinent topics for discussion and debate. More attention needs to be paid to courses and workshops designed to hone reviewing skills. Library school education provides training in understanding children and in selecting materials, but a more professional standard in reviewing would be encouraged by additional training in literary and artistic evaluation and by a more conscious consideration of the role and function of reviewing.

RESEARCH ON BOOK REVIEWING

Research on children's book reviewing is an area in which much could be done from both a historical and a contemporary viewpoint. There have been a few historical studies[16] and some interest in the contemporary scene.

Top of the News (Winter 1979) featured articles on reviewing including studies on the adequacy of reviews. One of these, by Rosemary Weber, examined the reviewing of children's books and young adults' books published in 1977 in the most important reviewing journals.[17] The journals published 7,611 reviews covering 3,915 different books. Of these books, 55 percent were reviewed in only one journal with up to an additional 21 percent being reviewed in only two journals. While *SLJ* and *Booklist* had a much wider coverage than any of the other journals, it appears from this study that no single reviewing journal is sufficient for the book selector who uses reviews as a primary means to build collections.

In another approach to the journals, Virginia Witucke examined reviews for the "Notable Children's Books" of 1972, 1973, and 1974.[18] *SLJ, Booklist,* and the *Bulletin of the Center for Children's Books* each reviewed at least 75 percent of these highly selective titles. Witucke examined the rate of coverage, the promptness of appearance, and the characteristics of reviews. Not surprisingly, the number of critical themes per review was greater in *The Horn Book* and the *New York Times Book Review* than in other journals in which the reviews were much shorter and more descriptive. In a companion study of the reviewing of science books, Witucke found that the "Outstanding Science Trade Books" received less coverage than the notable books, although the top six reviewing journals each reviewed at least 40 percent of these titles.[19]

Phyllis Kennemer examined 209 reviews to discover to what degree the comments were descriptive, analytical, or sociological.[20] The results indicated that the reviews in the *Bulletin of the Center for Children's Books* were the most descriptive, those in *SLJ* contained the most sociological comments while those in *Booklist* and *The Horn Book* were the most concerned with literary analysis.

In a 1983 study of *SLJ* book reviewers, Kathleen Carver queried four areas of their work: the review's aspects (literary criticism, plot content, recommendations); the reviewer's role (critic or reviewer, objectivity); practices (reading or discussing the books, reading additional information); background (personal and professional).[21] Reviewers chose to give priority to literary quality and plot content in their reviews over other items such as comparisons to other titles, illustrations, recommendations, and use of the book. Reviewers reported that editors frequently queried reviews and did sometimes persuade reviewers to re-examine their judgments. Very few respondents (3 percent) saw their role as that of critic, more (30 percent) saw themselves as reviewers, and most (65 percent) saw themselves as mixtures of critic and reviewer. Most of the reviewers were practicing librarians with an altruistic attitude towards the voluntary service of reviewing and a positive attitude toward the books reviewed. Carver concludes that her data "unequivocally reinforced the confidence which librarians and others have historically placed in the objectivity and professionalism of book reviewers."[22]

There is always room for further examination. The recent interest in quantitatively examining children's book reviewing has largely established expected results but has also pointed to some provocative findings or peripheral areas for further investigation. In reflecting on the historical aspects, there is room for more research to document the past or examine the legacies that influence reviewing today. In reflecting on the contemporary scene, the exploration into books and reviews, librarians as reviewers and users, the role and function of reviewing and the relationships between these areas has yet to be fully exploited.

Potential research topics grow naturally from some of the studies cited. For example, some reviewers have stated their preference for reviewing fiction,[23] and there is general agreement that picture books and fiction are reviewed more often than nonfiction. So a study of the adequacy of the reviewing of nonfiction would be helpful to the profession. Then, too, within the reviewing of fiction itself, the determination of a bias toward the reviewing of particular genres would explore unknown data. The whole question of personal characteristics, which received some attention from Carver, is open for much more work. Since research on book selection in public libraries indicates that many librarians avoid buying books which might be objectionable to some members of the community, a study of the effect of reviewers' warnings of the controversial nature of some titles is indicated. No one has as yet studied the effect of reviews on the sales of children's books. A study similar to one done by Judith Serebnick on the purchasing of potentially controversial adult books could profitably be duplicated in the children's department.[24] Serebnick found that the number of reviews was more important in a purchase decision than was the favorable or unfavorable content of the review. Would this be true for children's titles? The collection of data on the generation, adequacy, and impact of reviews is a fruitful area to add to the literature on book reviewing. The literature to this time has consisted chiefly of opinion pieces which offer insights into the value of reviews or into the practice of evaluation and selection as related to reviewing. It is now time to increase the knowledge base with research which adds another dimension to the qualitative literature.

Reviews of children's and young adults' books are a part of the professional literature and are so important to collection development for young patrons that they constitute a valid and valuable area for examination. Because of the changing environment and the multiplicity of issues in reviewing for children, this area offers considerable scope for study. It is imperative to comprehend the nature of those ten thousand or more reviews that librarians may see in a year as they build collections for young patrons.

NOTES

[1]*The Bowker Annual* (1985), 499, reports figures from seven library journals, *Publishers Weekly* and six newspapers.

[2]*Encyclopedia of Library and Information Science*, 1978 ed., s.v. "Reviews and Reviewing," by Priscilla Moulton.

[3]Barbara Elleman, ed., Children's Books, in *The Booklist* 81 (July 1985): 1551, commented on the years of reviewing since the first issue (September 1905) which noted twenty children's books.

[4]Anita Silvey, ed., "The Mysterious Book Review Process," *The Horn Book* 56 (March/April 1985): 143.

[5]Ann A. Flowers, children's librarian and regular reviewer, stating her view on reviewing for *The Horn Book* 61 (March/April 1985): 238.

[6]"To Our Readers," a brief note in *Kirkus Reviews* 53 (15 October 1985).

[7]George A. Woods, "Reviewing Books for Children," in *Book Reviewing*, ed. S. E. Kamerman (Boston: The Writer Inc., 1978), p. 54.

[8]Virginia Witucke, "A Comparative Analysis of Juvenile Book Review Media," *School Media Quarterly* 8 (Spring 1980): 153-60.

[9]Lynda G. Adamson, "And Who Taught You Children's Literature?" *The Horn Book* 61 (September/October 1985): 631-32.

[10]As quoted by Bertha M. Cheatham, "News of '85," *SLJ* 31 (December 1985): 25.

[11]Betty Carter and Karen Harris, "The Children and the Critics: How Do Their Book Selections Compare?" *School Library Media Quarterly* 10 (Fall 1981): 54-58.

[12]Lillian H. Smith, *The Unreluctant Years* (Chicago: American Library Association, 1953), 33.

[13]Roger Sutton, "Librarians and the Paperback Romance," *SLJ* (November 1985): 25-29. In writing about the review media in his article, Sutton notes the practice of *VOYA: Voice of Youth Advocates* in letting many of its reviews of series be written by the teenagers, because, as co-editor Dorothy Broderick says "a book has a right to be reviewed by someone who's basically sympathetic to its point of view."

SLJ in its annual policy statement (September 1984) noted its then new practice of recording teen romance and participation series in separate columns. Subscribers identified that they wanted such titles briefly noted rather than critiqued. Editors were pleased because this decision allowed for more concentration on hardcover titles. In Sutton's article, while *LJ/SLJ* editors repeat their general opinion that they have "better things to do" than devote excessive time to romances, an *SLJ* editor also mentions that librarians do ask for reviews of these books, wanting to know which are best and which have controversial content.

[14]A recent study by David Jenkinson, "The Censorship Iceberg: The Results of a Survey of Challenges in School and Public Libraries," *School Libraries in Canada* 6 (Fall 1985): 19-30, notes some of the titles challenged in school libraries. These titles are similar to many in other censorship cases.

The *Newsletter on Intellectual Freedom* (Office for Intellectual Freedom, American Library Association) reports censorship activity in libraries, noting incidents, studies and their findings, and books that are targets for censorship.

[15]John W. Stewig, "Picture Books: What Do Reviews Really Review?" *Top of the News* 37 (Fall 1980): 83-84.

[16]The most notable historical study is Richard Darling's *The Rise of Children's Book Reviewing in America, 1865-1881* (R. R. Bowker, 1968).

[17]Rosemary Weber, "The Reviewing of Children's and Young Adult Books in 1977," *Top of the News* 35 (Winter 1979): 131-37.

[18]Witucke.

[19]Virginia Witucke, "The Reviewing of Children's Science Books," *Collection Building* 4 (1982): 19-30.

[20]Phyllis K. Kennemer, "Reviews of Fiction Books: How They Differ," *Top of the News* 40 (Summer 1984): 419-22.

[21]Kathleen Carver, "Book Reviewers: An Empirical Portrait," *School Media Quarterly* 12 (Fall 1984): 383-407.

[22]Ibid., 402.

[23]Ibid.

[24]Judith Serebnick, "Book Reviews and the Selection of Potentially Controversial Books in Libraries," *Library Quarterly* 51 (October 1981): 390-409.

Claire England and Adele M. Fasick

Book Reviewing in Canada

The purpose of this article is to consider certain library-related characteristics of book reviewing in Canada. The study will concentrate on those serials whose primary purpose is to provide reviews of new Canadian titles and will focus on the use made of them in the selection process.

"A review, even a bad one, is the cheapest form of promotion and often the most elusive."[1] This quotation is taken from the introduction to a *Quill & Quire* article by Diane Pullan entitled "The Ins and Outs of the Book Pages."[2] The article, published in January 1979, was based on an informal survey of ten English-language daily newspapers and five consumer magazines (*Books in Canada, Canadian Forum, Maclean's, Quill & Quire*, and *Saturday Night*). The survey of book reviews in the ten dailies from mid-August to mid-September 1978 indi-

cated that 243 books had been reviewed by 128 reviewers and that 119 titles or approximately 50 percent of the new books had been Canadian. The October 1978 issue of the four monthlies was examined. *Books in Canada* contained fifty-seven reviews and notices; *Canadian Forum* published seven reviews by seven reviewers, five of them reviews of Canadian titles, two of imports; *Quill & Quire* reviewed thirty-two new imprints using twenty-seven reviewers; *Saturday Night* had three Canadian reviews by three reviewers. *Maclean's* which had just become a weekly, published reviews of four Canadian titles and nine foreign titles, written by nine reviewers, in the four mid-season issues sampled. Taking the number of books reviewed over the four-week period, as well as figures provided by editors, the numbers in table 1 indicate how many books were estimated to be reviewed during a year in these sources.

Table 1.

Source	Number of Reviews Canadian Titles	Foreign Titles	Total	Estimated Numbers of Reviews per Year Calculated by *Quill & Quire*
	4-week period	1979		
Dailies (10)	119	124	243	3,159
Books in Canada	57[a]	-	57[a]	900[a]
Canadian Forum	5	2	7	100
Maclean's	4	9	13	150
Quill & Quire	32	-	32	900
Saturday Night	3	-	3	40-50

[a]reviews and notices

A good portion of the books reviewed, especially in the dailies, were imported titles and several of the dailies reviewed the same book. Some of the other findings of the survey were equally interesting: the timeliness of the reviews, following the appearance of the books, extended over several months; only *Canadian Forum* and *Quill & Quire* consistently reviewed books from smaller Canadian presses; there was little consistency among the titles reviewed and it was rare to see a book receive more than two reviews, even when it was appearing on best-seller lists; and the same title, if reviewed more than once, received different treatment. The focus of Pullan's article was the value of reviews as a means of promoting Canadian books; the reactions of Canadian publishers and authors to reviews and reviewers were its main concern.

Using the methodology described in the *Quill & Quire* survey, this author reviewed the book section in five of the ten dailies (one of the dailies had ceased publication) and in the five periodicals during the same time period in 1984. The results are described in table 2.

Table 2.

Source	Number of Reviews Canadian Titles	Foreign Titles	Total	Differences in Number of Reviews between 1979 and 1984 Survey Period
	4-week period	1984		
Dailies (5)	134	92	226	+109[a]
Books in Canada	18	1	19	-38
Canadian Forum	3	-	3	-4
Maclean's	7	14	21	+7
Quill & Quire	33	14	47	+15
Saturday Night	1	1	2	-1

[a]Author's note: Several factors militated against a study of the book reviews in dailies in this article. The most important are: (1) this article concentrates on publications whose major purpose is the review of new titles; (2) the Halpenny study revealed that most libraries did not rank the use of dailies in first or second place and some did not rank them at all (see page 9); (3) it is impossible to know how *Quill & Quire* in 1979 differentiated between Canadian and foreign titles and, therefore, to make a comparison with the count taken in 1984; (4) a title by title study is needed to assess the role of dailies in the review of Canadian publications; there appeared to be substantial duplication in the choice of titles reviewed by different dailies.

By verifying the figures for the two journals with the greatest number of reviews, *Books in Canada* and *Quill & Quire*, the author learned that the annual estimates in the earlier survey were high. *Books in Canada* published approximately 300 reviews a year in 1978 and now publishes between 450 and 500. *Quill & Quire* publishes approximately 450 reviews a year.

By comparing these figures with the number of titles reviewed in the 1979 and 1985 editions (covering the 1978 and 1984 imprints) of *Canadian Book Review Annual* (*CBRA*), which attempts to be comprehensive in reviewing the year's English-language publications, it is possible to chart the growth of this section of the publishing industry in Canada and to estimate what percentage of new Canadian publications are being reviewed in the sources

mentioned (see table 3). *Canadian Book Review Annual* selects its titles for review according to the following criteria: all trade books carrying a Canadian imprint and a copyright date of the year; all reprints of books originally published before 1975; paperback editions of books not reviewed in *CBRA* when published in hardcover; selected federal government publications; English translations of French-Canadian and foreign-language titles; and selected educational titles with obvious trade appeal. *Canadian Book Review Annual* began in 1975. This evaluative guide, through its authoritative two hundred- to five hundred-word signed reviews by subject specialists, "surveys the year's publishing and assists librarians, booksellers, and teachers in selecting Canadian books for their clients and students."[3]

Table 3.

Category of Publication	Year and Number of Titles		Percentage of Growth in Publications Reviewed between 1979-1984
	1979	1984	
1. Reference Materials	34	119	+350.0
2. Humanities and Applied Arts	153	321	+209.8
3. Literature and Language	291	485	+166.7
4. Social Science	161	270	+167.7
5. Science and Technology	36	90	+250.0
Total	675	1,285	+190.4

As the number of Canadian books reviewed by the sources surveyed by *Quill & Quire* in 1979 and again by this author in 1984 did not remotely reach the totals reflected for the same years in *Canadian Book Review Annual*, it becomes apparent that a review, although the cheapest form of promotion, is indeed increasingly elusive. A detailed study of which titles have been reviewed would be a necessary prerequisite to determining which types of publication are not receiving attention through reviews. To ensure a valid comparison, it would also be necessary to define consistently the term "Canadian books." The term is commonly used to identify a Canadian imprint, regardless of the subject and publishing company, or a book written by a Canadian author, regardless of the country of publication.

The paucity of timely reviews of all new Canadian publications has been confirmed by two recent studies, *Canadian Collections in Public Libraries* and "The Canadian Book and the Public Library."

Canadian Collections in Public Libraries (*CCPL*) is the report of research intended to address a long-felt need to obtain a significant body of statistical and other information about actual holdings of Canadian print materials in Canadian public libraries. The study surveyed fifteen libraries serving communities differing in size and nature. A master list of 4,620 Canadian books and 239 periodicals in English for 1977-1979 and 1981 was checked against the libraries' catalogs; interviews and a questionnaire provided a wealth of additional information about the libraries' selection policies and procedures, their use of aids to selection, the promotion of

Canadian titles and the influences upon their choice of new publications.

The *CCPL* questionnaire asked two questions related to selection tools and elicited responses relevant to the significance of book reviews. According to Francess Halpenny, of the five types of selection tool:

(i) reviews; (ii) non-evaluative tools; (iii) publishers' information; (iv) other aids; (v) readers' requests, 11 of the 15 libraries (4 small, serving a population from 10,000-49,999; 4 medium, serving a population from 50,000-99,999; and 3 large, serving a population of 100,000 and over) ranked reviews as most important. Three libraries ranked publishers' information as most important (1 small, 2 large); one library put "other aids" in the lead, referring to information received through its provincial library system in the form of title and index pages. Second place was given to readers' requests by six libraries (1 small, 3 medium, 2 large); to publishers' information by four libraries (2 small, 2 medium); to non-evaluative tools by three libraries (1 small, 2 large) and to reviews by two libraries (1 small, 1 large).[4]

In summary, reviews were ranked in first or second place by thirteen of the fifteen libraries and readers' requests, likely based on reviews from the various media, played a significant role in selection for six libraries.

The second question provided seven sub-categories under "reviews" and asked for identification of those used and a ranking of importance. The sub-categories were:

(i)   book pages of large dailies and regional papers
(ii)   periodicals that primarily review books and periodicals, e.g. *Books in Canada*
(iii)   periodicals that devote a significant space to books and periodicals, e.g. *Quill & Quire*
(iv)   periodicals in subject areas, e.g. *Harrowsmith*
(v)   university quarterlies
(vi)   library serials (*CM: Canadian Materials for Schools and Libraries; Reviewing Librarian; Canadian Selection; Emergency Librarian*; etc.)
(vii)   *Our Choice* (Children's Book Centre)

In the ranking, items (ii) (e.g. *Books in Canada*) and (iii) (e.g. *Quill & Quire*) appeared among the top three selected by 13 of the 15 libraries; of the two remaining libraries, one had (ii) among the top three and another (iii). Of the 11 libraries which had given reviews as their top overall category, 10 marked (ii) and (iii) among the top three in the sub-category, and 3 other libraries, which had placed their categories differently, repeat this grading for sub-categories (ii) and (iii): a strong vote. This ranking is endorsed by statements in the interviews pointing to the importance of the reviewing periodicals which offer short reviews in some quantity and publish more frequently, usually monthly. Regret was, however, expressed, as the profiles report, that the speed and coverage of reviewing in Canadian periodicals still does not compare with the service provided by American counterparts. Well-known Canadian authors may not be greatly affected—they "sell" themselves—but with the host of others the situation is different. Any improvement in the reviewing picture in Canada would obviously have an effect upon the process of selection in public libraries....

Sub-category (vi) under Reviews, dealing with "library serials",

appeared among the top three ranks for 11 of the 15 libraries, and they thus come out as important aids. Again, in the interviews the delay between publication of a title and appearance of a review, which is likely to be greater with quarterlies in this group than with monthlies, was noted as a problem. The disappearance of one, *In Review*, about the time CCPL was doing its checking, was by almost everyone bewailed; its coverage in reviews, its information on authors, its index are being missed. It was suggested to us that *Canadian Books for Young People* should be brought up to date and issued regularly as there was nothing comparable to it for quick reference (including the section on French titles). Another work of this group, *Canadian Book Review Annual* appears yearly and inevitably more after the fact. It should be of assistance as a check on what was available for selection in the given years".[5]

However, only 8 of the 15 libraries (1 small, 4 medium, and 3 large) held the 1975-1977 volumes.

To take a different type of reviewing, item (i), book pages of large dailies and regional papers are not checked as being used by 4 libraries, but are marked as used by 6 libraries; 5 libraries put this item among the top three in the sub-category: 1 library (medium) put it first, 4 libraries (1 small, 1 medium, 2 large) put it third. The libraries who gave a ranking to this item are located in or near urban areas where major newspapers are published. Item (iv), periodicals in subject areas, was checked as being used by 7 libraries, one of which ranked the item in third place. *Our Choice* was marked as being used by 6 libraries, with two of them giving it a rank specifically as an aid for their children's collection.[6]

The findings of the Halpenny study are confirmed by the research conducted by a group headed by Basil Stuart-Stubbs in one of three related studies carried out for the federal Department of Communications and distributed under the title *Development of Options for*

Action in Key Sectors of Canadian Book Distribution. The specific objective of the Department of Communications in commissioning the study of the Canadian book and the public library was "an increase in the range of Canadian-authored titles offered by public libraries and an upgrading of libraries' display and promotion of their Canadian collections."[7]

The survey, conducted in January and February 1984, "aimed at discovering how Canadian public libraries select, acquire and promote Canadian books, and at obtaining the views of public librarians on whether the situation should be improved, and if so, how."[8]

Of the 991 public libraries reported by Statistics Canada to be in existence in 1981, a total of 145 were targeted as those which, in every province and territory, reached the largest number of readers, held the greatest number of books, and accounted for the largest number of loans. Three groups of libraries composed this total: public libraries in urban areas; regional library systems; and provincial library services which deliver books to citizens who do not have access to a local library. Eighty-two libraries completed the questionnaire, which asked many basic questions about holdings, circulation, governance, acquisitions, and budgets before honing in on the questions related to Canadian publications: their selection, acquisition, and promotion. The question most relevant to this article concerned the deterrents to the selection of Canadian books.

> Twelve of the respondents stated that there were no deterrents. Ranked in the order of frequency with which they were checked, the other 70 respondents marked any of the following which they deemed appropriate:
>
> (i)   absence of Canadian books on subjects relevant to patrons' interest: 55
> (ii) limited book funds: 41
> (iii) low patron demand for Canadian books: 29
> (iv) few timely reviews of Canadian books: 22
> (v)   lack of advertising of Canadian books: 15
> (vi) lack of publishers' catalogues specializing in Canadian books: 7

In addition, libraries contributed their own deterrents:

> (vii) poor quality of Canadian books (design, binding, editing, content): 7
> (viii) lack of information re: local/regional publishing: 3
> (xi)   short print runs: 2.[9]

Book reviews were also mentioned as a means of promoting the Canadian titles acquired by the library. In the final chapter of the report, where the authors comment on their findings and make recommendations, specific mention is made of the importance of book reviews:

> There is no question that a good review in a widely-read publication precipitates orders from bookstores and libraries, and demand from the public in the same outlets. Even a bad review generates sales and interest. An absence of reviews can condemn a book to obscurity.[10]

The authors of this study make further observations and suggestions for particular studies and consultation on book reviewing:

> We know that in the case of English-language books public librarians rely heavily on reviews in *Quill & Quire* and *Books in Canada.* There has been no French equivalent to the Green or Beta reports to determine the facts, but it is probable that *Livre d'ici* performs the same function for public librarians in Quebec. What we definitely do not know is how adequate these journals are in their coverage by review of the totality of Canadian trade, regional and scholarly publishing. What percentage of new titles fall by the wayside? This is a question that deserves further research. It would be possible, for example, to check the 1982 spring lists of all publishers against reviews published in those journals to see what was omitted. It would be a piece of drudgery, but it could be done. Upon completion of such an investigation, one would know how efficient or deficient our main reviewing journals were. Or the question could be approached more directly if less scientifically by consulting with the book review editors

of those journals and asking them about their selection and rejection policies in light of the space available to them in their publications.

However the question is approached, there is no question that reviews are of major importance to the promotion of Canadian books, and any increase in the number of reviews would be desirable. The Canada Council has already supported a number of projects directed to this end. There are a host of related problems, such as the availability of competent reviewers, and especially ones that will meet deadlines, and the circulation of reviews once they are published. To deal with all such matters, consultation seems the advisable route.

Recommendation: That the Department of Communications and appropriate officers of the Canada Council consult with the book review editors of the major book reviewing periodicals to obtain their views on the effectiveness, shortcomings and problems of their publications, with a view of taking measures to strengthen and improve the reviewing of Canadian-authored books.[11]

Both the Halpenny and the Stuart-Stubbs et al. studies found that non-evaluative tools were used by public librarians. However, their conclusions were the same. In Stuart-Stubbs et al. the following observations are made:

It should be noted that public librarians use many other tools for the selection of Canadian books, including the national bibliography *Canadiana*, and one of its byproducts, *Forthcoming Books*, which is issued as a supplementary sheet in *Quill & Quire*. However, the Beta and Green reports suggest that these other means of selecting books are less frequently used: reviews and publishers' catalogues are of primary importance, providing the earliest information about new books. It is also worth noting that public librarians generally select books not by an examination of the books themselves, but from an examination of other publications.[12]

Having demonstrated the importance of timely reviews to the selection of Canadian works for public libraries, it may be useful, at this point, to identify the most significant characteristics which pertain to the symbiotic relationship among writers, publishers, and readers in Canada, and to the role of reviewing tools in assisting librarians and readers to select new Canadian titles.

Canada is a vast, sparsely populated country of 25.5 million people, a large percentage of whom live in urban areas within one hundred miles of the U.S.-Canadian border. It is a federal state, composed of ten provinces and two territories, whose history of recognizing the distinctiveness of its two predominant founding nations, Great Britain and France, was reinforced in 1969 by a national policy of official bilingualism. Canada has two primary sets of authors, those who express themselves in English and those who express themselves in French. The former are scattered in every province from Newfoundland to British Columbia, the latter are concentrated in but not confined to Quebec. The Canadian nation has two identifiable groups of readers, those whose mother tongue is English and those whose mother tongue is French, although for an increasing number of Canadians (over 3 million in the 1981 census), the first tongue is neither of Canada's official languages. Finally, the two publishing industries, who make possible the contact between the author and the reader and who complete the triangle, are also distinct. The capital of English-language publishing is Toronto, but there are independent, hardy Canadian publishers in every province from Newfoundland to British Columbia. The center of French-language publishing is Montreal, but French-language publishing is limited neither to that city nor to the province of Quebec. In summary, Canada is a vast country with a small population of authors, publishers, and readers, divided into two major language groups. The smallness of the market and the dominance of larger countries, the United States, Great Britain and France, in the Canadian book trade are realities which both communities face.

Governments within Canada provide financial assistance to Canadian authors, book publishers, and magazine publishers including most of those who support the literary experience by promoting books to readers through criticism and reviews. *Books in Canada* was created in 1971 "to bring every worthwhile book to the attention of readers wherever there is a library or a bookstore and honestly to point to its virtues and its faults in relation to other Canadian books and even to other imported books of its kind."[13]

Supported by the Canada Council and the Ontario Arts Council, it is published nine times a year and approximately twenty-five thousand copies have been distributed free by bookstores which buy copies in bulk. In May 1986, on its fifteenth anniversary, *Books in Canada*, which reviews both adult and children's English-language publications (including translations of French-Canadian publications), will become available only through subscription or through purchase in bookstores or newsstands.

In November 1974, *The Atlantic Provinces Book Review* was created out of the same set of general concerns as *Books in Canada*: "there was a tremendous interest in books in Canada, and especially in books about Canada [but] many Canadians were having difficulty finding out about the books being published in Canada."[14] However, its aim was at once narrower and broader. The *Review* was to act "as an enabling device and focus interest for everyone connected with books in the four Atlantic Provinces" (Newfoundland, Nova Scotia, New Brunswick and Prince Edward Island). It promised "to give every book published in the region some sort of coverage."[15]

The *Atlantic Provinces Book Review*, although larger — in recognition of the growth in the publishing industry in the Maritimes — has remained true to its original aim and appearance. Published four times a year in tabloid format at St. Mary's University in Halifax, it is distributed free through bookstores, libraries, universities, schools, museums, and other interested institutions and is available as a supplement for newspapers and magazines. It has the support of both the federal and Nova Scotia governments.

Lettres québécoises: revue de l'actualité littéraire, another regional reviewing tool, supported by the Canada Council and the Ministère des Affaires culturelles of Quebec, has recently celebrated its tenth anniversary. It appears four times a year and contains articles on all literary genres and interviews with French-Canadian authors. It compares most closely in intent with *Books in Canada*. In existence from 1962 to 1983, *Livres et auteurs canadiens* (changed in 1969 to *Livres et auteurs québécois*), provided, during its first decade, an annual review of literary publishing, including children's literature, and in its second decade broadened its scope to include all types of French-Canadian publishing. Similar in aim to "Letters in Canada," the annual review of English- and French-language publishing in the

summer issue of *University of Toronto Quarterly*, this revue of French-language titles published by the Université Laval described in greater detail the major works of the year. Its first edition contained 50 signed reviews and its final volume over 640 reviews, an increase of almost 1300 percent in twenty-one years. This increase attests to the growth of the French-language publishing industry and to the broader scope of the review. Its demise is due to the lack of continued financial support and the presence of *Lettres québécoises* and *Livre d'ici*, the Quebec book trade magazine, which appears ten times a year with some assistance from the Canada Council. Like *Quill & Quire*, which has the support of the Ontario Arts Council, *Livre d'ici* includes a section on forthcoming books entitled "Livres à paraître." These sections provide a non-evaluative identification of new titles based on Cataloguing-in-Publication data.

While this decade has seen the cessation of two well-respected reviewing journals, *Livres et auteurs québécois* and *In Review*, a quarterly and then bimonthly review of current children's literature, it has also witnessed the birth of *SÉLECTION: revue critique/French Book Review Journal*. Published by the Libraries and Community Information Branch of the Ontario Ministry of Citizenship and Culture, *SÉLECTION*, appearing first in December 1984, is a bilingual review journal which identifies and describes

> French language books in all subject areas of interest to both Francophone and English-speaking children and adults in Ontario interested in reading French language books.... Its objective is to provide a reliable bibliographic tool to assist libraries in meeting community needs. *SÉLECTION* appears three times a year and is updated by supplements. Arranged by broad categories of fiction and non-fiction and then organized by the headings used in the Dewey classification, *SÉLECTION* expects to review about 800 titles a year and is sent free to all Ontario public libraries. While its emphasis is on current Canadian publications, foreign titles in print are also reviewed.[16]

The attention paid to children's literature, both by the publishing industry and as a subject of professional and academic interest has increased in recent years. This interest has been manifested in several ways, but particularly in the appearance of regular sections in general magazines and also of specialized periodicals. *Quill & Quire* has initiated a special section entitled "Y.A.K.: Media for Young Adults and Kids" which appears every second month and *Books in Canada* has a regular children's feature. *CCL: Canadian Children's Literature* began as a quarterly journal of criticism and review in the spring of 1975. Financed in part by the Ontario Arts Council, the Social Sciences and Humanities Research Council, and the University of Guelph, it is now a bilingual periodical with the added title, *Littérature canadienne pour la jeunesse.* The National Library publishes *Notable Canadian Children's Books/ Un choix de livres canadiens pour la jeunesse,* an annual annotated bibliography of the best children's literature, chosen by two committees of experts.

Lurelu, also assisted by grants from the federal and provincial governments, has been dedicated to Quebec children's literature since its inception in 1978. It began as a quarterly distributed free, but is now published three times a year and available only by subscription. *Des livres et des jeunes* is published for teachers, parents, and professionals by the Association canadienne pour l'avancement de la littérature de jeunesse and has also appeared since 1978, with backing from two levels of government and support from the Université de Sherbrooke.

The *Reviewing Librarian* has been published four times a year by the Ontario School Library Association since 1978. The initialed reviews are arranged in sections according both to the Dewey Decimal Classification and to age groups: primary, junior, young adult, senior, and adult. *Emergency Librarian* is a professional journal for teachers and librarians working with children and adults, which has a regular review section in each of its bimonthly issues (five issues a year). This periodical has developed in size, complexity and design since its first issue in 1973. *CM: Canadian Materials for Schools and Librarians* is the Canadian Library Association's annotated critical bibliography. It began as an annual in 1971 in response to the need to make known and accessible Canadian materials produced for the Canadian student. It is now published six times a year, its reviews organized by subject.

The list of reviewing journals in this article is not intended to be exhaustive. Indeed, two of the categories of reviewing tool identified in the Halpenny study have received little attention: periodicals in subject areas (e.g., *Harrowsmith* and *Canadian Historical Review*) and the university quarterlies (e.g., *University of Toronto Quarterly* and *Revue de l'Université d'Ottawa*). While many of the Canadian

periodicals in these categories do have a regular book review section, their primary purpose is not to act as the promoter of new Canadian titles through reviews. Moreover, it would be difficult within the parameters of this article to treat the reviewing practices of so varied a group of journals as the subject, professional, and scholarly serials now available in Canada. It is useful to note, however, that *Canadian Periodical Index* does identify all book reviews found in the journals it indexes.

This article has relied heavily on the findings of a 1979 survey in *Quill & Quire* and of two recent studies, *Canadian Collections in Public Libraries* and "The Canadian Book and the Public Library." Certain limitations in the evidence are clear. The *Quill & Quire* survey was informal and some of its statistical findings are inaccurate. The Halpenny study, although the most scientific and thorough, surveyed only fifteen public libraries, none of which were located in Quebec, because a portion of the research was based on the checking of a master list of English-language adult and children's titles against the catalogs of the libraries. The Stuart-Stubbs et al. report summarized the findings of a larger sample of public libraries, including some in Quebec, but its findings are based on a set of questions for which the respondents did not always have statistical evidence. The latter studies through analysis raised many questions and put forward observations and recommendations which will lead, it is hoped, to more efforts to understand and to improve the communication and awareness among authors, publishers, and readers, assisted by such intermediaries as librarians, booksellers, translators, and critics.

This consideration of the state of book reviewing in Canada has brought many questions to the surface. It is interesting to speculate whether teacher-librarians, college librarians, and academic librarians would respond to the questions posed in the Halpenny and Stuart-Stubbs et al. studies in the same way that the public librarians did. Would it not be informative to know how librarians in Quebec assess the reviewing tools of French-language materials? Are librarians who appear to use and value timely succinct reviews themselves contributing to the review of new Canadian publications?

More information, both quantitative and qualitative, about the role of the federal and provincial governments in promoting and encouraging the reading of Canadian publications would be useful. The *Report of the Federal Cultural Policy Review Committee* indicates that "the federal government has provided support directly to writers and publishers, leaving readers—the largest group—more or less alone."[17] It has been noted in this article, however, that most of the reviewing tools, through grants to publishers, have received and do receive financial assistance. While governments are not implicated in what titles are reviewed and how a publication is treated, those governments which support the continuation of tools to promote Canadian publications are influencing the accessibility of information on new publications.

There are several aspects of book reviewing in Canada that have received only passing consideration — the timeliness and comprehensiveness of reviews, for example. This article has not attempted to discuss some of the other pertinent questions related to the subject — the reviewers, the quality of the reviews, and the reactions of readers themselves to the major reviewing tools. Indeed, this complex and interesting topic has had but a cursory review.

NOTES

[1]"The Pundits of the Book Pages," *Quill & Quire* 45, no. 1 (January 1979): 1.

[2]Diane Pullan, "The Ins and Outs of the Book Pages," *Quill & Quire* 45, no. 1 (January 1979): 6, 8-9.

[3]Dean Tudor and Ann Tudor, *Canadian Book Review Annual 1984* (Toronto: Simon and Pierre, 1984), unpaged.

[4]Francess Halpenny, *Canadian Collections in Public Libraries* (Toronto: Book and Periodical Development Council, 1985), 204.

[5]Ibid., 205-6.

[6]Ibid., 207.

[7]Basil Stuart-Stubbs et al., "The Canadian Book and the Public Library," in *Development of Options for Action in Key Sectors of Canadian Book Distribution* ([Ottawa: Department of Communications], August 1984), 1.

[8]Ibid., 2.

[9]Ibid., 102-3.

[10]Ibid., 128.

[11]Ibid., 128-29.

[12]Ibid., 129-30.

[13]Val Clery, "Books in Canada: Editorial," *Books in Canada* [1, no. 1] (May 1971): 5.

[14]Jim Lotz, "Editorial Statement," *The Atlantic Provinces Book Review* [1, no. 1] (November 1974): 1.

[15]Ibid., 1.

[16]"Foreword," *SÉLECTION: Revue critique/ French Book Review Journal*, 1, no. 3 (1985).

[17]Federal Cultural Policy Review Committee, *Report* (Ottawa: Department of Communications, 1982), 197.

REFERENCES

Atlantic Provinces Book Review. Halifax: St. Mary's University. [v. 1, no. 1], November 1974- . Quarterly. ISSN 0316-5981.

Books in Canada. Toronto: Canadian Review of Books Ltd. March 1971- . 9 issues a year. ISSN 0045-2564.

Canadian Book Review Annual. Edited by Dean Tudor and Ann Tudor. Toronto: Simon and Pierre, 1975- . Annual. ISSN 0383-770X. (Published by Peter Martin Associates from 1975 to 1979 inclusive.)

Canadian Books for Young People/Livres canadiens pour la jeunesse. Edited by I. McDonough. University of Toronto Press, 1980. 205p. ISBN 0-802-04594-4.

Canadian Forum. Toronto: Survival Foundation. v. 1, no. 1, October 1920- . Monthly. ISSN 0008-3631.

Canadian Periodical Index. Ottawa: Canadian Library Association. v. 1, 1947- . Monthly. ISSN 0008-4719.

Canadiana. Ottawa: National Library of Canada. v. 1, no. 1, 1951- . Monthly. ISSN 0008-5391.

CCL: Canadian Children's Literature/Littérature canadienne pour la jeunesse. Guelph, Ontario: Canadian Children's Press. v. 1, no. 1, Spring 1975- . Quarterly. ISSN 0319-0080.

CM: Canadian Materials for Schools and Librarians. Ottawa: Canadian Library Association. v. 1, 1971- . 6 issues a year. ISSN 0317-4654.

Des Livres et des jeunes. Sherbrooke: Des libres et des jeunes. v. 1, no. 1, novembre 1978- . 3 issues a year. ISSN 0706-795X.

Emergency Librarian. Toronto: EL. v. 1, no. 1, 1973- . 5 issues a year. ISSN 0315-8888.

Federal Cultural Policy Review Committee. *Report.* Ottawa: Department of Communications, 1982. 406p. ISBN 0-660-11228-0.

"Forthcoming Books." A supplement distributed in *Quill & Quire.* Monthly.

Green, Deidre E. *Final Report of the Library Information Project.* [Toronto: Canadian Book Information Centre, 1977]. 69 lv.

Halpenny, Francess G. *Canadian Collections in Public Libraries.* Toronto: Book and Periodical Development Council, 1985. 280p. ISBN 0-9692164-0-8.

Harrowsmith. Camden East, Ontario: Camden House Publications. v. 1, no. 1, May/June 1976- . Monthly. ISSN 0381-6885.

In Review. Toronto: Libraries and Community Information Branch (formerly Provincial Library Service). v. 1, no. 1, Winter 1967- v. 16, no. 2, April 1982. ISSN 0019-3251.

Jarvi, Edith, et al. *Canadian Selection: Books and Periodicals for Libraries.* Toronto: University of Toronto Press, 1978. 1060p. ISBN 0-8020-4554-5.

Lettres québécoises: revue de l'actualité littéraire. Montréal: Éditions Jumonville. v. 1, no. 1, mars 1976- . Quarterly. ISSN 0382-084X.

Livre d'ici Livres et auteurs Lurelu. Montréal: Livre d'ici. v. 1, no. 1, décembre 1975- . 10 issues a year. ISSN 0714-9948.

Livres et auteurs québécois. Québec: Les Presses de l'Université Laval. [v. 1], 1961-[v. 21], 1982. Annual. ISBN 2-7637-7034-7.

Lurelu. Saint-Jérome: Association Lurelu. v. 1, no. 1, 1978- . 2 issues a year. ISSN 0705-6567.

Maclean's. Toronto: Maclean-Hunter. v. 1, no. 1, 1911- . Weekly. ISSN 0024-9262.

Notable Canadian Children's Books/Un choix de livres canadiens pour la jeunesse. Ottawa: National Library of Canada. 1973- . Annual. ISSN 0715-2612. (Edited originally by Sheila Egoff and now by Irene E. Aubrey.)

Our Choice. Toronto: Canadian Books Centre. 1978. Annual.

Public Libraries in Canada: A Study Commissioned by the Canadian Book Publishers' Council. Toronto: Beta Associates, May 1982. 122p.

Quill & Quire. Toronto: Key Publications Ltd. v. 1, no. 1, 1935. Monthly. ISSN 0033-6491.

Reviewing Librarian. Toronto: Ontario Library Association. v. 1, no. 1, November 1974- . ISSN 0318-0948.

Revue de l'Université d'Ottawa. Ottawa: L'Université d'Ottawa. v. 1, no. 1, January/March 1931- . Quarterly. ISSN 0041-9206.

Saturday Night. Toronto: Saturday Night Publishing. v. 1, July 22, 1911- . Monthly. ISSN 0380-867X.

SÉLECTION: revue critique/French Book Review Journal. Toronto: Libraries and Community Information Branch, Ministry of Citizenship and Culture. v. 1, no. 1, December 1984- . 3 issues a year. ISSN 0826-7855.

Stuart-Stubbs, Basil, et al. "The Canadian Book and the Public Library." In *Development of Options for Action in Key Sectors of Canadian Book Distribution.* [Ottawa: Department of Communications, August 1984]. various pagings.

University of Toronto Quarterly. Toronto: University of Toronto Press. v. 1, no. 1.- . Quarterly. ISSN 0042-0247. (The summer issue contains "Letters in Canada.")

Gwynneth Evans

Contemporary American Minor Library Publications

INTRODUCTION

Miscellaneous ephemeral publications have been with us for some time, and libraries and library organizations have been notorious producers and consumers of such publications for many years. In recent years the proliferation of library associations and organizations, combined with advances in technology which permit information to be produced more rapidly and less expensively, has brought us an absolute flood of information of all kinds and in all formats. The quantity of miscellaneous ephemeral publications produced by libraries and library organizations and available to librarians, whether they want them or not, is perhaps surpassed only by the quantity of mail-order catalogs that we receive at Christmas time. All of this "library junk mail" is, presumably, produced for a purpose in an attempt to communicate useful information to librarians, library users, governing boards and bodies, and others. Some of it is well produced; some is not. Some communicates useful information effectively; some fails to do so. Attractive or ugly, good or bad, needed or not, it just keeps coming. We both produce and consume such miscellaneous ephemeral publications with little thought to just what they are and what real purpose they serve.

We tend, as I have done, to describe this material as ephemeral publications but we should be somewhat more precise. In the world of antiques and collectibles the term *ephemera*

has come to have a very specific meaning as books such as Chris E. Makepeace's *Ephemera* (Gower, 1985) make abundantly clear. Ephemera are material carrying a verbal or visual message that is printed, or otherwise reproduced, usually in something other than a standard book, pamphlet, or periodical format. Ephemera are usually flimsy or insubstantial and consist of transient documents produced for a specific purpose and not intended to last beyond that immediate purpose. Libraries and library organizations certainly produce their share of ephemera as one who collects library ephemera can testify. Announcements of building dedications, calling cards, compliments slips, floor plans, gift acknowledgment forms, notices of meetings, posters, and the other thousands of pieces of topical information that we produce in all sizes and shapes to fill a specific need fall into that category.

At the other end of the spectrum, and clearly not ephemeral in any sense of the word, is the standard body of our professional literature which includes books produced by trade publishers, national journals, and a variety of other documents. We have established means of dealing with that material. It is typically advertised and sold through formal channels, evaluated and reviewed in standard sources, acquired and processed through an organized system, and made available for use in an orderly fashion. It is a major component of our professional life and thought.

Between the ephemerality of a dedication program and the permanence of a major national library journal lies a vast world of what can best be characterized and defined as minor library publications. Specific examples of the kind of items that constitute this category of minor library publications will be enumerated in detail below. In broad terms the category can be defined as encompassing a wide variety of items usually in a standard book, pamphlet, or periodical format that are printed, or otherwise reproduced, by a library or library organization. These items, which are usually distributed free of charge, or sometimes sold for a nominal fee, are generally aimed at a particular body of potential readers and are intended to convey practical information of an immediate nature to those potential readers. The newsletters which seem to dominate the field are only a representative example of the wide range and variety of material that constitutes this body of minor library publications.

We all know and love them. If we are responsible for their production and distribution we are, of course, absolutely convinced of their value. In fact, however, we know very little about this enormous body of material and tend, both as producers and consumers, to treat it in a casual fashion. We need to give more thought to how we can effectively incorporate such material into our professional service and our professional growth and development. We too often fail to think seriously about such publications and we have largely, especially from the perspective of consumers, neglected them in our standard professional literature. There is a small but growing body of both conventional wisdom and literature that deals with the production of these minor publications. There are both handbooks and workshops for the editors of newsletters. A number of articles describing and evaluating the publications programs of individual libraries have been published. For the most part, though, our lack of understanding, as producers, is enormous. Our failure to understand our purpose in producing such items, how to produce them, how to distribute them, and their value to our intended audience contributes in many ways to the problems we then face as consumers of that same material. To date there has been, as best I can determine, absolutely no attempt to examine these minor library publications from the standpoint of a consumer and user. In dealing with these items we have given, it seems, almost no thought to the basic questions involved in dealing with any printed material. We have nonstandard practices and, both as individuals and institutions, idiosyncratic techniques for dealing with basic matters relating to the content and value, acquisition and selection, internal distribution, retention and recording, and the disposition of these minor library publications which are, in fact, a major component of the professional information sources that we deal with.

This initial examination and consideration of minor library publications is based on extensive personal experience as a consumer of such publications as well as a careful recent examination of the accumulation, use, and disposition of such publications in one academic library and a more cursory examination of the material received in several other libraries of different types. These observations, which contain a few practical suggestions, are intended to offer, for the first time, some useful guidance to other librarians as they wrestle with this flood of minor library publications whose growth seems limitless.

CATEGORIES

While these minor library publications come in all shapes and sizes, are issued with varying frequency, are reproduced in a variety of ways, and consist of a wide assortment of material, they do, for the most part, fall into several distinct categories. By far the most numerous of these publications are newsletters of various kinds. Issued to convey current information to a particular group of people, the newsletter has become ubiquitous. Every librarian must receive at least two or three newsletters a week. Most libraries of any size issue an internal staff newsletter of some kind, and many libraries issue more general newsletters designed to inform users, and other interested parties, of library happenings. If there is a friends of the library group it may issue its own newsletter. Most library associations and organizations, and especially library networks and other cooperative groups, rely heavily on newsletters as a primary means of informing participants about what is happening. The numerous recently established user's groups, which consist of libraries tied together by their common interest as users of a particular automated service or system, all issue newsletters to communicate with their membership. Libraries, such as state libraries, that themselves serve a wider body of libraries, commercial vendors, and a wide range of special interest or topical groups, including the many committees of national, regional, and state library associations, all issue newsletters designed to inform their own special constituency of news that is of particular interest to them. There is no shortage of libraries, and library-related organizations, issuing newsletters and no end to the procession of newsletters that crosses our desks.

The next most common body of these minor publications can be loosely categorized as reports. The annual report, whether produced largely for internal or more for external use, is a good example as almost every library issues, and most seem to distribute, such a document. Now it has become more common than it once was for library associations and organizations, again especially those that are of a cooperative nature, to issue annual reports to their constituents. In addition to these reports, which typically recount the past year's accomplishments — but seldom the failures — and provide detailed statistics about the operations of the issuing agency, other kinds of one-time or special reports are now more widely available. Accreditation reports, self-studies, committee reports, research reports, and the like are issued in great profusion.

Bibliographies, especially those based on special collections within a library or produced as part of a program of bibliographic instruction, are frequently published directly by libraries. Other kinds of catalogs, such as exhibit catalogs, and guides to individual collections, such as locally produced serials lists, fall into this same general category. Groups of libraries may produce cooperative guides or catalogs, such as union lists of serials, and library associations and organizations may issue publications in a bibliographic series of some kind. With this category of material should also be grouped the more general guides to a library's collections, and especially a library's special collections, that are frequently published (often in a more elaborate format than most minor library publications).

In general, however, more than enough guides and handbooks are published for them to form a separate category of their own. Here are to be found the typical guide to the collections and services issued by most libraries of any size for their users. Many larger libraries issue handbooks and manuals of various kinds for their staff to aid them in their understanding of the operation of the library and to assist them in their work. Many library associations and organizations also issue various guides and manuals which range, for example, from directories of members to manuals on shared cataloging policies.

Even with these several categories, there remains, as one might expect in dealing with such material, a large body of miscellaneous material that fails to fall into any single neat category. This miscellaneous assortment is by no means limited to but includes news releases and other announcements of activities, events, and happenings; summaries of studies distributed to those who have responded to a questionnaire on a subject; announcements of products and services by commercial vendors or library associations and organizations; publications based in some fashion on the contents of a library's collections; and almost anything else that may strike the fancy of somebody with access to or control of the printing budget and resources of a library or library association or organization.

CONTENT AND VALUE

Except for the occasional publication of an item such as a piece of poetry, minor library publications are primarily of a topical nature in terms of their content and value. They are regarded, in some ways incorrectly, as being truly ephemeral. Aimed, for the most part, at a particular narrowly defined audience, these publications are mainly intended to provide that audience with information and news about current events, people, places, and subjects. The content is clearly of a practical nature. If any category of library materials deserves the Shavian appellation of how-I-run-my-library-good it is definitely these minor library publications. We read them because they tell us the things we need and want to know about the libraries where we work, the associations or organizations to which we belong, or a subject in which we have a current interest. There is nothing duller than a newsletter from another library. It is full of arcane references to people we don't know and don't care about. The newsletter from *our* library, on the other hand, is fascinating because it contains interesting and useful information about the place where we work and people we know. The content of these publications is most often truly of local interest and their value is to the limited audience to whom the publications are directed.

As a class, and even sometimes as individual pieces, such publications do have a broader value sometimes for their content and sometimes for their approach or format. We can, and do, use these publications in a secondary fashion to educate and inform ourselves in a variety of ways. The newsletter from another library may, for example, contain information about an activity or program that may seem suited to our library. Some of the practical suggestions contained in a report may have a wider application especially if we are dealing with the same problem or are carrying out a similar project. An annual report may contain comparative information of a statistical nature that we can put to good use. The approach to presenting information, the manner and style of the publication, and even the content may sometimes serve as models for us. We may use such publications to help us develop our own programs, reports, and publications.

These publications, as a class, are a gold mine of library humor. The staid standard professional journals, both at the national and the state level, tend to regard library humor as a subject which is generally not worthy of their attention. The editors of minor library publications are far less constrained and conventional. Much of the best library humor is of a brief and topical nature and, for that reason, is often better suited to library newsletters and other minor library publications. Much of the library humor that appears in these publications is of a highly localized nature. It is often intelligible to, and appreciated by, only a small local audience. Much of it is bad. Some of it has a broader appeal and a small quantity of it is excellent. An occasional minor library publication may be, or contain, a work of historical or literary merit.

Almost all of these publications appear on the surface to have little permanent value and we tend to treat all of them as though that were the case. Only the editor and the publisher (e.g., the library) tend to regard such material as having any long-term historical value. In fact for library historians, especially those with an interest in the social history of institutions, minor library publications contain much information of permanent value that can be of use in historical research. The historian writing a biography of a prominent librarian, for example, can find a wealth of minor and personal information, not otherwise readily available, in the annual reports, newsletters, and other minor publications of the libraries, and library associations and organizations, with which the person was affiliated. The history of a library cannot be written without examining the annual reports of that library and its other minor publications. In fact, the history of a library, or a biographical sketch of its librarian(s), may be published by the library as an incidental publication. If anyone ever deigns to write a comprehensive history of library humor, or to produce a bibliography on that subject, minor library publications, and especially library newsletters, will constitute a primary source of enormous value.

So while we properly regard these publications, individually and as a class, as being of limited short-term value for a specialized audience, and use them with that understanding, we should not fail to recognize that they may, both because of their content and their format, have a wider current audience and that they may, for some highly specialized reasons, indeed even have some permanent value.

SELECTION, ACQUISITION, AND DISTRIBUTION

Selection of minor library publications is, to all intents and purposes, hardly a major problem. We are all, in fact, inundated by these materials which appear, often unbidden, on our desk with alarming regularity and in such quantities that probably even the most avid librarian reads only a small fraction of the minor library publications that he or she regularly receives. We are selected; we do not select. Most of these publications come to us because of our affiliation with, or expressed interest in, a particular library or library association or organization. The library where we now work, and sometimes that where we once worked, selects us to receive everything as a matter of course. If our library belongs to a local system, or a regional, state, multi-state, or national network, they select us to receive all of their minor publications. The commercial vendors with whom our library deals select us to receive minor publications telling us all about their people, products, and services. Sometimes we generate user groups to affiliate ourselves with other libraries using the same vendor, and those user groups then select us to receive yet another body of publications. Membership either as an individual or as a library in local, regional, state, multi-state, and national library associations, and the components of those associations, selects us to receive yet another enormous body of minor library publications both directly from those associations, and their components, and from other associations or libraries with access to their mailing lists. Finally there is that mysterious body of material which, despite our best efforts to halt the flow, finds us and regularly appears unbidden and for no apparent reason. Most minor library publications are received without any initiative on our part, are free of charge, and come to us on a regular basis. It is difficult, if not impossible, to stop receiving such publications even those we no longer want or need.

It is extremely difficult to engage in any true selection of such items. What we do not receive automatically, we may not know about. These materials are not listed in standard bibliographies and guides to the professional literature; there is no established mechanism by which they may be acquired; and they are almost never reviewed in library journals. We would find it difficult to acquire a greater quantity of these publications, even those that are for sale, if we should want to. A very few of these publications are noted from time to time in the news columns of library journals especially if they are attractive or otherwise catch the eye of the editor. To find out about the availability of such items, one is generally forced to read the vast volume of minor library publications, especially newsletters, which one receives for that is most often where the information about other such items appears. One could, if one dared, undoubtedly greatly enhance the acquisition of minor library publications by sending, as some libraries are occasionally foolish enough to do, a mass mailing to other libraries and library associations and organizations asking to be placed on their mailing list to receive annual reports, newsletters, and other similar minor publications. That is *not* a recommended process for the selection and acquisition of such materials.

The appropriate distribution and use of such material once it is received is still another problem. Because of the quantity of material that we all receive, its ephemeral nature, and the lack of good sources of information about its availability or its content, the effective internal distribution of these publications is an important factor in their use. In reading such publications one must be alert not only to the listing of other publications of potential interest but also to information that may be of interest or value to a colleague within one's own library or elsewhere. One can never be certain, in part because of the almost random distribution of such publications, that he or she may have seen that same item. It pays to make a regular practice of notifying others when you see a minor library publication, or something in such a publication, of potential interest to them. In the same fashion, especially because the distribution of such materials from external sources seems to be almost random in nature, it pays to regularly route, or otherwise make available to your colleagues, the minor library publications that you receive. One never knows when they may find something of interest to them in what you may regard as a useless publication.

It is, then, difficult to deal with the selection, acquisition, and distribution of these minor library publications in any reasonable, organized fashion. They come to us on a regular basis in such quantities that we seldom want more. We often assume that others get, and perhaps even read, the same publications, and, because they seem incidental to our work, we tend to deal with them in a casual fashion without giving proper attention to their proper selection, acquisition, and distribution.

RETENTION, RETRIEVAL, AND DISPOSITION

As much use as we give them and as useful as they may be, these minor library publications are, in almost all libraries, seldom treated as though they were in any way normal publications. That is, in part, because we treat them as disposable reading material and, in part, because they are addressed to us as individuals, often by virtue of our position, rather than to the acquisitions or serials department where they might receive more formal treatment. Even when they are addressed to individuals in the acquisitions or serials department, they may be ignored as regular publications perhaps on the theory that, since they are addressed to an individual, they are simply working tools and that somebody else will take care of normal library procedures for those items which are, after all, often received in multiple copies. For whatever reasons in most libraries, as best I can tell, minor library publications are seldom, if ever, dealt with as though they were serious publications with any kind of lasting value.

Some library school libraries may acquire, catalog, and otherwise treat these publications in a serious fashion and most, but by no means all, libraries are likely to subject their own publications to regular processing treatment. For the most part, we treat most minor library publications far more casually. They are seldom, if ever, checked in, recorded, cataloged, classified, labelled, and shelved with other publications. Instead they are treated, often appropriately, as contemporary ephemeral working publications of some value to us in our day-to-day work but of no value to our users and of no value on a permanent basis. Once we have read them, or decided not to read them, we may either simply throw them away or send them along to another library staff member who we think may have some interest in a particular item. At best we may retain these publications for an indefinite period of time in some haphazard manner on a shelf in an office or the staff lounge, or in a vertical file that is seldom used or weeded. If they are retained, these publications are seldom kept in order. If, as it often happens, issues disappear, nobody cares because, except for a very short time after receipt, we seldom refer to these publications. If the occasional minor library publication, such as a bibliography or a handbook, appears to be significant, it may sometimes get sent along for cataloging and addition to the collection. Even specialized publications with some recognized value are far more likely just to get routed to what seems to be an appropriate person or department for their action. There such items may well languish in a backlog, get placed unprocessed on a shelf of working tools, or end up in a seldom-used vertical file. Minor library publications of a serial nature are not indexed in standard indexing and abstracting sources such as *Library Literature*. Those of a monographic nature are not usually cataloged by the Library of Congress; they may not even be entered into the OCLC or RLIN database unless somebody in the originating library or library organization happens to think to do so. It is, therefore, often difficult to locate and retrieve minor publications within a short time after their publication. Our memory is likely to serve as the only catalog or index to these publications and their location. We may not know what has happened to these publications once we have finished with them. We are not likely to keep track of their location and disposition. It is likely, then, to be difficult to locate an item again even if we do remember something about the content that prompts us to attempt to retrieve it. Almost all minor library publications are issued unbound and there seldom appears to be a reason to bind either an individual item or a completed serial volume. Finally, even if any of these publications are retained and maintained in some reasonable fashion, they are very likely to be discarded periodically as a matter of routine, or since shelf or file space is at a premium.

This may sound like a cynical attitude towards a significant body of material but it is meant, I would suggest, to describe what happens in most libraries. It is not necessarily meant to describe recommended practices. As working tools with a perceived, and actual ephemeral value, minor library publications are regarded as something less than standard publications and are treated in a desultory fashion. If these publications are given standard library treatment, it is likely to be because an individual sees that these items have some lasting value but even that treatment is likely to cease if the individual leaves or loses interest in the orderly treatment of minor library publications. They may have greater value than we think. They do often deserve better treatment than we give them.

CONCLUSIONS AND SUGGESTIONS

For better or for worse, minor library publications have become an integral part of our professional life. It seems certain that they will continue to be issued in the same formats, and in even greater numbers, for some years to come. Some of the information disseminated in such publications may increasingly become available in electronic formats, including electronic newsletters, but there is little evidence, to date, that electronic forms are replacing or endangering paper forms. It is, in fact, the electronic information systems that seem to be contributing most directly to the continuing increase in these kinds of publications. Each provider of electronic library services produces its own annual report, its own newsletter(s), its own news releases and other information sheets, its own documentation, and its own special reports almost all of which are issued in paper formats. A significant switch to electronic formats would, in any case, be largely a switch in format and would, unquestionably, further increase the number and availability of such publications. We would still be faced with the same issues and questions.

As consumers of these minor library publications, we need to develop a better understanding of the information which they are intended to convey, the purposes which they serve, and the role that they can properly play in our professional work. We should give them serious thought and not treat them, as we tend to, simply as casual "junk" mail that crosses our desk to be disposed of according to the inclination of the moment. We need to consider how we can best integrate these materials into our work. To a large degree that means developing systematic programs in individual libraries for their acquisition, distribution, and disposition. That need not involve an elaborate set of policies and procedures. It does mean dealing with these publications in a carefully thought-out, conscientious manner using, for the most part, standard library practices and routines.

The development by consumers of an effective approach to these materials could benefit substantially by more careful thought by the producers of minor library publications and by some collective efforts. The content and the quality of minor library publications is, at best, highly uneven. It appears, in most cases, as though somebody simply has an idea that a newsletter, annual report, special report, or other publication should be issued for some reason and proceeds to issue it without much thought to the audience, the content, or the format. There have been several excellent articles on publication programs in libraries, but even those seldom deal adequately with the purpose of such publications. One of the few succinct statements on such matters appears in *Communication throughout Libraries*.[1] There are numerous publications, and some excellent workshops and other instructional programs, that deal with the production of newsletters and other minor publications. The availability of such information, and the current state of printing technology, means that almost any institution or organization should be able, with little effort and at modest cost, to issue publications in an attractive format. There is no excuse for the many low-quality and unattractive minor library publications that continue to be issued.

It would also be beneficial if the producers of minor library publications gave some thought to the distribution of their publications rather than simply adopting, as so often seems to be the case, a shotgun approach which involves either acquiring a variety of mailing lists or otherwise developing the most comprehensive mailing list possible. While we all regularly receive far too many publications, and often duplicate copies, there is no systematic way of determining what is being published. As was mentioned above, most of these publications are not indexed in *Library Literature*, or other professional indexes, and are not listed in standard bibliographies and directories. It is, of course, difficult to argue that they should be included in such sources because, in addition to being minor publications, so many of them are ephemeral, regularly change title and frequency, and are otherwise illusory and transitory. The provision in some of the standard directories of libraries and library associations of more information about whether or not the library or association issues, for example, a newsletter would be beneficial. The development of some organized repositories of minor library publications, perhaps in library network offices, would enable us to have a way of periodically examining what is being published and making some conscious selection choices. We should also be more assertive in asking to be removed from the mailing lists of publications that we do not wish to receive and in notifying the distributors of such publications when we regularly receive multiple copies of an item. Such repositories might also reduce the need for individual libraries to maintain files of such publications.

The most serious problem with access to these minor library publications has to do with the occasional special publication or report. The annual reports, newsletters, and other serial publications do regularly come to us, after all, without any effort on our part. They serve particular short-term functions and the failure to receive a particular title or issue may not matter much. Increasingly, however, important professional publications with a longer range value are published by libraries, by library associations and organizations, and even by individuals. Even if they are for sale, distribution and availability present serious problems. It is not economically feasible to advertise such publications, they are seldom listed in standard bibliographies, and information about them is difficult to come by in any systematic fashion. The issuing library, association or organization, or individual finds it difficult to identify appropriate channels in which it can be certain that the availability of such publications will be announced. The best that can be hoped for is that a notice sent to the major professional library publications may eventually result in a brief note about what the editor regards as a significant item appearing in a news column or special listing of materials. The lack of any organized source of information about such publications hinders both the producer, who may issue something of value but still be left with a large unsold inventory, and the potential consumer, who may be interested in a report on a particular subject but be unaware of its availability. The regular production and distribution by a library association or organization, or even a commercial source, of a cooperatively financed catalog of minor library publications, especially those of a non-serial nature with some more lasting value, would be of real benefit to producers and potential users alike.

Whether or not we individually or collectively make any effort to improve the production, distribution, and use of minor library publications, it is essential that we recognize the importance that these publications now have for librarianship. They represent a major source of current professional information that has a real contribution to make to our work. In addition to giving serious thought to the use that we make of these publications, we should encourage more analysis and review of individual publications and more general analysis and review of these publications as a class.

NOTES

[1]Norman D. Stevens, *Communication throughout Libraries* (Metuchen, N.J., Scarecrow, 1983), 103-7.

Norman D. Stevens

Ten Years' Work in Library History:
The Monograph from 1975 to 1985

In 1972, Sidney L. Jackson reviewed the availability of "Materials for Teaching Library History in the U.S.A.,"[1] and concluded:

> Altogether, historical scholarship has furnished teaching materials in English in more than sufficient amount for surveys, and reasonably well for the old libraries, and modern public libraries. It has not done so well for the academic library, service to children, the special library, the rural library, library education, or development apart from the United States and the United Kingdom. Feeble indeed is the monographic historical literature on aspects of library operation; treatment of the school library, and women in libraries, is almost nonexistent.[2]

Jackson's statement still has considerable accuracy even though there have been a number of factors present in the years covered by this review that have brought external pressure as well as publishing opportunity to those interested in library history. We find Harris and Davis commenting, in the preface to their bibliography,

> This guide should prove of special interest to scholars interested in the social, intellectual, and literary history of the country. In the past this group generally overlooked library and book history in their studies, viewing ideas as merely camouflage

for deeper motives, and they thus tended to ignore ideas in order to focus on social and, especially, economic forces in American history.[3]

On a more optimistic note, the compilers conclude—as some historians might not—that "the study of the origins, contents, and evolution of private and public libraries now plays an important part in the writing of American intellectual history."[4]

The focus of the following pages is to assess only one aspect of publication in library history, in one country, for a limited period. The survey will examine, through selective examples and an overall statistical summary, the publication of material on U.S. library history that could be considered "more than" journal publications, special reports, papers, or, in most cases, chapters in volumes of essays.

LIMITATIONS

Before beginning that review, two important limitations need to be noted. First, it is basically impossible to define the parameters of what might be included in the survey. Stam, in reviewing *Books and Society in History*[5] gave some idea of the scope of the issue when he wrote that "what comes across as most important is the growing interdependence of historian, bibliographer, sociologist, librarian, and literary scholar."[6] As the literature of library history is examined, certain categories do fall in place, but an examination of the materials reviewed in *The Journal of Library History* demonstrates the wide range of topics of interest, one must assume, to library historians. For example, the most recent issue (vol. 20, Fall 1985) of that journal includes reviews on a social history of the German book trade in America; a record of Carnegie libraries in Ontario; international book and library activities; two Festschriften; a quasi-autobiographical work; a study of library work for children and young adults in developing countries; a review of WPA activities; a volume on crime in the library; trends, collections, and sources of rare books; and the reading of soldiers during the Civil War.

Raabe, writing on "Library History and the History of Books: Two Fields of Research for Librarians,"[7] suggests that topics for study must first embrace all kinds of libraries and that individual library histories provide the foundation for the whole: "Research in library history, like any piece of historical work, proceeds from the investigation of the particular, the specific, the single case. The general presentation of interconnections can only be the result, the summary of a considerable number of individual studies and investigations."[8] Raabe then identifies individual subject areas that need historical consideration and are related to other key issues: (1) the history of holdings from private libraries as related to the methods used, i.e., acquisitions; (2) the history of catalogs and, in turn, the techniques of organization and retrieval; (3) the history of who make use of the library and their interests; (4) the history of the physical structures, the buildings, locations, plans, and their relationship to the society in which they were constructed; (5) the history of the staff, the librarians, and their impact on the profession; and (6) the history of library administration at all levels both within and without the institution—especially within our society. Raabe turns to book history in the same essay and identifies areas of research as including book manuscripts, book production, book illustration, printing bases, book bindings, book trade, criticism, and reading.

Such a classification, of course, is only one way of looking at the vast array of what might be counted in a review of a decade of monographic research and writing. Kaser, surveying "Advances in American Library History," uses a much simpler approach that covers, under the headings of academic libraries, public libraries, organization of materials, library associations and library education, some eighty-five titles including studies of individual libraries and librarians; a few broader, "horizontal" studies that provide a more comprehensive perspective; geographical studies; microanalytical studies; and revisionist studies.[9] (He ultimately concludes, in his survey that mainly focuses on the late 1960s

and mid-1970s, "recent studies in American library history—in general, although not in all cases—show a marked improvement over earlier work. They manifest greater scholarly rigor and acknowledge the importance of structure in research and writing, and the finer points of historical method.")[10]

Harris and Davis have developed the organization scheme that is often used.[11] Although their chapters do not dictate the analysis found in the remainder of this essay, they provide a logical way in which to establish a framework. Their chapters are (1) "Historiography and Sources," (2) "General Studies of American Library History," (3) "Private Libraries, Reading Tastes, and the Book Trade from the Colonial Period to the Present," (4) "Predecessors of the Public Library," (5) "Public Libraries," (6) "Academic Libraries," (7) "School Libraries," (8) "State Libraries," (9) "Special Libraries," (10) "Education for Librarianship," (11) "Library Associations," (12) "Special Aspects of American Librarianship," and (13) "Biographies of Librarians and Library Benefactors." Of course, a number of titles reviewed in library journals do not fit precisely any one of the thirteen categories, yet are relevant to effective understanding of library history. *The Journal of Library History* sees fit to review such titles as Mukerji's *From Graven Images: Patterns of Modern Materialism*, a study of the economic factors that served as a foundation to capitalism and modern materialistic culture.[12]

This survey has focused only on those titles that have a primary or, occasionally, secondary relationship to library history as a limited construct. Otherwise, the data become impossible to obtain or abstract—regardless of the profession's need to place library history within a generalized framework.

A second limitation must also be pointed out. Only in recent years have the appropriate indexes and reviews been generated to serve the library historian. It should not be surprising to hear Davis state, in his 1978 review of the 1976 publications, that "sources for studying library history became more accessible during the year because of the care with which the summary articles were documented. The authors' citations identified retrospective publications in such a way that the references themselves are frequently as important as the summaries."[13] If the library historian begins a literature review of relevant titles directed only to aspects of "library history," a select number of sources emerges as the most useful, and they are products, in general, of the past fifteen to twenty years. This limitation does not preclude use of basic indexes such as Cannons's *Bibliography of Library Economy, Library Literature*, and indexes of related fields, but it does admit the difficulty of any sure or simple identification of monographs specifically identifiable as library history. The nature of indexing and abstracting sources inhibits searching by such a generic mode.

Bibliographical control did take a major step forward in 1968 with the first of the periodical reviews of "The Year's Work in American Library History."[14] This series, which became a "Two Years' Work ..." in 1972, is still *the* key source for an overall assessment of what has been published. Wiegand, writing for the 1977-1978 review, emphasized that the Harris and Davis bibliography, cited earlier, "will quickly become a first source for library historians to consult before commencing research projects."[15] He also notes that their volume includes "only those articles, books, papers, master's theses, and doctoral dissertations (over 3,000 citations) which approach the field as conscious library history."[16] In addition, it should be noted that Harris and Davis begin their text with a section on historiography and sources citing ninety-three titles that they believe are germane. Of the ninety-three titles, a number are focused on historiography and are not bibliography per se. The point here is, of course, to re-emphasize the limitations inherent in a review of ten years' work. Relevant titles frequently eluded the authors of those annual or two-year reviews at the time of their analysis. When and if located, they were included in later issues. The last two-year review was being prepared at the time of the writing of this essay and it covered 1983 and 1984. For purposes of this essay, then, 1985 titles are limited and may not be reflective of the year's work. At the same time, certain publication patterns do emerge even if some titles were not identified in the sources consulted.

PUBLICATION PATTERNS

This review of monograph publication began with an examination of the 1975 year. Davis and Harris, in their analysis of the publications for the 1974-1975 period, concluded that they were observing a major expansion in both the amount and range of historical literature.[17] They cite 118 publications but it is important to note that of that number, only 32 titles fall outside of journal publication or chapters in books. Moreover, among the 32 cited in monographic style, they included papers published by the University of Illinois Graduate School of Library Science in its Occasional Paper series (e.g., Harris[18]), and a number of titles that tend to defy effective evaluation as library history, e.g., Stevens's collection *Essays for Ralph*

Shaw.[19] The authors noted three such publications and described them as "of some value to historians."[20]

In the years surrounding the nation's bicentennial and the American Library Association centennial, there was evidence of renewed interest in history and, of course, it was logical to publish either just before, during, or in the years immediately after 1976. This, to a degree, explains why few monographs are cited specifically for 1975 since many publishers and authors were looking to the highly "marketable year"—1976.

When the titles actually published in 1975 are isolated, only six emerge as basic library history contributions although all provide viewpoints and data that are of interest to the historian. A 1975 work by Edwin Wolf, 2nd, reflects an ongoing publication area: the history of the library of a noted collector and scholar.[21] Such works, whether simply a catalog or a more descriptive analysis, appeared regularly in the period from 1975 to 1985. As pointed out by Raabe, such a work "affords insight into the history of private libraries, in as much as they initially formed the basis of public libraries."[22] Ten years later, in 1985, this tradition is continued in the Columbia University Libraries volume, *The Rare Book and Manuscript Library of Columbia University.*[23] Raabe notes that "the study of specialized catalogues and means employed in making the holdings available, e.g. the compiling of manuscript catalogues, carries over into the field of the history of scholars."[24] The catalogs of the libraries of notable bibliophiles and historical figures, such as Thomas Jefferson,[25] offer opportunities for unique assessment as do those of specialized collections. Among the latter is the 1981 publication of Ball and Martin that dealt with rare Afro-Americana in the Adger Library.[26]

Although the published volume did not appear until 1976, a second publication pattern was anticipated in the 1974-1975 review when Davis and Harris cited Bentinck-Smith's "analysis of Archibald Cory Coolidge's central role in [Harvard's] development."[27] When Williamson reviewed this work, he succinctly pointed out that such a history "highlights once again how much we need a professional history of our premier academic library that will describe, analyze, and generalize Harvard's experience as it illustrates or contrasts with the typical university library experience in the United States."[28]

Two types of publication have already been noted; there are others that were indicative of what was to come. Among them were the first two volumes of the Heritage of Librarianship series.[29] The foreword of the first volume, edited by Harris, begins "with this volume Libraries Unlimited inaugurates its Heritage of Librarianship Series. This series is designed to provide modern librarians, both here and abroad, with carefully selected collections of the writings of prominent American and European librarians."[30] Although the series does not offer definitive studies of the subjects (Jewett, 1976; Spofford, 1976; Cutter, 1977; Dewey, 1978; Winsor, 1980), each includes a selection of the subject's writings as well as a critical essay by the well-known editors, each of whom has a strong library history background. Studies of other prominent individuals associated with librarianship occurred throughout the ten years surveyed. Sullivan, in 1976, published a well-received study of Carl H. Milam,[31] and Dale edited a series of his unpublished documents.[32] Boorstin sponsored a collective biography on the *Librarians of Congress, 1802-1974* that consisted of eleven studies of his predecessors.[33] Since the biographies were individually done, there was some unevenness in approach. Keyes D. Metcalf, in reviewing the title, noted that "there was no attempt to provide a summation or to compare the significance of the contributions...."[34] Among other noteworthy biographical studies of the period are Marion Casey's excellent study of Charles McCarthy, founder of Wisconsin's Legislative Reference Library;[35] Wiegand's subjective collection of academic library leaders;[36] and Gondos's dedicated study of J. Franklin Jameson, founder of the National Archives.[37] The decade obviously produced several studies that attempted to fill the numerous gaps in the biographical history of librarians, archivists, bibliophiles, and educators. One of the invaluable contributions of the period was the 1978 publication of the *Dictionary of American Library Biography* (*DALB*).[38] Danton, in his thorough and critical review essay, concluded that "the DALB is a splendid piece of work. It will be used for years to come, and it can be used with confidence.... [It] is likely to be one of the most consulted single-volume publications American librarianship has ever produced."[39] The 301 original, biographical sketches constitute "a comprehensive history of American librarianship and its institutions from about 1730 to about 1930-40."[40]

The limited monographic publication in 1975 did produce three other historical studies reflecting major themes in the broadly based field of librarianship. The first, *The Shaping of American Library Education*,[41] was described as a "scholarly little book, well documented and undergirded with notes and bibliography."[42] Library education was also addressed in succeeding years through Cramer's model history

of the Case Western library school;[43] a "timely and appropriate historical criticism of library education and research"[44] by Houser and Schrader; and Richardson's superbly detailed study of the Graduate Library School of the University of Chicago.[45]

Another aspect of library history published during the 1975 year was directed to special libraries and their individual histories. This began with Garland's centennial (1875-1975) history of the Boston Medical Library.[46] In 1979, Knox, writing on the Frick Art Reference Library, turned "what could easily have become a dull and dreary book ... [into] absorbing history."[47] Mount, in 1982, authored a careful analysis of the Engineering Societies Library,[48] and Richards produced a study of the New York Historical Society. Her 1984 work was "grounded in archival research, gracefully written, and elegantly argued,"[49] although, the reviewer noted, there were areas that might have been better developed, notably the library's impact on scholarly production or the effect of political attitudes on the library itself. The period also produced studies on the national library, the Library of Congress, other national institutions (the National Library of Medicine, the National Archives), and highly specialized collections such as the 1985 study of the Lilly Library at Indiana University.[50] It should probably be noted that these histories are often tied by publication to an anniversary year of the library and not to any other factor.

Still another "first" when categorizing types of study came with a 1975 analysis of the Missouri Library Association,[51] not especially well reviewed. Thomison's 1978 history of the American Library Association and Hindman's 1982 study of the Catholic Library Association were also part of this decade's efforts to synthesize different facets of library science.[52]

Finally, for such a slim year in terms of actual publications, one other title needs special note—McCrimmon's selection of nineteen essays that would illustrate American library philosophy.[53] Although the authors of the essays reflect four periods of our history (1897-1927, 1927-1942, 1949-1954, 1961-1972) and are highly respected authors/pioneers/leaders, McCrimmon is additionally noteworthy because of her goal: the essential obligation for authors and editors to attempt to comprehend broad perspectives. The 1975-1985 decade did see a significant attempt by the profession to address the larger issues. Whether it is Stone's 1977 outline/explication of *American Library Development, 1600-1899*,[54] noted for its "judicious compromise of brevity and adequacy";[55] Rogers and McChesney's introductory volume on *The Library in Society*;[56]

the recent history of library development found in *National Planning for Library Service, 1935-1975*;[57] the broad strokes of Metcalfe's 1876-1976 analysis of information retrieval;[58] or the commemoration of American library history published as a special issue of *Library Trends*;[59] the period was one of reflection and sensitivity to the need for the perspective that Shera called for when he stated that:

> the history of librarianship ... treats of the changes *within* the library and the impact of those changes upon the services of the library as one agency in the communication process.... The kind of historical writing for which we are here arguing would throw a strong light on librarianship today, and provide us with insight at a time when insight is sorely needed.... Not until such studies have been made can the profession speak with authority of the meaning of librarianship within its coeval culture.[60]

PATTERNS OF PUBLICATION— CENTENNIAL YEAR

The relative paucity of monographs published in 1975 was easily balanced by the publishers' and authors' rush to respond to the 1976 celebration. Depending on one's definition of a "book," it is possible to say that some twenty books (or at least lengthy essays) were published in that year. Some publication patterns, although they have existed throughout the writing of library history, were particularly apparent that year, i.e., the relatively brief histories of small public libraries. Often, as in the case of Helmrich's eighty-four-page history of the public library in Brunswick, Maine,[61] a reviewer would note that "although the public library ... is not a major institution, nor its community a large one, this library reflects much of the general advancement of libraries from the last quarter of the nineteenth century to the present day."[62]

Also published in the centennial year were a series of works that both assisted and occasionally limited a cohesive overview of library history. Among the resource titles were the last of the bibliographical checklists, by state, that the library school at Florida State University produced. Few would dispute the value of many of the checklists such as Kunkle's 182-page *Bibliography of the History of Libraries in California*, a 1976 offering, but supplemented in

succeeding years by such works as the 1983 compilation of Texas library history.[63] Although not primarily library history, the centennial edition of the *ALA Yearbook* merits note since it began an ongoing tradition of including overviews on library history activities.[64] In addition, the long-sought author index to Cannons's *Bibliography of Library Economy* was described as "essential to the success of scholarship."[65]

One of two[66] less successful centennial efforts was that of Ellsworth and Stevens who attempted to identify true landmarks of the profession by compiling forty-one papers published from 1876-1976. The work suffered from the lack of an analytical or summary conclusion as did the earlier-cited study of librarians of Congress. A second centennial compilation was based on eighteen original essays and it, too, was not completely balanced although the final chapter provides an overview of trends and issues in American librarianship for the past one hundred years.

The profession was more satisfied with the publication of the first edition of the *ALA World Encyclopedia of Library and Information Services* produced in 1980.[67] Although uneven in coverage of historical events, it stood up well to Danton's criteria and was judged as "a valuable addition to our professional literature and will undoubtedly be widely and intensively used."[68] Then, in 1982, Schlachter and Thomison provided an update on library science dissertations covering the period from 1973-1981.[69] In the same year, the *National Catalog of Sources for the History of Librarianship* was soundly applauded by Holley, who noted that "one can hardly imagine any embryo or aged historian who won't need access to NCSHL and its future editions."[70] A year later, 1983, *Libraries in American Periodicals before 1876: A Bibliography with Abstracts and an Index* brought, according to Harris, "the conclusion of a substantial collective bibliographic effort designed to provide comprehensive and up-to-date bibliographic coverage of the literature on the history of American libraries."[71] Throughout the ten year period, there were a number of specialized bibliographies produced for outstanding bookmen. These are not detailed here, but any peruser of that period would find basic source material such as those on Louis Round Wilson and J. Periam Danton, both published in the centennial year.[72]

Turning from this examination of special resources for the library historian, 1976 saw the publication of works that helped to define library functions and specializations. For example, Comaromi brought out his extensive history and analysis of the first eighteen editions of the Dewey Decimal Classification, and Pitkin provided a bibliographic history of serials automation.[73] Both works had their critics, but each made a contribution to the history of library organization that in succeeding years included Miksa's excellent study of *The Subject in the Dictionary Catalog from Cutter to the Present*,[74] and Maciuszko's valuable assessment of the first ten years of OCLC.[75]

Brewster's thoroughly documented study of postwar American technical assistance provides the "necessary basic background information on which to build."[76] Kraske, nearly ten years later, offered a different overseas perspective; he "recounts the role that the American library profession played from 1938 to 1949 in the promotion of cultural cooperation with other countries on the part of the United States government."[77]

One other title deserves some recognition during the centennial year. Related to library education, it was not noted earlier when discussing significant studies because Carl White's 1976 publication was a revision. Still, Reed reminds us that "out of his wisdom and scholarship would come answers that would make important reading for everyone interested in library education or in librarianship generally."[78] Centennial years need to be marked by that perception.

NEW AND OLD:
1977-1980

As is obvious from the selective title notations made up to this point in the essay, there were a significant number of noteworthy centennial monographs that reflect a variety of library history interests. The next four years produced areas of publication that had not been noted in either 1975 or 1976. Of course, the works continued to cover the spectrum of both quality and content. Wiegand summarized the period when he pointed out that "the profession needs more biographies, more monographs, and more articles based on meticulous research into primary sources materials...."[79] On the other hand, for purposes of reviewing the breadth and depth of works valuable to library historians, two titles, not mentioned before, deserve special recognition. Although there has been reference to the area of printing, Blumenthal's "prolonged and careful preparation"[80] of *The Printed Book in America* brings back to our attention the relationship of printing history and its protagonists to library history. Similarly, even the fourth edition of a landmark study, *Banned Books: 387 B.C. to 1978 A.D.*, indicates that "there are times when a mere recitation of historical events speaks more eloquently than the most inspired orator."[81] This classic leads logically to recogni-

tion of the work on censorship in American public libraries published near the end of the ten year period that was surveyed. Geller's superb history of

> the change in our professional attitudes toward censorship from 1876, when the newly founded American Library Association sought to avoid controversial literature and endorsed the concept of the librarian as a moral censor, to 1939 when ALA adopted its first Library Bill of Rights, provides a view of many librarians that standard biographical sources fail to reveal.[82]

It might be worthwhile to note, again, that histories of individual libraries, both short and long, were still in production as, for example, the short but well-done history — despite a dearth of citations — of the Dallas Public Library.[83] Even more valuable, although still lacking the total picture, is a competent history of the library of the Woman's College, Duke University, 1930-1972.[84]

One area that emerged in 1977 is important to emphasize since it reflects the ease with which whole areas can be overlooked for long periods of time. Smith published a historical survey of black academic libraries in 1977.[85] Although only partially library history, the fact that it exists becomes notable. In the period reviewed, no monographs that could be identified as history on other minorities served by libraries were noted and only two other titles on black history were cited and reviewed. One, edited by Phinazee, describes the black librarian in the Southeast,[86] and the second, by Joyce, surveys the development of black book publishing.[87]

Also tackled in a book-length approach during this period are three areas not mentioned previously. First, Adkinson[88] "inadvertently suggests a refreshing new perspective in library history by attempting to identify the general patterns of federal information machinery."[89] Next, a lengthy and valuable study by Hudak on *Early American Women Printers and Publishers, 1639-1820* provides biographical sketches on twenty-five women prominent during that period who obviously had been ignored in other compendia.[90] Although some of the anthologies cited earlier have included discussions focused on the role of women, the next five years after the 1978 study on women printers produced four studies. In 1979, Weibel and Heim edited a series of original essays on *The Role of Women in Librarianship, 1876-1976*.[91] Titles on women are often reviewed by women and in this instance, Lucille Wert[92] was highly critical of the volume noting, inevitably, the unevenness of the contributions, the unattainable goal "to provide a history of the first hundred years of a profession ..."[93] and compared it unfavorably to the theme articulated in the other major publication of that year, *Apostles of Culture*.[94] Garrison's highly acclaimed, equally criticized, and provocative analysis of the American public library system from 1876 to 1920 and the change from a masculine to a feminine profession produced a rash of responses continuing to date. Monographs on women are no less prone to mistakes than those on any other subject, and a slim collection of sketches by Lundy in 1980 is a prime example of what should not be published.[95] Wiegand, in opening the review of the 1979-1980 period, was correct in his admonition that "library editors and publishers should impose more rigorous standards of scholarship on authors...."[96] This may be true of the 1983 work on *The Status of Women in Librarianship: Historical, Sociological and Economic Issues*.[97] Rosemary Du Mont reviewed it with mixed conclusions and noted that she "came up with many instances where articles represented opinion as fact or fudged conclusions. In spite of that, the content is compelling."[98] Needless to say, future publications focused on women will also receive a most careful scrutiny, but this period did draw attention to an issue of major import to the profession.

Earlier, comment was made about the limited book-length attention given to minorities; the same might be said of those areas that serve special populations of the library including service to children, the literature of children, service to young adults, service to other special groups such as the disabled, and even service to adults. Tied into this area of import for library history would be publications on reading research. Altogether the ten year review does not provide much to note. Braverman, in 1979, traced the development of young adult services in three libraries;[99] Davis, in the same year, provided a specialized focus on *A Colonial Southern Bookshelf: Reading in the Eighteenth Century*;[100] Smith's earlier work on the history of children's literature was revised and enlarged in 1980;[101] the role of Daniel Nash Handy in the special library movement was addressed by Christianson;[102] Birge "traces the sporadic and uneven attempts by the library community to serve adult learners";[103] Karetzky provides a thorough and careful examination of the early years of reading research at the University of Chicago;[104] a handbook of issues on service for the blind and physically disabled was published in 1983;[105] and, in 1985, a historical analysis of the attitudes of librarians and the policies of public libraries toward fiction during the 1900 to 1950 period was published, updating an earlier work.[106] Although eight titles have just been identified, each tends to be *the* major work published during ten years. As noted by the reviewer of *Fiction in Public Libraries, 1900-1950*, "there aren't many books on the subject ... yet, it is such as obvious one."[107]

THE CLOSING YEARS:
1981-1985

As outlined in the opening section of this essay, a major source for identification of monographs is the ongoing reviews of "The Literature of American Library History" published in *The Journal of Library History*. Each of these articles has been completed approximately two years after the period reviewed due to the difficulty of identifying, obtaining, and reviewing many of the titles. The last review published covers the 1981-1982 monographs and also includes any titles not located for the earlier essays.[108] In the essay covering the 1979-1980 period, Wiegand had stated a concern about the drop in titles, but his coverage deals with all forms of printed materials. The number of monographs during that period was not reduced. Unfortunately, it is difficult to give precise figures since titles per se have not been the measure of organization. For example, seventeen titles were originally identified for 1978, nineteen for 1979, twenty-two for 1980, nineteen for 1981, and nineteen for 1982. Overall, 188 titles were initially identified. One hundred and one are cited in this review. Those numbers became meaningless as the books themselves were reviewed for their general quality or reflection of a publication pattern. As Wiegand also concludes, "the literature of American library history published in the past two years must receive mixed reviews."[109]

In completing the final years of the decade and concluding the review, certain aspects not noted in the earlier comments need to be clarified. To begin with, there have been many notable works during the decade that have looked to the areas outlined by Raabe at the beginning of this essay: manuscripts, book production, book illustration, printing, binding, the trade, and catalogs of all types. This essential area of research is exemplified by the 1981 work of John Tebbel.[110] The fourth volume of his masterful series on the history of book publishing in the United States that began with 1630 is finished, at least for a couple of decades, with the coverage from 1940 to 1980. This type of research, related to library history though it is, has been neglected by this reviewer, although it is regularly considered in *The Journal of*

Library History review essays. From 1975 to 1985, there were at least two titles on bookselling, nine on printing and bibliographical history, one on bookbinding, three on publishing including Meckler's 1982 work on micropublishing,[111] and seven titles that might be classified as catalogs or rare book collection checklists.

At the same time, the period did not uncover numerous sources dealing with the antecedents of current libraries. However, in 1980, Kaser produced a history of the circulating library in America[112] that suggested many opportunities for additional study and related this early library to other aspects of American cultural history.

Although they could have been included in the section on special services, three authors, Cole, Kaser, and Young produced works that discuss access to books and reading interests of American soldiers in three wars.[113,114,115] Kaser directed his attention to the Civil War period and offered an enjoyable but introductory assessment of the reading habits of the soldiers from both the North and the South. Young, in his *Books for Sammies*, considers the period of World War I and describes the effort to build, stock, and staff thirty-six camp libraries. Finally, Cole has compiled and introduced several short essays that briefly outline the efforts during World War II to provide access to books and reading by servicemen overseas.

Another topic that was touched on earlier, but only briefly, did emerge strongly in the last half of the 1975-1985 decade. In the opening pages, it was noted that comprehensive histories had to be built on the histories of individual libraries. Such a comprehensive history appeared in 1981 with the publication of *The University Library in the United States: Its Origins and Development*.[116] Young pointed out that "despite a heritage surpassing three centuries, the university library is generally neglected in institutional histories and only occasionally addressed in unpublished theses and dissertations."[117] Hamlin's work is the first integrated history of the American university library. A year earlier, in 1980, Thompson had edited a volume of fifteen essays,[118] but its international scope and its approach do not match the historical perspective of the Hamlin title. Coincidental to the Hamlin publication of 1981 was Shiflett's *Origins of American Academic Librarianship* that both looks at the origins of the academic tradition and then describes the professionalization of academic librarianship and the status of the librarian.[119] Still another title in this category is *The Carnegie Corporation and the Development of American College Libraries, 1928-1941*.[120] This assessment is a well-constructed narrative that examines the impact of the Carnegie philanthropy. Finally, a full-length study on undergraduate libraries in the United States and Canada traces the concept of separate collections and services.[121]

A number of studies specifically related to the public library have already been noted. One of the more thought-provoking is White's challenge to established perceptions about the public library.[122] Two other titles should be noted although they are not specifically "horizontal" histories relating to public libraries. The first, consisting of seven essays edited by Ring, is a study of library history projects funded by the WPA in seven major public libraries during the 1930s; the essays "are uniformly well-documented and well written."[123] The second, just published in 1985, is Shavit's analysis of the events leading to the amendment of LSCA in 1970; five libraries are examined in terms of the impact of that legislative change plus eight others are examined through quantitative data and interviews.[124]

At the beginning of this article, Jackson is quoted as stating that there are many works available to support the study of library history. This is certainly true when reflecting on the addition of the titles published from 1975 to 1985. However, there are some serious gaps in the "book" literature. Notable among the missing is school media programs. One title that might have been noted in conjunction with the works on women or with the biographical studies is a 1981 publication by Branyan.[125] Basically it is not cited because it is a simple, notebook reproduction of the author's dissertation. However, it *is* an examination of the women who promoted unified school library and audiovisual programs, 1950 through 1975. It also illustrates the researcher's problem in locating relevant sources unless formally published, advertised, disseminated, and reviewed.

Before ending the summary, it is requisite to provide a cursory breakdown of the topics of publication. The data that follow are somewhat deceiving since some titles clearly could be and have been used in more than one category. First, outside of the broad range of book production and distribution including catalogs of manuscripts and libraries that was summarized earlier, publication has been to a large extent classified by types of libraries: Approximately twenty-five titles discussed here are distinctly public library oriented; eighteen focus on special libraries; eighteen can be associated mainly with academic librarianship; and eleven deal with national institutions.

Second, the obvious categories of library functions or activities are evident: Seven titles recognize historical issues of organization and retrieval; two examine library automation; five consider aspects of censorship, nine focus on women and minorities; three discuss books and libraries for servicemen; nine examine problems of library education, five summarize the history of library associations; eleven deal with the relationship between federal policy here and overseas; and four fall into a "miscellaneous" classification. From these overall categories there is overlapping with general library history, responses to the centennial year, and the ongoing production of reference sources.

Separate from this rough classification, seven Festschriften have been noted; sixteen titles are reference works including collective biography, bibliographies, encyclopedias, yearbooks, etc.; and seventeen have a strong biographical thrust. The numbers noted in the preceding paragraph do not add up to the total production, 188 titles, because of their consideration in more than one category.

Finally, there has been no mention of those special insights provided to all library historians through the autobiographical commentaries of librarians or the various collections of writings or essays in honor of the famous. It seems most appropriate to close a decade of library history by noting just a few of the famous who did share their perceptions, often of several decades of library history, with their readers. Oboler characterized his own work as the "essays of an unorthodox academic librarian";[126] McShean described his trials as a "librarian's medium-rare memoir about censorship";[127] Ellsworth modestly provided an "unchronicle, mostly true account";[128] Metcalf analyzed seventy-five years of "random recollections of an anachronism";[129] Lyle went beyond his expectations;[130] Ready called his memoir, *Files on Parade*,[131] Benge entertained with *Confessions of a Lapsed Librarian*;[132] and Downs conservatively provided *Perspectives on the Past*.[133]

However, it was Shores who, in the opening year of this survey, 1975, provided the beginning and end of a ten year review of work in library history. His autobiography, *Quiet World: A Librarian's Crusade for Destiny*,[134] elicited many responses. Two reflect not only this essay but his world and ours. The first suggests a continuing theme in much of the work of library historians. Shore's study was described as "flawed as is the man ... overstated, uneven...."[135] So, too, is the monograph literature of our field. At the same time, "In all probability every librarian who reads it will find within [the literature or] *Quiet World* something with which he can identify; many will find that, for their own worlds, some things are left out."[136] And so stands the decade of 1975-1985.

NOTES

[1]Sidney L. Jackson, "Materials for Teaching Library History in the U.S.A.," *Journal of Education for Librarianship* 12 (Winter 1972): 179-92.

[2]Ibid., 192.

[3]Michael H. Harris and Donald G. Davis, Jr., *American Library History: A Bibliography* (Austin, Tex.: University of Texas Press, 1978), ix.

[4]Ibid.

[5]Kenneth E. Carpenter, ed., *Books and Society in History*, papers of the Association of College and Research Libraries Rare Books and Manuscripts Preconference, 24-28 June 1980 (New York: Bowker, 1983).

[6]David H. Stam, review of Carpenter (see Reference 3) in *College & Research Libraries* 45 (January 1984): 78.

[7]Paul Raabe, "Library History and the History of Books: Two Fields of Research for Librarians," *The Journal of Library History* 19 (Spring 1984): 282-97.

[8]Ibid., 286-87.

[9]David Kaser, "Advances in American Library History," *Advances in Librarianship* 8 (1978): 181-99.

[10]Ibid., 193.

[11]Harris and Davis.

[12]Chandra Mukerji, *From Graven Images: Patterns of Modern Materialism* (New York: Columbia University Press, 1983). Reviewed in *Journal of Library History* 20 (Summer 1985): 321-23.

[13]Donald G. Davis, Jr., "The Year's Work in American Library History—1976," *The Journal of Library History* 13 (Spring 1978): 187.

[14]Michael H. Harris, "The Year's Work in American Library History: 1967," *The Journal of Library History* 3 (October 1968): 342-52.

[15]Wayne A. Wiegand, "The Literature of American Library History, 1977-1978," *The Journal of Library History* 14 (Summer 1979): 320.

[16]Ibid.

[17]Donald G. Davis, Jr., and Michael H. Harris, "Two Years' Work in American Library History, 1974-1975," *The Journal of Library History* 11 (July 1976): 276-96.

[18]Michael H. Harris, *The Role of the Public Library in American Life: A Speculative Essay*, Occasional Paper No. 117 (Urbana, Ill.: University of Illinois Graduate School of Library Science, 1975).

[19]Norman D. Stevens, ed., *Essays for Ralph Shaw* (Metuchen, N.J., Scarecrow, 1975).

[20]Ibid., 287.

[21]Edwin Wolf, 2nd, *The Library of James Logan of Philadelphia* (Philadelphia: Library Company of Philadelphia, 1975).

[22]Raabe, 287.

[23]*The Rare Book and Manuscript Library of Columbia University: Collections and Treasures* (New York: Columbia University Library, 1985).

[24]Raabe, 287.

[25]Emily M. Sowerby, comp. and annotator, and The Thomas Jefferson Memorial Foundation, ed., *Catalogue of the Library of Thomas Jefferson*, 5 vols. (reprint, Charlottesville, Va.: University Press of Virginia, 1983).

[26]Wendy Ball and Tony Martin, *Rare Afro-Americana: A Reconstruction of the Adger Library* (Boston: G. K. Hall, 1981).

[27]Davis and Harris, 282, in reference to William Bentinck-Smith, *Building a Great Library: The Coolidge Years at Harvard* (Cambridge, Mass.: Harvard University Library, 1976).

[28]W. L. Williamson, *Library Quarterly* 47 (January 1977): 76.

[29]John Y. Cole, ed., *Ainsworth Rand Spofford: Bookman and Librarian* (Littleton, Colo.: Libraries Unlimited, 1975); Michael H. Harris, ed., *The Age of Jewett: Charles Coffin Jewett and American Librarianship, 1841-1868* (Littleton, Colo.: Libraries Unlimited, 1975).

[30]Harris, reference 29, p. vii.

[31]Peggy Sullivan, *Carl H. Milam and the American Library Association* (New York: Wilson, 1976).

[32]Doris C. Dale, ed., *Carl H. Milam and the United Nations Library* (Metuchen, N.J.: Scarecrow, 1976).

[33]*Librarians of Congress, 1802-1974* (Washington, D.C.: Library of Congress, 1977).

[34]Keyes D. Metcalf, "*Librarians of Congress, 1802-1974*: A Review Essay," *The Journal of Library History* 14 (Winter 1979): 54.

[35]Marion Casey, *Charles McCarthy: Librarianship and Reform* (Chicago: American Library Association, 1981).

[36]Wayne A. Wiegand, ed., *Leaders in American Academic Librarianship: 1925-1975* (Pittsburgh, Pa.: Beta Phi Mu; distr., Chicago: American Library Association, 1983).

[37]Victor Gondos, Jr., *J. Franklin Jameson and the Birth of the National Archives* (Philadelphia: University of Pennsylvania Press, 1981).

[38]*Dictionary of American Library Biography* (Littleton, Colo.: Libraries Unlimited, 1978).

[39]J. Periam Danton, " 'The Essence of Innumerable Biographies': A Review Essay on the *Dictionary of American Library Biography*," *The Journal of Library History* 13 (Fall 1978): 463.

[40]Ibid., 462.

[41]Charles D. Churchwell, *The Shaping of American Library Education* (Chicago: American Library Association, 1975).

[42]Edwin Castagna, review of Churchwell (see Reference 41), *The Journal of Library History* 11 (July 1976): 263.

[43]C. H. Cramer, *The School of Library Science at Case Western Reserve University: Seventy-Five Years, 1904-1979* (Cleveland, Ohio: School of Library Science, Case Western Reserve University, 1979).

[44]Glynn Harmon, review of L. Hauser and Alvin M. Schrader, *The Search for a Scientific Profession: Library Science Education in the U.S. and Canada* (Metuchen, N.J.: Scarecrow, 1978) in *The Journal of Library History* 14 (Winter 1979): 104.

[45]John V. Richardson, Jr., *The Spirit of Inquiry: The Graduate Library School at Chicago, 1921-1951* (Chicago: American Library Association, 1982).

[46]Joseph E. Garland, *The Centennial History of the Boston Medical Library, 1875-1975* (Boston: Boston Medical Library, 1975).

[47]Elizabeth Reuter Usher, review of Katharine McCook Knox, *The Story of the Frick Art Reference Library: The Early Years* (New York: Frick Art Reference Library, 1979) in *The Journal of Library History* 15 (Fall 1980): 501.

[48]Ellis Mount, *Ahead of Its Time: The Engineering Societies Library, 1913-80* (Hamden, Conn.: Linnet Books, 1982).

[49]Arthur P. Young, review of Pamela Spence Richards, *Scholars and Gentlemen: The Library of the New York Historical Society, 1804-1982* (Hamden, Conn.: Archon Books, 1984) in *The Journal of Library History* 20 (Spring 1985): 213.

[50]*The Lilly Library: The First Quarter Century, 1960-1985*, by the Lilly Library Staff and Professor Breon Mitchell (Bloomington, Ind.: Lilly Library, 1985).

[51]George N. Hartje, *Missouri Library Association, 1900-1975* (Columbia, Mo.: Missouri Library Association, 1975).

[52]Dennis V. Thomison, *A History of the American Library Association, 1876-1972* (Chicago: American Library Association, 1978); Jane F. Hindman, *The Catholic Library Association: The First Sixty Years, 1921-1981* (Haverford, Pa.: Catholic Library Association, 1982).

[53]Barbara McCrimmon, ed., *American Library Philosophy: An Anthology* (Hamden, Conn.: Shoe String Press, 1975).

[54]Elizabeth W. Stone, *American Library Development, 1600-1899* (New York: Wilson, 1977).

[55]David Kaser, review of Stone (see Reference 54) in *The Journal of Library History* 13 (Winter 1978): 62.

[56]A. Robert Rogers and Kathryn McChesney, *The Library in Society* (Littleton, Colo.: Libraries Unlimited, 1984).

[57]R. Kathleen Molz, *National Planning for Library Service, 1935-1975* (Chicago: American Library Association, 1984).

[58]John Metcalfe, *Information Retrieval, British and American, 1876-1976* (Metuchen, N.J., Scarecrow, 1976).

[59]Howard Winger, ed., "American Library History, 1876-1976," *Library Trends* 25:1 (July 1976).

[60]Jesse H. Shera, "What the Historian Has Been Missing," *Wilson Library Bulletin* 40 (1966): 639.

[61]Louise R. Helmrich, *A History of the Public Library in Brunswick, Maine* (Brunswick, Maine: Public Library Association, 1976).

[62]David C. Libbey, review of Helmrich (see Reference 61) in *The Journal of Library History* 12 (Fall 1977): 419.

[63]Hannah Josephine Kunkle, ed., *Bibliography of the History of Libraries in California. Journal of Library History Bibliography* No. 13. (Tallahassee, Fla.: *Journal of Library History* and School of Library Science, Florida State University, 1976); A. F. Skinner, *Texas Library History: A Bibliography* (Phoenix, Ariz.: Oryx Press, 1983).

[64]Robert Wedgeworth, ed., *The ALA Yearbook: 1976 Centennial Edition* (Chicago: American Library Association, 1976).

[65]Jesse H. Shera, review of *Cannons' Bibliography of Library Economy, 1876-1920: An*

Author Index with Citations, ed. Anne Harwell Jordan and Melbourne Jordan (Metuchen, N.J.: Scarecrow, 1976) in *The Journal of Library History* 12 (Winter 1977): 80.

[66]Dianne J. Ellsworth and Norman D. Stevens, eds., *Landmarks of Library Literature, 1876-1976* (Metuchen, N.J.: Scarecrow, 1976); Sidney L. Jackson, Eleanor B. Herling, and E. J. Josey, eds., *A Century of Service: Librarianship in the United States and Canada* (Chicago: American Library Association, 1976).

[67]*ALA World Encyclopedia of Library and Information Services*, ed. Robert Wedgeworth and others (Chicago: American Library Association, 1980).

[68]J. Periam Danton, " 'To Render Superfluous the Need to Consult Any Other Books': A Review Essay on the *ALA World Encyclopedia of Library and Information Services*," in *The Journal of Library History* 16 (Fall 1981): 541.

[69]Gail A. Schlachter and Dennis Thomison, *Library Science Dissertations, 1973-1981: An Annotated Bibliography* (Littleton, Colo.: Libraries Unlimited, 1982).

[70]Edward G. Holley, review of *National Catalog of Sources for the History of Librarianship* (Chicago: American Library Association, 1982) in *The Journal of Library History* 19 (Spring 1984): 326.

[71]Michael H. Harris, review of *Libraries in American Periodicals before 1876: A Bibliography with Abstracts and an Index*, comp. Larry J. Barr, Haynes McMullen, and Steven G. Leach, ed. Haynes McMullen (Jefferson, N.C.: McFarland, 1983) in *The Journal of Library History* 19 (Spring 1984): 325.

[72]*Louis Round Wilson Bibliography: A Chronological List of Works and Editorial Activities Presented on the Occasion of His Centennial Celebration, December 2, 1976* (Chapel Hill, N.C.: University of North Carolina Library, 1976); *J. Periam Danton: A Bibliography* (Berkeley, Calif.: School of Librarianship, University of California, 1976).

[73]John Phillip Comaromi, *The Eighteen Editions of the Dewey Decimal Classification* (New York: Forest Press Division, Lake Placid Educational Foundation, 1976); Gary M. Pitkin, *Serials Automation in the United States: A Bibliographic History* (Metuchen, N.J.: Scarecrow, 1976).

[74]Francis L. Miksa, *The Subject in the Dictionary Catalog from Cutter to the Present* (Chicago: American Library Association, 1983).

[75]Kathleen L. Maciuszko, *OCLC: A Decade of Development, 1967-1977* (Littleton, Colo.: Libraries Unlimited, 1984).

[76]Lester Asheim, review of Beverly J. Brewster, *American Overseas Library Technical Assistance, 1940-1970* (Metuchen, N.J.: Scarecrow, 1976) in *The Journal of Library History* 12 (Summer 1977): 321.

[77]Norman Stevens, review of Gary Kraske, *Missionaries of the Book* (Westport, Conn.: Greenwood Press) in *Wilson Library Bulletin* 60 (January 1986): 56.

[78]Sarah R. Reed, review of Carl M. White, *A Historical Introduction to Library Education: Problems and Progress to 1951* (Metuchen, N.J.: Scarecrow, 1976) in *The Journal of Library History* 12 (Spring 1977): 195.

[79]Wayne A. Wiegand, "The Literature of American Library History, 1977-1978," 340.

[80]Susan O. Thompson, review of Joseph Blumenthal, *The Printed Book in America* (Boston: David R. Godine, in association with Dartmouth College Library, 1977) in *The Journal of Library History* 14 (Winter 1979): 97.

[81]Sally A. Davis, ed., review of *Banned Books: 387 B.C. to 1978 A.D.* 4th ed. updated by Chandler B. Grannis (New York: Bowker, 1978) in *RQ* 25 (Fall 1985): 150.

[82]Norman Stevens, review of *Forbidden Books in American Public Libraries, 1876-1939* (Westport, Conn.: Greenwood Press, 1984) in *Wilson Library Bulletin* 58 (September 1984): 84.

[83]Larry Grove, *The Dallas Public Library: The First 75 Years* (Dallas, Tex.: Dallas Public Library, 1977).

[84]Betty Irene Young, *The Library of the Woman's College, Duke University, 1930-1972* (Durham, N.C.: Regulator Press, 1978).

[85]Jesse Carney Smith, *Black Academic Libraries and Research Collections: An Historical Survey* (Westport, Conn.: Greenwood Press, 1977).

[86]Annette L. Phinazee, ed., *The Black Librarian in the Southeast: Reminiscences, Activities, Challenges*, papers presented for a colloquium sponsored by the School of Library Service, North Carolina Central University, 8-9 October 1976 (Durham, N.C.: North Carolina Central University School of Library Science, 1980).

[87]Donald Franklin Joyce, *Gatekeepers of Black Culture: Black-owned Book Publishing in the United States, 1817-1981* (Westport, Conn.: Greenwood Press, 1983).

[88]Burton K. Adkinson, *Two Centuries of Federal Information* (Stroudsburg, Pa.: Dowden, Hutchinson and Ross, 1978; distr., San Diego, Calif., Academic Press).

[89]Wayne A. Wiegand, "The Literature of American Library History, 1979-1980," *The Journal of Library History* 17 (Summer 1982): 318.

[90]Leona M. Hudak, *Early American Women Printers and Publishers, 1639-1820* (Metuchen, N.J.: Scarecrow, 1978).

[91]Kathleen Weibel and Kathleen M. Heim, *The Role of Women in Librarianship, 1876-1976; The Entry, Advancement and Struggle for Equalization in One Profession* (Phoenix, Ariz.: Oryx Press, 1979).

[92]Lucille M. Wert, review of Weibel and Heim (see Reference 91) in *The Journal of Library History* 15 (Spring 1980): 226-29.

[93]Weibel and Heim, ix.

[94]Dee Garrison, *Apostles of Culture: The Public Librarian and American Society, 1876-1920* (New York: Free Press/Macmillan, 1979).

[95]Kathryn R. Lundy, *Women View Librarianship: Nine Perspectives* (Chicago: American Library Association, 1980).

[96]Wiegand, "The Literature of American Library History, 1979-1980," 291-92.

[97]Kathleen M. Heim, ed., *The Status of Women in Librarianship: Historical, Sociological and Economic Issues* (New York: Neal-Schuman, 1983).

[98]Rosemary Ruhig Du Mont, review of Heim (see Reference 97) in *The Journal of Library History* 20 (Summer 1985): 334.

[99]Miriam Braverman, *Youth, Society, and the Public Library* (Chicago: American Library Association, 1979).

[100]Richard Beale Davis, *A Colonial Southern Bookshelf: Reading in the Eighteenth Century* (Athens, Ga.: University of Georgia Press, 1979).

[101]Elva S. Smith's *The History of Children's Literature: A Syllabus with Selected Bibliographies*, rev. and enl. Margaret Hodges and Susan Steinfirst (Chicago: American Library Association, 1980).

[102]Elin B. Christianson, *Daniel Nash Handy and the Special Library Movement* (New York: Insurance Division, Special Libraries Association, 1980).

[103]James Hecht, review of Lynn E. Birge, *Serving Adult Learners: A Public Library Tradition*, ALA Studies in Librarianship No. 8 (Chicago: American Library Association, 1981) in *The Journal of Library History* 18 (Winter 1983): 100.

[104]Stephen Karetzky, *Reading Research and Librarianship: A History and Analysis* (Westport, Conn.: Greenwood Press, 1982).

[105]National Library Service for the Blind and Physically Handicapped, *That All May Read: Library Service for Blind and Physically Handicapped* (Washington, D.C.: Library of Congress, 1983).

[106]Esther Jane Carrier, *Fiction in Public Libraries, 1900-1950* (Littleton, Colo.: Libraries Unlimited, 1985).

[107]Ina Wise, review of Carrier (see Reference 106) in *RQ* 25 (Winter 1985): 273.

[108]Wayne A. Wiegand, "The Literature of American Library History, 1981-1982," *The Journal of Library History* 19 (Summer 1984): 390-425.

[109]Ibid., 417.

[110]John Tebbel, *A History of Book Publishing in the United States, Vol. IV: The Great Change, 1940-1980* (New York: Bowker, 1981).

[111]Alan Meckler, *Micropublishing: A History of Scholarly Micropublishing in America, 1938-1980* (Westport, Conn.: Greenwood Press, 1982).

[112]David Kaser, *A Book for a Sixpence: The Circulating Library in America.* Beta Phi Mu Chapbook No. 14 (Pittsburgh, Pa.: Beta Phi Mu, 1980).

[113]John Y. Cole, ed., *Books in Action* (Washington, D.C.: Library of Congress, 1984).

[114]David Kaser, *Books and Libraries in Camp and Battle* (Westport, Conn.: Greenwood Press, 1984).

[115]Arthur P. Young, *Books for Sammies: The American Library Association and World War I* (Lexington, Ky.: Beta Phi Mu, 1981).

[116]Arthur T. Hamlin, *The University Library in the United States: Its Origins and Development* (Philadelphia: University of Pennsylvania Press, 1981).

[117]Arthur P. Young, review of Hamlin (see Reference 116) in *The Journal of Library History* 17 (Summer 1982): 358.

[118]James Thompson, ed., *University Library History: An International Review* (London: Clive Bingley, 1980).

[119]Orvin Lee Shiflett, *Origins of American Academic Librarianship* (Norwood, N.J.: Ablex Publishing, 1981).

[120]Neil A. Radford, *The Carnegie Corporation and the Development of American College Libraries, 1928-1941* (Chicago: American Library Association, 1984).

[121]Roland Person, *A New Path: The History of the Undergraduate Library at U.S. and Canadian Universities* (Norwood, N.J.: Ablex Publishing, 1985).

[122]Lawrence J. White, *The Public Library in the 1980s: The Problems of Choice* (Lexington, Mass.: Lexington Books, 1983).

[123]Marion Casey, review of *Studies in Creative Partnership: Federal Aid to Public Libraries during the New Deal*, ed. Daniel F. Ring

(Metuchen, N.J.: Scarecrow, 1980) in *The Journal of Library History* 17 (Fall 1982): 516.

[124]David Shavit, *Federal Aid and State Library Agencies: Federal Policy Implementation* (Westport, Conn.: Greenwood Press, 1985).

[125]Brenda M. Branyan, *Outstanding Women Who Promoted the Concept of the Unified School Library and Audiovisual Programs, 1950 through 1975* (Fayetteville, Ark.: Hi Willow Research Publishing, 1981).

[126]Eli M. Oboler, *Ideas and the University Library: Essays of an Unorthodox Academic Librarian* (Westport, Conn.: Greenwood Press, 1977).

[127]Gordon McShean, *Running a Message Parlor: A Librarian's Medium-Rare Memoir about Censorship* (Palo Alto, Calif.: Ramparts Press, 1977).

[128]Ralph E. Ellsworth, *Ellsworth on Ellsworth: An Unchronicle, Mostly True Account....* (Metuchen, N.J.: Scarecrow, 1980).

[129]Keyes DeWitt Metcalf, *Random Recollections of an Anachronism, or Seventy Five Years of Library Work* (New York: Readex Books, 1980).

[130]Guy Lyle, *Beyond My Expectations: A Personal Chronicle* (Metuchen, N.J.: Scarecrow, 1981).

[131]William B. Ready, *Files on Parade: A Memoir* (Metuchen, N.J.: Scarecrow, 1982).

[132]R. C. Benge, *Confessions of a Lapsed Librarian* (Metuchen, N.J.: Scarecrow, 1984).

[133]Robert B. Downs, *Perspectives on the Past: An Autobiography* (Metuchen, N.J.: Scarecrow, 1984).

[134]Louis Shores, *Quiet World: A Librarian's Crusade for Destiny* (Hamden, Conn.: Shoe String Press, 1975).

[135]S. D. Neill, review of Shores (see Reference 134) in *Library Quarterly* 46 (April 1976): 216-17.

[136]"Editorial," *The Journal of Library History* 11 (January 1976): 5.

Laurel A. Grotzinger

A Century of Publishing at the American Library Association

Publishing at ALA is one hundred years old in 1986. The present phase began in 1968, when the association's executive director, David Clift, re-established a publishing department separate from his office. Clift recognized that ALA's publishing activities had become too large and complex to be defined merely as printing procurement and sales. Efforts to make ALA a professional publisher in structure as well as in output were thus formalized in 1968.[1] The publishing program's financial contribution to the association was recognized. But six years passed before a new ALA executive director, Robert Wedgeworth, was able to transform Clift's vision into reality. Clift had appointed William Rutter, who had held various jobs at Oxford University Press, to head the new publishing department. But Rutter departed two years later without leaving much of a mark, and his successor, John F. Gillespie, lasted barely a year in the turbulent political environment of ALA. The post was vacant for three years then, with the book section's executive editor, Pauline Cianciolo, acting as director without the title.

Donald E. Stewart, who became the director of publishing in 1974, had been managing editor of *Encyclopaedia Britannica*. He brought a thorough knowledge of reference book publishing to his new job and an eagerness to plan and edit major works himself. As an outsider, he also clearly saw how the organization's gov-erning structure retarded the timely production of books. The Editorial Committee, which had once been a significant asset to the association, could only meet four times a year to approve new book projects. In more competitive times, faster response was needed. In 1976, the Editorial Committee was absorbed into a new Publishing Committee, the committee of ALA's Council charged with giving advice on publishing matters. The practice of approving projects, formerly the role of the Editorial Committee, was delegated to staff, under the general guidelines of the Publishing Committee.

Stewart's editorial talents resulted in publication of three major works during his time. He and Executive Director Wedgeworth created an annual yearbook, designed to summarize the most significant library news of each year. Unlike the *Bowker Annual, The ALA Yearbook* develops articles in depth, contains half a dozen special reports on critical issues, reviews developments in all library associations and on the major topics of interest to librarians, and presents biographies and state reports. Wedgeworth edited the first ten editions of *The ALA Yearbook of Library and Information Services* (its title since 1984, replacing the more parochial *ALA Yearbook*), ably assisted by Stewart and Richard Dell, a former colleague of Stewart's at Encyclopaedia Britannica and currently editorial director at Doubleday's J. G.

Copyright © 1986 American Library Association.

Ferguson division. The newest edition is edited by ALA Deputy Director Roger Parent.

Another idea of Stewart's and Wedgeworth's was *The ALA World Encyclopedia of Library and Information Services*, published in 1980. This one-volume work concentrated on history, biography, and summaries of the state of the art from around the world. Sales were outstanding not only in the United States but also internationally, especially in the People's Republic of China and in Japan. The 1986 edition has an even broader international scope and demonstrates the association's continuing commitment to reference works in the library field.

In 1982, under the editorship of ALA headquarters librarian Joel M. Lee, *Who's Who in Library and Information Services* was published, the sixth edition of a directory that had been irregularly produced since 1933 under several imprints. The 1982 edition contains 18,000 accurate and up-to-date entries in a single volume; it is the only work of its kind in print.

Stewart was also involved in the prolonged and sometimes rocky negotiations that led, in 1978, to the publication of the second edition of the *Anglo-American Cataloguing Rules*. The first edition was published in 1967 under the editorship of Seymour Lubetzky and C. Sumner Spalding. The new edition was the product of five corporate authors: ALA, the Canadian Library Association, the Library Association (of the United Kingdom), the Library of Congress, and the British Library. The complexity of authorship and of publication was imposing, but after four years' work the three national associations successfully published *AACR2*, which quickly became ALA Publishing's best seller. It and its progeny, such as *Cartographic Materials: A Manual of Interpretation for AACR2, Cataloging Microcomputer Files: A Manual of Interpretation for AACR2, The Concise AACR2, Handbook for AACR2*, and *Guidelines for Using AACR2 Chapter 9 for Cataloging Microcomputer Software*, give ALA the strongest group of cataloging publications available from any publisher.

While Stewart oversaw special projects, a talented, experienced staff produced a variety of other publications. These professionals included Paul Brawley, *Booklist*'s editor since 1973; Herbert Bloom, acquisition editor since 1969; Helen Cline, the managing editor for books since 1973; Art Plotnik, *American Libraries* editor since 1975; and Howard White, in charge of *Library Technology Reports* from 1971.

American Libraries had experienced an upheaval during the 1970s that, while it resulted in a positive outcome, caused some pain. Gerald Shields had transformed the stodgy *ALA Bulletin* into the lively *American Libraries* during his time as editor from 1968 to 1973. His successor, Gordon Burke, in trying to assert his editorial independence, used a Washington stringer to discover if the National Commission for Library and Information Science (NCLIS) was a front for the "information industry" and opposed to the political stance of ALA. In the process, the efforts of ALA's Washington office were thought by its director, Eileen Cooke, and Executive Director Robert Wedgeworth to have been compromised.[2] Wedgeworth ordered Burke to fire the stringer, and Burke, along with three other editors, resigned. The result of the episode was a bifurcated structure, the editor reporting to the executive director for editorial matters and to the publishing director for budget and administrative matters. Helen Cline, managing editor in the books unit, was briefly moved into the editorial breach before Art Plotnik took over *American Libraries* in 1975. Plotnik is a writer who had worked at the Library of Congress and was associate editor of *Wilson Library Bulletin*. He brought a high degree of creativity and imagination to *AL*. By 1986, the magazine had by far the largest circulation, over forty-three thousand, of any library periodical in the country.

Another important Publishing personnel decision had been made by Wedgeworth in 1973. Edna Vanek, long-time editor of *Booklist*, retired, and Wedgeworth reached into the staff, appointing Paul Brawley, the *Booklist* nonprint editor, to the top spot. The journal had changed its trim size in 1969, and in 1974 Brawley began using colorful illustrations for the cover from books that the journal reviewed. These handsome covers have become a trademark. Many improvements were made in the magazine, so now, with a circulation of about thirty-five thousand, *Booklist/Reference Books Bulletin* lists over thirteen thousand items a year, including reviews of about six thousand books. Previously, *Reference Books Bulletin* was a separate unit although published in *Booklist*. It was successfully integrated administratively with the magazine in 1985 although *RBB* continues to use volunteer members as reviewers while *Booklist* uses paid staff.

Financial problems in 1981-1982, brought about in part by the most serious recession since the Great Depression, affected every unit of ALA. Donald Stewart retired in 1982. His successor is Gary Facente, an experienced publisher, formerly at Follett and McGraw-Hill. Armed with business management skills, Facente installed new financial controls, reorganized staff, automated order fulfillment, and focused more attention on marketing. He continued publishing major reference works, including Martha Williams's *Computer Readable Databases*, and concentrated more on *Booklist/RBB*, *American Libraries*, *Library Technology Reports*, and the publishing department's relationship with divisions and with the Joint Steering Committee for Revision of AACR.

In 1984, the Publishing Committee adopted a statement of principles, which sets forth four objectives: (1) to "publish books, journals, and other non-book materials to achieve timely and effective exchange of ideas and information among ALA members, the profession at large, and the publics served by the profession"; (2) to "cooperate with all units of the Association and with related organizations and agencies to provide access to materials on issues important to the Association"; (3) to "administer and seek funds that enable ALA members to publish materials for information professionals and for library users"; and (4) to "manage the Publishing Services offices effectively, and to educate ALA members about the role and responsibilities of the publishing unit of a complex, non-profit professional association."

Marketing of ALA Publishing products is centralized under the direction of Paul Kobasa, a librarian formerly employed at Greenwood Press. For books, a systematic program utilizing review copies and direct mail and space advertising informs librarians and wholesalers on a regular basis. ALA depends on authors to help identify special markets and suggest innovative ways to sell their books. Direct mail and space advertising are also used to promote subscriptions to *Booklist/RBB* and *American Libraries*. Emphasis is placed on the utility of these publications to practicing librarians. Both *Booklist/RBB* and *American Libraries* sell and give away reprints of special articles and lists. In recent years *Booklist/RBB* has expanded its special lists of recommended materials to include everything from foreign-language bibliographies and agricultural materials to the year's best software. Among notable special materials recently available through *American Libraries* is a special report on copyrighted videotape and software materials, written by ALA Counsel Mary Hutchings Reed and produced by ALA's capable copyright administrator, Donna S. Kitta.

Advertising has been an important element in the financial success of ALA publications. Commissioned sales representatives solicit ads, and as has been true for one hundred years, publishers and library vendors have supported ALA publications and recognized that their own self-interest is served through participation in ALA.

ALA's publications have for many years been available abroad. Beginning in 1980, ALA has exhibited at the Frankfurt Book Fair. Co-publication and prepublication arrangements for important works have been made in recent years, expanding the access to ALA materials for librarians worldwide, in spite of the inhibiting effect of a strong dollar.

Historically, ALA's publishing efforts have produced standard professional works and set standards for, as well as launched, other library publishers. Politics and concern about money often interfered with the enterprise, but the good will and energy of many people, combined with the needs of practicing librarians overcame these obstacles.

In 1886, the association established the Publishing Section, the first unit of ALA to have a separate identity. Its stated purpose was to "further cooperation among libraries by preparing and publishing bibliographies, indexes and special catalogs."[3] The founding of a separate publishing activity had been preceded by the efforts of about fifty librarians to revise William Frederick Poole's *Index to Periodicals*, which was issued in 1882, revised and published by Houghton Mifflin in 1893, leading eventually to the Wilson Company's *Readers' Guide*.[4] Among the early titles of the Publishing Section were John F. Sargent's *Reading for the Young: A Classified and Annotated Catalogue* (1890), Gardener M. Jones's *List of Subject Headings for Use in Dictionary Catalogs* (1895), Caroline M. Hewins's *Books for Boys and Girls* (1897), and J. N. Larned's *Literature of American History* (1902).[5]

A major activity of those early years was an attempt by the Publishing Section to facilitate cooperative cataloging among libraries. Between 1892 and 1901, ALA struggled with this task, finally turning it over to the Library of Congress.[6] Able now to concentrate on publishing, the section became successful in 1906; half the rent of the association's first space was being paid for by the Publishing Section. In 1911, Publishing took in the sum of $4,778.12, which, when added to the $4,000 interest on the Carnegie Fund, represented two-thirds of the association's income.[7]

Before 1900 most ALA publications were published by other organizations, although sponsored by ALA and prepared by its members. *Library Journal*, which had been founded by Melvil Dewey in 1876, prior to the founding of ALA, and owned by R. R. Bowker, was the official publication of the association until 1908. The movement to replace *Library Journal* with an ALA-produced official publication had started in 1904 but took four years to complete. Many of the strong personalities that peopled ALA's early years, including John Cotton Dana, were involved in the politics of beginning an official journal. Unfortunately, the *ALA Bulletin* not only hurt *Library Journal* but was unattractive and sometimes unreadable.[8]

Two important events happened in 1902. ALA President John Shaw Billings wrote to Andrew Carnegie requesting a subsidy for preparation of bibliographies, indexes, reading lists, and other literary aids. Carnegie donated one hundred thousand dollars and the result was that in February 1905, under the editorship of Caroline Garland, *Booklist* began. *Booklist* was primarily a review journal of current books of interest to public libraries. It was immediately popular, gaining three thousand subscribers even though it was frequently criticized for the lateness of its reviews. Also in 1902, the first edition of Alice B. Kroeger's *Guide to the Study and Use of Reference Books* was published. Kroeger was succeeded by three distinguished editors, Isadore Gilbert Mudge, Constance Winchell, and Eugene P. Sheehy. *Guide to Reference Books* was, and is, a keystone of ALA's book publishing efforts, both in terms of its utility to librarians and its profitability to ALA's publishing activity.

Prior to World War I, ALA Publishing continued to serve libraries and librarians with professional tools. During and immediately after the war, the association's energies were concentrated on raising money for purchase and distribution of over three million books for men in training camps, aboard ships, and in the field. A so-called Enlarged Program of Service designed to continue this high level of activity was proposed but failed miserably. Nevertheless, the association's work went on under a new executive secretary, Carl H. Milam, and with it, the publishing program. In 1921 the ALA Constitution was revised and one of the changes made the Publishing Section less independent. Previously, Publishing had had its own board and control of its own money. The new constitution set up a five-person Editorial Board accountable to the Executive Board.[9] Over the next forty years, this board initiated much of the work previously done independently by members. It, and the ALA in general, were subject to intensely critical remarks by the association gadfly, John Cotton Dana, who, in 1927, accused the leadership of using the publishing department to feather their own nests because they had been paid thirty thousand dollars to write library school textbooks.[10]

By 1930, though, the publishing program was a well-established fact of ALA life, produc-

ing the *ALA Bulletin*, *Booklist*, books, and pamphlets. A new publication, *Subscription Books Bulletin*, was founded in that year. Currently called *Reference Books Bulletin*, the journal was a departure from most ALA reviewing activities because it reviewed books that were not recommended. This has resulted over the years in several threats of lawsuits. In addition, the new publication was to alert librarians to shady sales practices of encyclopedia and subscription book companies. In practice, this responsibility did not last long.

In spite of the successes of the publishing section, political concerns once again entered Publishing's realm. In 1929 a special committee assessing the association's activities pointed out that not enough scholarly and bibliographic work was being done and that there was no comprehensive planning.[11] In addition to the former criticism from academic librarians, children's librarians criticized the publishing section for production of *The Winnetka Graded Book List*, written by Carelton W. Washburne, then superintendent of schools in Winnetka, Illinois, and funded by the Carnegie Corporation. Carl Milam had successfully tapped Carnegie to subsidize several important publishing projects during the twenties. The furor over publication of this list was a sensitive matter, putting the association's major benefactor at odds with its children's librarian members, with the publishing department in the middle, a place that would become increasingly familiar. But, by and large, the publishing program was making a significant contribution to library life. The Editorial Board formulated an idea for a new journal, which became *Library Quarterly* and was turned over to the Graduate Library School of the University of Chicago, where it flourished after a slow start.[12]

In 1936, Everett P. Fontaine took over as director of publishing. One of Carl Milam's closest associates, Fontaine had a ready wit and a penetrating understanding of the complex forces of ALA. Fontaine began transforming the ALA publishing office, a process of professionalism that though probably necessary nevertheless risked putting too much distance between the market and the department's products. Important monographs continued to be published, including new editions of *Guide to Reference Books*, Susan Grey Akers's books on simple cataloging, and the Junior Members Round Table's compilation of *Library Literature*, 1921-1932, later taken over by the H. W. Wilson Company.

In 1942, W. T. Couch, director of the University of North Carolina Press was hired as a consultant to review the publishing program. He was very supportive of the work being undertaken and especially the way in which the association balanced member participation with financial requirements. He did note that without subsidies, such publishing as was being done would likely lose money.[13] However, in spite of financial difficulties, important works continued to be produced. Although the Depression had curtailed the *Reading with a Purpose* series of booklets that were distributed to millions of library patrons from 1925-1932, other major titles were published, including the *ALA Glossary*, 1943 (not revised until 1983) and Mann's *Introduction to the Cataloging and Classification of Books*, also in 1943.

In 1947, another oversight committee once again gave mixed reviews to the publishing units, criticizing the journals, praising the books, and noting that the cash method of accounting inaccurately reflected the financial contribution made by the publishing department.[14] Carl Milam left ALA in 1948 to become librarian of the United Nations. Fontaine stayed until 1951, when he, too, moved to New York, in the employ of a for-profit publisher. He was succeeded by Pauline Love, who directed ALA Publishing until 1968.

The world was much changed after World War II. Hope for more funding for libraries as government became more centralized resulted in Joechel and Winslow's *National Plan for Public Library Service*. At the same time, the parochialism of the Cold War accelerated the association's work in the intellectual freedom area. A new generation of ALA leaders, among them Robert B. Downs, contributed such works as *Books That Changed the World* (1956). The association kept up with technology, producing films, filmstrips and records, and such books as *The Use of Television by the Public Library* (1950) and *Library Application of Punched Cards* (1952) by Ralph H. Parker. As the country grew, so did libraries, and librarians were helped by such books as Ralph McCoy's *Personnel Administration for Librarians* (1953), *Periodicals for Small and Medium-sized School Libraries* (8th ed., 1948), and Asheim's *The Core of Education for Librarianship* (1955). Members remained active authors; the Editorial Committee produced the *Subject and Title Index to Short Stories for Children* in 1955.

Standards blossomed in the 1960s, helped by infusions of federal money. *ALA Standards for College Libraries* was published in 1959 and the first edition of *Standards for Library Functions at the State Level* in 1963. *Standards for Children's Services in Public Libraries* was issued in 1965 and *Standards for School Media Programs* in 1969. In 1963, ALA's Association of College and Research Libraries began publishing *Choice*, which quickly became the most important selection tool for college and university libraries. During this period, the catalog of ALA books and journals carried the following information: "ALA publications are priced to cover only manufacturing and distribution costs...." It was not a surprise, therefore, when, in spite of significant growth in revenues, surpluses were minimal. The result was that the executive director, David Clift, decided to put ALA Publishing on a more professional basis, as noted at the beginning of this article.

Professionalism continues to be a basic tenet of ALA publishing policy. Being an ALA author has sometimes been more complex than writing for other publishing houses. The need for ALA to produce authoritative works sometimes causes delays in publishing manuscripts. But authors whose manuscripts have been subjected to the thorough procedures of ALA editors know that their work has benefited. Since many ALA books are the result of committee work, some ALA authors have felt that a degree of ambiguity existed regarding their compensation. This problem has been solved by the issuance of simple letters of agreement between the ALA Publishing Department and the unit producing a work. It's amazing how many problems evaporate when everyone works from the same assumptions and has the same expectations.

The physical production of ALA books and journals is one of the association's great strengths. Books are printed on acid-free paper, and the designs, though never flashy, are appropriate to the subject. Most of the association's journals are produced in the Central Production Unit where adherence to strong production values is a tradition, making ALA journals the standard in the field. During their term as journal editors, members get the equivalent of a course in design and copy styling.

The needs of the association will always affect the publishing department. Productive cooperation between Publishing and ALA divisions and offices has enabled Publishing to share its fulfillment and marketing capabilities resulting in more uniform and efficient service to members and customers. ALA is involved in a strategic long-range planning process in which Gary Facente participates on Publishing's behalf. With a new executive director, Thomas Galvin, the association can expect changes in focus, emphasis, and goals. Advances in publishing and information technologies are carefully monitored and evaluated in terms of how they can improve Publishing's procedures and major forthcoming projects. ALA Publishing's next century will, of course, be radically different from the last, but the high level of commitment and quality will remain unchanged.

NOTES

1. *ALA Bulletin* 62 (July/August 1968): 805.

2. *American Libraries* 5 (November 1974): 566.

3. Dennis Thomison, *A History of the American Library Association 1876-1972* (Chicago: American Library Association, 1978), 28.

4. Edward G. Holley, "ALA at 100," *ALA Yearbook 1976* (Chicago: American Library Association, 1976), 5.

5. Ibid., 6.

6. *Library Journal* 26 (January 1901): 4.

7. Everett O. Fontaine, "People and Places of the Milam Era," *ALA Bulletin* 58 (May 1964): 363.

8. Thomison, 54.

9. Peggy Sullivan, *Carl H. Milam and the American Library Association* (New York: H. W. Wilson, 1976), 12.

10. Thomison, 106.

11. Ibid., 116.

12. Ibid., 117.

13. Sullivan, 125-26.

14. "Preliminary Report of the Fourth Activities Committee to the Council," *ALA Bulletin* 42 (July/August 1948): 295-306.

Gary Facente

Part II
REVIEWS OF BOOKS

Reviews of Books

GENERAL REFERENCE WORKS

Bibliographies

1. Higgens, Gavin L., ed. **Printed Reference Material.** 2d ed. London, Library Association; distr., Phoenix, Ariz., Oryx Press, 1984. 740p. index. (Handbooks on Library Practice). $55.00; $29.95pa. ISBN 0-85365-995-8; 0-85365-776-9pa.

Volumes in the Handbooks on Library Practice series cover several aspects of British librarianship, e.g., medical librarianship, serials librarianship, university librarianship, picture librarianship. The present volume is as its title suggests, now in its second edition (first edition published in 1980), on printed reference material. In its 740 pages Higgins and several of his contributors (among them Denis Grogan, A. John Walford, and Malcolm Campbell) try to cover all aspects of reference librarianship, starting with some theoretical considerations (e.g., "The Reference Process," by Gavin Higgens) down to such topics as general and subject encyclopedias, biographical sources, directories, government publications, bibliographies of older material, and subject bibliographies. The coverage of material in this second edition is somewhat enlarged, with inclusion of three new chapters on printed visual sources, videotext information and communication systems, and indexes. Most other chapters have been substantially revised and updated but the underlying philosophy remains essentially the same. It is a practical manual for practicing librarians working in smaller institutions, introducing them to the most important reference sources with brief annotations. Essential bibliographical information is more or less complete, but entries provide no pagination for monographic works and very little for serials. Twenty-two chapters have their own brief introductions, usually rather simplistic.

Is there any practical value for American libraries? Any value is rather limited. This manual reminds us of Shores's text used in this country several generations ago. In comparison to Bill Katz, or even Cheney, this is a step backwards. However, for British librarians working in smaller institutions this compilation will provide useful assistance in identifying important, primarily British, sources. Coverage of American reference materials is inadequate and occasionally titles discussed are obsolete or replaced with better works. [R: JAL, July 85, p. 182]

Bohdan S. Wynar

2. McCormick, Mona. **The New York Times Guide to Reference Materials.** rev. ed. New York, Times Books/Random House, 1985. 242p. illus. index. $15.95. LC 84-40109. ISBN 0-8129-1127-X.

This guide was first published in hardcover as *Who-What-When-Where-How-Why Made Easy* (Quadrangle Books, 1971). The paperback edition, titled *The New York Times Guide to Reference Materials* (Popular Library, 1971), was updated in 1977. This revised edition, like its predecessors, is "intended to assist students and general readers in their search for information by offering a strategy for searching and an *introduction* [author's emphasis] to basic reference sources" (p. ix). In all editions the author has been Mona McCormick, formerly a reference librarian at the *New York Times* and now associate librarian, University Research Library, UCLA.

The arrangement of the work is simple and orderly, forming a logical procession. Part 1, "Finding Information," briefly discusses search strategy (i.e., orderly sifting through information for the pertinent and the best materials), library and online catalogs, terms and abbreviations used in reference materials, and computerized searching, including a selected list of more than one hundred databases. Part 2 introduces in six chapters reference books by type: almanacs and atlases, bibliography, biography, dictionaries, encyclopedias, newspapers, and magazines. The structure of each chapter follows a fairly uniform format: overview of the type of reference material under consideration, description (and sometimes comparisons and facsimile illustrations) of selected titles, and a bibliography of titles just described. Part 3—the largest section—applies the part 2 format to subject reference sources in twenty-two areas (e.g., art; books and literature; business, economics, and statistics; quotations; science and technology). Two areas—minorities and women's studies—are new to the edition. The fourth part is a chapter on critical thinking as applied to the research process. McCormick here announces (1) that "*finding* the information is not the most important part of research; what you *do* with it is" and (2) that certain attitudes are requisite to critical thinking: intellectual curiosity, personal honesty and objectivity, open-mindedness and respect for the viewpoints of others, flexibility, skepticism, persistence and orderliness. She concludes the chapter with the (a) cornerstones of evaluation of reference materials (authority, purpose, scope, audience) and (b) primary/secondary sources. The fifth part—"Organizing and Communication Information"—introduces researchers to (a) writing guides (Safire's *What's the Good Word?*, Strunk and White's *Elements of Style*, etc.) and publishing/marketing guides (e.g., *Literary Market Place, Writer's Market, Writer's Handbook*), (b) style manuals, (c) footnotes and bibliography, and (d) a sample term paper. The guide concludes with a selected bibliography of titles for further study and an A-Z index of authors, titles, and subjects of the more than five hundred sources treated. The index does not, however, include the databases cited earlier.

All in all, this guide generally succeeds in its stated purpose. And while no cutoff date is given, the volume lists a number of 1983 and 1984 editions/titles. A sampling of various sections does suggest the need for citing later editions and/or additional titles. Oxford companions (p. 86) to American literature, classical literature, and English literature are available in later editions (1983, 1984, 1985, respectively). There is a 1981 edition of *Random House Dictionary* (p. 45). Perhaps the entries for native Americans (pp. 128-29) should add the Smithsonian Institution's projected twenty-volume set, *Handbook of North American Indians* (1978-). *Survey of Current Business* (p. 98) has been the responsibility since its inception (1921) of the Bureau of Foreign and Domestic Commerce and now of the Bureau of Economic Analysis—but *not* of the Bureau of the Census as mentioned. The third edition of *McGraw-Hill Dictionary of Modern Economics* (p. 95) appeared in 1983. Another McGraw-Hill publication, *Encyclopedia of Economics* (1982), merits consideration for inclusion on the same page. Not mentioned (p. 94) is that a revised edition of Daniells's *Business Information Sources* (1976), in progress for a number of years, was published in 1985. The twelve-volume *Guide to American Law: Everyone's Legal Encyclopedia* (1983-1985) is surely a candidate for inclusion in the chapter on politics, government, and current events. [R: LJ, 15 Apr 85, p. 66]

Wiley J. Williams

3.   **Reference Books Bulletin, 1983-1984: A Compilation of Evaluations Appearing in *Reference Books Bulletin....*** By the American Library Association *Reference Books Bulletin* editorial board. Helen K. Wright, ed. Mary E. Gabel and Beth A. Nikels, comps. Chicago, American Library Association, 1984. 194p. index. $20.00pa. LC 73-159565. ISBN 0-8389-3296-7; ISSN 8755-0962.

This twelfth cumulation of evaluations produced by the American Library Association's *Reference Books Bulletin*'s editorial board has several new features. It has a new title: the last cumulation appeared as *Reference and Subscription Books Review*—until 1 September 1983 the title of the bimonthly *Booklist* insert where evaluations are first published. It has a reorganized table of contents: titles are arranged in the table of contents by format (bibliographies, dictionaries, encyclopedias, etc.); however, the text itself is still arranged alphabetically by title. There is a subject index in this cumulation and, for the first time reviews of online reference tools and of works appearing only in microform are included.

Cumulated in this edition are all the reviews that appeared in each issue of *RBB* from 1 September 1983 to 1 August 1984. The reviews, which are generally regarded in the profession as authoritative, are prepared by the *RBB* editorial board, using a committee approach. The board also selects the reference works to be evaluated, using broad criteria: "any work regardless of format, source or price, written in English, and of potential usefulness in home, school, public, or academic libraries" (p. xi). For each of the last few years, between four and five hundred works have been evaluated; or, approximately 25 percent of reference books published in the United States each year. Included in this cumulation, along with the evaluations, are three omnibus articles: "Biographical Reference Sources," "Desk Dictionaries," and "World Atlas Survey."

The main value of this cumulation is the convenient access to the fine reviews in *RBB* it provides. But, because it is fairly selective and relatively out-of-date by the time it is published, it is unlikely to serve as first court of appeal for acquisitions or reference work.

Heather Cameron

4. Wynar, Bohdan S., ed. **American Reference Books Annual. Volume 16: 1985.** Littleton, Colo., Libraries Unlimited, 1985. 670p. index. $70.00. LC 75-120328. ISBN 0-87287-426-5; ISSN 0065-9959.

The history and development of *ARBA* as a reference work were outlined at length in the 1985 volume of *Library Science Annual.* Many of the reviews which *ARBA* has received throughout the years discussing its comprehensiveness, its scope, its organization, and the quality of its critical annotations were cited and compared. *ARBA 85* continues in the tradition of the prior fifteen volumes with comprehensive coverage of reference books either published in the United States or having an exclusive distributor in the United States. In *ARBA 85*, 1,734 works are covered, most with 1984 imprints, a few from 1983. Reviews are both informative and evaluative, describing the purpose and scope of each work, comparing it to other, standard sources in the field, if any, and providing a qualitative analysis of content. The more than 300 reviewers are subject specialists and well-known in their respective fields; many are librarians of national reputation.

This sixteenth volume of *ARBA* has been redesigned. Reference publishing has been growing each year; to accommodate the steady increase of material, Libraries Unlimited has adopted a new, larger format and a double-column layout, which allow nearly 20 percent more material; the present volume, therefore, stands slightly taller, but is more slender than those from prior years. This arrangement also permits easier scanning and comparison of related titles.

Moreover, *ARBA 85* shows significant changes in arrangement of materials. Works are still classified under four major subject areas: "General Reference Works," "Social Science," "Humanities," and "Science and Technology."

"General Reference Works," arranged alphabetically, is subdivided by form: bibliographies, biographies, catalogs and collections, dictionaries and encyclopedias, handbooks and yearbooks, indexes, and so on. Within the remaining three parts, there are thirty-six chapters representing broad subject categories arranged alphabetically under each heading. Thus, under "Social Sciences" the reader will find, among others, chapters entitled "Economics and Business," "Education," "History," and "Law." Each chapter is subdivided in a way that reflects the arrangement strategy of the entire volume: First there is a section on general works, then there is a topical breakdown, which is further subdivided.

ARBA first discontinued its reviews of non-reference materials in Library Science in 1985; however, it has continued its coverage of reference materials in the field. Henceforward, both reference sources and all other materials of interest to the library profession will be included in *Library Science Annual.*

All libraries—public, academic, special, and school—will find *ARBA 85* helpful in the areas of reference, collection development, and acquisitions. The care with which each reference work is evaluated will be appreciated not only by librarians but also by researchers, booksellers, and students.   Shirley Lambert

5. Wynar, Bohdan S., ed. **Recommended Reference Books for Small and Medium-sized Libraries and Media Centers 1985.** Littleton, Colo., Libraries Unlimited, 1985. 253p. index. $30.00. LC 81-12394. ISBN 0-87287-494-X; ISSN 0277-5948.

Like its predecessors, the fifth volume is "designed to assist smaller libraries in the systematic selection of suitable reference books for their collection" (p. xi). To achieve this goal the editor chose 562 titles of 1,734 reviewed in the 1985 edition of *American Reference Books Annual.*

This "abridged" version of *ARBA* is aimed at librarians working with collections in small colleges, public libraries, and school media centers. As earlier reviewers of this work have noted, such designations appended to each entry guide the selection of reference works for such libraries. A listing of titles under each audience designation would facilitate such use. However, the user must remember, as the editor warns, that "such recommendations are somewhat arbitrary, since individual institutions vary in the size of their collections, reference needs, clientele, and budgetary allocations" (p. xi). If users limit their consideration to works designated for their particular type of library, public librarians would find 430 titles, college librarians 330, and school librarians 109 titles. Actually, school librarians will find additional titles of interest as the annotations point out potential users of each recommended title. Reviews are taken directly from *ARBA* and include full bibliographic data, price, LC number, ISBN or ISSN, and evaluative comments including remarks on the strengths and weaknesses of the title under discussion.

The new double-column format facilitates ease of use as does effective use of bolder typeface than found in previous volumes.

Although larger libraries will want to turn directly to *ARBA*, this work fills a void for coverage of reference materials useful to smaller libraries.   Phyllis J. Van Orden

Biographies

6.   **Marquis Who's Who Directory of Online Professionals.** Chicago, Marquis Who's Who, 1984. 829p. index. $85.00. ISBN 0-8379-6001-0.

One of a new group of Marquis biographical publications devoted to professional groups, this contains six thousand biographical sketches of online system specialists. The sketches contain typical biographical data such as address, birth date, education/career experience, publications, and memberships. In addition, they show the online functions being performed (searcher, consultant, educator, manager, etc.), online experience, systems and databases used, type of library and equipment, and subject expertise. There are indexes by online function, database subject expertise, and geographical location.

The sketches are typical of Marquis publications: biographee-supplied, much abbreviated, in small print. Questionnaires were mailed to members of professional societies, journal subscribers, attendees at conferences, and users of online services. The only criterion for inclusion was "employment in the industry or use of the industry's products and systems." This includes librarians, computer scientists, publishers, professors, consultants, market researchers, executives, and the like. This, then, is a directory, not a "who's who."

Who's Who in Library and Information Services (ALA, 1982) covers many of the same fields but is somewhat more selective in terms of qualifications for inclusion and is not focused on any one activity. It contains about twelve thousand shorter sketches, mostly from the library field. There is about a 20 percent overlap between the ALA book and this Marquis volume.

The reference value of this work will depend on the need to locate information about people involved with online information systems. [R: RBB, 1 Sept 85, p. 46; WLB, Mar 85, p. 502]

A. Neil Yerkey

Dictionaries and Encyclopedias

7.   Kent, Allen, ed. **Encyclopedia of Library and Information Science. Volume 38, Supplement 3.** New York, Marcel Dekker, 1985. 415p. illus. $55.00 (individual price); $45.00 (subscription price). LC 68-31232. ISBN 0-8247-2037-7.

A lengthy review of the main thirty-five-volume set and first two supplementary volumes of *Encyclopedia of Library and Information Science* was published in *ARBA* 85 (entries 527-29).

Allen Kent, who remains as executive editor for *Supplement 3*, has described the purpose of the supplements as follows: to update articles in the main set; to add new articles on topics currently important in the field; to add biographies of recently deceased prominent figures; and to include articles originally commissioned for the main set but not received in time for inclusion. All but the last of these categories relates to currency, so, one might reasonably expect that emphasis to be reflected in the contents of any supplementary volume. In *Supplement 3*, however, the overwhelming majority of contributions are on topics that might have been covered in the main set. One finds, for example, articles on the Arkansas Library Association, the Bollandists, *Booklist*, Connecticut Historical Society, the Indian Library Association and the literature and bibliography of horsemanship, to mention only a few. Of the twelve biographies, only three are for recently deceased individuals: Jesse Shera, Scott Adams, and Josef Stunnvoll. Only a few articles expand upon contributions to the original set. Curiously, one of these is a fifty-seven-page article on libraries in Chile. The other two, on EDUNET and the American Society for Information Science make no reference to the original articles. Topics of new or emerging interest to the profession that are treated include expert systems, display formats for public access catalogs, online encyclopedias, human-computer dialog and UNIX.

It is not clear how topics of new and emerging interest were selected and why so few are covered. Where are the contributions on microcomputers in libraries, end-user systems and services, videodisc technology? Why did Te-Chu Lee choose to focus on display issues related to public access catalogs? A comprehensive survey of OPACS would have been an important and timely contribution. Where are the biographies of Derek de Sola Price and Fritz Machlup, individuals whose work has had a substantial impact on library and information science?

One wonders, too, how articles to be updated were identified: why update an article on libraries in Chile?

On the positive side, the articles included are thorough and well documented, and the contributors are authorities in their subject areas. Topics and contributors reflect the international perspective or "one world" concept of library science that has become a hallmark of the *Encyclopedia*. One hopes that future supplements will place greater emphasis on currency so that they can serve as useful annual updates to the main set of this important encyclopedia.

Heather Cameron

8. Li, Heng. **Dictionary of Library and Information Sciences: English-Chinese/Chinese-English.** Munich, New York, K. G. Saur, 1984. 327p. $41.00. ISBN 3-598-10532-0.

Claimed to be the first bilingual dictionary for library and information sciences in English-Chinese, Chinese-English, this dictionary is a useful tool for translating selected library and information science terms to Chinese. The English and Chinese definitions of terms are very helpful. The main body of the dictionary is the English-Chinese section which provides, in alphabetical order, English terms with corresponding Chinese characters. The second section is a Chinese-English index using the Pinyin system for the Chinese language. Added at the end of the book are a list of acronyms and abbreviations, three appendices explaining the Chinese phonetic alphabet, and a bibliography.

Although the dictionary claims to contain more than 1,800 entries, it includes fewer terms than the pocket-sized English-Chinese dictionary *English-Chinese Dictionary of Library Science* (Beijing, Commercial Press, 1982). A random comparison of the two finds that the Li dictionary lacks many important terms such as *CODEN, PRECIS, precision ratio, recall ratio, Project INTREX, UNISIST,* and others which are in the pocket-sized dictionary. Another similar dictionary, *English-Chinese Library and Information Sciences Terminology* by Lucy Te-Chu Lee, published in Taipei in 1981 contains 5,480 entries, about three times as many as the title reviewed. For comprehensive coverage, all three dictionaries are needed. The pocket-sized dictionary, however, is probably the best of the three. Hwa-Wei Lee

9. Tayyeb, R., and K. Chandna, comps. **A Dictionary of Acronyms and Abbreviations in Library and Information Science.** 2d ed. Ottawa, Canadian Library Association, 1985. 279p. $20.00pa. ISBN 0-88802-195-X.

If the AAAAAA had been more active, compilers Tayyeb and Chandna would not have had to record so many widely ranging entries. For this acronym, third entry in the new edition of this dictionary, stands for Association for the Alleviation of Asinine Abbreviations and Absurd Acronyms. The new edition attempts to include as many French and Canadian abbreviations as possible. The number of abbreviations and acronyms is also expanded. Related entries range widely from reference book titles (e.g., *Grove, D.A.B.*) to such miscellaneous entries as *SIG,* "Special Interest Group" and *KISS,* "Keep it simple, Sir/Stupid." Although many of the entries will be found in other dictionaries of acronyms and abbreviations, this dictionary can be recommended for its well-searched contents, arrayed in such readable form. It will be helpful to those using the literature of library and information science. Frances Neel Cheney

Directories

10. Alvord, Katharine T., ed. **Document Retrieval: Sources & Services.** 3d ed. San Francisco, Calif., Information Store, 1985. 241p. index. $60.00 looseleaf with binder.

This work provides librarians and other searchers for information with a directory of companies, nonprofit information centers, and certain libraries which are sources for all types of published documents which might not be found through traditional means such as interlibrary loan. The directory lists 241 suppliers, 75 percent U.S. and the remainder Canadian, European, Asian, and African. Indexes arrange the suppliers by subject of materials covered, geographic location of the supplier, copyright compliance, and online ordering capability. Many suppliers are professional research firms with a variety of services. The chief value of the directory's entries is the provision of information on fulfillment time for orders, ordering procedures, rates or prices, and copyright compliance (how royalties are dealt with).

There is some overlap of coverage here with the *Encyclopedia of Information Systems and Services* (see *ARBA* 82, entry 148) and with *Information Industry Marketplace*'s "Information Retailing" sections (see *ARBA* 81, entry 37). Both provide more data on services and resources of the suppliers, but also lack the ordering information that this work includes. This is a reasonable reference work for expanding patrons' access to the ever-increasing amounts of grey literature being created today.

Leon J. Stout

11. **American Library Directory.** 38th ed. Edited by Jaques Cattell Press. New York,

R. R. Bowker, 1985. 2v. index. $119.25/set. LC 23-3581. ISBN 0-8352-2078-8; ISSN 0065-910X.

The updated thirty-eighth edition of the *American Library Directory* provides information on some thirty-three thousand libraries in Canada, the United States, and regions administered by the United States. The book is arranged alphabetically by state, region, or province, then by city, and finally by institution name. Most of the book consists of statistical information on public, academic, government, and special libraries, including name and address of the library, names of key personnel, and information on the library's holdings. In addition, budget, expenditures, subject interests, special collections, automation, and publications are frequently noted within each entry. Data were obtained from each library to provide accuracy.

A "Library Information" section concludes the work, including information on consortia, library schools, library systems, libraries for the handicapped, public library agencies, state school library agencies, interlibrary loan codes, United States Armed Forces overseas libraries, and United States Information Agency centers. An index listing libraries by name provides access to the library profiles.

The format and content of this standard work follow those of earlier editions (see *ARBA* 83, entry 111, and *ARBA* 85, entry 530). It continues to be a useful purchase for all libraries.

Gloria Palmeri Powell

12.   Biggs, Penelope T., ed. **Current Research for the Information Profession 1984/85.** London, Library Association; distr., Phoenix, Ariz., Oryx Press, 1985. 1v. (various paging). index. $91.00. ISBN 0-85365-906-0.

Current Research in Library and Information Science replaced *Radials Bulletin* in 1983 as a record of research in progress. Expanded to provide worldwide coverage and newly titled, it includes reports of ongoing research in English from thirty-six countries. Beginning with this volume (*1984-85*) periodical entries are cumulated and published as an annual record.

Research is treated in its broadest sense and a wide variety of investigations, studies, surveys, and evaluated innovations are included. Contributors include academics, students, and practicing librarians with emphasis on research reported in the current year, but work begun earlier is included until finished. Once the project has been completed and published, it would appear in *Library and Information Science Abstracts.*

Each entry includes the project title, lists researcher(s), and the institution where the research is being conducted. A brief description

of the project and its anticipated completion date complete the entry. Items are arranged by subject, in a complex faceted system divided into core and fringe areas. Author and subject indexes are provided.

The cumulation is useful as a guide to work in progress and analysis of entries can give a profile of types and subjects of research being conducted in a country or by a university. The way in which entries were identified for inclusion in the volume is not indicated. Was a questionnaire sent to likely contributors? Is this a listing of items reported elsewhere? The record is not complete and there is no way of knowing how complete it is. Such a compilation is a useful tool but it is difficult to determine how truly useful it is.   Ann E. Prentice

13.   Burwell, Helen P., comp. and ed. **Directory of Fee Based Information Services.** Houston, Tex., Burwell Enterprises, 1984. 203p. index. $18.95 spiralbound.

Since this publication was last reviewed (see *ARBA* 82, entry 145), it has grown from 89 to 203 pages, increased its coverage from 257 to 334 listings, and escalated in price from $6.95 (paper) to $18.95 (spiralbound). Information consulting is a profession growing in both popularity and profitability, it would seem.

The current edition of *Directory of Fee Based Information Services* conforms to the format of previous editions: entries are arranged alphabetically by states within the United States section, by countries (seventeen) in the international section. Each entry is numbered, and includes individual or company name, address, telephone and telex number, former name (if appropriate), key individuals, branches, date founded, areas of specialization, information services offered, and a brief statement submitted by the organization describing the firm and its services. Four indexes—company name, key personnel, subject, and service—provide handy access by entry number to the data contained in the text. Information is current as of January 1984.

The directory has several limitations. It is not comprehensive (nor does it claim to be so). A cursory check of Colorado's nine entries revealed the omission of at least two major information consulting companies. Furthermore, no price or price range information for services has been included, nor the number of employees per firm, both areas that might be determining factors in deciding which of several companies to contact. In addition, the brief descriptive paragraphs submitted by each firm occasionally lapse into useless hornblowing (e.g., "They know what to do—and what NOT to do—when bringing new ideas to bear on real world library problems). Overall, however, this is a helpful, well-organized, source that can be of use to both the library staff and their patrons in public and academic libraries. [R: RBB, 1 Feb 85, p. 762]

G. Kim Dority

14. Klement, Susan, ed. **Who Knows What: Canadian Library-related Expertise.** Ottawa, Canadian Library Association, 1984. 174p. index. $20.00pa. ISBN 0-88802-186-0.

This directory to 139 people (and firms) from across Canada—but mainly in Ontario and in Toronto, Ontario—has been "designed to help Canadian librarians find the experts who can assist them with their work" (p. vii). Most are librarians, but some are library-related, for example, management consultants to the field of librarianship, computer specialists, and architects. This book is highly useful to librarians who need advice on library procedures, and of course to anyone who needs library-related services of research, pictures, and statistics. It has been based largely on an earlier, 1976 book that Klement did for the Metropolitan Toronto Library Board, but that book was limited to Toronto. However, that book, unlike this one, did include a number of nonlibrary subject experts.

The contents for each entry include name, address, present position, specialties, experience, previous clients, education, availability, fees, and so forth. There are indexes by geography, by language, and by subject, and as well there is a copy of the questionnaire/profile (and instructions) that each entrant filled out. A review of all the entries reveals that while there are many bona fide and serious consultants and experts, there are also quite a few academics, retired librarians, and others who want to moonlight. The question is, of course: who or what is a consultant? [R: CLJ, Feb 85, p. 39]

Dean Tudor

15. Roney, Raymond G., and Audrey V. Jones, eds. **Directory of Institutions Offering Programs for the Training of Library-Media Technical Assistants.** 6th ed. s.l., Council on Library/Media Technicians, 1984. 106p. index. $18.00pa. (May be purchased from Council on Library/Media Technicians, c/o Myron Allman, Publication Chairperson, 20505 Cedarville Road, 11-4, Brandywine, MD 20613.)

This directory contains information on programs offered by ninety-one institutions. These programs can be used for credits toward an associate's degree or a certificate for library/media for technical assistants. It provides information on degree, name of person in charge, the number of faculty involved, and the number of

credits for each course. Any institution offering a bachelor's degree or above is omitted.

This directory is organized alphabetically by states and Canadian provinces. The appendix lists institutions located in the states and provinces as well as an alphabetical listing of the institutions. Some institutions offer only a few courses while other listings are quite extensive.

This directory would be useful for persons interested in library work or those already working in a library. The main value, as this reviewer understands it, would be for those living within the areas where the programs are offered. If one is going to travel any distance it would be better to study toward a master's degree in library science. Therefore, the *Directory*'s usefulness for most libraries is limited.

Mary Lee Morris

Handbooks and Yearbooks

16. **Advances in Librarianship. Volume 13.** Wesley Simonton, ed. Orlando, Fla., Academic Press, 1984. 264p. index. $32.00. LC 79-88675. ISBN 0-12-024613-9.

Advances in Librarianship does not attempt comprehensive annual coverage on a worldwide basis—an undertaking no longer possible, as the Library Association discovered more than a decade ago. Rather, the editor chooses a few key topics and invites experts to prepare comprehensive essays which review current developments in the light of past trends. The latest volume opens with Charles McClure's "Management Information for Library Decision Making," continues with Nancy Williamson's "Subject Access in the On-Line Environment," and concludes with C. D. Hurt's "Important Literature Identification in Science." In between are essays on community information services (Joan Durrance), IFLA (Robert Vosper), Latin America (Marietta Daniels Shepard), and two studies on collection development (Marcia Pankake, Paul H. Mosher).

The essays (except for the fact-and-acronym-laden piece on Latin America) are generally conceptual and issue oriented. McClure, for example, notes the problems arising from the fact that most computerized systems in libraries were designed for other purposes (e.g., inventory or bibliographic control) with management information as an afterthought. He draws distinctions between management information systems and decision support systems and notes the time lag between development of conceptual models and implementation. Durrance clarifies the distinctions between community information, local information, information and referral, and public policy information services. Similarly, the distinction between "selection" and "collection development" is explicated. Methods of trying to identify important literature are explored and the difficulty of predicting future usage is noted, but with an awareness of the value of community analysis and user studies in enhancing predictability of use. Reference features include a detailed table of contents, lengthy bibliographies, and a brief index. Generally, the writing is clear and enjoyable to read. The volume in hand can serve as a summary, a stimulus, and a guide. [R: C&RL, Sept 85, p. 449]

A. Robert Rogers

17. **The ALA Yearbook of Library and Information Services: A Review of Library Events 1984. Volume 10.** Chicago, American Library Association, 1985. 393p. $65.00. LC 83-8703. ISBN 0-8389-0434-3; ISSN 0740-042X.

The tenth edition of *The ALA Yearbook of Library and Information Services* continues the worthy goals of its predecessors: to survey in a comprehensive, authoritative manner the "events, activities, and individuals who have shaped 1984 for the field of library and information services," and to note and evaluate current trends that will effect the future of librarianship and information science.

Leading off this year's review is "Librarianship through a Rear View Mirror," a feature article by the editors that takes a retrospective stroll through the past decade's significant events and issues as recorded in the *Yearbook.* Funding difficulties, the rise of online databases, the ALA centennial celebration, copyright concerns, the embattled state of book publishing, literacy (and illiteracy) rates, preservation and security considerations, and the long-term effects of Proposition 13 are among the topics highlighted in this interesting (if occasionally depressing) overview of librarianship's battles over the past ten years. Following this article are brief sections on awards, biographies, obituaries, and notables, then the lengthy "Review of Library Events 1984," an alphabetically arranged (by title, which also indicates subject matter) compilation of some 140 articles, most several pages in length. Scattered throughout the "Review" section are twelve special reports, dealing with such topics as the ramifications of an independent national archive, 1984 themes in electronic publishing, the anticipated impact of American withdrawal from UNESCO, and the history and role of Canada's National Library. The fifty state reports conclude the yearbook. As in past volumes, all articles are signed, and the generous use of interesting and appropriate illustrations enlivens the text.

The ALA Yearbook continues to provide a well-organized, comprehensive (if expensive) overview of events and trends in librarianship. The publication's value, however, would be greatly enhanced by the availability of a cumulative index that would allow readers—not just editors—to peruse the significant events of the past ten years as recorded annually in its pages.

G. Kim Dority

18. **Annual Review of Information Science and Technology. Volume 19. 1984.** Martha E. Williams, ed. White Plains, N.Y., published for the American Society for Information Science by Knowledge Industry, 1984. 417p. index. $50.00. LC 66-25096. ISBN 0-86729-093-5; ISSN 0066-4200.

19. **Annual Review of Information Science and Technology. Volume 20. 1985.** Martha E. Williams, ed. White Plains, N.Y., published for the American Society for Information Science by Knowledge Industry, 1985. 360p. index. $52.50. LC 66-25096. ISBN 0-86729-175-3; ISSN 0066-4200.

Annual volumes of *ARIST* have been reviewed regularly in *ARBA*. Its purpose has remained constant over the years: to describe and appraise activities and trends in the field of information science and technology as substantiated by the literature. Approximately ten topics, selected on the basis of timeliness and an assessment of reader interest, are reviewed in each volume. The scholarly reviews, which may cover a one-year or multiyear period, provide the author's expert opinion regarding developments and activities within that area, while reviewing the key literature. Extensive bibliographies follow each chapter/topic, making *ARIST* the most important bibliographic guide to the general literature of information science and technology.

A wide range of topics is covered in volumes 19 and 20: a reflection perhaps of the growing sophistication and diversity in the information sciences. In addition to numerous articles on technologies and applications, such as those by Christine Borgman on psychological research in human-computer interaction, by Charles Goldstein on computer-based information storage technologies, and Karen Markey on visual arts resources and computers, are three thought-provoking pieces treating the impact of information technologies on privacy, economics, and international relations. These include Thomas Surprenant's "Global Threats to Information," Rein Turn's "Privacy Protection," and Donald Lamberton's "The Economics of Information and Organization."

A theme recurring in several articles in both volumes is the emerging importance of end-user systems and services. Sowizral states in "Expert Systems" that interest in expert systems is growing exponentially. Borgman notes that concurrent with the evolution of the computer from a programmer's tool to a general-purpose tool for the masses, has grown the demand for "user-friendly" systems. Tenopir in her article on full-text databases remarks that user studies reveal an end-user market for full databases but that research is needed to examine what search or display capabilities are desired and needed by users. Hildreth ("Online Public Access Catalogs") lists as one of the major research and design challenges for the rest of this decade the creation of user-system interfaces that are "more natural, helpful, and adaptive to a variety of users" (vol. 20, p. 273).

ARIST provides from year to year a unique overview of the key issues in information science and technology. By filtering the literature of a subject through the critical judgment of experts, who shape it into a meaningful context and identify influential works and emerging trends, *ARIST* offers a unique service to its readers.

Heather Cameron

20. **The Bowker Annual of Library and Book Trade Information.** 30th ed. Julia Moore and Dorothy Pollet Gray, eds. New York, R. R. Bowker, 1985. 768p. index. $69.95. LC 55-12434. ISBN 0-8352-1975-5; ISSN 0068-0540.

The thirtieth edition of this well-known work maintains its six-part format, organizing its articles and statistical reports under "Reports from the Field," "Legislation, Funding, and Grants," "Library/Information Science Education, Placement, and Salaries," "Research and Statistics," "Reference Information," and "Directory of Information." New to this edition are a field report, "Information Standards in 1984," and, in part 5's "Reference Information," a ready-reference section that contains a list of toll-free numbers for some four hundred U.S. publishers. As usual, the articles and reports are based on concrete, documentable facts and statistics, making this annual publication a reliable resource with which to back up such managerial concerns as budget and salary negotiations.

Especially noteworthy among this edition's articles and reports is a timely contribution by Thomas J. Galvin, former Dean of the University of Pittsburgh's School of Library and Information Science. In his "Trends and Issues in the International Library and Information Community," Galvin addresses the American information community's position on the United States' withdrawal from UNESCO, notes the increasing polarization of the geopolitics of information, and warns against our historic and continuing tendency to hold ourselves aloof from international library and information organizations.

Whether one uses *The Bowker Annual of Library and Book Trade Information* for its directory-type listings, its calendar of events, its statistical compilations, or the broad coverage of its industry overviews, the work continues to be a reliable, authoritative resource of interest to librarians and other information professionals.

G. Kim Dority

21. **Canadian Library Yearbook. Annuaire des bibliothèques Canadiennes.** Diane Gallagher, ed. Toronto, Micromedia, 1985. 420p. index. $55.00pa. ISSN 0827-3715.

This work was formerly known as the *Canadian Library Handbook*, first issued in 1979/1980. Its new title reflects a number of changes beginning in 1985. First, it is now to be available annually. Second, there is a longish section on Canadian library associations, and this section is unique since the National Library will not be publishing its *Directory of Canadian Library Associations* anymore, nor will the National Library be publishing a directory of library science periodicals from Canada. Both cuts were due to stern budget measures. Additionally, there are many unique library statistics here that will not be published by Statistics Canada (although it will continue to collect the material, the actual dissemination in print has been cut back because of expenses). And the annual reviews of library trends in Canada, formerly published by S. D. Neil, have been subsumed in this new work.

Thus, there is quite a bit of new stuff here, and that also includes a unique survey of librarians' and library technicians' salaries (mainly gleaned from articles in other library science periodicals), a library services directory to Canadian book wholesalers and to Canadian magazine subscription agencies, and a regional breakdown of the National Library trends (about forty pages) in the Atlantic provinces, Quebec, Ontario, and the west.

The older material remains, updated of course. There are a directory of fifty-five hundred public, government, university and college, and special libraries (with the chief librarian's name, address, phone number, and subject coverage, but nothing on content and services), some data on regional library systems and archives in Canada, plus information on Canadian library education. Good value for its Canadian tabular data.

Dean Tudor

22.   Horowitz, Lois. **Knowing Where to Look: The Ultimate Guide to Research.** Cincinnati, Ohio, Writer's Digest Books, 1984. 436p. index. $16.95. LC 84-20876. ISBN 0-89879-159-6.

There are many guides to reference books and search methodology which have been written for librarians, but very few such guides have been intended for laypeople. Horowitz's book is the latest and by far the largest example of the latter type.

A guide which presumes to instruct the general public in matters ordinarily left to the professionals must pass several tests. Is it clear? Is it interesting? Does it explain and not merely describe? Is it accurate without being pedantic? Is it assimilable rather than overwhelming? Horowitz, who has had considerable experience both as reference librarian and journalist, receives high marks on all the above tests except possibly the last. Her material is well arranged into easily discernible categories; the writing is lucid, fluent, and informal (without being irritatingly "jazzy"); she knows the good instructor's technique of supplying plenty of examples and summaries; most important, she herself is obviously most keen about her task and she communicates that enthusiasm to the reader.

Perhaps, indeed, Horowitz is too keen. In her desire to provide every possible help, she presents much more information than I feel most readers will want or be able to digest. On the other hand, it is only fair to note that the readers need not digest it all; the material is so well laid out as to make it easy for them to find the parts they want without having to read the whole. All this, together with the substantial assets of a modest price and pleasing format, makes *Knowing Where to Look* well worth knowing about. [R: JAL, May 85, p. 111; JAL, Sept 85, p. 232; JAL, Nov 85, p. 310; LJ, 15 Mar 85, p. 53]   Samuel Rothstein

23.   **Library Lit. 15—The Best of 1984.** Bill Katz, ed. Metuchen, N.J., Scarecrow, 1985. 346p. $20.00. LC 78-154842. ISBN 0-8108-1808-6.

John Berry, Mary Chelton, Arthur Curley, William Eshelman, Pat Shuman, and Bill Katz have selected thirty "best" articles to include in *Library Lit. 15—The Best of 1984.* The purpose of this annual compilation is still to recognize superior writing, research, and opinion and to alert the reader to some fine work dispersed among an increasingly voluminous literature.

As always, the collection is pleasantly eclectic. Articles on censorship and government secrecy are stitched together with contributions on academic library management, subject cataloging, and children's literature. Among the

contributors are librarians, publishers, university presidents, and journalists.

Library Lit. does not pretend to represent evenly intellectual activity in library science from year to year. Nonetheless, reading the collection is an enjoyable and stimulating experience.   Heather Cameron

24.   **Library Lit. 14—The Best of 1983.** Bill Katz, ed. Metuchen, N.J., Scarecrow, 1984. 372p. $20.00. LC 78-154842. ISBN 0-8108-1717-9.

Here is a standard work in its fourteenth year which always fulfills its purpose very well—to recognize and share the best articles chosen by a jury of writers and editors from a wide range of periodicals on the subject of libraries, librarianship, and related fields.

In this case John Berry, Mary K. Chilton, Arthur Curley, William R. Eshelman, and Pat Schuman along with Bill Katz are the jury who have selected thirty articles by a variety of international authors including not only library professionals but also those outside of our field. Among these are Richard DeGennaro on theory versus practice in library management, Luo Xingyun on libraries and information services in China, Ashley Montagu on the Nonesuch Press, Guy Marco on bibliographic control of library and information science, and Robert D. Stone on the legal implications of *Island Trees vs. Pico.*

Articles are selected on the basis of originality of thought, depth of research, and grasp of subject matter. Consideration is also given to scope, journal representation, timeliness, and just plain intuition by the jury members.

Nineteen journals are represented. *Library Journal* provides five articles followed by three in *Collection Building* and two each in *Daedalus, Public Library Quarterly,* and *Reference Librarian.*

The editor and jury members perform a valuable service in this annual compilation. We have an important, growing record of the best of our journal articles. Perhaps on some future anniversary of this publication, we can have a volume with selections of the best from the best in library literature. [R: JAL, May 85, p. 101; LJ, 15 Nov 84, p. 2134; VOYA, Apr 85, p. 72; WLB, Dec 84, p. 284]   George S. Bobinski

25.   Wynar, Bohdan S., and Heather Cameron, eds. **Library Science Annual. Volume 1: 1985.** Littleton, Colo., Libraries Unlimited, 1985. 204p. index. $37.50. ISBN 0-87287-495-8; ISSN 8755-2108.

The dramatic growth of the monographic and periodical literature of the library profession has prompted Libraries Unlimited to initiate a new, annual publication dedicated exclusively to reviewing the literature of librarianship. Commencing with the first annual volume, *American Reference Books Annual* has included reviews of both reference and nonreference monographs in library science. Reference publications in library science are still included in *American Reference Books Annual*, but beginning with volume 16 of that annual, coverage of other monographic literature has been shifted to *Library Science Annual*.

The scope of *Library Science Annual* is broad, and includes four major categories of information. The main body of the work provides reviews of *all* English-language library science monographs and reference books published during the year. Although volume 1 is principally devoted to works published in the United States and, to some extent, Canada, comprehensive coverage of publications from Canada, the United Kingdom, and other English-language countries will be introduced in subsequent volumes.

The second major component of this work is the systematic evaluation of English-language library science periodicals and indexing services. This will be implemented through the evaluation of selected titles each year. The third component consists of abstracts of the most significant doctoral dissertations of the year from librarianship and related disciplines.

In addition to the three types of literature for which individual reviews or abstracts are presented, each annual volume will include a section that consists of reports on various aspects of the production and distribution of knowledge in library science. Volume 1 includes several essays on library science publishing. The editors have stated that it is their objective "to attempt, over time, a permanent record of the intellectual activity in librarianship and to impose bibliographic control over the literature" (p. x).

The first volume of *Library Science Annual* is organized into four parts consistent with the four categories described above. Part 1 includes six essays on publishing in library science. Part 2 includes reviews of 253 reference and nonreference monographs in library science. This part is subdivided by topic with the topic headings selected to reflect terms and concepts common to library practice. Part 3 includes reviews of thirty-nine national, subject-oriented, and regional periodicals, as well as three indexes. Part 4 includes abstracts of thirty-two dissertations in library science. For convenience, all reviews and abstracts are numbered, using a single numbering system (a total of 327 in all). Access is provided through a detailed table of contents and through a combined author, title, and subject index.

The list of reviewers includes 145 persons, most of whom are well known in their respective areas of specialization. Each review is signed, and many include a list of references to other reviews of the same work. The reviews of the monographs are comparable in length and quality to those found in *American Reference Books Annual*. The periodical reviews are longer and more varied in nature. Some of the periodicals reviewed are old, well-established journals; for them a historical account of the journal is provided. Other periodicals, typically topical in nature, are examined more critically, with the objective of evaluating their value to the field. Dissertations are not reviewed, but rather, are abstracted by Gail A. Schlachter, following the same format as used in Schlachter and Thomison's *Library Science Dissertations, 1925-1972: An Annotated Bibliography* (Libraries Unlimited, 1974) and *Library Science Dissertations, 1973-1981: An Annotated Bibliography* (Libraries Unlimited, 1982). The dissertation abstracts are preceded by a brief but useful analysis of dissertation production for the year.

This work is a welcome expansion of the library science coverage formerly included in *American Reference Books Annual*. The extended coverage of the annual reviewing of monographic literature, particularly to works published outside of the United States is an important advance in the creation of better bibliographic control of the literature of librarianship. Also, the in-depth evaluation of library science periodicals and the ongoing abstracting of new dissertations that pertain to library science are valuable new additions to the coverage previously available. The identification of new dissertations should increase the use of these underutilized resources. One limitation in the coverage of dissertations is the decision to include only selected dissertations. It would be a greater contribution to bibliographic access to these publications if all were included, as with monographs.

The essays on aspects of library publishing are a valuable new resource. They will enable members of the library profession to better understand the characteristics of library science publishing, and to monitor changes as they occur. Of particular value is the decision to dedicate one essay in each volume to an in-depth examination of a major library publishing house. The publishing company covered in volume 1 is Scarecrow Press.

There is little to criticize and much to applaud in the decision by Libraries Unlimited to initiate this new publication. As noted in the introduction to volume 16 of *American Reference Books Annual*, it does indeed include information "beyond the purview of *ARBA*"

(p. xiv). This augmentation of the information previously included in *ARBA* makes this new annual series an indispensable resource for the professional collection of all types of libraries. If librarians use this as it is designed and intended to be used, it will make a major contribution toward providing bibliographic access to the resources that librarians require to meet their professional information needs. [R: JAL, Sept 85, p. 236; WLB, Sept 85, p. 70]

Gary R. Purcell

ACQUISITIONS

26. Lee, Sul H., ed. **Issues in Acquisitions: Programs & Evaluation.** Ann Arbor, Mich., Pierian Press, 1984. 133p. bibliog. illus. index. (Library Management Series, No. 8). $24.95. LC 84-61226. ISBN 0-87650-188-9.

This is a collection of papers presented at a 1984 Oklahoma City Conference on Current Issues in Library Acquisitions focusing mainly upon approval programs and vendor-library relationships. Gary Shirk's outstanding contribution of a model for evaluating vendor performance of approval programs includes a helpful rationale along with specifications. Also reported are three in-house, evaluative studies conducted by Texas A&M, the purported largest approval program consumer. The evaluative studies involve an analysis of interlibrary loan requests and university press acquisitions and a comparison of approval program receipts against an issue of *American Book Publishing Record.* Additional papers cover the ways to increase faculty participation in the approval program process, steps to be considered in automating the acquisitions function, and responsibilities that both parties have in developing successful approval-vendor/library relationships. This work is strengthened considerably by including strongly stated vendor prospectives. Of value to book vendors, academic acquisition librarians, and students of technical services. [R: AL, Apr 85, pp. 249-50; JAL, May 85, pp. 116-17; JAL, July 85, pp. 160-61; LJ, 15 June 85, p. 46]

Ann Allan

AUTOMATION IN LIBRARIES

General Works

27. **The Automation Inventory of Research Libraries 1985.** Maxine K. Sitts, ed. Washington, D.C., Systems and Procedures Exchange Center, Office of Management Studies, Association of Research Libraries, 1985. 1v. (unpaged). $40.00pa.

This publication found its origins in suggestions by some Association of Research Libraries (ARL) directors who felt the need for a document summarizing and comparing automation activities within their libraries. The resulting work contains the responses to a survey from ninety-two ARL members.

Libraries were asked to report on automation activities for seventeen identified functions such as acquisitions, circulation, cataloging, ILL, online catalogs, and collection development. For each function, respondents were asked to describe the status of the automation activity (whether or not work was planned, if a function was operational, if the function existed only in the main library or also in branches, who owned the hardware and software, and what patron access was). The two main sections of the document deal with this information. The first section is an alphabetical listing by responding institution. The second lists the specific function and under each, indicates which libraries are automating in this area. Short, informative comments made by individual respondents are also included.

In addition to the raw data received from the survey itself, the editor further analyzes these data regarding current automation and future trends. In these analyses, the most often reported uses for library automation are cited as are those functions for which libraries are planning to automate. The survey itself and matrix are included in the work.

While this directory was created primarily for the ARL libraries, its value cannot be underestimated for others involved in automation. It can help plot library automation trends both nationally and locally. More important, the *Inventory* can be used to identify individuals who can be contacted for information about particular vendors or systems.

No mention is made regarding possible updates or revisions of this document. Future editions of this work should already be in the planning stages due to the changing nature of library automation. This is an important and useful work, not only for ARL libraries but for any library involved with or considering automation. Marjorie E. Bloss

28. Daily, Jay E. **Staff Personality Problems in the Library Automation Process: A Case in Point.** Littleton, Colo., Libraries Unlimited, 1985. 147p. bibliog. $28.50. LC 85-19906. ISBN 0-87287-505-9.

Jay Daily has used the form of case histories to approach a difficult subject: interpersonal problems in library automation. Five case studies are recounted in letters sent from librarians to former professors in library school. In all but one, several letters make the case history. Unfortunately, there are no letters in response from the learned professors.

Each of the five cases is preceded by a history of automation illustrated in the story and followed by a summary of problems encountered, an analysis of what happened, and finally speculation on how the problems could have been prevented.

Several types of library settings are depicted — both a small and a large college library, two public libraries, and one specialized library.

This book was written, according to the author, to be used in library science classes in the management of technical services. Based upon the case histories, this reviewer believes if the book is to be used at all, it must be with librarians having working experience, not just textbook knowledge.

The case histories, to anyone with hands-on experience, will appear totally unrealistic. Anyone who has ever worked in a public library will get a good laugh reading case history number 5: The director hires a friend as cataloger at her library. Over dinner and a bottle of wine, the two librarians decide they need a computer and, even though it is not budgeted, order ten thousand dollar equipment the following day. The computer arrives within three days. (Please, who is this company?!)

As if that were not bad enough, the director and cataloger set forth to hire a new staff member. After they have narrowed the applicants to two choices, they decide they cannot choose between the two; thus the director offers both applicants jobs "half afraid both would accept or both refuse." Both accept, so the director plans to take book funds to pay salaries.

After thirteen years in the library profession, as both a student and a professional, I found this case history totally absurd! I've been involved in automation of two library systems in the past ten years and never have I encountered or heard of such situations. As a cataloger, I recommend this book for the Fantasy collection — not Library Science!   Janet R. Ivey

29. **Electronic Information Delivery Systems: Proceedings of the Library of Congress Network Advisory Committee Meeting April 18-20, 1984.** Washington, D.C., Network Development Office, Library of Congress, 1984. 79p. (Network Planning Paper, No. 9). $6.00pa. LC 84-600244. ISBN 0-8444-0465-9.

Whether or not we like the idea, and whatever our present state of preparedness, the information economy is not just coming ... it's here. The effects of that economy on libraries and library directors and planners are uncertain, but certain to be far-reaching and profound. In this context, numerous issues of change will need to be scrutinized carefully, with inferences and implications clearly drawn.

This "planning paper" is really a collection of eight papers, constituting a Library of Congress Network Advisory Committee program held in November 1984. The meeting at which that program took place provided a forum for some of the weightier issues confronting librarians of today and tomorrow, and the new roles such libraries and librarians would play in the future: Electronic information delivery systems, the publishing environment, online full text and its implications, abstracting and indexing services, changing acquisitions and access procedures, new equipment and applications, and computer-aided database searching.

This is the tenth in an ongoing series of Network Planning Papers published by LC, and their timely topics, attractive pricing and readable formats should give them widespread distribution. Some of these papers tend toward the dry and statistical, and none of them can be termed especially fun to read. Then there's the lack of an index, which would have made things more accessible, but all contain valuable information for decision-makers wherever electronic options are presented, and all deserve to be read by the widest possible audience.

                                Bruce A. Shuman

30. **Encyclopedia of Information Systems and Services: An International Descriptive Guide to Approximately 3,300 Organizations, Systems, and Services Involved in the Production and Distribution of Information in Electronic Form ..., 1985-86.** 6th ed. Detroit, Gale, 1985. 2v. index. $325.00/set. LC 82-18359. ISBN 0-8103-1537-8.

The fifth edition of this standard resource on the electronic information industry describes some thirty-three hundred organizations — approximately 35 percent of which are new to this edition — that provide bibliographic, full-text, numeric, and other types of computer-processed information. Because of the vast increase in material over the previous edition, the directory is now published in two volumes: *International*, listing more than eleven hundred foreign organizations from fifty-nine countries, and *United States*, with the latter volume including a combined master index to entries contained in both volumes. Each volume may be purchased separately. Other changes new to this edition include expanded and more detailed information being provided for each entry, especially in the area of publications; inclusion of brief or partial entries for organizations for whom complete information was not available (in previous editions, only those organizations submitting a completed questionnaire were listed); inclusion of the address or code through which an organization can be contacted through public electronic mail networks; and several indexing enhancements.

Entries describing such categories of information as videotex/teletext information services, abstracting and indexing services, magnetic tape providers, library and information networks, information-on-demand services, document delivery services, research projects, and electronic mail applications are arranged alphabetically by name of the parent organization. Twenty-two indexes, each introduced by a scope note, provide access to organizations by function (e.g., community information and referral, online/host services, personal computer-oriented services) and to specific subject, personnel, geographic location, database names, publications, and software.

Supplemented by the periodic *New Information Systems and Services*, the encyclopedia continues to be a valuable information resource. However, given the high price of this set, smaller libraries may want to consider purchasing only the United States volume ($190.00).

G. Kim Dority

31. Genaway, David C. **Integrated Online Library Systems: Principles, Planning and Implementation.** White Plains, N.Y., Knowledge Industry, 1984. 151p. illus. bibliog. index. (Professional Librarian Series). $34.50; $27.50pa. LC 84-15406. ISBN 0-86729-092-7; 0-86729-091-9pa.

The preface states that the purpose of this book is to "provide an overview of integrated online library systems and to outline some of the planning procedures, evaluations and selection criteria useful in acquiring and implementing these systems." The table of contents indicates that appropriate topics are covered: chapter 1, "Overview of Integrated Online Library Systems," chapter 2, "Planning for an IOLS," chapter 3, "System Evaluation and Selection," and chapter 4, "System Implementation and Acceptance." In addition, profiles of various system vendors and the possible uses of microcomputers are listed as topics to be addressed in this book. Various appendices are also included.

Initially it appeared that this brief paperback book might be valuable to those totally unfamiliar with library automation, but then the author's intended audience was noted: "all those involved in the selection and acquisition of such a system as well as all others interested in integrated online library systems." Given this intended audience, the book clearly warranted a more detailed inspection.

Closer scrutiny revealed the book to be poorly written, grossly oversimplified (especially for its intended audience), and lacking in useful information. Various important issues are either overlooked or slighted. Examples of these problems can be found in all parts of the book. Chapter 2, "Planning for an IOLS," begins by posing an excellent question: "First, the library must ask why it needs an integrated online library system," but no answers are provided. The index includes no references to "retro-conversion," although two brief references are found under "data conversion." Several paragraphs begin "First, ..." without being followed by a subsequent "Second, ..." Finally, chapter 2 summarizes its discussion of planning for automation with the astute observation that "Good planning is a time-consuming, often costly, undertaking."

As is typical with many Knowledge Industry publications, almost half of this short book (151 pages) is composed of survey documents and vendor directories. While descriptions of the various integrated system vendors would be valuable, the brief (generally one-page) noncritical annotations provided in this book are almost useless. Most of the actual text represents information which has been presented elsewhere in a more comprehensive and readable fashion. This book is too superficial to be of value to anyone truly interested in integrated library systems. [R: AL, Apr 85, p. 219; BL, 15 Apr 85, p. 1157; JAL, May 85, p. 102; LJ, 1 Mar 85, p. 50; LJ, 15 Mar 85, p. 46]

Greg Byerly

31a. Grosch, Audrey N. **Distributed Computing and the Electronic Library: Micros to Superminis.** White Plains, N.Y., Knowledge Industry, 1985. 205p. bibliog. index. (Professional Librarian Series). $36.50; $28.50pa. LC 85-7627. ISBN 0-86729-145-1; 0-86729-144-3pa.

This is a basic source for librarians and information specialists who want information about the current state of the art of distributed systems for libraries and information centers. In a chapter on the state of the art of computer applications and plans for the future, Grosch presents the results of a questionnaire distributed to U.S. and foreign libraries. Chapters are also devoted to trends in library automation, to communications technology, and to hardware and software developments. One chapter describes and analyzes commercially available integrated library systems and another discusses systems software for specific applications. There is a directory of installed systems arranged by library which includes basic facts about each system. This directory has its own index. There is an additional directory of names and addresses of suppliers as well as a glossary.

This is a carefully prepared, sensible guide for the novice in computer applications in libraries, replete with vitally important advice for library decision makers. There are other software directories, but this is particularly useful because of Grosch's critical analysis of commercially available systems and recognition that an ideal system for one library may not suit another. While directed towards the tyro, this book should be a valuable resource and reference tool for those with much more experience.

Margaret McKinley

32. Levy, Charlotte L., and Sara Robbins. **Library Automation: A Systems and Software Sampler.** Brooklyn, N.Y., CompuBibs/Vantage Information Consultants, 1985. 87p. index. (CompuBibs, No. 11). $15.50pa. LC 85-5757. ISBN 0-914791-10-9.

This guide lists 125 automated systems commercially available from thirty-eight vendors. System descriptions extracted from vendors' promotional literature are arranged in three sections: turnkey systems which include vendor-supplied hardware and software, integrated software systems, and separate, single-function systems. Systems range in size from NOTIS, designed for large research libraries, to Bookworm, intended for use in elementary school libraries. The summations are necessarily noncritical and, given the rapidity of change in this field, will soon be outdated. Since vendors' addresses and telephone numbers are included, libraries may ask vendors for current information about their systems. Notwithstanding these limitations, this is a worthwhile catalog for librarians shopping for automated systems, eliminating the need for tedious searches in periodical literature and software directories.

Margaret McKinley

33. **Library Systems Evaluation Guide.** Powell, Ohio, James E. Rush Associates, 1983- . 8v. index. $410.00/set; $59.50/vol. LC 83-9584. ISBN 0-912803-00-2.

The set provides a comprehensive methodology for managers to evaluate library automated systems as well as a wealth of reference information about system specifications, capabilities, and operational details and goals. Volumes 1 through 6 are available, and cover serials control, circulation control, public services, acquisitions, management services, and interlibrary loans. The last two volumes of the set will cover cataloging and systems integration.

Although the coverage of each guide is individualized for the specific topic covered and each guide can be used independently, the basic design, layout, and recommended methodology for evaluation are duplicated in all. Each guide consists of ten sections, covering the purpose and general description of computer-based applications to the topic and of the principles and applications of the methodology; lists of functions, features, and data elements; definitions; inventory of available systems; a selected bibliography; and an index.

The guides focus on online, interactive systems, including microcomputer-based, minicomputer-based and large mainframe-based systems. The evaluation methodology central to each guide includes setting objectives; examining documentation; comparing candidate systems with function and feature tables and checklists of data elements; and on-site and post-installation evaluations. The methodology stresses modifications for local site needs, and the guides provide both outline work charts for application in the review process and helpful data on generic system features and operational objectives.

The volumes available for this review are thorough and provide an excellent base of data and clearly presented procedure for use in an evaluation process. The price is reduced by purchase of the entire set and is low in comparison to the cost of either external consultants or staff effort to draw similarly thorough conclusions as offered by use of the guides. These guides are recommended for the desks of managers considering library automated systems and for the reference shelves serving interest in current library trends or system design.

Danuta A. Nitecki

34. Lovecy, Ian. **Automating Library Procedures: A Survivor's Handbook.** London, Library Association; distr., Phoenix, Ariz., Oryx Press, 1984. 247p. bibliog. index. $28.00. ISBN 0-85365-516-2.

Lovecy's work deals with the processes involved in the selection, introduction, and use of computerized systems in libraries. Following a very realistic and refreshingly honest introduction to the current capabilities and deficiencies of computers, he discusses their application to various library functions such as administration, acquisitions, circulation, and information retrieval. In each case, he presents the advantages and disadvantages of computerized systems in a very clear and concise manner. The reader is effectively guided through numerous options with a minimal amount of computer jargon.

LYMAN BEECHER BROOKS LIBRARY
NORFOLK, VIRGINIA

The final six chapters of the work provide a great deal of valuable information for making both administrative and conceptual decisions. The pros and cons of in-house development versus commercial procurement are explained, as well as the option of working with other libraries in a cooperative. Problems of dealing with staff attitudes and training, system installation and maintenance, computer crises, and interfacing the library user with computerized systems complete the text. A four-page bibliography, a glossary, and an index complete the volume.

Although Lovecy's advice comes from a British perspective, his work should be required reading for anyone considering library automation. His comments come from experience with actual situations as a "survivor."

Bill J. Corbin

35. Matthews, Joseph R. **Directory of Automated Library Systems.** New York, Neal-Schuman, 1985. 217p. index. (Library Automation Planning Guides Series, No. 2). $34.95pa. LC 84-25490. ISBN 0-918212-82-0.

This directory presents comparative data on thirty automated library systems and software packages on the market as of July 1984. Exhibit 1 of part 1 consists of general vendor information such as type of organization, total staff, number of staff in sales, systems development, software maintenance, hardware, operating systems software, number of current customers, and number awaiting delivery of systems. Exhibits 2 through 9 provide checklist data on the following functions supported by the systems: acquisitions, cataloging, online catalog, circulation, circulation database, equipment, serials, and reference. Each exhibit is a table noting whether specific features are available in each system and, if not, the expected date of availability.

Part 2 is a directory of all current customers of each vendor listing library, address, contact person, date of installation, number of terminals, and disc capacity of the system. Part 3 presents profiles of microcomputer software for library applications.

The *Directory of Automated Library Systems* is a useful, well-organized tool for an initial survey and preliminary screening of systems available on the market. The customer list is particularly useful, allowing one to contact automated libraries similar to one's own in size and type and to avoid the possible bias of vendors' referrals. Evaluative and performance data are not included, and the compiler patiently cautions the user of the directory that it does not constitute the final word in system selection.

[R: JAL, Nov 85, p. 318; LJ, 15 Oct 85, p. 56]

Joe A. Hewitt

36. Reynolds, Dennis. **Library Automation: Issues and Applications.** New York, R. R. Bowker, 1985. 615p. index. $37.50. LC 84-6272. ISBN 0-8352-1489-3.

It takes 615 pages, but this newest book on library automation does a very credible job of covering a rapidly expanding and increasingly unavoidable topic for librarians and library administrators. Library automation is broadly defined in terms of the "reusability of data and flexibility in manipulating it." While the technology of library automation is examined in detail, the book clearly believes that library automation "is as much a human process as a technological one."

The book is divided into three parts and sixteen chapters. Part 1, "History and Background," includes six historical and background chapters. Early manual and online technical support systems are described. The evolution of the public catalog and the development of information retrieval services and interlibrary lending procedures are also summarized. Part 2, "Planning and Preparation," provides a thorough overview of the basic approaches to selecting, acquiring, and installing an automated system. Retrospective conversion of bibliographic records to machine-readable format is concisely outlined in a separate chapter. Part 3, "Applications," offers practical examples of operational library automation and provides suggestions for implementing online catalogs, automating technical services, and providing online searches.

Three major themes are identified as being central to the approach of the book. First, while the actual technology involved will continue to change rapidly, certain "analytical and managerial considerations related to evaluation, selection, purchase, implementation, and ongoing use of systems" can be identified and employed by anyone involved in an automation project. Second, it is essential that all options be carefully considered in any planning process and that the "human consequences" be given high priority. Third, all potential applications of library automation must "be viewed within the context of the broader issues surrounding them in the external environment."

The only criticism of the book is the lack of a bibliography and the scarcity of references included at the end of each chapter. Regardless of the accuracy and insights provided by the author, most readers will want to consult other sources of information. In fact, the author admonishes readers to "use this book as a starting point for their own data gathering," but few such starting points are identified.

LYMAN BEECHER BROOKS LIBRARY
NORFOLK, VIRGINIA

This book can be used for two different, but very important purposes. As a general overview of library automation through the mid-1980s, it can serve as a basic resource for anyone with a general interest in library automation. However, it is arranged in such a fashion that anyone with a need for information on a particular topic concerning library automation (e.g., retroconversion or optical digital disks) can find exactly what is needed with minimal effort. In addition, the emphasis in the book on the "human elements" that determine the ultimate success of any automation project makes it required reading for those directly involved in planning and implementing any type of library automation. [R: JAL, Nov 85, p. 318]

Greg Byerly

Databases and Software

37. Chen, Ching-Chih. **MicroUse™ Directory: Software.** West Newton, Mass., MicroUse Information, 1984. 440p. index. $99.50pa. ISBN 0-931555-01-9.

This directory is printed from a new database produced by the editor with a grant from OCLC; the database will provide current information on microcomputers in libraries and information centers. Three other directories are planned; they will focus on hardware, applications, and library and information centers.

The main part of the directory consists of an alphabetic listing of software. Each entry includes the following elements: name, type (unfortunately, one must refer to the back of the volume for an explanation of the codes for type); vendor, address, menu-driven (yes or no), programming language, price, hardware, operating system, RAM requirements, peripherals required, and a very brief description. The indexes are type, vendor, hardware, operating system, and RAM requirements.

According to an article in the OCLC newsletter in February 1984 over four hundred library microcomputer application programs were entered into the database; this directory contains fifteen hundred entries, but the majority, unfortunately, are on word processing, spreadsheets, graphics programs, etc. These types of programs are well documented elsewhere, especially the selections here — Lotus 1-2-3, Flash Calc, Megawriter, Wordstar, Logo, and others. I believe that most users would prefer to have these entries eliminated, making the library programs more prominent and the cost much less. Maybe entries explaining how various libraries used these programs in an imaginative way would be appropriate.

This directory is obviously a computer printout; neither the type nor the format is very professional. The database has not been cleaned up for this product; the first four entries are actually nonsense. (Software unknown, vendor not indicated.) The descriptions are limited to 128 characters, probably to save disk space, and are not helpful at all.

There is a great need for more information on library automation, computer software, and so forth; this directory would be much more useful if it were limited to that field and the information on those products were more extensive. The price does not really justify the information contained.   Constance D. Williams

38. Gates, Hilary, comp. **A Directory of Library and Information Retrieval Software for Microcomputers.** Brookfield, Vt., Gower Publishing, 1985. 59p. index. $17.95pa. LC 84-24738. ISBN 0-566-03531-6.

Any directory on microcomputer software must be regarded as out-of-date even before it is published. This fact is recognized by the compiler of this work who intends to update the *Directory* on an annual basis or even more frequently if need warrants.

The *Directory* attempts to provide complete coverage of microcomputer software developed for library science and information work available predominantly in the United Kingdom. It excludes software developed or adapted by UK library schools for their programs. Also excluded are conventional software packages used in libraries but originally written for word processing, spreadsheets, and database management systems. The primary reason for omission is that such information is found in other sources like *The CP/M Software Directory; The International Software Directory on DIALOG; Micro Software Report: Library Edition.*

For the U.S. audience who may feel this work's information is limited, the compiler does include software from places other than the UK including U.S. companies and developers. Entries for all software are listed alphabetically by name. Under each is given the supplier's name and address, operating system, necessary hardware, system description, reviews of the system, and application of indexing terms. The work concludes with two indexes; the first, by function; the second, by hardware required to run the software.

Although software packages developed in the UK are the major focus of this work, its worth outside the UK should not be underestimated. Many of the packages are run on machines accessible to many libraries (various models of Apple, IBM, and TRS-80). This reviewer hopes the promise of revisions will be kept. An already well-done directory can only grow in usefulness as additional microcomputer software for library and information science is developed. [R: JAL, Nov 85, p. 312]

Marjorie E. Bloss

39. Hlava, Marjorie M. K., ed. **Private File Creation/Database Construction: A Proceeding with Five Case Studies.** New York, Special Libraries Association, 1984. 108p. $15.00pa. ISBN 0-87111-312-0.

This book is intended to be "a practical guide to the design, creation and maintenance of online bibliographic databases." As its title implies, the book focuses on bibliographic files of fairly small (mostly special library) collections. The editor, Hlava, and David Grossman have written the first two chapters (over half of the book) as introductions to the topic. The rest of the volume is composed of five brief case studies. The book was developed from workshops and seminars that the authors have given.

Although the book does provide an introductory overview of the topic, it falls short of its stated purpose. The first two chapters duplicate each other a good deal. They are not well organized and they don't provide nearly as much how-to-do-it information as they could. The five case studies are interesting and informative but very brief. Throughout the book, the authors provide an extensive list of considerations and problems. But they present few instructions on how to make decisions, how to solve problems, or how to answer the many questions raised.

There are some erroneous and misleading statements in the book. For example, to say that document information is never missing from its designated place in an automated system (p. 1) is most certainly false. Accidentally deleted files, lost data, input errors, and damaged storage media are all well known in systems environments. The implication that free-text searching is less expansive than index searching (p. 34) is also misleading.

There are also some discrepancies. For example, the first chapter of the book tells us that a computerized system is usually only practical if the document collection being automated exceeds five thousand (p. 2). But at least two of the five case studies are of databases which are smaller than that (five hundred to one thousand and twenty-five hundred). Some terminology is used in the book with partial or no definition (e.g., *inverted files, boolean operators, nesting, control vocabulary*, and much more).

Despite these shortcomings, the book does provide a useful, somewhat clear introduction to the topic of database construction. Although the book is not a thorough, how-to-do-it guide, the authors do convey expertise in the topic and the book is a recommendable starting point. [R: JAL, July 85, pp. 175-76]

James Rice

40. Nolan, Jeanne M., ed. **Micro Software Report. Volume III—1984-1985: Library Edition.** Westport, Conn., Meckler Publishing, 1985. 245p. index. $97.50pa. ISBN 0-88736-029-7; ISSN 8755-5786.

The three volumes of *Micro Software Report* provide a comprehensive listing of library applications software from 1981 to 1984. The programs in the third and largest edition appeared in source literature between July 1983 and July 1984. The entries in the first and second editions appeared between July 1981 and July 1982, and July 1982 and July 1983, respectively. Meckler is compiling a three-year cumulative index scheduled for release in the latter part of 1985.

The listings include both library-specific software and general applications software used in library management. Each entry includes the program title and producer, a brief description, an equipment list, review source(s), review citations ("favorable," "unfavorable," etc.) and the price (if available). Since prices change rapidly or vary depending on source, this information is apt to be approximate. A small percentage of entries name libraries using the programs. There is some overlapping, but each volume lists programs not found in the others. Programs only appear more than once if "they have been upgraded, expanded or revised in some way [or] cited or reviewed" during the covered period. Volumes 2 and 3 have expanded subject indexes and indexes by type of computer and/or operating system, as well as multiple review citations for many entries. Each volume includes a list of over sixty-five resources consulted in compiling the listings.

Inclusion does not constitute recommendation, but all the programs appear to be appropriate for library applications. Nolan has collected information from widely scattered, sometimes obscure sources, providing an enormously useful, time-saving selection tool that would make any search for a desired library program much easier. Although the purchase price places *Micro Software Report* out of reach for most small libraries, it is highly recommended for district and regional library/media centers, where it would be accessible to libraries within the system. As a footnote, librarians are urged to respond to the editor's request to submit corrections and additions for the next edition, in order to keep this valuable location tool current, and allow all to benefit from our shared experiences.   Betty Costa

41.   Palmer, Roger C. **dBASE II and dBASE III: An Introduction for Information Services.** 2d ed., rev. and enl. Studio City, Calif., Pacific Information, 1984. 1v. (various paging). (Professional Skills Series). $25.00pa. LC 84-20654. ISBN 0-913203-09-2.

This edition is a significant improvement over the first edition in terms of typography, arrangement of contents, and comprehensibility. The volume starts quite logically with an introduction to file and relational database management systems. Although considered by some to be passé, introduction to flowcharting would have been a welcome addition to this section. Many librarians need this additional method of organizing tasks prior to computerization. The next five sections deal with a crash course in dBASE II, file redesign, sorting and indexing of files, joining of files, and programming a catalog. Only the last section, consisting of nine pages, actually deals with dBASE III. The title of the volume is somewhat misleading in that the last section focuses on changes that must be made to earlier sections of the text in order to adapt dBASE II programs for use in dBASE III. An appendix discusses procedures for preparing dBASE II programs for use on an IBM Personal Computer. Annotated references to a few related information sources and a brief index complete the volume.

Considering the price of the volume, other publications such as Albert L. Peabody and Richard H. C. Seabrook's *dBASE II Programming* (Prentice-Hall, 1984) might be a better bargain for the novice. Certainly this edition would not be the volume of choice for dBASE III programmers. However, library and information science students and practitioners might be more comfortable with examples of bibliographic programming such as construction of a library catalog. The book certainly merits examination and will be of practical value in library science education as well as the workplace.   Andrew G. Torok

42.   Schmittroth, John, Jr., and Doris Morris Maxfield, eds. **Online Database Search Services Directory: A Reference and Referral Guide to Libraries, Information Firms, and Other Sources Providing Computerized Information Retrieval and Associated Services Using Publicly Available Online Databases.** Detroit, Gale, 1983-1985. 2 pts. index. $110.00pa./set. LC 84-642259. ISBN 0-8103-1698-6; ISSN 0741-0077.

This directory identifies 739 academic libraries, 207 special libraries, 99 public libraries, and 100 information-on-demand firms providing online search services to outside users in the United States and Canada. These organizations access 107 different online systems and over 200 different databases. A listing is provided of the most frequently accessed systems and databases. Information was gathered primarily through surveys, and from guides and directories and online user groups. The questionnaire used to gather the information is appended.

The main entries are alphabetical according to parent organization name. Information pertains to the organizations providing the service, rather than describing the systems and databases searched. Numerous other guides, such as Martha Williams's *Computer-Readable Data Bases* (ALA, 1985) should be consulted for such information. A detailed listing of the seventeen information fields for each entry was provided in a review of part 1 (see *ARBA* 85, entry 557). Some of the more interesting fields include approximate annual search hours, fee policies, turnaround time, and associated services. Access is provided via indexes of organization name and acronym, online system accessed, databases searched, subject areas searched, and personal name, and a geographic index. Indexes in part 2 cumulate the indexes in part 1 for the 1,145 entries. Although by no means comprehensive, the information will be of great interest to other searchers and provide valuable data sources for researchers.   Andrew G. Torok

43.   **Downloading/Uploading Online Databases & Catalogs: Proceedings of the Congress for Librarians February 18, 1985, St. John's University, Jamaica, New York.** Bella Hass Weinberg and James A. Benson, eds. Ann Arbor, Mich., Pierian Press, 1985. 136p. index. (Library Hi Tech Special Studies Series, No. 1). $39.50pa. LC 85-9414. ISBN 0-87650-195-1.

"Uploading" and "downloading" are terms found increasingly in the literature of information studies, and both terms refer to processing involved in transferring stored data from one computer to another. On February 18, 1985, St. John's University held its annual Congress for Librarians, where this volume's theme became the first in a projected series of Library Hi Tech Special Studies. On that occasion, fourteen professionals, publishers, librarians and educators, contributed to an understanding of both the opportunities and problems connected with this emerging field.

Sections in the *Proceedings* deal with terminology, hardware, software, applications, and copyright. Within these, the authors examine the nature, implications, and problems of downloading and uploading, potential risks, and the positions of two major online bibliographic utilities (OCLC and RLIN) on these practices which they may view with alarm, yet with which they must come to terms.

Benson's introduction helpfully defines terms. Subsequent papers deal with varied aspects of the practices under discussion, such as reference applications, printed applications, specific software products, and the downloading and uploading policies of twenty or so commonly used utilities. The papers are of varying length, complexity, and interest (a few are merely abstracts), but a good integrated index of both names and topics enhances the overall utility of the volume.

Not the last word or a definitive treatment of these topics — about which we will inevitably hear and read much more in years to come — but a useful point of departure, covering the things one must think about when contemplating capture or transmission of proprietary information. Therefore, recommended for professional collections. [R: JAL, Nov 85, p. 317]

Bruce A. Shuman

Microcomputer Use

44. Dewey, Patrick R. **Public Access Microcomputers: A Handbook for Librarians.** White Plains, N.Y., Knowledge Industry, 1984. 151p. illus. bibliog. index. (Professional Librarian Series). $34.50; $27.50pa. LC 83-26776. ISBN 0-86729-086-2; 0-86729-085-4pa.

Librarians have been inundated with books about microcomputers and their numerous uses in libraries (see Jane Beaumont and Donald Krueger's *Microcomputers for Libraries* reviewed in *ARBA* 84, entry 211) and Ching-chih Chen and Stacey E. Bressler's *Microcomputers in Libraries* (see *ARBA* 83, entry 243). This book deals with one specialized type of microcomputer in libraries: public access microcomputers. Microcomputers that are available to the public in a public library are becoming more familiar, but most libraries are only now developing actual programs for instituting such activities. This book can do much to facilitate this process. It is clearly written and jargon free, and it is logically arranged. The book is designed to both "inspire ideas and encourage readers to experiment" and "help them avoid many of the pitfalls and problems in the process."

Chapters 1 through 4 clearly summarize three basic issues: (1) identification of community needs and degree of service required, (2) selection of microcomputers and appropriate software, and (3) management of any public microcomputer facility. The remaining three chapters are perhaps the most valuable. Chapter

5 presents nineteen examples of actual public access projects already in existence. These brief descriptions provide practical and innovative examples of exactly what can be done by public libraries to encourage and support the use of microcomputers by patrons. Chapter 6 describes various computer-related activities for patrons that libraries have and can sponsor: computer clubs (including computer reading clubs), game days, computer fairs, contests and tournaments, classes and seminars, handouts, newsletters, etc. Electronic bulletin boards and access to remote database services (e.g., Dialog, BRS, The Source, etc.) are briefly described in chapter 7.

Six appendices are presented which identify selected microcomputer manufacturers, software companies, coinop companies, microcomputer newsletters and journals, and bulletin board software sources. A sample grant proposal is also included, as are a brief bibliography and a basic glossary.

This book will need to be supplemented by other books about selecting microcomputers and their potential uses in libraries. However, it does present a very concise overview of the specific topic of the public use of microcomputers and will be useful to any library considering making microcomputers available to the public. [R: CLJ, Dec 85, pp. 388-89; RQ, Spring 85, pp. 373-74]

Greg Byerly

45. **Essential Guide to the Library IBM PC. Volume 1: The Hardware: Set-up and Expansion.** By Nancy Jean Melin. Westport, Conn., Meckler Publishing, 1985. 275p. bibliog. index. $19.95 spiralbound. LC 85-10535. ISBN 0-88736-133-5.

Set-Up and Expansion is the first of a planned eight-volume set which is "in non-technical language for everyone from first-time user of microcomputers to the experienced computer whiz." Herein lies the volume's weakness: the publisher has tried to provide something for everyone and has created a presentation that will disappoint most. This volume provides first an introduction to the PC and to DOS. Then it covers memory and storage; input and output devices; modems; local area networks and mainframe connections; and general care and maintenance. The volume concludes with three appendices: (1) a list of DOS commands, (2) a directory of IBM-PC users groups and bulletin boards and a list of IBM-PC specific periodicals, and (3) a glossary of terms. The volume has an index. The general coverage is appropriate. But some sections of the volume are seriously flawed in the selection and presentation of the specifics. No attempt is made to separate the basic information for the beginner from the more advanced information for the experienced user. Further the choices of topic detail are not appropriate to PC-users' needs. For example, the introductory section on the history and general description of the PC-hardware never explains the terms *bit, processor, 8-bit processor, chip, hard disk drive, expansion slot, peripheral*, and many other basic terms. While many terms are defined in the glossary, the novice will be frustrated by the need to constantly refer to the back of the volume. At the same time there are pieces of information about Intel's 8088 chip, 16 vs. 18-bit [sic] processors, and applications software which are not particularly useful to the PC-user. In addition to the uneven and poorly selected text content, the volume has many useless photographs. This is epitomized by a poor quality photograph of a boxed PC with the caption "IBM boxes its computer and components carefully to avoid any damage to them." Finally there are typos, questionable advice and instructions, and poor writing. While much of the criticism above applies to the entire volume it is directed particularly to the early chapters. What quality the volume has is in the chapters on input and output devices which provide a well-organized explanation of the various types of equipment. However, many introductions to computers will cover these devices, all-be-it in a way less specific to the IBM PC. This volume is not recommended.   Thomas G. Kirk

46. Kazlauskas, Edward John. **Systems Analysis for Library Microcomputer Applications.** Studio City, Calif., Pacific Information, 1985. 104p. bibliog. (Professional Skills Series). $24.50pa. LC 85-9277. ISBN 0-913203-11-4.

Kazlauskas, a designer of microcomputer installations for libraries and records centers as well as a professor teaching courses in systems analysis and computer literacy, has designed this volume as an introductory text on systems analysis fundamentals for library microcomputer applications.

His stated purpose is to introduce basic systems methodologies for designing computer applications, assist those using existing general software for microcomputers, help those who are surveying their needs to choose a library-specific software, and give examples of systems drawn from the public library setting.

After defining *systems*, he presents a six-step analysis model. The model covers preliminary analysis, input analysis/design, output analysis/design, processing analysis/design, hardware and software selection, and other analysis/design issues.

The preliminary analysis covers problem isolation, constraints, user needs, and understanding of the organization and touches on organizational goals, problem definition, and the use of a management plan.

The input analysis/design includes form and file input, file analysis, input requirements, form design, and input screen design. Output analysis/design covers similar ground and also discusses cost-effectiveness and nature of the finished product.

Processing covers task analysis and flowcharting and microcomputer processing problems like amount of storage space needed and user-friendly interactions.

Hardware and software selection is self-explanatory dealing with criteria for selection, selection sources, and general guidelines.

Kazlauskas ends his six-step analysis with discussions of housekeeping routines, documentation, and implementation. The final pages of the book are devoted to a bibliography of articles and books on systems analysis and user needs and a list of software with addresses and annotations.

Systems Analysis for Library Microcomputer Applications is a very thorough and useful guide in determining the use of microcomputers in this setting and all the problems and planning inherent in such applications. While not providing any new information for those familiar with basic systems analysis techniques, it does summarize these for those new to this territory. [R: JAL, Nov 85, p. 314]   Daniel F. Phelan

47. **Microcomputers for Libraries: Product Review and Procurement Guide.** Powell, Ohio, James E. Rush Associates, 1984. 1v. (various paging). index. $115.00/yr. looseleaf with binder. LC 84-1961. ISBN 0-912803-09-6.

This looseleaf publication, updated quarterly, is intended as "a guide to microcomputer hardware, software, and systems that can serve as the basis for procurement decisions on the part of management in libraries and information services." Its fifteen sections include background and historical information on microcomputers; a somewhat technical description of microcomputer systems; a brief technology assessment; hardware specification summaries; a detailed discussion on software, including operating systems; nonevaluative source information for library applications software; a cross-reference section that lists software according to operating system and hardware requirements; a list of software vendors; a list of materials suppliers; procurement guidelines; and a nonevaluative section on resource literature. Dividers are included for two sections which as yet contain no material: peripherals and telecommunications (the latter topic is addressed briefly in the description of microcomputer systems). The appendices include a very short, unrelated glossary and an explanation of place value systems.

The guide does not seem to have been compiled with a clear audience in mind. It is not a review instrument, but contains a great deal of technical information that seems inappropriate for most library staff members. Although it is difficult to keep such hardware-specific information current, some of the information is quite dated. Most helpful to librarians would be the discussion of operating systems, the cross-reference hardware/software listings, and the procurement guidelines. The latter includes an excellent introduction comparing mini- or mainframe computer acquisition (where much of the burden of responsibility is on the vendor) and procurement of microcomputer systems (where the buyer assumes much greater responsibility). The guidelines, however, also place a major emphasis on hardware. The vendor lists might be more useful if cross-referenced to the hardware and software summaries. The purpose for the appendices is not clear.

This publication may be appropriate for large consulting firms or as part of a reference collection in a large library system. Overall, especially for small libraries, the same information is available from other sources and for less money.   Betty Costa

48.   Milliot, Jim, comp. **Micros at Work: Case Studies of Microcomputers in Libraries.** White Plains, N.Y., Knowledge Industry, 1985. 148p. bibliog. index. $36.50; $28.50pa. LC 85-241. ISBN 0-86729-117-6; 0-86729-116-8pa.

During the spring and fall of 1984, Knowledge Industry Publications conducted a survey of microcomputer use in libraries. The results of the survey are published in this book. Only 64 usable responses were returned from 220 questionnaires sent (a 29 percent response rate). Of these, 28 came from academic libraries (universities, high schools, and grammar schools), 25 from public libraries, and 11 from special libraries (government, corporate, and medical). The book is divided into four parts: an introduction by Allan Pratt; results of the microcomputer survey compiled by Jim Milliot; profiles of the returned surveys; and appendices, glossary, suggested reading list, and index. In the introduction, Pratt describes the current "micro reformation" and how the library is influenced by this reformation. In the second part the results of the survey are presented, but with not much statistical analysis. Numbers of different types of software owned by libraries, as well as numbers of different applications with microcomputers, are also presented. However, the compiler neither mentions the types of software being used nor indicates applications even

though this is an important issue in "micros at work." In addition, there is no mention of what types of modem were being used by libraries. The reader should not expect much from this part of the book except numbers and percentages from the survey.

Nevertheless, the profile of returned surveys is informative. In each profile or returned questionnaire, individual libraries describe how micros are being used. But the usefulness of each profile depends upon how much information was given by the respondent. Some of the important terms were left out in the glossary, for instance, Winchester disk/hard disk, monochrome display, etc. Finally, the suggested reading list is very useful to the novice. The book is a recommended reading for those who are planning to use micros in the library.

Mohammed M. Aman

49.   Stirling, Keith, ed. **Microcomputer Applications in Library and Information Services.** Philadelphia, Drexel University, 1984. 99p. (*Drexel Library Quarterly*, Vol. 20, No. 4). $10.00pa. LC 65-9911. ISSN 0012-6160.

Keith Stirling, issue editor, states, "Library and information services deal with two basic types of problems: 1) the organization and control of information sources and 2) intellectual access to information." Following the premise that "the five areas of application software already developed for microcomputers justify their permanent existence," he has selected eight articles on the ways micros offer librarians increased capabilities for dealing with these problems.

The first and longest article evaluates eight serials management programs commercially available in June 1983, and provides an excellent guide for selecting a serials system to meet any library's needs. Other selections provide practical guidelines for selecting microcomputer circulation systems, possibilities for using spreadsheets, and interesting ideas about the use of microcomputers in online catalog systems. One article describes methods for extending the capability of a word processor designed for English to include the diacritic marks essential to non-English Romance languages; two others discuss networking possibilities. The last article, by Stirling, describes a microcomputer program for training students to use the Dialog Retrieval System without incurring the expense of actual online searches.

This issue is a useful and interesting combination of general background information and practical advice. Librarians involved in the rapidly changing field of microcomputer utilization in library and information services, especially in the areas of service control and circulation, should find it quite helpful.

Betty Costa

Networks and Networking

50. Ahluwalia, Rajesh, and Roddy Duchesne. **Computerized Library and Information Network Contracts: Proposed Guidelines and Definitions.** Ottawa, National Library of Canada, 1984. 36p. bibliog. (Canadian Network Papers, No. 8). free pa. ISBN 0-662-53423-9; ISSN 0226-8760.

Upon recommendations from various sources, the National Library of Canada decided to define the terminology employed by libraries and services in negotiating contracts. The services include such businesses as database suppliers, vendors, bibliographic utilities, and communications carriers. The first eighteen pages here comprise an attempt at setting out the negotiations. Provision is made for interpretation, service description, scope of the contract, the obligations of both parties, the financial terms, audits, warranties, and termination of the contract.

The appendices contain the definitions; there are some thirty-nine items, such as "ownership," "protocol," "record," "user," "hit," "file," and "information provider." The last two appendices contain model contracts for both information retrieval facilities and library processing facilities. And, of course, the price is right: free for the asking on your letterhead.

Dean Tudor

51. **Local Area Networks and Libraries: The Los Angeles Chapter of ASIS Seminar Proceedings.** Wendy Culotta and others, eds. Studio City, Calif., Pacific Information, 1985. 174p. illus. index. $28.50pa. LC 85-6576. ISBN 0-913203-12-2.

The Los Angeles chapter of the American Society for Information Science designed its annual continuing education seminar for 1984 to assist information workers in gaining a better understanding of local area networks, or LANs. The fourteen contributors focused on planning, management, and use of LANs in different library environments and network approaches.

The published proceedings are arranged in three parts. Part 1 contains papers by California State Librarian Gary E. Strong and University of Florida Libraries Systems Specialist Nolan F. Pope. In part 2 are essays on wide-area networks by experts from California, Colorado, Sweden, and the United Kingdom, along with case studies of LANs at academic, public, and special libraries in California, and a look at the future. Part 3 is an index to the contents of this volume.

These proceedings provide a useful record of the state of the art in LANs as of 1984. Not overly technical, the papers present a good overview of local area networks and libraries. This practical book will be helpful to all librarians interested in new technologies. [R: JAL, Nov 85, p. 315]

Leonard Grundt

52. Luquire, Wilson, ed. **Experiences of Library Network Administrators: Papers Based on the Symposium "From Our Past: Toward 2000."** New York, Haworth Press, 1985. 131p. illus. (*Resource Sharing and Information Networks*, Vol. 2, Nos. 1 and 2). $22.95. LC 84-22428. ISBN 0-86656-388-1.

Also published as *Resource Sharing and Information Networks* (vol. 2, nos. 1 and 2, Fall/Winter 1984), this book shares that journal's short tradition of completely reproducing presentations and discussions of one of the library network symposiums organized by the editor, Wilson Luquire. This collection of papers arose from the April 1984 symposium, "From Our Past: Toward 2000" held in Chicago.

The five keynote papers present an excellent review of the development of major national, regional, and state networks as well as the NCLIS. James H. Kennedy writes of "The AMIGOS Experience: Development of a Successful Network." Alice E. Wilcox's paper, "Library Networks Circa 1984 or One Blind Person Touching the Elephant" focuses on the development of MINITEX. "The CLASS Experience" is represented by J. Michael Bruer. Frederick G. Kilgour reflects on "Experience and Expectation" with personal perspectives on OCLC. "The National Commission on Libraries and Information Sciences: Past Accomplishments—Future Prospects" is addressed by Alphonse F. Trezza. A transcription of audience questions and the panel discussion conclude the book.

The book's perspective is historic with timely conclusions. With the exception of Kilgour's OCLC Founder Trustee status, the speakers are no longer affiliated with the agency about which they spoke, and yet all played very influential roles in network development and in shaping today's resource-sharing activities. This may attest to the "risk-taking" characteristic identified in network personalities, a theme explored in the panel discussion. Among the recurring topics addressed throughout the book is the difficult issue of network governance and directions for document delivery.

Meeting its intent to recreate the symposium's flavor through inclusion of all commentary and pictures, the book presents a good personalized contribution to the history of library network development and offers easy, armchair professional reading. [R: JAL, May 85, pp. 124-25]   Danuta A. Nitecki

New Technologies

53. Binder, Michael B. **Videotex and Teletext: New Online Resources for Libraries.** Greenwich, Conn., JAI Press, 1985. 160p. illus. bibliog. index. (Foundations in Library and Information Science, Vol. 21). $23.75; $47.50 (institutions). LC 85-5246. ISBN 0-89232-612-3.

This excellent introduction to videotex and teletext begins with a historical look at early systems. The author carefully defines the terminology of the industry and builds on these foundations to give the reader a comprehensive picture.

Chapter 3, "Fundamentals of Teletext Systems," is a particularly well-written chapter that provides a step-by-step analysis of the components of a typical teletext system. Teletext is compared to videotex and the advantages of each are explored.

Chapters 4, 5, and 6 look at British, French, and Canadian systems respectively and include discussions of Prestel, Antiope Teletext, Antiope Videotex, and Telidon.

Chapter 8, the largest section of the work, deals with videotex and teletext use by libraries. Anyone who regularly reads *Information Today* knows that capturing the latest information in this field is a formidable task. Binder does a good job of covering the basics. OCLC's channel 2000 and Vietron are thoroughly covered.

Text throughout the book is enhanced with tables, diagrams, and figures. It should serve as a good basic primer to study of videotex and teletext. [R: JAL, Nov 85, p. 312]
        Judith A. Copler

54. **Optical Disk Technology and the Library. Technologie du vidéodisque et la bibliothèque.** Ottawa, National Library of Canada, 1985. 51p. (English); 55p. (French). bibliog. (Canadian Network Papers, No. 9). free pa. ISBN 0-662-53811-0; ISSN 0226-8760. SN 12-1/9-1985.

Another in the excellent, timely series of papers devoted to reporting on progress related to network development, this overview of optical disk technology with illustrative library applications also includes a report on the National Library of Canada's Videodisc Demonstration Project. Typical of each of the papers in the series, the report is succinct, well organized, and well documented with references to sources of information and for sources to help the reader keep track of this area which is experiencing rapid change. In part 1, "The Technol-

ogy and Its Applications," terms are defined and comparisons are made of various storage systems. Discussion of applications in libraries is short. Part 2, on the demonstration project, provides more detail on all phases of the project. Evaluative as well as descriptive, the information about producing a videodisc with a variety of materials and formats to demonstrate various uses of the medium, including interfacing the videodisc with a microcomputer, is useful for those considering other similar projects. The potential for use of this new technology for document storage and delivery in the network environment is tremendous. Again the lack of standardization and continuing development of expensive, competing systems will affect the patterns of library use probably for the forseeable future.
        JoAnn V. Rogers

55. Saffady, William. **Video-based Information Systems: A Guide for Educational, Business, Library, and Home Use.** Chicago, American Library Association, 1985. 240p. illus. index. $30.00pa. LC 84-21567. ISBN 0-8389-0425-4.

Saffady has demonstrated in earlier works (on micrographics and library automation) that he has a special gift for explaining technical subjects with great clarity. The present work attempts to summarize for information specialists, business system analysts, librarians, and other interested persons, major developments and the most important facts associated with current video technologies.

He devotes chapters to display equipment (including receivers, monitors, projection, and high definition TV); videocassette recorders and video cameras; videodisks; cable, satellite, and other video delivery systems; videotext; facsimile transmission; videoconferencing; and data display terminals. He describes operating principles, applications, and possible future developments. Each chapter concludes with an excellent bibliography. Readers who may be called upon to participate in the selection of video systems and hardware will be grateful for the detailed coverage afforded to equipment and for the realistic evaluations of current alternatives and options.

While Saffady seeks to provide a state-of-the-art survey, he concedes that the book reflects conditions in early 1984. Some technologies have experienced important changes or rapid development since then so that a few parts of the book (e.g., the section on optical disk storage systems) are noticeably incomplete. However, this is an unavoidable shortcoming. A readable and valuable publication. [R: LJ, 15

Nov 85, p. 68; VOYA, Dec 85, p. 341; WLB, Oct 85, p. 60]   Joseph W. Palmer

Online Public Access Catalogs

56. Bausser, Jaye. **Online Catalogs: Issues and Concerns.** Syracuse, N.Y., ERIC Clearinghouse on Information Resources, Syracuse University, 1984. 40p. bibliog. $6.00pa.

This ERIC document appears to be based on a number of the author's articles that appeared in the *RTSD Newsletter* over a three-year period. Some of the issues and concerns identified include authority control, subject access, retrospective conversion, resource sharing, standards, and education. The author indicates she intends the text to be used by librarians and systems designers involved with online catalog development as well as administrators seeking information about online systems in general.

As a *very* general overview, this pamphlet could be used by the groups identified above. One would hope, however, that the generalities in it would be old hat and somewhat superficial to such people. A more appropriate group might be library science students looking for a quick summation of the major issues concerning online catalogs. A bibliography containing only the most obvious works is included, as is a list of acronyms. There is no index.

As a pamphlet goes, this is not a bad little book. The information it contains, however, is quite basic and not overly detailed. As a result, its audience will be limited to those who know little about the subject or who need a quick refresher. [R: JAL, Sept 85, p. 248; RQ, Winter 85, p. 278]   Marjorie E. Bloss

57. Matthews, Joseph R. **Public Access to Online Catalogs.** 2d ed. New York, Neal-Schuman, 1985. 497p. illus. bibliog. index. $35.00pa. LC 84-20706. ISBN 0-918212-89-8.

This is "a primer on public access online catalogs" and "is *not* intended to be an authoritative comparison of existing online catalogs."

The book is divided into two parts. The first part (ca. 100 pages) consists of seven chapters examining the online catalogs' developments; their variety of design; their components; their operation; their effects on staff, patrons and services; planning and implementation of them; and their future. The author is himself a renowned authority and researcher on the topic, but draws practical conclusions from the findings of many published studies he cites. The presentation however is consistently clear and easily understandable to the novice reader, while still interesting and informative to those already exposed to the topic. Photographs,

occasional illustrations, and frequent subheadings contribute to the ease of use and understandability of the potentially complicated subject presented.

The second part (ca. 400 pages) includes detailed individual profiles about forty-eight operational online catalogs. Each entry presents information in directory fashion about the background of the online catalog, the computer system environment, the library environment, patron use, the database, system operation, user training aids, the potential for system transfer, and samples of screens used to communicate with the user of the catalog. Data were provided by the libraries and vendors. The profiles are arranged alphabetically by name of the online system. In addition, two summary lists of the forty-eight catalogs are provided, one indicates their type of hardware, the other is arranged by the developing library vendor. A glossary of well-selected and briefly defined terms, an extensive bibliography, and an index conclude the volume.

The book documents Matthews's talent for synthesizing a wealth of information on a current automation topic and presenting it in an easy-to-use and well-organized manner. Its information is not restricted to any single library environment. This will serve as a major reference tool about online catalogs as well as an invaluable textbook for both the new student and the seasoned professional seeking guidance for planning the selection and implementation of an online catalog system. [R: JAL, July 85, p. 174; JAL, Nov 85, p. 300 and 312]

Danuta A. Nitecki

Online Searching

58. Feinglos, Susan J. **Medline: A Basic Guide to Searching.** Chicago, Medical Library Association, 1985. 138p. bibliog. index. (MLA Information Series). $20.00pa. ISBN 0-912176-19-9.

This helpful guide is intended primarily for new MEDLINE database searchers, although experienced searchers can make good use of it as a review. It is short and practical, providing only basic material; however, more detailed information is available from other sources, notably the training sessions sponsored by the National Library of Medicine and some commercial database vendors.

Six chapters and a section of appendices are provided. The chapters present background and introductory material, instructions on how to use medical subject headings, selected aspects of search software, search strategy formulation, and sample search strategies. Among the appendices are a directory of MEDLINE vendors and database access software, a list of search aids produced by the National Library of Medicine, and lists of topical subheadings. A glossary has been included.   Theodora Andrews

59.   Li, Tze-chung. **An Introduction to Online Searching.** Westport, Conn., Greenwood Press, 1985. 289p. bibliog. index. (Contributions in Librarianship and Information Science, No. 50). $27.95. LC 84-6686. ISBN 0-313-24274-7.

This book provides an excellent compilation of a great deal of diverse information in an organized, readable, and understandable text. Despite certain shortcomings that will be discussed later, Tze-chung Li has done a good job of sequencing. He begins with an introduction to the guides and information sources for online searching and a survey of its history and development. Then he explains concepts such as vocabulary control, free-text searching, precision and recall, boolean operators, and so forth. An overview of the online industry is followed by an introduction to the implementation and management of an online search service. The final two-thirds of the book is devoted to introducing the actual use of DIALOG, ORBIT, BRS and some of the rudiments of a few other search services.

Li also discusses some of the more advanced aspects such as microcomputer-based searching, uploading, downloading, and the need for more standardization. Some important topics are (perhaps justifiably) omitted or only briefly mentioned. These include end-user searching, translator (or universal) languages, integrating online searching with reference service, the fee or free issue, and television-based online systems.

The major shortcoming of this book (one over which Professor Li had little or no control) is that it is already slightly out-of-date and will become more so very quickly. For example, DIALOG version 2 came out about the same time as this book was published and many of Li's examples are dated. Perhaps monographic publishing is not the best communication vehicle for such a volatile topic as online searching. But Li's conceptual and theoretical development is sound, clear, and should be useful for some time.

Much of the tutorial information that Li provides is available from various sources, especially the vendors. But as he points out, this book brings it together in a more uniform format. The price is high but possibly worth it for the organization and ease of understanding this book will provide. Librarians who want a self-teaching guide and library and information science students will find this book to be very useful. It could also serve successfully as a textbook with careful classroom support for

certain courses depending on their level and scope. [R: BL, 15 Apr 85, p. 1158; JAL, July 85, p. 174; JAL, Sept 85, p. 232; JAL, Nov 85, p. 312; LJ, 15 June 85, p. 46; RQ, Winter 85, p. 274]   James Rice

BIBLIOGRAPHY

60.   Harner, James L. **On Compiling an Annotated Bibliography.** New York, Modern Language Association of America, 1985. 40p. bibliog. $5.00pa. LC 85-3009. ISBN 0-87352-138-2.

As general editor of the Renaissance volumes in G. K. Hall's Reference Guide series, James L. Harner has probably seen more bibliographies—good and bad—than most people have. He is also the compiler of several excellent annotated secondary bibliographies and is, therefore, well qualified to write a guide to the preparation of such a bibliography.

Harner's guidelines are straightforward, clear, and practical, from the preliminary considerations through the final writing. Some of his recommendations may seem obvious (e.g., determining whether the particular bibliography is needed), but anyone who uses bibliographies extensively knows that many of the bad ones have ignored basic considerations. Organization of a bibliography is often a problem; Harner explains several systems, pointing out the advantages and difficulties of each.

Perhaps the most valuable part of this small book is the section entitled "Planning Your Research." Even an experienced bibliographer can waste a lot of time and effort; Harner's suggestions for planning will cut down on this waste. His advice on compiling and writing the entries obviously comes from one who has actually done the work. The book concludes with sections on editing the finished work, preparing the index, and writing the prefatory material.

Preparing a bibliography is often viewed as second-class scholarship. Harner demonstrates that the task requires "determination, meticulousness, energy, time, critical acumen, and literary detective skills"—in short, much the same abilities as are required of any sound scholarship. Anyone considering an enumerative bibliography project should first spend an evening reading and studying Harner's little book. It is a sound and reliable guide to the preparation of a bibliography.

Philip R. Rider

61.   Williams, William Proctor, and Craig S. Abbott. **An Introduction to Bibliographical and**

Textual Studies. New York, Modern Language Association of America, 1985. 106p. illus. $27.50; $14.50pa. LC 84-18975. ISBN 0-87352-133-1; 0-87352-134-Xpa.

This extremely useful little book is grounded on the dicta of the bibliographer W. W. Greg that "the process of transcription is characterized by variation" and that "such variation may be assumed to be universal, every transcription introducing some variants ... in all but the shortest texts." The variations that occur in the process of producing and reproducing books and other texts are the *raison d'être* for the bibliographical and textual studies described in this introductory work.

The "bibliography" which this book describes is not the reference bibliography with which librarians, teachers, and students are so familiar. It is *analytical* bibliography, defined by the authors as that "branch of bibliographical investigation, often used as an umbrella term to cover all forms of physical bibliography, that concerns the physical embodiments of texts as evidence of the process that produced these embodiments and of the relations between them. For analytical bibliographers," the authors continue, "the book is a physical object." Thus the excellent chapter on analytical bibliography is followed by a discussion of descriptive bibliography, which details just what a book says about itself, how it is put together, what it contains, what it is made of, how it is packaged, and what is known about its printing and publishing history. This information helps make sense of the two samples of descriptive bibliography, which might otherwise intimidate the scholar or librarian ignorant of the principles of bibliographic description.

The chapter on "A Text and Its Embodiments" traces the life of a text (1) from the handpress period and (2) from the machine-press period. This chapter is followed by a discussion of textual criticism, which "lies midway between literary criticism, which focuses on works, and bibliography, which focuses on books as books." Indeed, the authors emphasize throughout the book that biblioigraphical and textual criticism should precede literary criticism, and even those who do not engage in bibliographical study must know how to use its products. This work provides, in its small scope, that know-how, and is an excellent complement to those sometimes inpenetrable works of bibliographical scholarship which appear in the "Reference Bibliography" at the end of the book. Highly recommended for all academic libraries. [R: JAL, Nov 85, p. 322]

Edwin S. Gleaves

CATALOGING

General Works

62. **Foundations of Cataloging: A Sourcebook.** Michael Carpenter and Elaine Svenonius, eds. Littleton, Colo., Libraries Unlimited, 1985. 276p. index. $27.50. LC 85-10333. ISBN 0-87287-511-3.

This anthology of cataloging articles is designed for library science students and faculty. There is very little overlap in the content between this work and other books of readings. The seventeen articles focus on the key descriptive cataloging issues spanning 150 years. Included are outstanding contributors to Anglo-American cataloging theory such as Panizzi, Jewett, Cutter, Lubetzky, and Verona, along with current important figures like Gorman and Malinconico. The articles are arranged in chronological order, with each having an introduction written by the editor as well as a list of suggested readings. In their entirety the articles reflect the theoretical challenges and controversies associated with descriptive cataloging: corporate authorship, authority control, code development, catalog objectives, automation requirements, standardization, and bibliographic versus literary units. This book of readings is made particularly useful due to its excellent index and the fact that a companion volume exists that is devoted to the other major area of cataloging: that of subject analysis. The companion volume, *Theory of Subject Analysis: A Sourcebook*, is organized in the same manner. Together the articles in the two works represent the foundations of Anglo-American cataloging as we know it today.　　　Ann Allan

63. Olson, Nancy B. **Cataloging Service Bulletin Index: No. 1-28, Summer 1978-Spring 1985.** Lake Crystal, Minn., Soldier Creek Press, 1985. 76p. $10.00pa. LC 84-645709. ISSN 0739-3393.

Nancy B. Olson has been compiling the *Cataloging Service Bulletin Index* annually since the 1982 issue, covering numbers 1-16. This is an alphabetical index which provides access to the *Cataloging Service Bulletin* by topic and by AACR2 rule number. The *Bulletin* itself is useful to catalogers as it contains LC's AACR2 rule interpretations, changes in subject headings and in the *Subject Heading Manual*, and other news and notes from the Library of Congress. It is, therefore, important that an index provide easy and accurate access to its contents.

The content arrangement of the latest issue of the *Index*, covering *Bulletin*s numbers 1-28, has not changed much from that of previous years. However, this year's index was produced on a Macintosh XL computer, and printed on an Imagewriter printer. This new printer makes a much better looking product, with upper and lower case and smaller type, instead of the upper case only of the previous issues. The column headings "Bulletin No.," "Page," "Index term" have been dropped in the new layout, except for the first page. As the index runs to seventy-six pages, it would have been advisable to print these column heads on every page. Another minor criticism of something which first appears in this issue is the fact that continuations of headings onto another line run flush with the left-hand margin, which means they break up "Bulletin No." and "Page" columns. They should have been indented slightly to the right of the beginning of the "Index term" column, as had been done in previous issues. This would enhance even more the appearance which has been helped by the use of this new printer.

To summarize, this is an essential and inexpensive tool for all those who subscribe to the *Cataloging Service Bulletin.*

Barbara E. Brown

64.   Salinger, Florance A., and Eileen Zagon. **Notes for Catalogers: A Sourcebook for Use with AACR 2.** White Plains, N.Y., Knowledge Industry, 1985. 347p. bibliog. index. (Professional Librarian Series). $34.50; $27.50pa. LC 84-21770. ISBN 0-86729-099-4; 0-86729-098-6pa.

Broader than their first work, *Monograph Cataloging Notes*, this book covers the construction, wording, and appropriateness of cataloging notes for all types of library materials covered in *AACR2* with the exception of early printed monographs. To be used by catalogers in conjunction with *AACR2*, this collection of examples of notes does not contain the rationale behind their development or application. The *LC Cataloging Service Bulletin* and the Library of Congress cataloging records are the chief source of the author's information. Instead of basing notes for chapter 4, "Manuscripts," on *AACR2*, the authors use the Library of Congress's guide by Henson entitled *Archives, Personal Papers and Manuscripts.* Chapter 9, "Machine-Readable Data Files," could have been more complete but the authors lacked access to the 1984 ALA *Guidelines.* Organized numerically by chapter and within by rule number, *Notes for Catalogers* includes a brief but key bibliography and an extensive subject index.

This will be a must purchase for the cataloging departments of all libraries doing original cataloging and for library schools training would-be catalogers. [R: JAL, July 85, p. 179]

Ann Allan

65.   Wallace, Danny P. **The User Friendliness of the Library Catalog.** Champaign, Ill., Graduate School of Library and Information Science, University of Illinois, 1984. 42p. (Occasional Papers, No. 163). $3.00pa. ISSN 0276-1769.

The term *user-friendly* is frequently used in connection with online public access catalogs and other automated library systems designed for public use. Wallace applies the concept of user friendliness to the card catalog and to traditional cataloging practice. A number of long-standing and largely unresolved issues are interpreted in the light of the idea of user friendliness. Among these are the purpose of the catalog, the form of the catalog (card vs. book or COM), the basic arrangement of the catalog (dictionary vs. divided), the content of catalog records, and the nature of catalog entries. Wallace concludes that while the literature bearing on these issues clearly shows a concern for the user, "this concern has been mostly unsystematic and has resulted in the implementation of methodologies and systems that have sometimes been of questionable value and almost always based on untested assumptions regarding the needs and wants of catalog users." Although brief, this work represents a thorough review of the relevant literature and provides a useful historical context to current discussions of user friendliness in online catalogs.

Joe A. Hewitt

66.   Wynar, Bohdan S., and Arlene G. Taylor. **Introduction to Cataloging and Classification.** 7th ed. Littleton, Colo., Libraries Unlimited, 1985. 641p. illus. bibliog. index. (Library Science Text Series). $35.00; $21.50pa. LC 85-23147. ISBN 0-87287-512-1; 0-87287-485-0pa.

For over twenty years, successive editions of this text have appeared, and it is probable that a majority of those currently cataloging have had much of their basic training with "Wynar." The present, seventh edition is the second to be undertaken by Taylor, and the content, organization and presentation continue to improve with each version.

The section on descriptive cataloging under AACR2 has been altered extensively to provide more discussion and explanation and less direct repetition of the rules themselves. LC rule interpretations have been incorporated in a number of cases, making it easier for students and practitioners to create records which conform to general national practice. MARC formats and some coding information have been included, although newcomers to the field probably would benefit from a more thorough treatment.

The section on the subject approach to information has been updated, but continues to be a considerably more summary presentation of both classification and subject headings than that for descriptive cataloging. In view of the increasing attention being given to subject access of various kinds and in varying types of catalogs, an augmented discussion of this important aspect of cataloging is to be desired.

The emphasis on computer-based cataloging has increased, although students will need considerably more information than given here before they will be comfortable preparing cataloging information for input via a terminal—and the field has moved so rapidly that, despite the updating, there is no index entry for "microcomputers."

The typography and layout have been improved, and the book is easy to use. "Wynar" (or, increasingly, "Taylor") should continue as a frequently used textbook—while waiting for the eighth edition.   C. Donald Cook

Authority Control

√ 67. Burger, Robert H. **Authority Work: The Creation, Use, Maintenance, and Evaluation of Authority Records and Files.** Littleton, Colo., Libraries Unlimited, 1985. 126p. illus. bibliog. index. $23.50. LC 85-6791. ISBN 0-87287-491-5.

Basic information on the purpose, creation, and operation of authority files (both manual and automated), previously scattered widely, has now been brought together in the first general text specifically devoted to this topic. It is timely in view of the increased attention being given to standards for computer-based records.

The book is divided into "General Principles," "Creating Authority Records and Implementing Authority Systems," "Use and Maintenance of Authority Systems," "Measurement and Evaluation," summary descriptions of several major operating systems, discussion of future trends, and a substantial appendix on the LC MARC authorities format.

Personal names, corporate and conference names, geographic names, uniform titles, and series or serials are included, but (except as these types of headings may be used as subjects) there is no consideration of subject authority control; coverage is more limited than the title would imply.

Not unexpectedly, almost two-thirds of the text deals with computer-based authority work, and most of the discussion is helpful. Although there is wide use of authority control through bibliographic utilities, the complex problem of varying authorities for different clients is not addressed. Imbedded in the discussion of the MARC format are suitable explanations of

more elaborate reference and history structures and the recording of source information and catalogers' supporting notes; the relatively brief presentation of the manual authority file scarcely suggests that these types of information are often needed. Bi- or multilingual authority control is not considered. Most of the book treats the topic at a middle level of sophistication; in some cases assuming knowledge which the novice or student will not have, in others providing explanations which are not needed by the experienced cataloger.

The book partially fills a gap which existed in the professional literature, but it is to be hoped that this may be, in effect, the precursor of a more comprehensive work in the future.
        C. Donald Cook

Classification and Classification Schemes

68. Anderson, Jacqulyn, comp. **How to Classify and Catalog Media: Technical Processes Guide 2.** Nashville, Tenn., Broadman Press, 1984. 92p. illus. $5.95 spiralbound. LC 84-21426. ISBN 0-8054-3709-6.

69. Anderson, Jacqulyn, comp. **How to Process Media: Technical Processes Guide 1.** Nashville, Tenn., Broadman Press, 1984. 64p. illus. $5.95 spiralbound. LC 84-21436. ISBN 0-8054-3710-X.

Intended to give basic guidelines on library technical processing to nonprofessional personnel, usually volunteers, in church media libraries, these two handbooks serve a useful purpose. Hardly a substitute for professional coursework, they can, nevertheless, be used as study guides as well as manuals of practice. The manual on processing gives direction in preparing materials for circulation. The manual on cataloging and classification gives directions in the use of standard tools suggesting that church libraries use the eleventh abridged edition of the Dewey Decimal Classification System combined with the 200 class for religion from the nineteenth unabridged edition. It also suggests use of the *Sears List of Subject Headings*. This standard approach will provide the most useful access to the materials in the collections. Illustrations of practice and explanations of various facets of the processes, such as the explanation of the 200 class of Dewey, focus on topics concerned with Christian religion. Broadman Press is affiliated with the Southern Baptist church.
        JoAnn V. Rogers

70. Austin, Derek, and Mary Dykstra. **PRECIS: A Manual of Concept Analysis and Subject Indexing.** 2d ed. London, British

Library, 1984. 397p. index. £8.50pa. ISBN 0-7123-1008-8.

PRECIS is a method of subject indexing developed for the *British National Bibliography* in the early 1970s. Other indexing agencies such as the National Film Board of Canada have since adopted PRECIS techniques, and the author reports growing international interest in the system. This new edition is proffered in response to questions raised in library school courses and indexing workshops held in several countries. While the basic structure and components of PRECIS (PREserved Context Index System) are thoroughly delineated in this manual, the specific properties, codes, and "operators" of the system are also detailed. Although the foreword notes that some recent codes developed for the use of PRECIS in other languages are not included, it explains that extra procedures have been added and some complex solutions to indexing problems have been streamlined since the first edition. Since the production of a PRECIS index includes both human indexing and the use of a machine-held thesaurus, a number of chapters explain the technical aspects of thesaurus construction. The presence of exercises at the end of most chapters as well as the systematic approach and frequent examples seem to make this title most useful as a text, although the eleven-page index could provide some limited quick-reference access in environments where PRECIS is used. Those seeking in-depth detail on PRECIS will find it in this manual.   Mary Ardeth Gaylord

71. **Canadian Subject Headings.** 2d ed. Ottawa, National Library of Canada, 1985. 477p. index. $22.20pa. ISBN 0-660-11786-X.

The first edition of this work (see *ARBA* 80, entry 207), published nearly eight years ago in 1978, but with a 1976 cutoff date, is now out-of-print. Intervening changes in subject analysis make a significant impact on this second edition, but in no way affect its stated goal of compatibility with the ninth edition of *Library of Congress Subject Headings* (see *ARBA* 82, entry 258) and its supplements. The new Canadian list is designed, as before, to complement that work as needed to express concepts either uniquely Canadian, or of major interest to Canadians. Its approximately 20 percent increase in bulk permits it to expand the number of "representative" headings for use as examples of subject retrieval in their special fields.

Related to this aim is the greater application of pattern headings, free-floating subdivisions, numerous instructions on the interpretation, use, and construction of headings, and similar LCSH devices. Forty-five pages of introductory material include extended comments

on divergencies from LCSH, cross-references, Canadian acts, treaties, geographic names and chronological subdivisions, the relation to the *Répertoire de vedettes-materière* (9th ed., RVM, 1983), and similar aids. An index to specific points discussed, and a glossary of terms employed in *CSH 2* complete the English portion, which is followed by a parallel French introduction and an English-French three-page bibliography. Regular supplements are planned. The first will list all *CSH 1* headings which have been changed or cancelled in *CSH 2*. American as well as Canadian libraries will find this a useful addition to the growing arsenal of subject analysis tools.   Jeanne Osborn

72. Castonguay, Russell. **A Comparative Guide to Classification Schemes for Local Government Documents Collections.** Westport, Conn., Greenwood Press, 1984. 144p. bibliog. index. $35.00. LC 83-26594. ISBN 0-313-24208-9.

What should we do with these government documents? Eventually, almost all library directors are asked or ask this question. Academic libraries are likely to have collections of U.S. federal, international, state, foreign and local documents. Public libraries usually have U.S. federal, state, and, with luck, a good collection of local documents. Special libraries have some of all of these types. Should we classify and integrate them into the collection, catalog them, keep them separate or ... what?

This work is a unique and excellent beginning to providing answers to this troubling issue, particularly as it applies to local government documents. It is not *the* answer, but it certainly sheds much-needed light by providing information about the nature of the issue and the alternatives available to those who want to do more than simply toss local documents in a vertical file as a temporary stop-over to the trash can.

The issue of local documents is well posed in the first chapter. The local document is defined and the current state of knowledge regarding problems of acquisition, bibliographic control, reference, publicity, retention, and organization are well reviewed. The focus of the work, however, is on the organization and indexing of the local documents collection. Seventeen different classification systems that have been used for arranging local documents are carefully described and evaluated. These systems range from widely used ones, such as LC and DDC, to those used in only one or two places, such as the Harvard University and University of Makerere systems. Examples of applications of each system are given and strengths and weaknesses noted. When published analyses of the systems have appeared these are cited and discussed. Comparisons are made across systems when appropriate. The author is careful to distinguish between the archival-based systems and the subject-arrangement systems and the advantages and disadvantages of these two distinct approaches to arrangement.

As noted earlier, this work is unique—and has long been needed. It brings together in one source the currently available options for handling local documents and judges them according to a systematic set of criteria. In general, the evaluations are excellent and provide a basis for making a decision about use. In a few cases, however, the evaluations needed more critical attention to appropriateness for application to documents from several jurisdictions. A summary of the evaluation section, by way of advice to the library director struggling with the decision of how to organize and access all the library's government documents, would have been a useful addition.

The last section in the volume, "Indexing of Local Government Documents," is both useful and disappointing. It does print out some of the thesauri available for use in indexing documents and discusses a few of the automated indexing systems that are being used. It is unfortunate that this section was not expanded to discuss other thesauri, indexing systems, and online databases appropriate to local documents problems. A brief evaluative discussion that integrated this section on indexing with the comparative analyses of the classification schemes would have been very useful.

Fortunately, the absence of these desired "enhancements" do not detract from this valuable work. While it is probably too much to expect every library director to read it, it should certainly be read by every documents librarian before any decisions are made regarding the arrangement and indexing of local documents and their relationship to the rest of the library's collections. [R: LJ, 1 Nov 84, p. 2014]

Robert V. Williams

73. **DC& Decimal Classification: Additions, Notes and Decisions.** Albany, N.Y., Forest Press/Lake Placid Education Foundation, 1985. 87p. (*DC&*, Vol. 4, No. 5). free pa.

The first issue of volume 4 of this title was dated June 1980. It and successive issues form a supplemental updating service for the *Dewey Decimal Classification and Relative Index*, nineteenth edition (see *ARBA* 80, entry 210), just as earlier volumes 1-3 did for *DDC* editions 16 through 18. Forest Press sends copies free of charge to all edition 19 purchasers who return the postcard enclosed in volume 1 of the set.

The Press also honors requests in writing from Abridged Edition 11 purchasers.

The format of each *DC&* issue is fairly standard. First comes news of administrative changes; newly released schedules (e.g., extensive revisions, separately published, or foreign-language editions); pertinent committee work; exhibits, conferences, workshops, etc.; price changes; letters from the field; and the like. All this is followed by a list of corrections, changes, and new numbers which usually occupies some three-quarters of each issue, and is arranged by *DDC* volume and page. Blank pages are appended for user notes. The service is crucial for keeping primary volumes of the edition up-to-date, particularly in view of soaring costs, both of time and of money, needed to develop fully revised new editions of such a comprehensive, detailed classification scheme.   Jeanne Osborn

74. **DDC, Dewey Decimal Classification. 004-006 Data Processing and Computer Science and Changes in Related Disciplines.** Julianne Beall and others. Albany, N.Y., Forest Press/Lake Placid Education Foundation, 1985. 66p. index. $10.00pa. LC 85-1667. ISBN 0-910608-36-9.

The "001.6 : Data Processing" section of the 1979 *Dewey Decimal Classification and Relative Index*, nineteenth edition (see *ARBA* 80, entry 210) was nearly identical to its 1971, eighteenth edition predecessor, but eight years is a long time in the rapidly expanding computer field. The present revision/expansion discontinues that one-page schedule in favor of a fourteen-page development of three previously unassigned sections: 004-006. It further cancels the nineteenth edition subsection "621.38195 : Computers in General," moving and elaborating that sequence into 621.39, which had formerly housed a waste-basket collection: "Other Branches of Electrical Engineering." This second move may prove less satisfactory, since the subsections "621.393 : Rural Electrification," "621.394 : Electrification," and "621.396 : Conduction and Induction Heating," are left like islands in an inhospitable sea. However, for a notoriously overcrowded class 600, the operation, while not promising full recovery, offers an acceptable prognosis for the patient's survival.

New locations range from "Data Security," and "Micro- and Supercomputers," through "Artificial Intelligence" and "Computer Graphics." The revision offers an index to topics, which carries references to post-nineteenth edition locations (e.g., "384.34 : Electronic Mail") as well as to scattered nineteenth edition locations (e.g., "519.7 : Programming Mathematics"). It carries also its own "Manual of Application," and a glossary of some 150 terms, a table of corrections, changes, and new numbers from the basic three volumes of *DDC19*, and from the 1982 *Manual on the Use of the Dewey Decimal Classification: Edition 19* (see *ARBA* 84, entry 152).   Jeanne Osborn

75. Dershem, Larry D., comp. **Library of Congress Classification Class K Subclass K Law [General] Cumulative Schedule and Index.** Littleton, Colo., published for the American Association of Law Libraries by Fred B. Rothman, 1985. 288p. index. (AALL Publications Series, No. 24). $60.00 looseleaf. LC 85-1885. ISBN 0-8377-0122-8.

The American Association of Law Libraries issues a number of very helpful publications designed for law librarians and other professionals whose library collections contain legal materials. The publications in the AALL series range from law librarianship handbooks to manuals on LC classification schedules for legal materials.

This new publication is the twenty-fourth in the series, and it complements two earlier series' publications on LC classification, both of which were compiled by Dershem. These earlier works are a cumulative index to Subclass KF (no. 18) and a cumulative schedule to Subclass KF (no. 20). Both concern classification schemes for books on the law of the United States. The author's new publication cumulates Subclass K, Law (General), by updating the 1977 LC schedule on Subclass K. This publication concerns the classification scheme for legal materials on general topics of law, rather than the law of the United States. Thus, broad legal subjects, such as jurisprudence and comparative law, are classified in the new publication. The author plans to update the cumulative schedule quarterly, following the publication of each *LC Classification Addition and Changes List.*

A valuable compilation which provides needed updating for the schedule for general law subjects. Helpful for law catalogers, especially those who do original cataloging.

Susan Beverly Kuklin

76. **A Dialogue on the Subject Catalogue: J. M. Perreault, "A Representative of the New Left in American Subject Cataloguing": A Review Essay on Sanford Berman's *The Joy of Cataloging*, with Response by Sanford Berman.** Champaign, Ill., Graduate School of Library and Information Science, University of Illinois, 1984. 64p. (Occasional Papers No. 161). $3.00pa. ISSN 0276-1769.

Since information organization for retrieval is central to librarianship, it is fitting that librarians debate cataloging theory and practice. This slim volume embodies a rather

vociferous exchange between two leading representatives of the cataloging world: J. M. Perreault of the University of Alabama Library in Huntsville and Sanford Berman of the Hennepin County Library, Minnesota. Unfortunately, as their editor observes, their exchange generates somewhat more heat than light, but it will serve to bring to many librarians and to students of librarianship the current burning issues in cataloging—issues which affect all of librarianship.

The volume begins with Perreault's extended review of Berman's recent *The Joy of Cataloging* (Oryx Press, 1981). But even the title of the review is unnecessarily provocative. Why should Berman's attempts to taylor access points to the vocabulary of his public and to reduce the use of derogatory terms for groups of persons qualify him as "a representative of the new left"? But Perreault does offer important concerns, centered on systematic consistency, predictability, and conflicts between "proper" terminology and actual usage. Although subject cataloging dominates the discussion, some passing attention is given to minor aspects of AACR2.

Unfortunately, Berman responds not with a reasoned essay but by refutations of particular points, followed by Perreault's rebuttals, not once, but for three rounds, until they, apparently, give up trying to convince each other of anything.

These are important issues, and librarians, especially catalogers, will benefit from, and perhaps even enjoy, exposure to this match.

James D. Anderson

77. Dykstra, Mary. **PRECIS: A Primer.** London, British Library; distr., Halifax, School of Library Service, 1985. 262p. bibliog. index. $15.95pa. ISBN 0-7123-1022-3.

The author suggests that this primer be used as an introductory text or companion volume to the more detailed, "comprehensive or advanced" title Derek Austin's *PRECIS: A Manual of Concept Analysis and Subject Indexing* (see entry 70). While the author admits that this primer has "of necessity drawn from" the *Manual*, she sets out to introduce the information specialist, student, or beginning indexer to the PREserved Context Index System (PRECIS). Originally developed for the *British National Bibliography*, PRECIS has also been used in the batch-mode production of printed, alphabetic subject indexes at the National Library of Australia and UTLAS (University of Toronto Library Automation Systems). The bulk of this volume offers textbook-style discussions of the indexing syntax and thesaural relationships which are unique to PRECIS.

Interspersed with examples and illustrations, most chapters end in exercises aimed at the student, although the last chapter briefly addresses current Canadian and British applications of PRECIS in online retrieval. A seven-page index assists the reader in quickly locating a particular topic, and makes this volume of possible reference value to those producing or using a PRECIS index. While in some ways an abbreviated approach to part of the information found in Austin's *Manual*, this primer retains a detailed focus of primary use to the student or researcher needing a technical outline of PRECIS methods. [R: JAL, Nov 85, p. 311]

Mary Ardeth Gaylord

78. **L.C. Subject Headings Weekly Lists: A Working Cumulation 1984.** Lists 1-19. Detroit, Gale, 1985. 249p. $225.00pa. ISBN 0-8103-1796-6; ISSN 8755-366X.

Throughout the year, the Library of Congress releases information on new, changed, and cancelled subject headings and references in its *Library of Congress Headings Weekly Lists.* In some cases, further revision of headings is made, so the weekly lists will not always have the final approved headings or references. Final versions of headings and references are published in the annual *Supplement to Library of Congress Subject Headings* and updated editions of *Library of Congress Headings in Microform,* although these publications do not always appear on a timely schedule. Issued monthly, the approximately fifty weekly lists for 1984 cost $65.00. Gale Research Company has begun cumulating the weekly lists into a single alphabetical sequence. The first installment covers lists 1-19, 1 January-7 May 1984. Cumulation is to continue throughout the year. For this convenience, Gale is asking $225.00 for 1984 and $335.00 for 1985.

The Gale cumulations will make information on new subject headings more easily available. An explanation is needed, however, of the symbols used by the Library of Congress to indicate changes and references. Catalogers will know what they mean, but reference librarians and others may need a little assistance.

James D. Anderson

79. **Library of Congress Classification, Class K, Subclass KD, Law of the United Kingdom and Ireland: Cumulative Schedule and Index.** Larry D. Dershem, comp. Littleton, Colo., Fred B. Rothman, 1985. 431p. index. (AALL Publ. Series No. 25). $75.00 looseleaf. LC 85-25597. ISBN 0-8377-0124-4.

This is a looseleaf cumulation of the Library of Congress classification schedule KD (Law of the United Kingdom and Ireland). It

will be updated quarterly, upon publication of the Additions and Changes bulletin issued by the Library of Congress, and purchasers of the volume are entitled to three updates free of further charge.

The typeface is good quality typescript, and the text occupies only two-thirds of each page. This leaves a lot of room for expansion. A slight error in printing caused four sheets to be mismatched: page 199 is backed by page 204; page 203 by page 200; page 423 by page 428; and page 427 by page 424. Dividers are provided to separate the different sections of KD and the index. It would be a good idea to provide another divider for the tables of form subdivisions, to separate them from the schedule KDK (Republic of Ireland).

Because it provides in one sequence up-to-date access to the class KD, this cumulation would be of great use to those libraries which have large collections of books concerning the law of the UK, and which, therefore, require fast access to the correct classification number when cataloging new books.

The price is reasonable for those who would use it frequently. Others may be satisfied with copies of the LC class KD schedule, published in 1973, along with the Gale cumulation of additions and changes through 1983 and any more recent cumulations, also the latest issues of *Additions and Changes* published by the Library of Congress.

Of course, using the cumulation is much easier, as one does not have to interpret instructions such as "Change table number"; "Add table number"; "Delete 's' from 'products'." This work has already been done.

Barbara E. Brown

80. Momeni, Mahvash K. **Adaptations of DDC in the Middle East.** Champaign, Ill., Graduate School of Library and Information Science, University of Illinois, 1985. 41p. bibliog. $3.00pa. ISSN 0276-1769.

Strong evidence of the continuing vitality of the *Dewey Decimal Classification and Relative Index* (see *ARBA* 80, entry 210) is its wide use in translation and/or adaptation throughout the world. This study of the four translations (Arabic, Farsi, Hindi, and Turkish) most prevalent in the Middle East recognizes primarily the sociological factors such as religion, language, customs, history, etc., which necessitate local adaptation, but argues for a universal "MEDCC" (Middle Eastern Edition of DDC) to be used through the area. In developing its thesis, it first reviews the historical backgrounds of the four existing translations. Then it analyzes comparatively all major adaptations in each DDC class except 000 Generalities, 500 Pure Sciences, and 600 Technology, where it assumes only minor differences caused by sociological factors. It closes with summaries of the significant characteristics, the shortcomings, and future needs of existing MEDCCs, and makes specific recommendations for MEDCC development. The recommendations include avoidance of letters in the notation, closer cooperation with the Decimal Classification Editorial Policy Committee, and use of recommended options and other practices from the more recent editions of official DDC schedules wherever possible. The text is accompanied by twelve illustrative tables and a four-page bibliography.   Jeanne Osborn

81. Reed-Scott, Jutta. **Issues in Retrospective Conversion: Report of a Study Conducted for the Council on Library Resources.** Washington, D.C., Bibliographic Service Development Program, Council on Library Resources, 1984. 57p. $3.00pa. LC 84-15548.

Relatively short, this report of a CLR-sponsored study, is thorough in meeting its objectives of assessing current levels of retrospective conversion and of exploring key issues facing libraries wishing to convert bibliographic records to machine-readable form economically and effectively.

The report is organized into four parts. The first section provides an overview and framework for review, including a definition of retrospective conversion, a summary of past efforts, a description of current activities, and a projection of future trends. The second part presents major approaches to retrospective conversion and library strategies for it. The third part addresses general issues and problems, including the economics of retrospective conversion and the quest for a national database. The final section offers five new initiatives toward a national strategy for retrospective conversion, six specific recommendations, followed by a three task implementation strategy. A selected bibliography and a brief description of the ARL National Collection Inventory Project conclude the report.

The report advocates that U.S. research libraries become actively responsible for developing a coordinated program with the Library of Congress and bibliographic utilities. It recommends establishing priorities for converting records, developing a fund-raising plan to support the conversion, adopting agreed-upon standards, and giving high priority to implementation of the Linked System Project. The report's recommendations have been actively undertaken under the sponsorship of the CLR and ARL.

This documentation provides an excellent summary and update for both librarians directly involved in managing retrospective conversion projects and those wanting to stay abreast of current professional issues. [R: LJ, July 85, p. 160; WLB, Mar 85, p. 495]
          Danuta A. Nitecki

82. **Subject Thesaurus for Bowker Online Databases.** New York, R. R. Bowker, 1984. 571p. $25.00pa. ISBN 0-8352-1889-9.

The book provides over eighty-five thousand subject headings, including more than thirty-four thousand with cross-references, for three R. R. Bowker databases: BOOKS IN PRINT, ULRICH'S INTERNATIONAL PERIODICALS DIRECTORY, and AMERICAN MEN AND WOMEN OF SCIENCE. The subject headings list for BOOKS IN PRINT contains headings from various sources and these are listed separately: the Library of Congress Subject Heading File, the Children's Books in Print Subject Heading File, the Forthcoming Books Subject Heading File, and the Paperbound Books Subject Heading File. Each subject heading listed is followed by a number in brackets which represents a searchable numeric code for that exact heading. Scope notes and cross-references are also provided whenever necessary.

It is significant to note that Bowker's philosophy of assigning subject headings is to be "explicit rather than general." The need to search past the main entry and to consider the typically numerous subheadings is emphasized. For example, the topic of journalism has thirty-eight subheadings and twenty-two *see also* references in the Library of Congress Subjects list. Differences between the subject headings used in these various Bowker databases also become readily apparent when studying this book. For example, Children's Subjects lists Clocks and Watches--Vocational Guidance, while Library of Congress Subjects uses Clock and Watch Making—Vocational Guidance.

The stated aim in producing this book was to "provide the online searcher of Bowker's databases with a comprehensive yet concise guide to the searchable subjects and their numeric codes used on the databases." It accomplishes this goal, but the value of the publication needs to be considered. While reference librarians and online searchers might profit from reading the preface, few practical uses of this publication can be imagined. Most online searches of these Bowker databases will not require the extensive breakdown of assigned subject headings provided in this thesaurus. In most cases searchers will rely on the free-text searching capabilities of BRS and DIALOG or, if the exact subject heading is known, a search of the appropriate print volumes will be suggested. Recommended only for those search services which maintain an extensive collection of search aids. Greg Byerly

83. **Theory of Subject Analysis: A Sourcebook.** Lois Mai Chan, Phyllis A. Richmond, and Elaine Svenonius, eds. Littleton, Colo., Libraries Unlimited, 1985. 415p. index. $36.00. LC 85-15978. ISBN 0-87287-489-3.

Theory of Subject Analysis is a collection of writings, for the most part excerpts from books and reprints of journal articles which are well known and widely cited, and which focus on the theoretical and philosophical rather than the practical and technical. The editors have defined subject analysis broadly to include vocabulary structuring (i.e., construction of tools such as classifications) and subject indexing, which in general and contemporary terms, refers to the indication of topic by any meaningful string of alphanumeric characters. The selections, arranged chronologically in order to show the history or development of ideas and concepts, begin with an excerpt from Charles A. Cutter's *Rules for a Dictionary Catalog* (1876) and end with a 1982 reprint on the "Complimentarity of Natural and Indexing Languages." Each selection is preceded by an editor's note which ensures continuity and usually provides a historical setting or offers insight on what follows. In the note preceding "Subjects and the Sense of Position" (Patrick Wilson), the editors imply that we have not routinely troubled to "address and pursue with philosophical rigor fundamental questions about the way we organize information." This volume can certainly play an important role in assisting those who wish to do just that.

Theory of Subject Analysis performs the service of collecting significant thought on the topic of subject analysis in one place for the use of students, teachers, and practitioners. It has a personnel/corporate name index and a subject index. It is intended to stand as a companion volume to *Foundations of Cataloging: A Sourcebook* (Libraries Unlimited, 1985).

Jeanne Somers

Special Materials

84. Baker, Barry B., and Lynne D. Lysiak, eds. **From Tape to Product: Some Practical Considerations on the Use of OCLC-MARC Tapes.** Ann Arbor, Mich., Pierian Press, 1985. 121p. bibliog. index. $29.50. LC 85-60594. ISBN 0-87650-191-9.

Papers presented at an April 1982 conference sponsored by the Resources and Technical Services Section of the Southeastern Library Association (and subsequently updated through December 1983) afford a technical and a practical guide to the use of OCLC archival MARC tapes for local systems and COM catalogs. This volume contains twelve papers divided into four sections: "Tape Uses and Format," "Tape Processing," "Products: Problems and Solutions," and "Maintenance Considerations." It includes bibliographic citations for each article, a selected bibliography and an index. The meat of the volume is the twenty-five-page paper by Michele I. Dalehite, project analyst at SOLINET, "MARC Format on Tape: A Tutorial," and probably worth the price of the book. In a technical but clear and well-illustrated discussion, Dalehite details the structure of an OCLC record down to the bit and byte levels, the specific differences between OCLC-MARC and Library of Congress MARC, and the problems in converting records from the extended ASCII (American Standard Code for Information Interchange) used by OCLC to EBCDIC (Extended Binary Coded Decimal Interchange Code) used by IBM hardware. The other articles add details on using the archival tapes for producing a COM catalog (a lengthy exposition of Georgia State University's experiences) and in local systems using CLSI, DataPhase, and a NOTIS-based system as well as a locally developed system. These will be of interest to readers concerned with the specific uses, but the overview of the OCLC-MARC tapes, the "Tutorial," and two papers on tape processing should serve anyone considering using the tapes (although the discussion focuses on SOLINET procedures). [R: JAL, Nov 85, p. 316]

Hwa-Wei Lee and K. Mulliner

85. Crawford, Walt. **MARC for Library Use: Understanding the USMARC Formats.** White Plains, N.Y., Knowledge Industry, 1984. 221p. bibliog. index. (Professional Librarian Series). $36.50; $28.50pa. LC 84-23376. ISBN 0-86729-120-6; 0-86729-119-2pa.

As Henriette Avram notes in her foreword, "this publication should provide the basis of understanding for those new to MARC, as well as those who have experience with MARC ... useful to librarians at all levels, technicians involved in library automation, and students and teachers in library schools." It offers the first comprehensive work on MARC and is written in an understandable style, supplemented by helpful, illustrative figures and examples.

The book is arranged in twelve chapters, offering a detailed exposition of MARC formats, their application to different material types (e.g., books, serials, manuscripts, music) and their utilization for authorities and holdings, as well as for links between records and fields. A historic review of the development of USMARC and a summary of the extensions of MARC by the bibliographic utilities are presented. A practical discussion of the use of MARC in the library environment is addressed, including focus on strategies for retrospective conversion. The three appendices include (1) a full, though annotated, reproduction of the "USMARC Formats: Underlying Principles" approved in 1982 by MARBI and the USMARC advisory group, (2) perhaps the first published glossary of MARC and related terms, and (3) a lengthy though selected bibliography and reading list. An index concludes the volume.

There are numerous more technical documentations on MARC, geared primarily for catalogers (e.g., *MARC Formats for Bibliographic Data*) as well as guides provided by such services as OCLC, RLIN, WLN, and UTLAS. This book, however, offers an excellent overview, with sufficient detail to inform librarians who will need a basic understanding of MARC to deal with vendors and to consider automated systems for local applications such as online catalogs. Danuta A. Nitecki

86. Dodd, Sue A., and Ann M. Sandberg-Fox. **Cataloging Microcomputer Files: A Manual of Interpretation for AACR 2.** Chicago, American Library Association, 1985. 272p. illus. index. $37.50. LC 85-1359. ISBN 0-8389-0401-7.

The proliferation of microcomputer software in recent years has presented a real challenge to catalogers—especially in the schools, public libraries, and undergraduate libraries where collections are growing most rapidly. Chapter 9 of *AACR2* was written with mainframe computers in mind. In 1984, some assistance was provided by ALA's publication of *Guidelines for Using AACR2 Chapter 9 for Cataloging Micro-computer Software*, but controversies remain and less experienced catalogers sorely need guidance in understanding and applying the rules.

Help is provided by this excellent manual which was prepared by authors who are both experts and practitioners. Dodd wrote *Cataloging Machine Readable Data Files: An Interpretative Manual* (ALA, 1982) and both authors participated in the preparation of the *Guidelines* and of the MARC format for machine-readable data files. They have written a comprehensive, detailed, very understandable guide which incorporates their own very helpful suggestions for handling the special problems of physical and file description. After a brief overview of microcomputer hardware and software, the authors present a rule-by-rule examination of chapter 9 which explains, interprets, and applies the

original text and also relevant sections of the *Guidelines.* There follows a detailed chapter on the application of chapter 21 ("Choice of Access Points"), chapters on classification and subject headings, and finally twelve step-by-step cataloging examples. Catalogers who have been struggling with the new technology may well find this much-needed book an answer to their prayers. Joseph W. Palmer

87. Hoduski, Bernadine Abbott, ed. **Cataloging Government Documents: A Manual of Interpretation for AACR2.** Chicago, American Library Association, 1984. 259p. index. $49.00. LC 84-6499. ISBN 0-8389-3304-1.

In the past, government documents have been the forgotten children of library catalogs. They have generally been relegated to separate uncataloged collections or stuffed into vertical files that only the most knowledgeable could effectively use. In the few instances in which libraries did catalog them, they were frequently given overly simple cataloging that did not adequately reflect their complex origins from multiple corporate and personal authors. The implementation of AACR2 did little to change the situation and, in some ways, had a further negative effect on the willingness of libraries to give adequate cataloging to these materials. While this problem has been most apparent for U.S. federal documents, it is even more severe for state, local, international, and foreign national government documents.

In recent years several things have happened that have had positive results towards changing this situation. The most significant was the decision in 1976 by the Superintendent of Documents to begin using AACR in *Monthly Catalog* bibliographic records. The availability of these records through OCLC and other networks has made cataloging data easily accessible for most libraries. These events should encourage libraries of all types to give adequate cataloging to their government publications.

The publication of this manual is a timely contribution to this small trend and will, with luck, give it stimulus. The work is the result of a concerted effort by a special committee of ALA's Government Documents Roundtable (GODORT). The end product is a highly useful guide to the cataloger struggling to apply AACR2 to government documents.

Organization of the manual follows the rule format of *AACR2.* Explanations are a combination of the AACR2 rules themselves and additional comments specifically oriented towards applying the rule to government publications. Examples of applying the rules to documents are abundant and varied. The level of explanation from rule to rule and chapter to chapter in

AACR2 varies but the ones most pertinent to documents problems are well covered. References are given to Library of Congress rule interpretations that do not appear in *AACR2* itself. Particularly useful are the examples given to the handling of reports series code numbers and the explanations for the origins of these numbers (and other mysterious codes) by the various government agencies. An excellent index provides rapid access for those requiring information about the handling of a specific type of document or a vexing bit of information on the title page of a document.

Overall, the work is admirable. One could wish for more extensive treatment in some areas, such as the chapter on machine-readable data files, and for greater attention in the examples to international government bodies, but these can wait for a later edition, which will likely be necessary as changes occur in AACR2 rules and as the frequency and use of machine-readable files and international documents increases. This work should rightfully be (despite the high price) in a handy place on the desk of all original catalogers. [R: C&RL, Sept 85, p. 444; JAL, Nov 85, p. 299; LJ, 15 Apr 85, p. 60]

Robert V. Williams

88. Olson, Nancy B. **Cataloging of Audiovisual Materials: A Manual Based on AACR2.** 2d ed. Mankato, Minn., Minnesota Scholarly Press, 1985. 306p. illus. bibliog. index. $34.50pa. ISBN 0-933474-38-5.

If one were to wait until all of the problems associated with cataloging nonprint materials and entering them into records of the bibliographic utilities were solved, catalogers would never have the opportunity to receive the help that this manual provides. The first edition of this work, which is about half the length of this second edition, focuses on a limited number of cataloging examples and provides short explanations of a few parts of the description for each. The most significant change in this second edition is the inclusion of much more extensive discussions of the reasons for choices made. Olson's approach in the second edition provides the cataloger with a generalizable learning experience in addition to a specific example. This is a great improvement, although the user may find it more time-consuming to use. Once the principles are learned, however, the cataloger will find that a better understanding of the process is more valuable than numerous examples from which one must infer the principle in order to catalog the item in hand. Library of Congress Rule Interpretations as well as other guidelines relevant to different types of materials also are well integrated into the text and discussions.

In addition to the expansion of chapters from the first edition, new chapters on microcomputer software and serials are added, along with a useful chapter dealing with general considerations applicable to most nonprint. This is a practical and useful guide for catalogers containing enough new material to make purchase worthwhile. [R: JAL, Sept 85, p. 250; LJ, Aug 85, p. 71]

JoAnn V. Rogers

89. Olson, Nancy B. **Cataloging of Audiovisual Materials: A Manual Based on AACR 2, Supplement: Coding and Tagging for OCLC.** Mankato, Minn., Minnesota Scholarly Press, 1985. 78p. $15.00pa. ISBN 0-933474-39-3.

Meant to accompany the second edition of *Cataloging of Audiovisual Materials*, this supplement is a collection of the catalog cards in that work, but in OCLC input form. The illustrations appear exactly as they would look on the screen of an OCLC terminal, complete with fixed and variable fields, codes, tags and delimiters, and full bibliographic information. Included are examples for three OCLC formats, *Sound Recordings, Audiovisual Media,* and *Machine-readable Data Files.* Brief comments follow some of the examples interpreting more difficult applications of the OCLC documentation. Also included is a valuable wall chart that displays the coding of the 007 field used to set forth the physical description of an item. Olson explains the relationship between elements, fields, and records along with the purpose of codes, tags, delimiters, and indicators. Two OCLC user groups are promoted.

The illustrations are arranged in the same sequence as in the main volume and contain page references to it at the top of each record. A table of contents or an index by type of material would have been helpful as would headings across the top of the pages. A separate sheet of corrections accompany the text and point out a major error made when the second and third lines of the fixed fields were reversed. For libraries that are OCLC members, this supplement will be useful to input operators and/or catalogers in their catalog departments, depending upon which group is responsible for tagging functions. It will also be of significant value to students when as a part of their curriculum, they must catalog nonbook materials and work in the OCLC format. [R: LJ, 15 Nov 85, p. 68]

Ann Allan

90. **Photographic Cataloging Manual.** [By] Diana Shih and Miriam Tam. New York, Department of Library Services, American Museum of Natural History, 1984. 72p. $10.00 spiralbound.

This is a manual of the American Museum of Natural History's rules and procedures for the descriptive and subject cataloging of its million-image photographic collection. The collection deals with scientific, social, and historical subjects rather than with art. The manual is based on Anglo-American cataloging rules supplemented by the Library of Congress's rules for cataloging graphic materials; it is not written solely for the trained librarian.

The entire contents of the photographic collection were surveyed for two years with funding from the U.S. Department of Education Title II-C program, the National Endowment for the Humanities, and the Exxon Foundation. Gathering and surveying materials in individual collections with online access to both names and subjects was accomplished by a subsequent one-year grant from the U.S. Department of Education.

The descriptive cataloging section deals with photographs at the collection level whereas the subject cataloging portion deals with photographs at the subcollection or series level. An appendix describing the software developed for the project and an appendix containing worksheets are included.

Although this manual is a working document for the museum, the system used can be adopted and adapted by similar collections and can be useful for museum curators, archivists, and their staffs.   Kathleen J. Voigt

91.   Shaw, Sarah J., and Lauralee Shiere. **Sheet Music Cataloging and Processing: A Manual.** [Canton, Mass.], Music Library Association, 1984. 51p. illus. (MLA Technical Reports, No. 15). $11.75pa. LC 84-20734. ISBN 0-914954-34-2.

The authors prepared this guide for use with the Sheet Music Cataloging Project at Brown University. In this project, approximately forty-eight hundred sheet music titles were cataloged. The categories cataloged were World War I songs, World War II songs, songs by and about Afro-Americans, and musical settings of nineteenth-century American poetry. The project was carried out through the RLIN database, utilizing the MARC format, but the procedures can be applied directly to OCLC as well.

Since this booklet is an actual procedures manual, readers are taken step-by-step through the authority search procedures and field-by-field through the MARC format, with indications as to exactly how decisions should be made. Secondary sources to check for authority work are noted for all types of information included in the cataloging record, such as photographs, illustrations, and various types of corporate authors. Sample authority search cards

and entry cards can be found in the appendix. For libraries currently involved in cataloging sheet music collections, or for those which are contemplating such cataloging, this clearly written guide can be of assistance. Some procedures, such as those for authority checking, may also be useful for other libraries. [R: JAL, May 85, p. 117]   Allie Wise Goudy

92.   Weidow, Judy. **Music Cataloging Policy in the General Libraries.** Austin, Tex., The General Libraries, The University of Texas at Austin, 1984. 112p. (Contributions to Librarianship, No. 8). $15.00pa.

Music Cataloging Policy in the General Libraries presents a helpful guide for libraries seeking to develop their own music cataloging policies. For many catalogers who deal with music materials, and for paraprofessionals working with OCLC input. The author has presented the policies for music cataloging in effect at the University of Texas at Austin, and, for original catalog policies for scores and sound recordings, has provided a rationale for those decisions in the form of LC rule interpretations gathered from the *Cataloging Service Bulletin* and the *Music Cataloging Bulletin*. OCLC input standards for editing and original cataloging, based largely on communication with OCLC and AMIGOS, are also thoroughly covered. Sections on policies and procedures for authority work and authority file development may be especially useful for libraries grappling with changes resulting from AACR2. Ample examples are included, and the policies are clearly written. Although the manual certainly doesn't cover all questions which might arise, nor does it apply to all libraries, it does provide a framework for libraries desiring to write policy manuals or to "see how someone else does it." This should prove to be a very useful publication.   Allie Wise Goudy

CHILDREN'S AND YOUNG ADULT SERVICES

93.   **Coordinators of Children's and Young Adult Services in Public Library Systems Serving at Least 100,000 People.** Chicago, Association for Library Service to Children, American Library Association, 1984. 62p. $7.50 spiralbound. ISBN 0-8389-6774-4.

This nationwide directory is paperbound, the pages hinged by a plastic spiral. The print is large and well spaced in an easy-to-read format. Information tabulated alphabetically by state is printed in three vertical columns. In the left-hand column, the entry for the state library agency includes city and zip code, name of agency, and street address, followed by tabulation for each library system identified within the specific state. Information in the second column concerns the status of a coordinator position in children's services; young adult services in the third column. "No Position" means that there is no budgeted position; "Position Open" indicates a current vacancy.

Quoting Ann Carlson Weeks, executive director of the Association for Library Service to Children, "By indicating the geographical and organizational deficits and disparities of leadership in public library service to children and young adults, it is hoped that the *Directory* will continue to provide an impetus for the planning and development of stronger and more equitable public library service to youth throughout the U.S." The publication succeeds in accomplishing this, although the statistics would have been strengthened by the inclusion of the history of positions in each of the systems. Denver Public Library, for instance, employed a coordinator until 1981; such information for other systems would have lent more clarity to the overall trends indicated in the directory.

The directory stands as an important aid in planning the growth and development of library services, and as a tool in job search strategies. Purchase of the directory is recommended for children's and young adult departments in public and special libraries, teaching facilities, such as graduate schools in librarianship, and planning and evaluation offices where staff is concerned with the growth of library services to children and young adults.   Barbara Sproat

94. **Meeting the Challenge: Library Service to Young Adults.** Andre Gagnon and Ann Gagnon, eds. Ottawa, Canadian Library Association, 1985. 158p. $15.00pa. ISBN 0-88802-193-3.

Experts on library services to young adults have gathered ideas and experience to be shared during International Youth Year 1985.

A good historical overview given by L. J. Amey shows concern for young adult library services throughout Canada. Services range from good to very good—Saskatoon is qualified by Amey as "a model of progressive young adult library service."

Eva Martin reminds us of the radical changes that took place in the past ten years in services to teens. Martin stresses that services for YA are legitimate and important. They require an organized structure. Goals and objectives should be developed keeping in mind the community to be served. Input from YA themselves should be encouraged so that their

needs be well known. Marion L. Pape writes about barriers to services: funding, low esteem for young adults, lack of services supported by the library administration, school/public library cooperation and youth participation.

Well-known Ken Haycock says that to accomplish its mission the school library should "assist students to develop skills to process and use information effectively" (p. 31). Expectations for teacher-librarians are very high and support staff is essential. The school resource center should serve as learning laboratory.

The next two chapters are devoted to surveys of young adults and libraries. The first one reported by L. J. Amey studied the impact of print, nonprint, and mass media resources for young adults in their daily lives. Amey qualifies the YA as an information seeker. The second survey of the Regina Public Library reported by Williams Murray is on the informational and recreational needs of YA. This study shows how the library is still being used in its most traditional role: borrow books and do home work. Fewer than 20 percent of the YA used the library in a nontraditional role.

One of the most outstanding chapters of this publication is Sarah Landy's on "Teen Parents and the Role of the Library." It is very encouraging to find this chapter in a book on library services. Every librarian must read this chapter carefully and think it over and discuss it with his/her organization. It gives the reader an overview of and an insight into a dilemma of our society.

The third part of this book deals with collections. This is one of the best sections of this fine book. Jenkinson writes one of the finest accounts of Canadian novels as one that "captures the nuances of our country" (p. 93). Elliott then goes on to show how challenging it is to work as a school librarian and gives an overview of nonfiction materials for collection building. Fleming makes a plea for the classics: those landmarks of the past, still of interest to a minority that cannot be ignored. Deane reviews nonprint services, and White looks at selection tools and important information gathering strategies.

The only small defect of this book, if there is any, is the cover. It could have been much more attractive to be in tune with the dynamic approach of the publication. On the whole the book is a real gem and the Gagnons should be commended for collecting such fine pieces of writing.

Camille Côté

CHILDREN'S LITERATURE

Anthologies

95. **Poetry Anthologies for Children and Young People.** By Marycile E. Olexer. Chicago, American Library Association, 1985. 285p. index. $40.00. LC 85-6033. ISBN 0-8389-0430-0.

This book selection aid analyzes approximately three hundred selected anthologies of children's poetry. Volumes chosen for inclusion represent collections around a specific theme or character, rather than titles of general anthologies. Anthologies described here were selected for three age categories: preschool and primary grades, intermediate grades (4-6), and junior high grades (7-9). In addition to choosing a balanced list grade-wise, Olexer also attempted to include a representative number of titles for each type of poetry (i.e., haiku, ballads, nursery rhymes, etc.). Most books included are still available for purchase and were recommended or reviewed favorably in reputable publications. Criteria for inclusion are stated in the introduction.

Entries are arranged in three parts which correspond to the three grade levels. Each part is divided into two sections: anthologies of many poets' works and collections by a single poet. Part 1 has an additional section of nursery rhymes. Titles are alphabetical by author/compiler within each section. Information in each entry includes a complete bibliographic citation (ISBNs, LC numbers, and prices are not included), as well as a specific grade level designation. The annotations are well written and packed with information. They average about 350 words each in addition to sample or representative verses. Contents of anthologies are carefully described, and there are critical comments about the book's format, illustrations, design, style, and print readability, as well as the mood or tone of the poems, quality of the poetry, length of the verses, related similar titles, emphases of the poetry (story content vs. rhythm and rhyme, etc.), curricular uses, and special features such as inclusion of biographical notes, tips on whether the poems should be read to or read by the children, etc.

The interesting analyses coupled with the profusion of sample poems (almost 300 titles appear in the acknowledgments section) make this a very readable reference book. Its theme approach should be very useful to classroom teachers, school library/media specialists, and other professionals interested in children's literature. Two bibliographies are included. The first provides a briefly annotated list of books and magazines which served as sources of the poetry anthologies analyzed. The second one lists all additional recommended titles which appear in the text, but were not analyzed. An author/title index and a very important subject index contribute to making this a highly recommended selection guide. [R: WLB, Dec 85, p. 66]   Lois Buttlar

Bibliographies

96. Carroll, Frances Laverne, and Mary Meacham, eds. **Exciting, Funny, Scary, Short, Different, and Sad Books Kids Like about Animals, Science, Sports, Families, Songs, and Other Things.** Chicago, American Library Association, 1984. 192p. index. $10.00pa. LC 84-20469. ISBN 0-8389-0423-8.

"I Want Something to Make Me Laugh," "I Want a Short Book," and other typical demands provide the categories covered in this annotated bibliography.

Approximately one thousand titles for readers in grades two to five are identified; usually five to fifteen titles per category. Fifty librarians were involved in composing annotations designed to appeal to children.

Standard bibliographic information is provided for each entry. The index is for author and title; subject access is provided by the table of contents. A few titles appear in more than one list where appropriate.

The lists are not exhaustive but ring of titles that one would recommend to and that would be liked by children. Librarians and children will find these handy starting lists to which they will want to add new and/or other favorite titles. [R: BR, Sept/Oct 85, p. 54; EL, Sept/Oct 85, p. 31; SLJ, Sept 85, p. 44; SLMQ, Summer 85, p. 223; TN, Spring 85, p. 305; WLB, May 85, p. 624]   Phyllis J. Van Orden

97. Cascardi, Andrea E. **Good Books to Grow On: A Guide to Building Your Child's Library from Birth to Age Five.** New York, Random House/Warner Books, 1985. 130p. illus. index. $6.95pa. LC 85-7114. ISBN 0-446-38173-X.

It is the goal of Cascardi's well-intentioned work to assist and encourage parents "who want to be involved in reading to their children the best possible choices from the myriad books for pre-readers suddenly flooding the market" (introduction). To that end, she has drawn on the experiences and personal favorites of children's librarians, leaders of local parenting groups, book reviewers, and booksellers, specializing in children's materials to identify some three hundred "good" books for babies, toddlers, and preschoolers.

Included in the selection are fiction, informational books, concept books, illustrated classics, holiday tales, poetry, boardbooks, pop-ups, cloth books, photo books, wordless picture books, and familiar storybooks. The books are grouped according to generally accepted developmental stages for pre-readers, taking into consideration the child's physical and intellectual needs, responses to stimulation, attention span, etc. The developmental groupings range from birth to six months (thirty-one titles); six months to one year (thirty); one year to eighteen months (twenty-five); eighteen months to two years (forty-five); two to three years (fifty-three); three to four years (fifty-four); and four to five years (forty-nine). Entries give title, author, illustrator, publisher, date of publication, and, in most cases, price. Descriptions, usually several sentences in length, give an affectionate plot or content summary and identify, when appropriate, the work's special characteristics.

With the wealth of materials available to librarians on quality books for children, it is doubtful that there would be much of a need for this book as a reference or acquisitions tool. There is no subject index, the book is highly selective, not sturdily bound, and is somewhat casual about what constitutes a "good book." In addition, the author's primary credentials appear to be enthusiasm and a commendable belief in the importance of bringing together babies and books. However, for parents unsure of their own literary judgment; uncertain as to which books might match their child's interests and abilities; or unaware of more sophisticated selection aids, Cascardi's *Good Books to Grow On* offers an encouraging "first step" towards developing in young ones a love of reading.

G. Kim Dority

98. Caughey, Margaret, ed. **Children's Choices of Canadian Books. Volume 3.** Ottawa, Citizens' Committee on Children, 1984. 166p. index. $7.00pa. ISBN 0-9690205-2-X.

The differences between the evaluations of adults who review books for children and those of the children who read the books have long troubled people concerned with selecting books for children. *Children's Choices of Canadian Books* is the result of an attempt to collect children's opinions about the books published for them. Like the two previous volumes of this series, the books presented have been evaluated by a volunteer group of almost five hundred children aged four to fourteen. Since no attempt was made to select a group which would be representative of Canadian children as a whole, there is little doubt that these volunteers are children whose enjoyment of reading is greater than that of the average child. Nonetheless, they are a diverse group of children from the Ottawa area whose opinions are worth reading.

The approximately 250 books covered are divided into six groups based on their popularity; thus they range from the nineteen which about 90 percent of the children ranked high, to 10 which were almost universally disliked. Books in the largest group (82) were enjoyed by about 75 percent of the children in the appropriate age group. Marginal symbols are used to indicate the amount of Canadian content in each book, the availability of a French-language edition, portability, and whether books are notably "easy reading" and/or adult favorites. The annotations, which are about 100 to 150 words in length, describe the book and the readers' responses to it.

The result of this method of evaluation is a book which will be useful to librarians, teachers, and parents, although it would be unfortunate if book selectors put too much emphasis on choosing books from the high-popularity sections since several books listed in the last three categories had a very high appeal to a limited group of children. The comment under one of the group 5 books was "Readers who like Indian stories found these tales interesting and exciting. Readers who do not like Indian stories disliked these ones as well." Historical fiction and Indian legends tend to be found in the groups of less popular books, but surely librarians want to provide these books in addition to the light reading which is popular with almost all children.

A change of format is promised which will make *Children's Choices* available as a semi-annual periodical beginning in mid-1985. In either format it is appropriate as a supplementary selection aid.

Adele M. Fasick

99. Dale, Doris Cruger. **Bilingual Books in Spanish and English for Children.** Littleton, Colo., Libraries Unlimited, 1985. 163p. index. $23.50. LC 84-28916. ISBN 0-87287-477-X.

Including picture books, readers, textbooks, fiction, and nonfiction titles from the preschool to the sixth grade level, this source provides a wealth of information for the practitioner or bilingual scholar. Its purpose is to provide a "historical record of the total extent of the publication of bilingual books in Spanish and English for children from 1940 through 1982." Therefore, out-of-print and in-print titles are included, as well as those recommended or not recommended. Excluded from consideration are activity and coloring books, grammars, curriculum materials, young adult books, and audiovisual materials.

Organization is in several parts with various indexes (name, title, series, subjects in English, subjects in Spanish) concluding the work. Section 1 provides an interpretive bibliographic essay preceding a list of book dealers, publishers, bibliographies, library catalogs, and research collections. Part 2 lists 254 titles by decade (1940 to 1980), with citations to reviews followed by well-written critical annotations, including comments on the illustrations, binding, and readability, but not availability.

This source has undertaken a mammoth task and succeeded admirably. Scholars will appreciate the chronological approach for identifying patterns and trends, and practitioners will be grateful for the concise annotations and listings of review citations. [R: BL, July 85, p. 1564; BR, Nov/Dec 85, p. 52; EL, Sept/Oct 85, p. 31]   Ilene F. Rockman

100.   Dreyer, Sharon Spredemann. **The Bookfinder: A Guide to Children's Literature about the Needs and Problems of Youth Aged 2 and Up. Volume 3: Annotations of Books Published 1979 through 1982.** Circle Pines, Minn., American Guidance Service, 1985. 703p. bibliog. index. $44.50; $17.95pa. LC 85-70307pa. ISBN 0-913476-48-X; 0-913476-49-8pa.

Bookfinder 3 continues the work begun in *Bookfinder*s *1* and *2* describing and categorizing 725 books in this volume according to 450 psychological, behavioral, and developmental topics of concern to children and adolescents.

The unique split-page format of the former volumes is not used in this work. Instead, the volume is arranged like other reference tools with the main section containing the annotations followed by the indexes: subject, author, and title. The hardcover edition also includes a cumulated subject index to all three volumes.

Each entry in the annotation section includes full bibliographical information for each book, a listing of primary and secondary themes, an annotation, commentary, reading level, and other forms available, such as braille, large print, cassette, or paperbound.

The subject index lists the themes and indicates relevant titles giving the annotation number. New topics used in *Bookfinder 3* are anorexia nervosa, epilepsy, school mainstreaming, parental custody, and school retention.

This work will be useful to library media specialists, teachers, psychologists, guidance counselors, parents, and anyone who is attempting to match children with books in an effort to help them cope with specific behavioral and developmental needs and problems. [R: BL, July 85, pp. 1544 and 1564; SLJ, Nov 85, p. 40]
                                        Sara R. Mack

101.   Elleman, Barbara, ed. **Children's Books of International Interest.** 3d ed. Chicago, American Library Association, 1984. 101p. index. $7.50pa. LC 84-20336. ISBN 0-8389-3314-9.

This bibliography, compiled from its second edition and from annual lists published by the International Relations Committee of the Association for Library Service to Children, focuses on collection development and individual reading guidance. In addition to quality, child appeal, and availability, criteria for titles were that they either incorporate universal themes or depict the American way of life. There are nine categories of books ranging from picture books and fiction to science and nature books. Each book has a relatively short, nonevaluative annotation.

Given the restricted number of entries (approximately three hundred) and the requirement that all titles be in print, the compilers achieved a fairly balanced bibliography. There may be some question on individual titles (e.g., why select *I Am the Cheese* instead of *The Chocolate War* for Cormier?), and some authors, for example Milicent Selsam, are omitted. The brief annotations do occasionally suggest additional works by an author. *Light* and *Truck* are mentioned under Crews's *Freight Train*. The helpful index offers access to individual titles under each author entry.

In general, this title achieves its stated purpose by suggesting accepted, familiar titles. [R: RBB, Aug 85, p. 1641]   Carol A. Doll

102.   Freeman, Judy. **Books Kids Will Sit Still For: A Guide to Using Children's Literature for Librarians, Teachers, and Parents.** Hagerstown, Md., Alleyside Press/Freline, 1984. 210p. illus. bibliog. index. $11.95pa. LC 83-21414. ISBN 0-913853-02-X.

A rationale and suggested techniques for sharing books with elementary school children accompany a briefly annotated bibliography of over one thousand titles. Chapters include discussion of and tips for identifying appropriate books, reading aloud, booktalks, and creative dramatics. Most titles have been "kid tested," and the author's enthusiasm for books and children strongly supports her chatty style.

In places the annotations are too brief to convey the book's content, mood, or style well enough for potential users to judge its appropriateness. **Apt. 3** by Ezra Jack Keats is simply described: "Sounds of an apartment house, Introspective and a good spur for discussion." Guidewords or other indicators on each page would help to identify sections of the bibliography quickly, and facilitate its use. Numerous illustrations from books listed enhance and enliven the bibliography. Unfortunately, pictures do not match the location of their titles in the bibliography. The illustration from *Stories Julian Tells* is on page 48; the book is listed on page 82. So, the title index must be consulted.

Some heading other than "Read-Aloud Fiction" would be more appropriate since some titles included are nonfiction, for example *Look Again* by Tana Hoban. However, there does seem to be a good mixture of titles up to 1982, and numerous genre are represented — contemporary realism, historical fiction, folklore, and fairy tales, poetry, joke books, fantasy, science fiction.

Overall, this is a nicely balanced bibliography, enthusiastically presented, which is suited for a person with some knowledge of children's books. [R: EL, Sept/Oct 85, p. 33; SLJ, Jan 85, p. 38]   Carol A. Doll

103. Gillespie, John T., and Christine B. Gilbert, eds. **Best Books for Children: Preschool through Middle Grades.** 3d ed. New York, R. R. Bowker, 1985. 595p. index. $34.50. LC 85-17417. ISBN 0-8352-2131-8.

This volume contains eleven thousand titles (ninety-two hundred individual entries and eighteen hundred related titles identified in the annotations), all currently in print. Over half the entries are new to this edition which is designed for preschool through advanced sixth grade readers.

Items are arranged by thirty-five main subject categories and over five hundred subcategories ranging from "Alphabet Books" and "Mathematical Puzzles" to "Play Production" and "Bionics and Transplants." Fiction books are included. Most individual entries include an entry number, author, title, suggested grade levels, an illustrations note (and sometimes the illustrator's name), publication date, publisher, price, editions (paperbacks and library editions are included), and a one-line annotation describing the general plot or contents. If the work has won an award, this is noted, as are other books in a series. Additional recommended titles on the same topic appear with certain entries. Included titles were chosen upon three recommendations from well-known selection guides, annual bibliographies of note, and generally used review periodicals.

The author/illustrator, title, biographical subjects, and subject indexes use entry numbers rather than page numbers.

Although comments are brief, the arrangement is convenient and all the volumes are recommended by reputable sources. This is a useful compilation for selecting, collection building, preparing bibliographies, and locating books on a particular subject for a patron or a curriculum need.   Eleanor Elving Schwartz

104. National Council of Teachers of English. Committee on the Elementary School Booklist. **Adventuring with Books: A Booklist for Pre-K-Grade 6.** new ed. Dianne L. Monson, ed. Urbana, Ill., National Council of Teachers of English, 1985. 395p. index. $9.75pa. LC 85-18762. ISBN 0-8141-0076-7.

Librarians, media specialists, and teachers who have relied on the NCTE booklists in the past will be happy to know that this new volume continues the high standards set by earlier editions.

Seventeen hundred new children's books have been annotated and categorized for use by those persons who are interested in bringing children (prekindergarten to grade 6) and recommended books together. Selecting on the basis of literary and artistic quality, the committee chose from approximately seven thousand titles published between 1981 and 1984 those having characteristics which appeal to children. They were also concerned that the listed books about minorities be accurate and of good quality.

The book is arranged in fifteen major categories such as "Books for Young Children," "Traditional Literature," "Modern Fantasy," and "Historical Fiction," each further subdivided into more particular subject areas. Author and title indexes help to locate specific titles. Following each major category, quality books of the past are listed without annotation.

Each title is annotated with a content statement and critical comment. Appropriate age level is indicated and award winning titles are noted. New to this edition is the noting of those books which appear on the annual Teachers' Choices list from the NCTE/Children's Book Council Joint Committee and the Children's Choices lists from the International Reading Association/Children's Book Council Joint Committee.   Sara R. Mack

105. **Notable Canadian Children's Books: 1975-1979 Cumulative Edition.** Ottawa, National Library of Canada, 1985. 103p. illus. index. $10.75pa. ISBN 0-660-53040-6.

Canadian children's literature has been developing its own character and identity, separate from the influence of the United States, helping create and support Canadian authors and illustrators and meeting the unique English/French bilingual needs of Canadian readers.

There are forty-six English-language books listed here. The list of French-language books contains fifty-five titles. All books are annotated in both English and French. The annotations summarize each book, describe the art media and technique used, and report on any awards given to the book.

Since there are some books printed in both English and French languages, they appear and are annotated in both of the lists.

Indexes are categorized by author, illustrator, subject, geographical area, and award.

Not only is this resource of notable Canadian children's books specific for Canadian readers, it will also be a useful tool for the U.S. teachers and librarians interested in providing multicultural literary experiences for U.S. children.   Norma J. Livo

106. Roman, Susan. **Sequences: An Annotated Guide to Children's Fiction in Series.** Chicago, American Library Association, 1985. 134p. index. $17.50. LC 84-244447. ISBN 0-8389-0428-9.

Not the usual bibliographic listing of titles in series, this volume deals with children's book sequences and sequels. Sequences, according to the author, show the development of character and plot through each novel, and the stories are closely related to each other. A sequel, on the other hand, will have the same characters as those of an earlier book, but the stories may exhibit only artificial unity.

This work contains both sequences and sequels which have been carefully selected from the best in children's fiction. It is skillfully organized for optimum use. Arranged alphabetically by author each entry includes a brief description of the series explaining its merits and identifying a broad reading/interest level. The titles, publishers and dates of the books are listed with brief annotations in the order in which they should be read. If there are other books related to the series but not really a part of it, these are mentioned in a note at the end of the entry.

The three indexes—title, main character, and series—add to the usefulness of this fine work.

Teachers and librarians will find it an invaluable guide for acquisitions and reading guidance for readers from grade three through young adult. [R: BL, July 85, p. 1565; RBB, 1 Oct 85, p. 208; SLJ, Sept 85, p. 44; WLB, Sept 85, p. 81]   Sara R. Mack

107. Schon, Isabel. **Books in Spanish for Children and Young Adults: An Annotated Guide. Series III.** Metuchen, N.J., Scarecrow, 1985. 208p. index. $16.50. LC 85-2196. ISBN 0-8108-1807-8.

According to the preface "this book is intended to serve as a guide to any adult—teacher, librarian ... who is interested in selecting books in Spanish for children of preschool through high school age. Most of the books included in this guide were published since 1982 and come from Argentina, Bolivia, Chile, Colombia, Costa Rica, Cuba, Ecuador, Mexico, Peru, Puerto Rico, Spain, the United States,

and Venezuela" (p. x). Each volume is provided with an annotation and a symbol that shows whether Schon considers the book to be outstanding, marginal, or not recommended. The preface also appears in Spanish. The first appendix is a listing with addresses of "Book dealers in Spanish-speaking countries" (not always quite accurately arranged by country for the Cuban dealer has a New York address). The second appendix is "United States Book Dealers" (specializing in books in Spanish). There is an author index as well as a title index.

Where numerous books from the same country are listed, Schon divides them into "Fiction," "Biography," "Careers," "Cooking," "Folklore," "Geography," "History," "Language," "Poetry," "Politics," "Religion," "Science and Technology," "Sports," and "Theater." The material is arranged first by country and then classified by topic where this is desirable.

The United States and Spain would seem to have produced in this period the most books for this age group that the compiler finds to be outstanding. She gives a not recommended rating to the three books from Bolivia.

There is little said about the compiler's method for choosing the books examined. For example, numerous Spanish translations are appearing of the work of Jack London many of which are suitable for children of this age group. None of these appear. Her list of dealers is on the skimpy side. She lists eleven dealers for twelve countries. She includes only one dealer from each country, though she recommends the same one for both Bolivia and Ecuador. She does not explain her choice of countries. Does Nicaragua publish no books in this field or were they impossible to obtain? One could ask the same question for other countries whose children's books are not discussed.

Schon's critical annotations should be extremely useful and the volume fulfills the compiler's purpose. [R: EL, Sept/Oct 85, p. 31]
Hensley C. Woodbridge

108. Schon, Isabel. **A Hispanic Heritage, Series II: A Guide to Juvenile Books about Hispanic People and Cultures.** Metuchen, N.J., Scarecrow, 1985. 153p. index. $13.50. LC 84-13964. ISBN 0-8108-1727-6.

This is an annotated reference book of Spanish American books published since 1979 in English for students from kindergarten through high school. The book is intended mainly as an aid for librarians and teachers who want to introduce students to Hispanic America through works available in English. The countries represented are Argentina, Bolivia, Chile, Costa Rica, Cuba, Dominican Republic, Ecuador, El

Salvador, Guatemala, Honduras, Mexico, Nicaragua, Panama, Peru, and Venezuela. Welcome additions are sections on Latin America, Puerto Rico, and Spain. Unexplained omissions are Paraguay and Uruguay. The section promised in the preface on the Hispanic-heritage people in the United States is loosely included in the section on Latin America.

While the book contains several English translations of works by Spanish American authors, for the most part the books included are by English-speaking authors. This point underscores the scarcity of and need for translations, but it is also a warning for users of this book to develop their own means to increment the information in it, and to think of the book as only an introduction to a rich and diverse area of the world. School libraries, some public libraries, and those academic libraries that collect children's literature would be advised to acquire this book. [R: JAL, May 85, p. 107; RBB, July 85, p. 1524]

Antonio Rodriguez-Buckingham

Biographies

109. **American Writers for Children before 1900.** Glenn E. Estes, ed. Detroit, Gale, 1985. 441p. illus. bibliog. index. (Dictionary of Literary Biography, Vol. 42). $88.00. LC 85-15990. ISBN 0-8103-1720-6.

A companion volume to John Cech's *American Writers for Children, 1900-1960* (see *ARBA* 85, entry 1025) this volume has the same excellent coverage and format. For each of fifty-two authors from the nineteenth century there are a list of selected books, a portrait, an interestingly written bibliographical account, illustrations from the author's books, and additional helps such as listings under bibliography, biography, references, and papers. Included are such well-known writers as Jacob Abbott, Louisa May Alcott, Horatio Alger, Joel Chandler Harris, Helen Hunt Jackson, Howard Pyle, and Kate Douglas Wiggin. At the end of the volume are two useful sections: "Checklist for Further Reading" and a cumulative index of the first forty-two volumes of *Dictionary of Literary Biography*, the *Dictionary of Literary Biography Yearbook*, 1980-1984, and the Dictionary of Literary Biography Documentary series, volumes 1-4. A list of contributors is also provided.

Biographical accounts are interestingly interwoven life events about and commentaries on literary works by the authors included. Random reading indicates the contributors and editor have successfully made this a uniform characteristic. The companion volumes are reminiscent of Anne Commire's *Yesterday's Authors of*

Books for Children (see *ARBA* 78, entry 1102) and *Something about the Author* (see *ARBA* 77, entry 1163). However, while the two volumes of *American Writers for Children* are more literary and readable in style, they are not so inclusive in coverage as the Commire titles.

A strong binding, good quality paper, excellent print, and clear reproductions of photographs and illustrations make this an inviting book for users, especially for libraries. *American Writers for Children before 1900* is strongly recommended for all who are interested in children's authors.

Ruth E. Bauner

110. Roginski, Jim. **Behind the Covers: Interviews with Authors and Illustrators of Books for Children and Young Adults.** Littleton, Colo., Libraries Unlimited, 1985. 249p. bibliog. index. $23.50. LC 85-18129. ISBN 0-87287-506-7.

In this readable, personalized work each of the twenty-two interviewees is presented through a brief biographical note, a "Prelude" (impressions of the interviewer), an edited recording of the question/answer interviews conducted from 1983 to 1984, and notes to works or individuals mentioned in the interview. An extensive bibliography of each author/illustrator's works through 1984 provides the interviewee's role (i.e., author, editor, etc.) and name or pseudonym used for each work, its title, publisher, and publication date. Works recognized through 1984 are listed with the award and/or honors, which are further identified in appendix B. Additional sources of biographical information are listed for most interviewees. Bibliographies were compiled by Muriel Brown, children's literature specialist at the Dallas Public Library.

The author (p. ix) acknowledges similarities with other tools, such as inclusion of biographical information, listing of works, and use of interviews. This biographical source is unique with the interviewer's impressions and the question/answer interview format creating a "you are there" feeling for the reader.

Appendix A lists names and addresses of library collections housing original works by these biographees. A "Bibliography of Awards Information" is on page 245, and there is a "Bibliography of Bibliographic Sources" on pages 248-49.

Indexes could bring information together. For example, appendix A notes that Jean Fritz's works are in two library collections, but that information is not acknowledged in the biographical introduction to her chapter. A subject index would provide access to portions of the interviews dealing with various aspects of the creation and production of children's books addressed.   Phyllis J. Van Orden

Handbooks

111. Rudman, Masha Kabakow. Children's Literature: An Issues Approach. 2d ed. New York, Longman, 1984. 476p. bibliog. index. $30.00; $16.95pa. LC 83-22217. ISBN 0-582-28398-1; 0-582-28397-3pa.

When the first edition of *Children's Literature: An Issues Approach* was published in 1976, Rudman's practice of bibliotherapy was described as a course that served to "crown didacticism and make literature subservient" in a *Horn Book* magazine editorial that engendered a lively epistolary debate in the magazine's 1977 volume. Now armed with documentation to defend the concept of bibliotherapy, Rudman seeks to quiet her critics and update her work. From the point of view of an educator, Rudman recommends as an "additional approach to the study of children's literature" the practice of using books to help children solve personal problems and become aware of societal concerns.

The issues discussed are: family, sex, gender roles, heritage, special needs, old age, death, and war. Each issue covered includes an introduction, a section that cites particular books as examples of how the issue is handled, suggestions for activities for teachers or other counselors, a description of related activities for adults to use with children, a reference list of sources relating the topic to children's books, which Rudman compiled with the aid of review journals and experts in the field. A chapter on methodology, a list of children's book awards and publishers' addresses and, most valuably, a list of reference books on children's literature round out the competent volume.

Sally Holmes Holtze

Indexes

112. Children's Book Review Index. Master Cumulation, 1965-1984. A Cumulated Index to More Than 200,000 Reviews of Approximately 55,000 Titles. Gary C. Tarbert and Barbara Beach, eds. Detroit, Gale, 1985. 5v. $350.00/set. LC 75-27408. ISBN 0-8103-2046-0; ISSN 0147-5681.

The improved access to reviews of children's books provided by the *Children's Book Review Index* is of real value to those doing retrospective selection of such material, preparing book talks and other informational programs, and responding to requests to review the original selection of a particular children's book for a library collection as well as to the growing body of scholars and students doing research in children's literature. This comprehensive master cumulation provides information about more than two hundred thousand reviews for almost fifty-five thousand different books that have appeared in 372 different periodicals. The five compact volumes present a brief listing by author and then title, or just title where there is no author, along with a simple coded index to where the particular book was reviewed. It is perfectly easy to locate the information in this index and then to locate the review in a particular journal.

However, the existence of the *Children's Book Review Index* raises some troublesome questions. All of the information in this master cumulation is derived from, and can with some greater effort be found in, the *Book Review Index*. An annual volume of the *Children's Book Review Index* is also published (see *ARBA 83*, entry 1144) and this cumulation includes the information from those volumes. This latest master cumulation extends and supplants an earlier, only slightly less expensive master cumulation of the *Children's Book Review Index* for the period 1969-1981 (see *ARBA 83*, entry 1143). This seemingly endless recycling of the same information in different formats benefits the publisher but not the consumer. Should you buy this master cumulation or wait a few more years for the next larger, more comprehensive, and more expensive master cumulation?

Norman D. Stevens

113. Children's Magazine Guide: Subject Index to Children's Magazines. Volume 38: Number 1. Patricia Kennelly Sinclair, ed. Madison, Wis., Pleasant T. Rowland, 1985. $22.50/yr. (11 issues plus semiannual cumulations); $27.50/yr. (foreign countries). ISSN 0743-9873.

Close to fifty periodicals for both children and adults are included in this unique source – the only commercially published subject index for children's magazines. Separate sections cover the citations for juvenile articles, and such standards as *Chickadee* and *Scienceland* for preschoolers; *Cricket* and *Ebony, Jr.* for elementary age children; and *School Library Journal* and *Teaching and Computers* for adults are included. Adult titles constitute only 25 percent of all titles, and eliminated from consideration are those magazines "published essentially to promote toys and television programs."

Organization is logical and typeset entries are easy to read. An announcements section precedes the body of the index and provides descriptions of new, ceased, or merged titles. The children's index follows next, alphabetically arranged by subject, with headings in boldface capital letters. Full citations are indented below.

At the conclusion of these entries are grey pages which index the professional journals for teachers and librarians, often including appended teaching activities. *See* and *see also* references are standard, the front cover provides a list of abbreviations and magazines indexed, and the back cover contains instructions for reading a sample entry. Semiannual cumulations occur in February and August. A valuable purchase for the nominal price.

Ilene F. Rockman

COLLECTION DEVELOPMENT AND EVALUATION

114. Angiletta, Anthony M., and others, eds. **The State of Western European Studies: Implications for Collection Development. Selected Papers from the Symposium on Western European Studies and North American Research Libraries....** New York, Haworth Press, 1984. 273p. (*Collection Management*, Vol. 6, Nos. 1/2). $29.95. LC 84-12803. ISBN 0-86656-354-7.

The conference from which papers are published in this volume was held in May 1983 and was sponsored by the Western European Area Studies Center at the University of Minnesota. In the introduction to this volume Clara M. Lovett, Chief of the European Division at the Library of Congress, states that "the editorial committee strove to identify those symposia contributions illustrating most clearly and cogently research trends, publishing trends, or issues of collection development and bibliographic control of Western European materials. We were less concerned with comprehensive geographical and topical coverage than we were with stimulating further debate on the state and needs of Western European studies" (p. xviii). This editorial decision resulted in rather randomly selected topics presented in three major parts: (1) "The State of Western European Studies: Trends in Scholarship and Publishing" (pp. 3-78), (2) "Collection Development for Western European Studies" (pp. 79-158), and (3) "Bibliographic Control of European Materials" (pp. 159-263). This volume includes twenty-one articles ranging from "Perspectives on Book Publishing in the German Democratic Republic" by G. P. Hueting and "The Scandinavian National Bibliographies as Tools for Research and Book Selection" by R. G. Selleck to "Outguessing History: Collecting Sources Today for the Scholars Tomorrow" by A. F. Peterson and "Medieval Studies and North American Research Libraries" by R. R. Ring. It is rather unfortunate that the editors and authors did not provide a precise definition of their major concept "Western European Studies" as well as of "area studies" in terms of its topical and geo-

graphic comprehension. The same relates to the other major term "bibliographic control" of West European materials.

Some published articles contribute to better understanding of some aspects of collection development for Western European studies. And it should be pointed out that published conference papers are rather uneven in terms of methodology and coverage. For instance, Clara M. Lovett in her article "Modern Italian Studies and Research Libraries in the United States" (pp. 135-43) failed to explain her survey methodology.

The lack of name and subject indexes and of a separate bibliographic section limits the reference value of this publication. Martha L. Brogan in her "Afterword" stated that one of the major shortcomings of this symposium was "the lack of teaching faculty" and many participants "expressed a desire for greater representation and involvement of researchers" (p. 247). The future conferences, according to Brogan, would be held at locations accessible to researchers and faculty. This is a wise decision on the part of organizers of future gatherings.

Lubomyr R. Wynar

115. Curley, Arthur, and Dorothy Broderick. **Building Library Collections.** 6th ed. Metuchen, N.J., Scarecrow, 1985. 339p. index. $18.75. LC 84-23665. ISBN 0-8108-1776-4.

The author entry for this book may tend to obscure the fact that it is simply another edition of the familiar textbook originally prepared by Mary Carter and Wallace Bonk and later revised by Rose Mary Magrill. The organization, contents, wording and bibliographies of this edition are much as they have been before. Considering the wide popularity of "Carter and Bonk" in library schools, this is probably for the good; one wishes, however, that the basic contributions of Carter, Bonk, and Magrill had been acknowledged on the title page.

The main changes in the sixth edition, apart from rephrasing of the wording, have been (1) Adding new chapters on "Why Libraries Exist" and "Philosophy and Framework of Collection Development." These stress the importance of basing effective collection development on a precise definition of the library's goals and a close study of the community's needs. The chapter "Studying the Library's Community" is accordingly expanded. (2) Deleting most of the appendices, on the not wholly acceptable argument that this material is available elsewhere. (3) Bringing bibliographies and factual information up to date, though not, it would appear, later than 1983. (4) Giving more emphasis to nonbook materials. (5) Integrating the material on selection by subject, formerly a separate chapter, into the basic selection chapters.

The new editors are well known and well qualified. Their reinterpretations and revisions will give *Building Library Collections* the vitality and currency for continued usefulness. [R: JAL, Sept 85, p. 256; RQ, Fall 85, p. 151]

Samuel Rothstein

116.   Futas, Elizabeth, and Sheila S. Inter, eds. **Collection Evaluation.** Champaign, Ill., Graduate School of Library and Information Science, University of Illinois, 1985. 1v. (various paging). (*Library Trends*, Vol. 22, No. 3). $8.00pa. ISSN 0024-2594.

A surprising range of topics is covered in this issue; many of the articles have titles that do not appear to be related to collection evaluation. For example, "Evaluation of Software" or "Looking for Tutors and Brokers" would seem out of place; however, all the essays do to a greater or lesser degree tie into collection evaluation. The eight authors, including the issue editors, are all well known to anyone interested in collection development. William McGrath's "Collection Evaluation—Theory and the Search for Structure" is an excellent article, and should be required reading in any course on collection development. McGrath points out the lack of a theoretical foundation for collection evaluation and then briefly describes some techniques that could be employed to begin to build a sound base. Rose Mary Magrill does her usual sound job of reviewing the literature in "Evaluation by Library Type." "Evaluation of Online Databases and Their Uses in Collections" by Barbara Rice provides a logical argument in favor of treating online databases as just another element in the collection as well as an overview of the system readily available for use in the library. The last three pages of her article look at how one might use online bibliographic databases in collection evaluation. Jane Hannigan's article "Evaluation of Microcomputer Software" is perhaps the only article that does not directly address collection evaluation. Her article is primarily concerned with describing categories of existing software (electronic mail and word processing for example) and how to evaluate them in terms of library needs. Research results are presented in Tony Stankus's "Looking for Tutors and Brokers: Comparing the Expectations of Book and Journal Evaluators." His methodology involves analyzing one thousand reviews in *Choice* during 1983. As might be expected, he found differences in the expectations of reviewers of books and journals; books are expected to function as a tutor and journals are expected to dispense facts/information as a broker. "A Way of Looking at Things" by Bill Katz reviews the many collection evaluations methods which are currently conducted by collecting information about different points of view about the collection—average user, specialist, or library staff, for example. The Magrill and Katz articles make a nice combination to get an overview of present practices. Selection and deselection (weeding) are really the focus of Lee Ash's "Old Dog; No Tricks: Perceptions of the Qualitative Analysis of Book Collections." The last two pieces by the editors treat a subject not often covered in collection evaluation—input from the entire library staff: Elizabeth Futas's "Role of Public Services in Collection Evaluation" and Sheila S. Inter's "Responsibilities of Technical Service Librarians to the Process of Collection Evaluation." A collection well worth reading regardless of how long you have been in the field or what your duties are in the library. [R: JAL, Nov 85, p. 320]

G. Edward Evans

117.   Halpenny, Francess G. **Canadian Collections in Public Libraries.** Toronto, Book and Periodical Development Council, 1985. 280p. bibliog. $50.00 spiralbound (Canada); $125.00 spiralbound (elsewhere).

Canada is very much concerned with maintaining its "cultural identity." Thus the issue of the extent to which its public libraries should and do stock Canadian publications is a matter of considerable debate, often acrimonious. This study tries to promote better understanding of the issue by supplying "adequate research data" about "the actual holdings of Canadian print materials in Canadian public libraries" and also on their policies for acquiring Canadian books and periodicals (e.g., priorities).

The study is massive (four years; a staff of some sixty; a checklist of nearly five thousand items; about one hundred pages of statistical data) but, surprisingly, is rather limited in scope. It does not include French-language publications or pubic libraries in French Canada. The sample of libraries is small (fifteen) and no claims are made for its being truly representative of Canadian Anglophone public libraries as a whole; in fact, it is admitted that the "mode of inquiry would resemble a case study method." Hence, perhaps, no firm conclusions or recommendations are offered but only a chapter of "reflections." As a result there appears to be an imbalance between the mass of data collected and the tentativeness with which the findings are delineated and interpreted.

Nevertheless two important "messages" do come through: (1) interest in Canadian publications is growing; (2) those who would like to see that interest become much greater (most obviously, Canadian authors and publishers) should take proper account of the cardinal fact that Canadian public libraries must be actuated primarily by the needs and circumstances of their particular communities. In short, the familiar dilemma of local demand versus "obligation" (quality) operates here as elsewhere.

Samuel Rothstein

118. Kohl, David F. **Acquisitions, Collection Development, and Collection Use: A Handbook for Library Management.** Santa Barbara, Calif., ABC-Clio, 1985. 408p. bibliog. index. (Handbooks for Library Management, Vol. 2). $35.00. LC 85-6023. ISBN 0-87436-433-7.

One of six volumes in the Handbooks for Library Management series; a new and highly interesting set of volumes designed for librarians needing quantitative information on topics such as cost of materials, use made of popular journals by high school students, most frequently used selection aids, and hundreds more. Quantitative research located in 34 library journals published in North America from 1960 through 1983 has been carefully selected for inclusion; research published in monographs and found in dissertations is not included. When information is available, research data are divided by type of library: academic, public, school, and special. Organization facilitates use data and complete bibliographic information are provided.

The format used translates all research included here into a standard formula: brief description of study (location, date, population size, response rate), the actual quantitative findings, and, when necessary, editorial comment. Annual cost figures reported in *Publishers Weekly* and *Library Journal* are not included (*LJ* is one of the titles surveyed, however). A serious oversight is not including journals such as *Database, Online,* and *Information Technology and Libraries*. Nevertheless, the handbook serves as an excellent annotated index to library literature and suggests topics for additional research. [R: JAL, Nov 85, p. 321; RQ, Winter 85, pp. 269-70]   Milton H. Crouch

COLLEGE AND RESEARCH LIBRARIES

119. **Australian Academic Libraries in the Seventies: Essays in Honour of Dietrich Borchardt.** Harrison Bryan and John Horacek, eds. St. Lucia, Australia, New York, University of Queensland Press, 1984. 331p. bibliog. index. (University of Queensland Press Scholar's Library). $32.50. LC 83-3557. ISBN 0-7022-1883-9.

This is one of the few festschrifts ever published in Australia and honors Dietrich Borchardt, foundation librarian at the La Trobe University and founder of the *Australian Academic and Research Journal,* a man well known internationally through IFLA activities. The work is a welcome addition to the literature on Australian academic librarianship in the 1970s. It provides rich source materials for comparative international library studies, especially, as related to networks, national information policy, cooperation, and resource sharing. It is noteworthy that many developments in Australian academic libraries parallel those in the United States; for example, a downward trend in collection development and library building and the struggle for an appropriate national information policy, effective networks, and adequate funding. Interesting insight into the library profession in Australia and its problems is given in essays dealing with the librarian's status in academe and staffing patterns in academic libraries.

The book, however, deals mostly with the past and does not address the future. Information on automation and new technologies is minimal.

It seems that recent Australian academic library development is more closely related to that of the United States than to that of the British.

Recommended for all library schools and academic libraries and other research libraries collecting materials on international librarianship.

Hannelore B. Rader

120. Boll, John J. **Shelf Browsing, Open Access and Storage Capacity in Research Libraries.** Champaign, Ill., Graduate School of Library and Information Science, University of Illinois, 1985. 34p. (Occasional Papers, No. 169). $3.00pa. ISSN 0276-1769.

A professor at the School of Library and Information Studies of the University of Wisconsin-Madison states, in this well-documented paper, that shelf browsing is not so important for information retrieval as most librarians think. He urges greater use of sized shelving and less use of classed shelving as an alternative to constructing new library buildings and expansions at research institutions. As a solution to space pressures, Boll encourages more academic libraries to follow the lead of Princeton, Cornell, Texas, California, and other universities in developing compact storage annexes. An historical perspective and currently employed criteria for selecting items for storage are presented.

This inexpensive, handsomely printed pamphlet deserves to be read by all librarians concerned with the need for more shelf space at a time when capital funding is declining.

Leonard Grundt

121. Council on Library Resources, Inc. **Twenty-ninth Annual Report/1985.** Washington, D.C., Council on Library Resources, 1985. 71p. index. free pa. ISSN 0070-1181.

The Council on Library Resources is essentially a catalyst for the development and performance of academic and research libraries. Through it, libraries, societies, organizations, and individuals concerned with the importance of libraries can further their own priorities. Three components that serve to unify the council's activities are research, library operations and services, and librarianship itself.

Part 1 of this annual report reviews the programs in each of the above-mentioned areas: The expansion of research programs will enable a fuller exploration of topics related to information and its use. Today's new technology can foster greater benefits for both society and individuals. Projects in the second category will lead to better-informed decisions regarding library resources and the improvement of access to information. Finally, programs are documented that are designed to assure the high level of staff education essential to library performance. Various appendices include lists of committees, publications, program guidelines, and grant application procedures.

The financial statements in part 2 give a clear picture of CLR's income and expenditures, and active projects. An index follows, which helps access the information contained in this report.

CLR, as an agent, can assist in shaping the future of academic and research libraries by helping them define their objectives and obligations in appropriate ways. Anita Zutis

122. Cronin, Mary J. **Performance Measurement for Public Services in Academic and Research Libraries.** Washington, D.C., Office of Management Studies, Association of Research Libraries, 1985. 36p. bibliog. (Occasional Paper, No. 9). $15.00pa.

The director of libraries at Loyola University, Chicago, examines some of the realities involved in using performance measurement techniques to evaluate public service activities in academic and research libraries. She analyzes performance measurement from three different perspectives. In part 1 of this paper, a general background on current evaluation theory is presented. Building upon this theory, part 2 applies performance measurement to existing library activities through a model. Finally, part 3 briefly looks at the forces for and against

public services performance measurement, and future trends. Illustrations help clarify the text. This pamphlet concludes with an excellent bibliography including a selection of items from library literature related to performance measurement; publications dealing with public services are grouped according to function (circulation, reference, etc.), and particularly useful methodologies or approaches are noted in brief annotations.

With accountability being demanded more and more, academic library managers have to learn how to measure and evaluate performance in their institutions. This paper will help those libraries that can afford to buy it. [R: JAL, July 85, p. 171] Leonard Grundt

123. Haka, Clifford H., and Nancy Stevens. **A Guidebook for Shelf Inventory Procedures in Academic Libraries.** Washington, D.C., Office of Management Studies, Association of Research Libraries, 1985. 24p. bibliog. (Occasional Paper, No. 10). $15.00pa.

Expanding upon a "Research Notes" article in the March 1985 issue of *College & Research Libraries* written by Clifford H. Haka and Nancy Ursery, this paper elaborately describes procedures used by the University of Kansas in 1980-1981 to conduct an inventory of the main library at that institution. A short review of the principal types of inventories (in-stack and out-of-stack), a discussion of pilot inventories, and an assessment of the costs and benefits of shelf inventories are provided. Eight flowcharts and numerous other illustrations help to make the text easier to understand. In an appendix, the results of a 1980 survey of ARL academic library members regarding inventory practices are summarized. A brief, selected bibliography concludes this publication.

Prepared as part of the OMS collaborative research/writing project, this useful, albeit expensive, pamphlet should encourage more large academic libraries, as well as smaller ones, to conduct inventories in order to reduce the discrepancy between the holdings listed in the catalog—whether automated or not—and the materials actually available on the shelf. [R: JAL, Nov 85, p. 308] Leonard Grundt

124. Heintze, Robert A. **Library Statistics of Colleges and Universities 1982.** Washington, D.C., National Center for Education Statistics; distr., Washington, D.C., GPO, 1984. 83p. $3.25pa. S/N 065-000-00216-7. NCES 84-218.

There will be twenty fewer subject reports in the 1980 census of population than there were in the 1970 census due to "fiscal constraints." An example of a report not now included in the census is the "Older American." Also, other recurring statistical reports, sponsored by the federal government, will be issued less frequently. The result is increasing frustration among those who need social data to conduct research or measure policy outcomes.

Library Statistics of Colleges and Universities 1982 is an important source of national statistical data on libraries and their use. Unfortunately, it to is somewhat out-of-date and, therefore, researchers must, in many cases, rely on serial publications such as *Library Journal*, or annual handbooks, especially the *Bowker Annual of Library and Book Trade Information*; or, for the larger university libraries, the Association of Research Libraries' *ARL Statistics* (also published annually). In any event, the 1982 edition of *Library Statistics* is useful and quite inexpensive. This edition was published in the fall of 1984 based on information gathered via the Higher Education General Information Survey (HEGIS) and the Library General Information Survey (LIBGIS) in 1982 by the National Center for Education Statistics. The previous *Library Statistics* report was produced from information gathered in 1979. The first section of the report compares college libraries for 1978-1979 and 1981-1982 on holdings (a 34.7 percent increase, mainly in microforms); acquisitions (down 11.9 percent); expenditures (up 34.4 percent, primarily in wages/benefits); FTE staff (up only 1.4 percent); and circulation (up only 0.4 percent, although interlibrary loans were up 34.1 percent and reference questions up 64.8 percent). One of the big losers, to no one's surprise (I assume), is receipts from government grants which were down almost 24 percent.

The remaining section of *Library Statistics* contains thirty-three tables ranging in topic from the total number of books held, by institutional control, type, and size to the average number of hours the main library is open. An appendix is included which explains the National Center for Education Statistics' institutional classification scheme.

Richard H. Quay

125. Irvine, Betty Jo. **Sex Segregation in Librarianship: Demographic and Career Patterns of Academic Library Administrators.** Westport, Conn., Greenwood Press, 1985. 171p. bibliog. index. (Contributions in Librarianship and Information Science, No. 53). $29.95. LC 84-21228. ISBN 0-313-24260-7.

The purpose of this book is to answer questions "regarding the intra-occupational sex segregation of academic librarianship" (preface). The author collected data by questionnaire and from published sources on the top administrators (i.e., directors, associate direc-

tors, and assistant directors) of the ninety-nine academic library members of the Association of Research Libraries in 1980. She finds that men held 69 percent (256) of all administrative positions in the population of 371, and women, 31 percent (115). The book is written in a serious, methodical style characteristic of monographs based on doctoral dissertations. Copious notes and tables are provided along with an extensive bibliography. The tables unfortunately are rather faint and reproduced from typescript.

After ploughing through the findings on personal characteristics and family background, mobility and career history, role models and mentors, and professional affiliations and activities, the reader discovers that the author was surprised to find that there were fewer significant differences by sex among administrators than expected. She concludes that historically, role models for academic library administrative positions have not favored women but a significant change has occurred during the period 1970-1980 and she hopes that it will continue. This volume complements other studies on the topic of sex segregation. It will be useful mainly for courses on the administration of academic libraries and the role of women in librarianship. [R: JAL, Sept 85, p. 260; LJ, 1 Sept 85, p. 148; WLB, Oct 85, p. 59] Helen Howard

126. Kirk, Thomas G., ed. **Increasing the Teaching Role of Academic Libraries.** San Francisco, Calif., Jossey-Bass, 1984. 102p. index. (New Directions for Teaching and Learning, No. 18). $8.95pa. LC 83-82744. ISBN 0-87589-791-6; ISSN 0271-0633.

This eighteenth volume in the New Directions for Teaching and Learning series is the first to deal specifically with the role of academic libraries. The series is billed as "paperback sourcebooks," but there is no word from the series editor describing the purpose of the series or its intended audience. The editor of this volume, Thomas Kirk, states that it "is intended to provide a compact overview of the expanding area of library service" (p. 2). The concept of library service which is singled out for treatment is that of the teaching library. The core component of a teaching library is identified as "a comprehensive bibliographic instruction program" (p. 6), the purpose of such a program being to teach how to find, evaluate, and use information effectively.

Authors of individual chapters cover the following: conceptual and pedagogical issues, alternatives to the term paper, ways to gain faculty support, a description of eleven "leading" bibliographic instruction (BI) programs, project LOEX (Library Orientation Exchange), and a concise guide to the literature of bibliographic instruction. Only in his concluding remarks does the editor express his hope that the chapters of "this sourcebook" will make teaching faculty and administrators of colleges and universities more aware of bibliographic instruction activities being provided by their own and other academic libraries. This volume is unlikely to achieve these objectives. Although each chapter contains valuable references to the literature, and to specific BI programs, the text is uneven and prone to generalities. [R: LJ, 1 Mar 85, p. 68]   Helen Howard

127.   Lee, Sul H., ed. **Access to Scholarly Information: Issues & Strategies.** Ann Arbor, Mich., Pierian Press, 1985. 120p. (Library Management Series, No. 9). $24.50. LC 85-60595. ISBN 0-87650-189-7.

This collection of articles presents prominent librarians' opinions and a review of the literature on "how research libraries deal with the problems of access to information in the 1980's."

Eight contributors address the topic from traditional library perspectives. Herbert S. White's opening essay, "Ownership Is Not Always Availability ...," challenges the emphasis placed on collections as the key element to satisfy user needs. David Kaser reviews "The Role of the Building in the Delivery of Library Service." Kenneth G. Peterson's examination of the "... Impact of Collection Development, Reference Services and Preservation on Access to Library Resources," is followed by Helen S. Spalding's summary of "Recent Developments in Technical Services...." Carolyn Bucknall offers a model for information delivery and communication as basis for her considering "Conjuring in the Academic Library: The Illusion of Access." Donald E. Riggs reviews effects of copyright legislation on the "Reduction in Access and Rights." Robin Downes highlights the development of "Electronic Publishing and the Scholar's Workshop." The book concludes with Robert A. Seal's bibliography of about 250 citations on the topic published since 1975, organized into seven sections corresponding roughly with the book's earlier contributions. Additional references appear in notes after each article.

Overall, these articles appear as personal responses to a buzzword. Two papers open with reference to citation reviews on how "access" is used in recent literature. The issue is generally described, but the book does not advocate many creative strategies for action. The absence of any reference to current concerns about the impact of federal budgetary cuts on publishing and distribution of information produced by government agencies and the resulting consequence on national information policies is disappointing. The categorization of some citations and the exclusion of others in the bibliography are puzzling. The lack of an index precludes effective reference use of the volume. [R: RQ, Winter 85, p. 269]   Danuta A. Nitecki

128.   McElroy, A. Rennie, ed. **College Librarianship: The Objectives and the Practice.** London, Library Association; distr., Phoenix, Ariz., Oryx Press, 1984. 427p. index. (Handbooks on Library Practice). $50.00. ISBN 0-85365-785-8.

The term "college" is applied in Great Britain to any nonuniversity institution of tertiary education such as polytechnics, specialist monotechnics, and schools of education. This book is a collection of essays that deal with the management and user needs of the college library, and with the relationship between such libraries and their parent institutions. The discussions center around five themes: (1) the librarian as educator entrusted with the managing of special resources, (2) the librarian as promoter of the library within the college community, (3) the need to bring media and state-of-the-art information technology to the library, (4) the concern felt in Great Britain that the management of educational resources is being taken away from educators, and (5) the belief that the librarian must serve as the ambassador of the library in and out of the college community. The five themes are brought together in the book in three parts: the educational environment, the colleges and their libraries, and librarianship practiced in the college sector.

This book is indeed food for thought for librarians, and for teachers and students of librarianship, particularly, though not exclusively, those in the English-speaking world. It is an indispensable tool in libraries that support programs in library and information studies. [R: C&RL, July 85, pp. 371-72]

Antonio Rodriguez-Buckingham

129.   Moran, Barbara B. **Academic Libraries: The Changing Knowledge Centers of Colleges and Universities.** Washington, D.C., Association for the Study of Higher Education, 1984. 97p. bibliog. (ASHE-ERIC Higher Education Research Report, No. 8). $7.50pa. LC 85-61910. ISBN 0-913317-17-9; ISSN 0737-1292.

Change has become the dominant theme for most organizations today. The concept, however, is largely "oldhat" to higher education and librarianship. For three decades education has been on a virtual roller coaster ride experiencing dramatic fluctuations in environmental factors such as enrollment and funding. The rapid changes have been equally severe for libraries, as they have struggled to provide for increases in demand for service and for expanded quantities of information during a period of erratic monetary support.

Barbara Moran reviews more than 180 publications as a means of identifying the major changes that will confront academic libraries over the next several years. Her analysis of issues includes historical background as well as carefully framed predictions of future directions.

The book is structured around four major topics: "New Technologies," "Management," "Personnel," and "Collections and Cooperation." Issues within these broad topics include bibliographic utilities, online public access catalogs, the electronic library, organization of academic libraries, status of academic librarians, participation in governance, resource sharing, and preservation of library materials, plus many more.

In her concluding chapter, Moran presents four recommendations designed to help academic libraries meet the challenges facing them during the rest of this century. Her recommendations stress the need for libraries to plan for future development, the importance of faculty's and administrators' assisting in the planning, the requirement for adequate financing, and the necessity of joining in more cooperative ventures.

While directed toward academic libraries, the issues covered in this publication are relevant to all types of libraries. Hence, all librarians would find this book valuable and well worth the modest price. [R: JAL, Nov 85, p. 308]   P. Grady Morein

130. Spyers-Duran, Peter, and Thomas W. Mann, Jr., eds. **Financing Information Services: Problems, Changing Approaches, and New Opportunities for Academic and Research Libraries.** Westport, Conn., Greenwood Press, 1985. 197p. bibliog. index. (New Directions in Librarianship, No. 6). $29.95. LC 84-15729. ISBN 0-313-24644-0.

Librarians are often too consumed by the daily challenge of coping with technological, economic, and organizational change to reflect on the financial ramifications of their environment. For example, do the new technologies and information services require a modest realignment of resources or is a fundamental restructuring necessary to remain operationally effective and economically viable? These and related questions are addressed in twelve essays originally presented as conference papers by specialists in business, education, computer science, and librarianship at an international symposium, "Contemporary Issues in Academic

and Research Libraries," held in Boulder, Colorado, during February and March, 1984.

The volume is divided into three sections. Section 1, "Problems," outlines the recent austerity besetting many academic institutions; the decline in funding levels in British university libraries; and suggestions for financial planning in academic libraries. Section 2, "Changing Approaches," focuses on resources sharing; the relationship between costs and services; formula funding; new approaches and rationales for budget determination; and total resource budget planning. Section 3, "New Opportunities," deals with library automation and economics, networks, external contracting, and grantsmanship. A useful bibliography of recommended titles is appended.

Published conference papers are often uneven in quality and this collection confirms the generalization. Only two papers, Paul Kantor's on costs and services and Daniel Lester's on formula funding, are based upon original research. For stimulating insights, consult the essays by Maurice Glicksman, Murray Martin, Richard McCoy and David Weber, and Jo An Segal. Recommended as a convenient synopsis of current problems and directions in the area of financial planning. Only time will adjudicate the editors' bold claim that these essays will greatly influence future academic library development. Perhaps more research and less description is needed to advance the fiscal reformation of academic libraries. [R: JAL, Nov 85, p. 308; LJ, 15 Sept 85, p. 60; LJ, 15 Nov 85, p. 42]

Arthur P. Young

131. Spyers-Duran, Peter, and Thomas W. Mann, Jr., eds. **Issues in Academic Librarianship: Views and Case Studies for the 1980s and 1990s.** Westport, Conn., Greenwood Press, 1985. 206p. index. (New Directions in Librarianship, No. 7). $29.95. LC 84-15733. ISBN 0-313-24645-9.

The fourteen essays in this volume were first presented at a conference, "Contemporary Issues in Academic and Research Libraries," held at Boulder, Colorado, in early 1984. As one would expect, these essays range widely in interest; that any will have lasting significance is unlikely.

That is not to say some are not useful and/or informative. Donald Frank's description of the development of a performance evaluation system at Texas Tech is workmanlike and could serve as a useful model. Donald Simpson on electronic publishing provides a competent overview with a good discussion of implications for academic libraries. On the other hand, the essay on LC's optical disk program is quite dated. Fred Batt, on "Faculty Status for Academic Librarians," gives an efficient summary of the literature. His own position is provocative, though somewhat self-consciously so. Glyn Evans on the "Public Sector/Private Sector Interaction" is most interesting, but his topic is not really an issue for academic librarianship. E. R. Reid-Smith introduces the concept of "informatacy" — the acquired ability to understand and use data and information." Except for the term, he doesn't say much that's new, but the essay is well done. W. B. Raymond, on the preparation of academic librarians, thinks library schools have not been doing a good job — they should make research their primary focus and reinstate the thesis. This reviewer disagrees, but appreciates his argument. The other essays lack interest or originality. The editors should either have exercised more control over the content of the presentations or been selective about which ones to publish.

Evan Ira Farber

132. Stubbs, K. L. **Quantitative Criteria for Academic Research Libraries.** Chicago, Association of College and Research Libraries, American Library Association, 1984. 137p. $19.00 spiralbound; $15.00 spiralbound (ACRL members). ISBN 0-8389-6788-4.

This research project plunges directly into a discussion of data gathering; therefore, it is difficult to identify the purpose of the study. The project uses the U.S. government-accumulated HEGIS (Higher Education General Information Systems, only identified as HEGIS) data from 1978-1979 from approximately three thousand institutions. The intent is to identify "research" libraries. Stubbs finds "a cluster of libraries assumed to support research." Using quantitative characteristics of those institutions, Stubbs measures other libraries against these characteristics to determine if they, too, should be classed as research libraries.

Employing statistical tools such as the cluster analysis technique combined with others — both the discriminant analysis and principal component analysis — a component score for each library is identified. A second technique of identifying research libraries which satisfy a certain number of the criteria established is also discussed.

An appendix list, by state or territory, of the 2,943 libraries shows each library's rank, score, volumes held, gross volumes added, circulation, total expenditures, and total staff.

The volume is useful for comparative purposes and will be of interest to academic library administrators. [R: LJ, Nov 84, p. 299]

Robert D. Stueart

COMPARATIVE AND INTERNATIONAL LIBRARIANSHIP

133. Ahmad, Nazir. **University Library Practices in Developing Countries.** London, KPI; distr., Boston, Routledge & Kegan Paul, c1984, 1985. 207p. illus. index. $59.95. LC 84-4366. ISBN 0-7103-0058-1.

For most of us, knowledge of the Arab Muslim world has been recently acquired, encouraged by events of the last few years in some of the Arab countries. This book, intended for librarians but useful to anyone interested in the educational systems, is a good addition to the literature on the Muslim world in general as well as to the literature of library science.

The purpose of the work is to present "a penetrating analysis of contemporary procedures, practices, applications and operations of university libraries in eight Arab Muslim countries" (p. xv). These eight countries (Nigeria, Malaysia, Pakistan, Sudan, Qatar, Jordan, Kuwait, and Saudia Arabia) are geographically dispersed and represent a variety of stages of economic development but all have in common dominant or large Muslim populations. A total of twenty-four university libraries, varying in size as well as subject specialization, are represented in the descriptions of practices. Moderately systematic treatment is given to all the major library functions: organization, management, staffing, information services, selection and acquisition, collection development, building planning, and cooperation. The author uses as sources for each chapter information gathered from personal visits, interviews, survey data and, most frequently, documentation and published reports provided by the library. Frequent and effective use is made of charts, tables, photographs, and floor plans of the libraries.

Overall, the work is well done. It is particularly effective as a synthesis of the thought and practices of at least a portion of the library profession in the Muslim world. It is not, unfortunately, the "penetrating analysis" that the author says he intended. Indeed, the book is something of a mixture between a description of what the practices actually are in these twenty-four libraries and what the author thinks they should become. Very frequently, for example in the chapter on management and staffing, the author will quote Western writers on what good library management ought to be but then fail to tell us whether it really is that way in these libraries or why it does not or should not meet his stated criteria. The author seems to be writing for two different audiences, the Western reader who wants to know the situation, and the Muslim university librarian, who needs to know what good library management is like. It is often difficult for the reader to separate reality from desire.

Despite this problem, and it is a major one, the book is useful because of the scarcity of literature on the topic. Its most useful feature is that it draws together in one place a lot of scattered information and synthesizes the thought and work of university librarians in Muslim countries. The notes section is extensive, and the book is well indexed. The price is high for such a small volume but it will fill a large gap in our knowledge about the library profession in these countries. [R: JAL, May 85, p. 105; JAL, Sept 85, p. 232; JAL, Nov 85, p. 305]

Robert V. Williams

134. A Directory of Rare Book and Special Collections in the United Kingdom and the Republic of Ireland. Moelwyn I. Williams, ed. London, Library Association; distr., Phoenix, Ariz., Oryx Press, 1985. 664p. index. $135.00. ISBN 0-85365-646-0.

This directory contains descriptions of over five thousand rare book collections found in institutions, National Trust properties, and private houses throughout the United Kingdom and the Republic of Ireland. The information is arranged first by region, and then in alphabetical order by the name of the institution. Information includes address, telephone number, business hours, conditions of admission, research facilities, and, often, a brief history. The origin and history of each collection is noted, together with information on size, and a summary of contents and subject fields found in the collection. When possible, details of catalogs and published references follow each listing.

The editor defines "rare" as "all printed matter before 1851, as well as later collections of rare material such as first editions, limited editions, and ephemera" (introduction). He notes that " 'special collections' in libraries of whatever date imply rarity, and on this basis, these collections also have been included where they have been adjudged to be relevant and appropriate" (introduction). A list of abbreviations and acronyms appears at the beginning of the book and a list of contributors follows the text. The comprehensive index provides access to the institutions listed and to subject.

The entries are very readable and interesting. They would provide helpful background for scholars trying to determine a collection's usefulness. The references at the end of the entries include publication data and are most helpful, especially for large institutions, such as Oxford. This book is printed in easy-to-read type and has a sturdy binding. It would be a useful guide to those needing information on rare books or special collections in the United Kingdom and the Republic of Ireland.

Gloria Palmeri Powell

135. European Communities Information: Its Use and Users. Michael Hopkins, ed. London, Mansell; distr., New York, H. W. Wilson, 1985. 304p. index. $41.00. LC 84-20138. ISBN 0-7201-1701-1.

This compilation consists of fourteen papers which are grouped under two parts: (1) the nature of European Communities information and (2) sources of European Communities information and their use. The European Community consists of three main organizations— European Coal and Steel Community, European Economic Community (the Common Market), and the European Atomic Energy Community—and their related institutions (Commission, Council, European Parliament, Court of Justice, Court of Auditors, and Economic and Social Committee).

The first part of Hopkins's compilation includes six papers by senior European Community information and publishing officials on the following topics: the publications policy and program of the European Communities (EC); the role of the Office for Official Publications of the EC; the general information policy of the EC; disseminating the results of EC research; European Parliament information; and the library and documentation services of the Commission of the EC. The second part is concerned with EC information from the external user's point of view. Papers in this part were prepared by British government officials and librarians and include three which examine the way in which EC membership by Great Britain since 1973 has affected the British Parliament, local governments, and the business community; the EC information needed by these activities; and the sources which best meet those needs. A fourth paper describes grants and loans available to Britons from the European Communities. These four papers have limited value for an American audience. A valuable paper on use of EC information in British universities and polytechnics reflect similar use and needs in American academic institutions. The final three papers are bibliographic in nature and discuss sources of legal, statistical, and agricultural information of the European Communities.

LeRoy C. Schwarzkopf

136. International Librarianship Today and Tomorrow: A Festschrift for William J. Welsh. Joseph W. Price and Mary S. Price, comps. Munich, New York, K. G. Saur, 1985. 174p. $32.50. ISBN 3-598-10586-X.

The value of a festschrift depends on the intrinsic merit of the individual contributions and the degree to which those contributions interconnect—that is, is it a genuine monograph or just a miscellany? The William Welsh festschrift, compiled in honor of the deputy librarian of Congress, ranks high by the first criterion and does reasonably well by the second.

The contributors to *International Librarianship* are very well known—so much so that the editors apparently saw no need to identify or describe them. Perhaps they were right; names like Daniel Boorstin, Harrison Bryan, Martin Cummings, Else Granheim, Warren Haas, Preben Kierkegaard, Herman Liebaers, Guy Sylvestre and Alexander Wilson speak for themselves. Perhaps more important, the papers appear to have been written especially for this volume, not (as with so many festschriften) hauled out from some dusty desk drawer. As a result, these essays are up-to-date, pertinent to present-day concerns and well documented. Several of them are especially good examples of the welcome arts of compression and expression; they take large subjects and convey their essence in less than a dozen readable pages. Indeed, conciseness is a virtue which pretty well all these sixteen contributors have in common.

The papers cover aspects of the library scene in some ten different countries—hence the title of the volume is appropriate enough. However, no central theme dominates the collection and it will, therefore, take a very good memory or some future assiduous indexer to make these contents useful beyond the first reading. *International Librarianship Today and Tomorrow* is a very good festschrift but still only a festschrift.

Samuel Rothstein

137. Libraries in the United Kingdom and the Republic of Ireland 1985. Marion Colthorpe, ed. London, Library Association; distr., Phoenix, Ariz., Oryx Press, 1985. 171p. index. $22.00pa. ISBN 0-85365-916-8.

Now in its eleventh edition, *Libraries in the United Kingdom and the Republic of Ireland* continues to serve as a unique directory of libraries and librarians in the nations represented. Included are public, polytechnic, and academic libraries as well as selected national, government, and special libraries. The criteria for selecting the latter is not explained. Worthy of note is the inclusion of schools of librarianship.

The entries include library addresses, telephone numbers, and many telex numbers. The names of the chief librarians or the assistants in charge are given. A thorough index makes the directory easily accessible.

Libraries in the United Kingdom and the Republic of Ireland will be a worthwhile reference source to American libraries requiring mailing information for the libraries of these nations.

Jefferson D. Caskey

138. The Library Association Conference Proceedings Brighton 1984: Librarianship without Frontiers. David R. Bartlett, ed. London, Library Association; distr., Phoenix, Ariz., Oryx Press, 1985. 134p. ISBN 0-85365-996-6.

The British Council, now celebrating its fiftieth anniversary, has a network of 111 libraries with more than 2 million volumes and approximately 400,000 borrowers. On this base, the council has had a strong influence in developing national public library service in countries in Africa and Southeast Asia. The influence of council libraries as information resources for the English-speaking in other countries, particularly students, has been an important element in the development of those countries. Several papers in the *Proceedings* describe this library development, the best outlines the development of public library service in Malaysia where colonial roots of library service have served as the basis for impressive development of public libraries, library education, and a library association. Papers describing the role of the printed word in global English and the importance of carrying the British book overseas, "very British" in tone, make useful points. Other papers describe the need for librarians to be involved in social change and the role of the British Library and the Library Association in providing information service in a fast changing world. The paper outlining the influence of the British on European librarianship provides one country's view of its influence on its neighbors.

From these well-written papers, one gains an international perspective on the growth and development of public librarianship worldwide. We in the United States need more exposure to the world view of librarianship.

Ann E. Prentice

139. Loveday, Anthony J., and Gunter Gattermann, eds. **University Libraries in Developing Countries: Structure and Function in Regard to Information Transfer for Science and Technology. Proceedings of the IFLA/ UNESCO Pre-Session Seminar for Librarians from Developing Countries. Munchen, August**

16-19, 1983. Munich, New York, K. G. Saur, 1985. 183p. (IFLA Publications 33). $20.00. ISBN 3-598-20397-7.

The organizers of the conference correctly selected the theme mentioned in the title as a key factor in the national development of Third World countries. The fourteen papers cover a wide spectrum of useful topics including problems for university libraries functioning in a national system in developing countries, the example of Brazilian libraries in the acquisition of foreign periodicals in developing countries, collection building and information services for material in agriculture and medicine relevant to Third World use, new information technologies available in the industrialized world, and the application of automation to the library of the National Autonomous University of Mexico.

Each paper is well edited and organized, beginning with an abstract and introduction and ending with a conclusion. References are also provided at the end of each paper as well as an informative summary of the conference discussions. The publication ends with the recommendations and resolutions adopted by the participants and transmitted to the Professional Board of IFLA.

An important acquisition for any library with a strong collection in comparative librarianship or in academic librarianship. Many of the problems and needs identified for Third World countries have not as yet been resolved in the industrialized nations.

George S. Bobinski

140.   Vieira, Anna da Soledade. **Environmental Information in Developing Nations: Politics and Policies.** Westport, Conn., Greenwood Press, 1985. 174p. bibliog. index. (Contributions in Librarianship and Information Sciences, No. 51). $35.00. LC 84-10728. ISBN 0-313-23432-9.

Although the bulk of Vieira's work is given over to an analysis and description of politics and policies, the work also serves as a handy directory and guidebook to sources of information relating to the crises in the environment. Arranged in six chapters—with epilogue, appendix, bibliography, and index—the work opens with an overview of environmental pollution and development, reviewing physical sources of pollution as well as political, technological, and social factors which are contributing to pollution. This review is followed by a brief and useful description and comparison of the major ideologies governing environmental pollution—conservationism, developmentalism, and ecodevelopmentalism.

Vieira proceeds to describe information activities of international organizations, and reviews United Nations international conferences on the environment. In a subsequent chapter treating environment in the Third World, the author attempts to show the relationship between environmental policies and politics, governmental actions, and public awareness. Not until the midpoint of the volume are we exposed to an essay on the design of environmental information systems in developing countries, wherein the implications of underdevelopment and the implications of environmental policy are jointly explored. Then follows a review of environmental information systems in the Third World, focusing on Brazil, Mexico, Egypt, and India as somewhat representative of the past, present, and future. The author compares the approaches of each country, with implications for the Third World.

In the concluding chapter, Vieira discusses new development orientation, present status, and trends of environmental information; and makes predictions for the future, with a focus on the importance of the information professional. As a whole, the work attempts an almost encyclopedic approach. Although it fails in this respect, it remains adequately comprehensive in its treatment of the subject. No other work to date brings together so succinctly such a variety of information on the subject of environmental information in developing nations. Consequently, students and researchers in relevant disciplines will find multiple uses for Vieira's treatment of the subject. Citations in chapter notes, as well as the separate bibliography, should prove quite useful to selection librarians trying to identify important documents for the study of environmental information. Recommended for all college and university libraries. [R: WLB, Dec 85, p. 57]   Edmund F. SantaVicca

CONSERVATION

141.   Merrill-Oldham, Jan. **Conservation and Preservation of Library Materials: A Program for the University of Connecticut Libraries.** Storrs, Conn., University of Connecticut Library, 1984. 65p. bibliog. price not reported.

Why publish in 1984 a conservation manual which was written in 1981? The University of Connecticut apparently feels that its preservation plan can be of some use to other libraries engaged in planning for the conservation of their collections. The document was written after a year-long survey of the university libraries' preservation needs. It is divided into several chapters on environmental control; "inherent vice" (mainly acid in paper problems); handling and storage of material; repairs, binding, and other conservation work; training and outreach; and program planning. Each chapter contains descriptions of several problems or situations in the libraries with each description followed by a recommendation to alleviate the situation. For example, the explanation of the importance of temperature control is followed by a recommendation that the libraries be kept at 60°-70°F and that temperature variations be closely monitored. If all 215 recommendations were implemented, the university would have a comprehensive conservation program indeed.

A short list of references follows the text. Since there is no separate index, the table of contents must serve as index. This manual will be useful to librarians who wish to write a similar plan. Although it is specific to the Connecticut libraries, its advice applies to many collections. It is not a complete preservation manual by any means and does not replace Swartzburg's *Preserving Library Materials* (Scarecrow, 1980) or the Cunhas' *Conservation of Library Materials* (Scarecrow, 1983). But it will give other librarians ideas to consider when beginning or expanding their own preservation programs.   Linda S. Keir

142.   Merrill-Oldham, Jan, and Merrily Smith, eds. **The Library Preservation Program: Models, Priorities, Possibilities. Proceedings of a Conference....** Chicago, American Library Association, 1985. 117p. index. $8.95pa. LC 84-28270. ISBN 0-8389-3315-7.

This collection of papers was first presented at an April 1983 conference at the Library of Congress for "top-level library managers." The main body of papers discusses incorporation of preservation into existing library systems, determination of preservation needs at three universities and the Library of Congress, and the funding of preservation. The conference sponsors managed to attract virtually all the important names in the field, and thus the papers reflect some of the best programs in the country including those at Yale, Stanford, Berkeley, Columbia, Southern Illinois, and the Library of Congress. Taken together the papers give a library administrator a good idea of the work involved in establishing a first-class preservation program. Of particular interest are articles by David Weber of Stanford on the financing of his program and by David Stam on obtaining funds for preservation. Introductory articles by William Welsh and Rutherford Rogers look at the preservation problem and past efforts to deal with it. Pamela Darling provides a look to the future, outlining eight goals for a national preservation effort. Her commonsense approach to the problems and opportunities facing libraries provides a fitting ending to the volume.

Reflecting the original conference's purpose, this book is most useful to library administrators whose job it is to find the money, staff, and facilities necessary to establish and maintain a preservation program. It does not address specific problems and treatments as Merrill-Oldham's previous book, *Conservation and Preservation of Library Materials: A Program for the University of Connecticut Libraries*, and many others do. This volume is valuable, however, precisely because it focuses on administrative and financial questions and because it talks to the people who can effect change in their institutions. [R: JAL, July 85, pp. 179-80; LJ, 1 June 85, p. 104; RQ, Winter 85, p. 276]   Linda S. Keir

143.   Middleton, Bernard C. **The Restoration of Leather Bindings.** rev. ed. Chicago, American Library Association, 1984. 266p. illus. bibliog. index. (LTP Publication, No. 20). $25.00pa. LC 83-15371. ISBN 0-8389-0391-6.

As the author notes in his preface, the field of binding restoration has experienced a number of changes during the twelve years since the first edition of this work was published, not the least of which is an increased awareness of preservation problems and solutions. Middleton has taken that awareness into account, particularly in his expanded bibliography, but he is more concerned with advances in techniques and materials which have affected the craft of fine bookbinding. A comparison of the first and second editions shows many small but important changes where the author has updated the information in accordance with new research, particularly in the treatment of leather.

The major addition to the new book is the chapter on antiquarian books which discusses the practical, aesthetic, and moral issues involved in rebinding rare books and describes the construction and binding of old books. People interested in antiquarian books who will never be bookbinders will find this chapter informative and thought provoking. Illustrations in this chapter and throughout the book help clarify textual explanations.

This well-written but technical book will be useful to the practicing book binder and conservator. Because of its additions and revisions it should be preferred over the first edition. [R: C&RL, Nov 85, p. 531; JAL, Mar 85, p. 43]
                     Linda S. Keir

144.   **Preservation of Library Material: A Report of the Collection Preservation Committee.** Toronto, University of Toronto Library, 1984. 38p. $5.00pa.

This report details the activities and recommendations of a Collection Preservation Committee appointed by the University of Toronto's chief librarian. The committee's charge was "to address the problem of physical deterioration of the collections in Robarts, Sigmund Samuel and Science & Medicine, and the departmental libraries on the University of Toronto President's budget, and to report to the Collections Development Committee and the Library Advisory Council in March 1983." The committee (1) surveyed the collections to assess their physical condition, (2) considered the physical environment in the library including temperature, humidity, lighting, cleanliness, shelving and storage, and handling by staff and patrons, (3) proposed policies for the conservation and restoration of the collections, with an indication of priority, (4) indicated costs to carry out proposals, and (5) prepared the report.

Among other useful information, the report describes a computer-generated sampling scheme for surveying the collection which produced the following information: location; total number of items checked; number of monographs and serials; number of paperback monographs; number of items needing to be repaired, recased, or rebound; number of items with paper fair, fair-brittle, and brittle; and number of items containing loose or torn pages or a considerable amount of underlining. Actual survey results are given as are cost estimates for addressing each problem. Mass deacidification and the preservation of material in microform are also given consideration.

Even though this report addresses the specific needs of the University of Toronto Library, many of the findings, methods, and recommendations can be applied to similar situations in other libraries.

Dean H. Keller

145. Westbrook, Lynn. **Paper Preservation: Nature, Extent, & Recommendations.** Urbana, Ill., Graduate School of Library and Information Science, University of Illinois, 1985. 74p. bibliog. (Occasional Papers, No. 171). $3.00pa. ISSN 0276-1769.

Every year about one percent of the books in research libraries become brittle and can no longer be circulated. Nearly all (97 percent) of the books printed in this century have a life expectancy of fewer than fifty years. Lynn Westbrook in an exhaustive paper with over three hundred references tackles the gigantic problem of paper preservation under its many facets: nature of preservation problems; causes of paper deterioration; professional commitment; technology; cost; care; education; and local, national, and international plans. She demonstrates how preservation problems are linked to such library operations as resource sharing as well as to shrinking budgets, cooperative cataloging, printing, and

publishing. Every document of our libraries is vulnerable to all kinds of enemies—biological, physical, human—but the major causes of paper deterioration are acid, temperature, light, and fungus.

There is no easy solution; even experts in the field find themselves in conflict. Although a great number of librarians are aware of this problem, they have yet to take strong action. Technology is there to offer partial solutions in the forms of microforms, permanent paper, and deacidification. Professionals have still to come to grips with cost, care, archival quality, and readers. Currently a number of research facilities are working together on various facets of the problem. Westbrook makes clear that there is a need for continual research and budget allowance because we know that preservation can no longer be dismissed as a luxury program. This paper is a detailed look at a problem that plagues our libraries. It offers readers a thoughtful analysis and an extensive bibliography.

Camille Côté

COPYRIGHT

146. Hébert, Françoise, ed. **Copyright: Proceedings of the Workshop Held at the Annual Conference of the Canadian Library Association, June 7, 1984, Toronto, Ontario.** Ottawa, Canadian Library Association, 1985. 66p. $10.00pa. ISBN 0-88802-192-5.

The proceedings reported on here were organized after a round table discussion held at the annual conference of the Canadian Library Association, in Toronto. Françoise Hébert, a Toronto librarian, convenor of the CLA Copyright Committee, put this workshop together to help librarians answer a simple question: "Exactly what can we copy legally?" The publication is in three parts. Part 1, "Copyright Today," is presented by Françoise Hébert and guest Wanda Noel, practicing lawyer specializing in copyright law. The Canadian Copyright Act of 1924 is defined here and briefly explained. Participants of the discussion express their views on various hypothetical situations likely to occur in libraries. Among issues discussed are fair dealing; current awareness; issues on art and music; reserve in libraries; and recent technological developments with computers and videotapes. Short to-the-point answers provide well-documented information from a legal point of view.

The second part of the volume is a presentation by A. A. (Frank) Keyes of "From Gutenberg to Telidon," a white paper on copyright. Proposals are made for revision of the Canadian copyright law *and* of the government's intention to provide increased support by new copyright policies. There are also proposals to change the copyright law to provide greater protection to creators. A discussion between Noel and Keyes follows. The last part is a panel discussion on reprography collectives, a hot topic treated very seriously by four experts: Teeple, a member of the CLA Copyright Committee; Hébert, the convenor; Pitman, chairman of the Toronto publishing firm of Copp, Clark, Pitman; Woods, a member on the Board of the Writers' Copyright Agency of Canada Trust and a representative of the League of Canadian Poets to the Book and Periodical Development Council Task Force on Reprography Collectives; and finally Bruce Couchman, a lawyer and policy analyst with Consumer and Corporate Affairs Canada. Because of the importance of this issue, the last part is probably the best part of the document.

The style of the whole publication is lively and the presentation is pleasant. This is a fascinating volume on a topic that is most difficult to treat. Françoise Hébert succeeded in producing a readable, concise document with legal jargon applied to life situations (case studies). Every librarian, in Canada and elsewhere, should read this document. [R: CLJ, Dec 85, p. 385]

Camille Côté

147. Miller, Jerome K. **The Copyright Directory. Vol. I: General Information.** Friday Harbor, Wash., Copyright Information Services, 1985. 104p. index. $23.00pa. LC 84-29227. ISBN 0-914143-02-6.

Miller has a well-deserved reputation as an expert on compliance with the very complex U.S. copyright law. This is the first of three volumes he is publishing that will aid in compliance; volume 1, *General Information*, is now available, volume 2, *Copyright Attorneys*, is promised in 1986, and volume 3, *Rights and Permissions Officers*, will be issued in 1987. Volume 1 covers government agencies, copyright clearinghouses, rights and permissions agencies, associations active in copyright matters, cleared music and sound effects libraries, stock shot (photographic) libraries, and consultants and speakers. The volume ends with a law firm index, a legislative coalition index, and a personal name index.

In each case, entries provide official name, address, and telephone number; many entries also provide a personal name for contact purposes and a short annotation (twenty-five to fifty words) indicating the scope or nature of the organization. Each section has a one- or two-page introduction providing an overview of the topic. A worthwhile publication.

G. Edward Evans

EDUCATION AND PROFESSIONALISM

148. **Changing Technology and Education for Librarianship and Information Science.** Basil Stuart-Stubbs, ed. Greenwich, Conn., JAI Press, 1985. 188p. index. (Foundations in Library and Information Science, Vol. 20). $23.75; $47.50 (institutions). LC 84-21330. ISBN 0-89232-515-1.

This is the proceedings of an invitational conference, hosted by the School of Librarianship, University of British Columbia, 2-4 June 1983 and sponsored by the Council on Library Resources. The conference can be considered the third of a series of conferences intended to foster communication among directors of academic libraries and library and information science educators concerning areas of mutual interest and concern. The first conference of the series, held 13-17 December 1981 at Lake Arrowhead, was the Academic Libraries Frontiers Conference which identified the areas of interest. The second conference, held at Wye Plantation, 28-30 June 1982, concentrated on personnel-related issues of research libraries and of research library and information science education. This third conference assesses the impact of changing technology in order to assist librarians, associations, and educators in making plans for the next decade.

The proceedings include the full text of the six theme papers: "Changing Technology, Scholarly Communication and the Research Library" by John B. Black, "Changing Technology and the Personnel Requirements of Research Libraries" by Carlton Rochell, "Current Developments in Education for Librarianship and Information Science" by Edward G. Holley, "Essential Program Requirements for the 1980s and 1990s" by Bernard Franckowiak, "The School, Its Faculty and Students" by Michael Buckland, and "Strategies for Adapting to Constant Change" by Robert D. Stueart. Theme papers are followed by formal commentaries and synopses of informal group discussions. There are three final conference summaries written from the information scientists', the research library directors', and the educators' points of view.

Theme papers, though they contain no startling revelations, are organized authoritative overviews of the topics covered. Most theme papers and some commentaries include lists of references cited. The commentators view the themes from varying perspectives; accounts of group discussions held by the thirty-two conference participants augment understanding of the issues discussed. The author and subject indexes provide useful access points to the contents. This proceedings deserves wide reading by academic librarians and library and information science educators. [R: JAL, Nov 85, p. 305]

Virginia E. Yagello

149. Fang, Josephine Riss, Paul Nauta, and Anna J. Fang, eds. **International Guide to Library and Information Science Education: A Reference Source for Educational Programs in the Information Fields World-wide.** Munich, New York, K. G. Saur, 1985. 537p. bibliog. index. (IFLA Publications 32). $46.00. ISBN 3-598-20396-9.

This volume contains a wealth of information of great value to the library profession worldwide. The result of years of work initiated by the IFLA Section on Library Schools and Other Training Aspects, the *Guide* presents data concerning degree requirements, professional qualifications, and educational systems from countries spanning the globe.

The *Guide* is arranged alphabetically by country. A brief introductory description of the education system for each nation precedes individual program listings, which appear alphabetically by place. Entries include name, address, name and title of school director, year of founding, administrative structure, program details (entrance requirements, number of students, language of instruction), teaching staff, physical resources, continuing education, and professional status.

In compiling this volume, the editors have met their objectives of determining international professional qualifications, providing a basis for comparison and evaluation, encouraging the mobility of librarians across national boundaries through exchange and cooperation, and presenting an international guide to library education.

The arrangement of individual entries within countries by place name makes the *Guide* somewhat awkward to use at times, and the editors admit to the datedness of some of the information. Nevertheless, the ambitiousness of the project, the comprehensiveness of coverage, and the value of the included information make this volume a welcome addition to reference collections. Highly recommended.

John W. Collins III

150. **Financial Assistance for Library Education: Academic Year 1985-1986.** Chicago, Standing Committee on Library Education, American Library Association, 1984. 48p. index. free pa. ISBN 0-8389-6792-2.

This long-running annual title is a valuable tool for prospective students who wish to explore awards available in library education. The awards listed include those pertaining not only to the MLS but also to the library technical assistant level, and to bachelor's degree, sixth year certificate, doctoral, and continuing education programs.

The book is divided into two sections. The first section is arranged by state and includes information on financial assistance offered by state and provincial library associations, educational institutions, and local libraries in the United States and Canada. The second section lists national and regional awards offered in the United States and Canada. Both sections give the following: granting body and/or name of award; program level; type of assistance and number and amount of scholarships; academic and other requirements; and where to apply. A list of ALA accredited library schools and an index of awards by level of program are also provided.

Frank Wm. Goudy

151. **Librarian/Author: A Practical Guide on How to Get Published.** Betty-Carol Sellen, ed. New York, Neal-Schuman, 1985. 247p. index. $24.95. LC 85-4953. ISBN 0-918212-83-9.

The library science literature has grown dramatically in recent years. Librarians are writing more books for more library science publishers and contributing more articles to an ever-increasing number of journals. Sellen hopes to facilitate the publishing process for would-be author/librarians in this enjoyable handbook.

Librarian/Author is a collection of original articles on a wide spectrum of pertinent issues such as the author-editor relationship, book contracts, selecting a publisher, and writing a journal article. Informative lists of both library science journal and book publishers are included as well as the American Library Association's *Guidelines for Authors, Editors and Publishers of Literature in the Library and Information Field*. Librarian/authors, editors, publishers, and professional writers are represented among the contributors, many of whom like Pat Shuman or Art Plotnik will be well known to the general library community.

For the most part, the articles offer practical information and helpful advice. A good investment for the inexperienced or bashful would-be author.

Heather Cameron

152. **Library and Information Science Education, Statistical Report, 1985.** State College, Pa., Association for Library and Information Science Education, 1985. 1v. (various paging). $25.00pa.

This sixth annual compilation, analysis, interpretation, and reporting of information about graduate library and information science programs provides extensive data about those schools which are members of ALISE (Association of Library and Information Science Education). With a response rate of 97 percent from ALISE members and 26 percent from associate members, data from nearly all accredited and a percentage of unaccredited programs are included. The period covered is the 1983-1984 academic year except for faculty salary data which reflects salaries as of 1 January 1985. The report based on questionnaires sent to each school is divided into six sections: faculty, students, curriculum, income and expenditure, continuing education, and a summary and comparative analysis which ties the several sections together to form a profile of library/information science education.

Information is presented in tables, which provides the reader with comparative data on topics ranging from size of student body, to research dollars awarded, to average entry-level salary for assistant professors. Narrative accompanying the tables is in most cases brief and to-the-point although in some instances it would benefit from careful editing.

The compilation provides a comprehensive picture of the various schools individually and as part of the whole. The data provide opportunity for extensive analysis from which a picture of library/information science education today and over time can emerge. It is an essential management tool for those involved in the educational component of the library/information science profession and of interest to anyone wishing descriptive information about schools and programs.   Ann E. Prentice

153. Lindsey, Jonathan A., and Ann E. Prentice. **Professional Ethics and Librarians.** Phoenix, Ariz., Oryx Press, 1985. 103p. bibliog. index. $32.50. LC 83-43244. ISBN 0-89774-133-1.

Professional Ethics and Librarians by Jonathan A. Lindsey and Ann E. Prentice is a timely publication. It introduces the documentary history of American library codes of ethics within the general context of professional codes and the specific framework of recognizing that librarians are increasingly assuming the role, in this technological age, of purveyors of information to clients, to whom they are responsible. In emphasizing the currency and relevance of this

subject the authors within the first chapter, point to three factors: the amount of information available to the information specialist in computerized databases and the capability of manipulating the data in diverse ways; the cost of literature searches to clients; and the accountability expected from professionals in both the private and public sectors.

The second chapter traces the history of the American Library Association's official statements on ethics in 1929, 1938, 1975, and 1981, and provides the texts of these codes and other library codes which informed these official statements. To further the debate and to encourage refinement of the code, the authors have provided a chapter for the comments of nine American library leaders on the 1981 Statement on Professional Ethics.

Chapter 4 emphasizes the application of the code by laying out a series of cases which were presented by the Professional Ethics Committee during a program at the annual meeting in 1981 and by citing ethical questions raised by other professional groups which are relevant to the library profession.

Finally, a selective bibliography and index complete this compendium of information on codes of ethics for librarians. While the text is written from the American perspective, it does raise many aspects of an issue which librarians in every country must tackle. Those interested in the subject will find a wealth of references as well as several models. They will not, however, learn the viewpoint of either author. [R: AL, Apr 85, p. 224; JAL, Nov 85, p. 301; LJ, Aug 85, p. 71; RQ, Winter 85, p. 279]

Gwynneth Evans

154. Smith, Linda C., ed. **Professional Competencies—Technology and the Library.** Champaign, Ill., Graduate School of Library and Information Science, University of Illinois, 1983 [1984]. 138p. index. $15.00. LC 84-6047. ISBN 0-87845-070-X.

Speakers at the twentieth annual Clinic on Library Applications of Data Processing addressed the human side of information technology, considering how professional roles and responsibilities in all types of libraries are being affected by technological change. Their presentations have been collected in this volume.

Coverage is as follows: Jose-Marie Griffiths provides a planning framework for analyzing and developing the competencies of any information professional. Kathryn Luther Henderson analyzes competencies called for in job announcements for technical services librarians, including an extensive bibliography. Danuta A. Nitecki discusses competencies for public services librarians, and Richard T.

Sweeney looks at public librarians, proposing six general competencies in information technology and behavior. Carolyn Gray presents an articulate plea for development of an informed and interested library staff in combination with good technological design. Hillis L. Griffin discusses the unique skills required of special librarians. Linda Baskin offers practical ideas for in-service training in computer use, suggesting that one must not be impressed by the "computer mystique." In two essays, Evelyn H. Daniel and Julie Carroll Virgo look at formal professional education and the role of the professional association in continuing education.

The University of Illinois's annual clinics on library data processing are well known and well regarded. This one meets the high standards so firmly established. The essays are all thoughtful and practical. These papers should be carefully read and thoroughly considered by all professionals, especially those who provide guidance for others. [R: BL, 15 Jan 85, p. 683]

Margaret McKinley

155.　United States. National Commission on Libraries and Information Science. **Library and Information Services in a Learning Society: Annual Report 1983-84.** Washington, D.C., National Commission on Libraries and Information Science; distr., Washington, D.C., GPO, 1985. 87p. $2.50pa. LC 73-643728. ISSN 0091-2972. S/N 052-003-00991-9.

The NCLIS was established, in 1970 by the National Commission on Libraries and Information Science Act, to aid both the executive and legislative branches in national library and information-related matters. It also works with public and private sectors in the information industry in attaining mutual goals.

In 1984 the commission published several reports stressing the importance of libraries and information processing in a "Learning Society," and their crucial role in developing greater productivity. Policy and planning activities include the improvement of access to ever-changing library/information services necessary to support a program of lifelong learning.

Sections on personnel, administration, and future plans follow. Several appendices list the commission's goals, projects, publications, former members, and fiscal statement. The public law creating the commission is reprinted, completing this informative annual report.

Anita Zutis

HISTORY

156.　Carrier, Esther Jane. **Fiction in Public Libraries, 1900-1950.** Littleton, Colo., Libraries

Unlimited, 1985. 384p. bibliog. index. $27.50. LC 85-4269. ISBN 0-87287-459-1.

A good chronicle of librarians' attitudes towards fiction, based on evidence found in *Library Journal*, the *ALA Bulletin*, and *Public Libraries* between 1900 and 1950. Chapters 1 and 2 introduce readers to the subject. Chapters 3 and 4 discuss two sides of the same question: Should public librarians stock all kinds of fiction, or just "high quality"? Chapter 5 concentrates on the fuzzy distinctions separating censorship from book selection. Chapter 6 covers librarians' efforts to "improve" reading, and chapter 7 focuses on fiction for children and young adults. A summary chapter yields an obvious conclusion: the library profession could not agree upon the kinds of fiction public libraries should stock.

Carrier deserves credit for emphasizing this conclusion. It is regrettable, though, that she ignores the question of why this problem persisted? To answer that question adequately would require contact with scores of books recently written by library historians and social science and humanities scholars on such highly relevant subjects as censorship, the influence of literary canons, and the tendency of popular fiction to reinforce the dominant culture. Carrier has largely restricted her research to sources contemporary with the period under study. Furthermore, instead of analysis, she offers a narrative which often reads like an extended annotated bibliography of sources on the subject, only infrequently interrupted by underdeveloped summary paragraphs. As a chronicle, *Fiction in Public Libraries* will be helpful; as history, it needs a much broader framework to augment understanding of "the fiction question" in our profession's history. [R: Choice, Dec 85, p. 588; LJ, Dec 85, p. 74; RQ, Winter 85, pp. 272-73]

Wayne A. Wiegand

157.　Downs, Robert B. **Perspectives on the Past: An Autobiography.** Metuchen, N.J., Scarecrow, 1984. 225p. illus. bibliog. index. $17.50. LC 84-5589. ISBN 0-8108-1703-9.

The accomplishments of Robert B. Downs as a librarian are legion, both on the national scene and on an international scale. His publications, honors, and offices held alone represent the best the profession has to offer. In light of his highly productive life, Downs's autobiography is most disappointing.

Downs was an administrator, educator, researcher, publisher, and surveyor; simply put, he was a giant in the library field. He is still active as a researcher. He directed library programs at the University of North Carolina, New York University, and, for twenty-eight years, at the University of Illinois. He wrote over thirty-five books and seemingly uncountable articles and surveys. Even Downs's retirement in 1971 did not end a productive career. His many achievements are obvious from a reading of his own story. Yet, too much of the autobiography is excerpts from printed sources which recount Downs's career. An exchange with columnist James J. Kilpatrick, for example, over the issue of intellectual freedom is told only in previously published sources. While the autobiography is a significant contribution to the developing literature of librarianship, it is unfortunate that Downs's "perspectives" do not reflect more fully his devotion to libraries.

The small volume is divided into twelve chapters, each dealing with a topic ranging from Downs's administrative career to his ideas on intellectual freedom. In each, Downs relates his views on the issue and provides supporting evidence, usually in the form of anecdotes. It is here that the author's account is generally taken from printed sources. This is where the autobiography could have benefitted from Downs's personal reflections. The book also includes a brief but useful chronology, a selected list of writings, and an index. [R: AL, Apr 85, p. 249; JAL, May 85, p. 103; LJ, 1 Feb 85, p. 78]

Boyd Childress

158. Harris, Michael H. **History of Libraries in the Western World.** compact textbook ed. Metuchen, N.J., Scarecrow, 1984. 289p. index. $15.00. LC 83-20133. ISBN 0-8108-1666-0.

When a text is the only one of a kind in print and has been around since 1965, it is used and even commended despite its flaws and disappointments. Furthermore, critics feel a bit sheepish because they realize the magnitude of the task of preparing a one-volume text on the history of libraries—an assignment tantamount to producing a world history perceived through library-colored glasses. Those who saw virtues in the third edition (co-authored with Elmer D. Johnson, 1976) will likely find them in this slightly revised, but further "compacted," edition. It is still about the only place to go.

However, critics who despaired over the 1976 edition (see *JLH* 12 [Fall 1977]: 403-8) will find further grounds for dismay in this "compact textbook edition," for there is far more "cutting" than "pasting." Not only has the former final chapter, an attempt at general philosophical interpretation, been dropped as needless redundancy, the rest of the twelve-chapter text has been cut by more than one-tenth, ranging from two or three pages per chapter in the first two parts dealing with ancient and medieval libraries to as many as nine pages in each of the European chapters in the part devoted to modern libraries. About twenty

pages alone were eliminated by drastic reduction of the end of chapter bibliographical references. Though the preface justifies this procedure by mentioning the existence of newer bibliographical guides, the "Additional Readings" omit significant works such as the *Annual Bibliography of the History of the Printed Book and Libraries*, 1970- (1973-) and the continuing volumes of *British Library History: Bibliography*, 1962- (1972-). The favoring of current works rather than classic treatments from any given period will be less instructive for students. The reduction of the previously meager index to 5½ pages is symbolic of the reduced utility of this effort. (The expanded second edition, 1970, 521 pages, contained an index of 18 pages.)

In sum, if one cannot get real historical interpretation in any case, then a factual handbook has at least encyclopedic value; the second edition is still best for this. A standard text on this topic, up to the highest standards, has yet to be written. This should be a high priority for the profession. Until it appears, however, Harris's work will be used, cited, and found in all types of libraries—because it is the only such work available in print. [R: JAL, Nov 85, p. 306]

Donald G. Davis, Jr.

159. Kaser, David. **Books and Libraries in Camp and Battle: The Civil War Experience.** Westport, Conn., Greenwood Press, 1984. 141p. illus. bibliog. index. (Contributions in Librarianship and Information Science, No. 48). $27.95. LC 84-507. ISBN 0-313-24483-9.

This slim monograph is a neatly constructed and executed survey and analysis of the reading experiences of Civil War troops, North and South. Four short chapters deal with "Reading by American Men in 1860" (pre-war factors affecting reading and channels that supplied material, "What Civil War Soldiers Read" (the various kinds of reading—purposeful, religious, newspapers and magazines, escape), "Reading in Wartime Settings" (camp and battle, libraries and reading rooms, hospitals, prison camps), and "Sources of Soldiers' Reading Matter" (military, personal, commercial, religious, and charitable). An "Afterword" suggests the wide-ranging effect of the veterans on popular book and magazine production, the public library movement, and the development of military libraries.

The lucid organization of the study is supported by thorough research in the printed primary sources, notably memoirs and regimental histories, as well as relevant secondary literature. Consequently, dozens of well-chosen examples effectively underpin the structured themes. That the sources lead the author to greater concentration on the North (see treatment of the U.S. Christian Commission) is understandable. The thirteen illustrations, most drawn from contemporary materials, add much to the study. In his typical blend of scholarship and readability, Kaser fulfills his task in the now-expected fashion, from personal preface to summing up. This work will appeal to Civil War and library and literary history enthusiasts alike. [R: WLB, Feb 85, p. 416]

Donald G. Davis, Jr.

160. Kraske, Gary E. **Missionaries of the Book: The American Library Profession and the Origins of United States Cultural Diplomacy.** Westport, Conn., Greenwood Press, 1985. 293p. bibliog. index. (Contributions in Librarianship and Information Science, No. 54). $35.00. LC 84-27914. ISBN 0-313-24351-4.

Taking its title from Melvil Dewey's call in 1919 for American librarians to become active in the international arena as "missionaries of the book," this study documents the activities of the American library profession, especially during the years 1938 through 1949, in relating books and libraries with the cultural and diplomatic objectives of the U.S. foreign policy. With the cooperation and support of such private foundations as the Rockefeller Foundation and the U.S. State and War Departments, the American Library Association attempted to develop in numerous countries American-style libraries which would be "arsenals of democracy," free from governmental propagandistic activities — libraries which would strengthen cultural relations throughout the world.

Special interest was directed toward Latin American countries, China, and various European countries. But as World War II developed and in the Cold War years which followed, the governmental supporting departments saw these libraries mainly as an instrument in achieving their foreign policy concerns. The libraries were largely redesigned to serve as information centers, and book collections were developed more to counter propaganda directed against the United States. ALA involvement diminished and the United States Information Agency later assumed major responsibility for these programs.

The international interests of ALA were directed not only toward libraries as such but also toward training national librarians either in the United States or in overseas library schools, and in the postwar years toward assisting foreign libraries in obtaining American wartime publications and American libraries in finding foreign printed material.

This book, first prepared as a doctoral dissertation, is thoroughly researched and well documented, with an index (mostly personal and corporate names), extensive chapter footnotes, bibliography, and in an appendix a listing of "ALA International Projects, 1938-1949."

Esther Jane Carrier

161. Miksa, Francis. **The Development of Classification at the Library of Congress.** Champaign, Ill., Graduate School of Library and Information Science, University of Illinois, 1984. 78p. bibliog. (Occasional Papers, No. 164). $3.00pa. ISSN 0272-1769.

The early efforts to provide subject access to the Library of Congress's collections have been scantily described. Miksa shows the origins of the earliest classification in Bacon's *Advancement of Knowledge* (1604), as modified in the *Encyclopédie*, and, with the acquisition of Jefferson's library, the significant alterations by that sapient bibliophile. In 1897, John Russell Young fell heir to a million-piece backlog, and it was clear that a new classification system was needed. J. C. M. Hanson and Charles Martel undertook the job. Miksa describes lucidly the residual Jeffersonian influence, the contributions of the Cutter scheme, and the formative years of the new classification in the early Putnam era, 1901-1911. From this point Miksa provides an orderly account of the constant revision that has striven for universality both in coverage and application. In his concluding sentences Miksa suggests a review of the whole idea of classified shelf arrangement (Georg Leyh challenged it long ago, at least for research libraries). However, classification of some sort has been recognized as necessary from the Babylonians and Callimachus to our own time, and shelf classification is surely essential in the present state of technology for heavily used works. Miksa's history of the LC experience is also a guide to the theory and utility of classification in general, and it is highly suggestive of guidelines for the future.

Lawrence S. Thompson

162. Stokes, Roy. **Henry Bradshaw 1831-1886.** Metuchen, N.J., Scarecrow, 1984. 272p. index. (The Great Bibliographers Series, No. 6). $22.50. LC 83-20445. ISBN 0-8108-1679-2.

This is Stokes's second contribution to the series and both scholars and bibliophiles will appreciate the magnitude of the effort to organize the work of Henry Bradshaw, the eminent Cambridge librarian and bibliographer of the nineteenth century. The text is divided into three major sections, the first entitled "Commentary," being a forty-page analysis of Bradshaw's productivity. This proves to be a well-organized analysis of the various stages of his writing career in chronological sequence, and is carefully documented with notes, references, and reviews. Part 2 is a thirty-four page check-list of Bradshaw's published writings beginning with the year 1862 and continuing through 1981. It is clear that the bibliographer has remained a source of interest and inspiration for contemporary scholars who continue to reveal his wisdom and sagacity through publication of his letters and papers originally presented to the Cambridge Antiquarian Society. The largest portion of the text is reserved for the final part, which presents excerpts from eighteen of his works as originally published in 1889 by Francis Jenkinson, Bradshaw's successor as university librarian at Cambridge. Arranged in chronological order of their origin, these eighteen essays show not only Bradshaw's depth as a scholar but his effectiveness as a bibliographer, since many of his theories "have been assimilated into the corpus of bibliographical work." The volume concludes with an index of both names and subjects which should prove useful to the reader. Ron Blazek

INFORMATION SCIENCE

163. Garfield, Eugene. **The Awards of Science and Other Essays.** Philadelphia, ISI Press, 1985. 572p. illus. index. (Essays of an Information Scientist, Vol. 7). $30.00. LC 77-602. ISBN 0-89495-044-4.

The series note is the essential clue to the contents of this book; like the previous six volumes in the series, it faithfully reproduces the fifty-two essays (almost all by Garfield himself) published weekly in *Current Contents* for 1984. In addition the appendix reprints seven Garfield papers which originally appeared elsewhere, plus his doctoral dissertation.

Does this material deserve to be collected and preserved in book form? Or, to put it more directly, is the book worth the $30.00 it costs? My answers are mixed. If your library does not get or keep *Current Contents* or has a special interest in information science as a field of study, then definitely yes. If your library already has this material in its original form and is not sufficiently interested in Eugene Garfield's opinions, analyses, musings, and observations to pay for them twice, then no. I am personally inclined to opt for buying the book, since I consider Garfield's writings to be novel, intriguing, and informative enough to be worth "collecting" in both senses of the word. There can be very few scholars in information science with Garfield's breadth and sparkle.

One last point: the title is somewhat misleading. As a publishing ploy, each volume in this series is from now on to be given its own title as a way of suggesting its "uniqueness." But in fact the rest of the contents bear little

relationship to the title. So libraries should buy this book or not on exactly the same basis that they applied to its six predecessors. [R: JAL, Nov 85, p. 317] Samuel Rothstein

164. **The Information Economy in the U.S.: Its Effect on Libraries and Networks: Proceedings of the Library of Congress Network Advisory Committee Meeting November 14-16, 1984.** Washington, D.C., Network Development and MARC Standards Office, Library of Congress, 1985. 59p. (Network Planning Paper, No. 10). $7.50pa. LC 85-10608. ISBN 0-8444-0502-7.

This book is the product of a two-day meeting of the Library of Congress Network Advisory Committee on the topic of the effect of the emerging information economy upon libraries and library networks. The objective of the meeting, and of this publication, was to introduce the basic concepts which underlie the economic research which has proclaimed the arrival of the information sector in the United States economy. The treatment of the effects of that economic shift, despite the title, is *extremely* limited.

The bulk of the publication is devoted to a paper by economist Sherman Robinson, which describes the key research efforts which have been undertaken in the field of the economics of information. Robinson describes the groundbreaking research which Fritz Machlup published in 1962 as *The Production and Distribution of Knowledge in the U.S.*, and also the research conducted a decade-and-a-half later by Marc Porat and Michael Rubin in the nine volume *The Information Economy*. The research techniques employed in each study are compared, and discrepancies in the findings of the two studies are explained.

This is a good reference tool for those seeking a brief explanation of the research techniques used to measure the information economy. However, it falls far short of promise as an explanation of the effects of that economic shift upon libraries. [R: JAL, Nov 85, p. 316] Michael Rogers Rubin

165. **The Infrastructure of an Information Society. Proceedings of the First International Information Conference in Egypt, Cairo, 13-15 December 1982.** Sponsored by the Egyptian Society for Information Technology and the American Society for Information Science. Bahaa El-Hadidy and Esther E. Horne, eds. New York, Elsevier Science Publishing, 1984. 643p. index. $69.00. LC 84-10141. ISBN 0-444-87549-2.

The purpose of this international conference, cosponsored by the Egyptian Society for

Information Technology (ESIT) and the American Society for Information Science (ASIS), was to discuss the infrastructure of the information society, with an emphasis on developing countries. This volume of the conference proceedings includes fifty-four papers presented at the conference, with ten abstracts provided when the full papers were not available.

There are several problems evident in this volume. One problem is that there is an unevenness in the quality and substance of the presentations included. For example, the papers by J. M. Griffiths, S. A. Wolpert, M. Okenfeld, E. H. Levine et al., W. R. Feeney, S. A. Khalifa, H. E. Elshishiny, N. V. Weber, E. El Shooky and E. Bahgat, M. J. Ruhl, and K. Warnken were all too brief and contained few or no references.

A second problem is that the abstracts do not serve any good purpose when they appear in place of the papers, especially when the authors were at the conference to present their papers.

A third problem is that the method of printing was such that the papers appear in the volume just as the authors typed them so that as a result, there are many typographical errors. It is obvious that the two editors were not careful in screening or editing the papers nor persistent about obtaining the full papers from their authors. Not all papers included in this volume were presented at the conference since some of the speakers as well as the moderators withdrew or were forced to withdraw from the program for reasons described in the introduction. This fact should have been stated by the editors. The book has an author index, but no subject index.

Because of these problems in the volume, I feel that this volume is highly priced for its substance and contents.

Mohammed M. Aman

166. **Libraries and the Information Economy of California: A Conference Sponsored by the California State Library.** Robert M. Hayes, ed. Los Angeles, Calif., University of California at Los Angeles, Graduate School of Library and Information Science, 1985. 335p. bibliog. $20.00; $12.00pa. LC 85-1277.

This book represents perhaps the first major attempt to measure the size of the so-called "information sector" within the economy of anything less than a full nation. California is the focus of this effort, which had as its objective to foster "the development and use of information as both a public benefit and an economic resource in California."

The book largely consists of several papers prepared for and presented at the conference on the book's topic, which was held in March 1984. Among the papers are contributions by Rep.

George Brown, "National Policy Concerns"; Carlos Cuadra, "Information Technology"; Robert Chartrand, "Information Needs"; and a particularly interesting piece by Robert Arnold, "Information Activities in California." Arnold succeeds in measuring the economic size of the information sector in California. Robert M. Hayes acted as the editor for these papers, and also prepared an excellent introduction, which provides a very useful framework and background.

This is a very important book for several reasons. The measaurement of the information sector in California is valuable in its own right. Much more important, however, is the effort to go beyond measurement to address the important public policy issues that flow from the emergence of the information sector as a major component of the economy of a region. Readers new to the idea of the information sector as an economic factor, and readers long acquainted with that concept will both find this book to be an excellent reference source for understanding the economic concepts and the public policy issues that surround the "information economy." [R: WLB, Sept 85, pp. 70-71]

Michael Rogers Rubin

167. Parkhurst, Carol A. **Proceedings of the 48th ASIS Annual Meeting, 1985, Volume 22.** White Plains, N.Y., published for the American Society of Information Science by Knowledge Industry, 1985. 393p. index. $22.50pa. LC 64-8303. ISBN 0-86729-176-1; ISSN 0044-7870.

This ASIS annual meeting addressed five recurring themes which had appeared in *Annual Review of Information Science and Technology* volumes: distribution, communication, and hardware; databases: organization and access; information products and services; management, policy, and politics; and human factors. Contributed papers accepted by a panel of referees number seventy; an additional twelve papers submitted for special interest group sessions also appear in the volume. As anticipated, the range of papers is sufficiently diverse to suit varied interests and needs. The wide range of topics include, for example, electronic document delivery, criteria for selection of hardware and software, and impediments to database access. Several papers consider human information-seeking behaviors and differences in styles of online interaction, which seem to have clear implications for the development of improved interactive online systems. Indeed, several attempts in this direction are reviewed and discussed, thus informing the reader about the state of the art.

Perusal of selected papers may afford insights to such circumstances as human adaptation to imminent technological change and to a number of other concerns currently pervading the field. The concept of libraries as requisite providers of information in electronic form, and the notion of access to online information via gateway and linking systems are commanding increasing attention in the information field.   Ray Gerke

168.   Poole, Herbert. **Theories of the Middle Range.** Norwood, N.J., Ablex Publishing, 1985. 159p. bibliog. index,. (Libraries and Information Science Series). $29.95. LC 84-28402. ISBN 0-89391-257-3.

The purpose of this volume as stated in the foreword is to "set forth a new research paradigm for the field of library and information studies by attempting to describe behavioral principles buried in a group of information use studies ... and to use these principles for the purpose of theory construction." The data are drawn from ninety-seven investigations reviewed in volumes 1-7 and 9 of the *Annual Review of Information Science and Technology* which dealt with the behavior of scientists and engineers working in formal information settings. The title of this volume is drawn from articulation of statements known as middle-range theories, first attributed to R. K. Merton in *Social Theory and Special Structure* (Free Press, 1968). An extensive bibliography, an author index, and a subject index complete the volume.

The work can be best described as relating to the intellectual foundations of information science, at best a shaky and often controversial area. Arguments posed in this text are derived from real-world data, thus presenting a credible, if somewhat philosophical, series of theories which will be of great interest to information scientists and librarians concerned with the foundations of their profession.

Andrew G. Torok

169.   **Representation and Exchange of Knowledge as a Basis of Information Processes. Proceedings of the Fifth International Research Forum in Information Science (IRFIS 5). Heidelberg, F. R. G., September 5-7, 1983.** Hans J. Dietschmann, ed. New York, Elsevier Science Publishing, 1984. 433p. illus. index. $55.75. LC 84-10337. ISBN 0-444-87563-8.

The International Research Forum in Information Science has been meeting in biennial conferences since 1975. The papers presented here, from the fifth conference held in Heidelberg in 1983, provide an overview of basic and application-oriented research in information science. Topics and issues discussed include knowledge representation and organization, self-organizing documentation systems, tax-

onomies, automatic abstracting systems, communication, readability of scientific papers, user studies, online information retrieval, the impact of technology on information needs, and even the political prospects of information technology. As such the work is an interesting compendium of theoretical considerations and work in progress from German, British, American, Dutch, Finnish, Australian, Italian, and Swiss scholars. A simple, but useful, seven-page subject index has been included.

The papers are presented in photoreproduced form from nonserif typescript. The work, however, is marred by a multitude of typographical errors and a binding which, in this review copy, is already breaking loose.

Glenn R. Wittig

INTELLECTUAL FREEDOM

170.   Bouchard, Robert F., comp. and ed. **Guidebook to the Freedom of Information and Privacy Acts. 1985 Supplement.** New York, Clark Boardman, 1985. 398p. $26.50pa.

The *Guidebook to the Freedom of Information and Privacy Acts* and its 1985 supplement contain a wide range of materials pertaining to the laws of both the federal and state governments on this topic. The *1985 Supplement*, for example, contains a newly updated "Short Guide to the Freedom of Information Act" which discusses the federal act, and recent court cases which have interpreted it. At the same time a later chapter contains a state-by-state review of the laws which govern public access to state government files. In between are a variety of materials on the regulations issued by each federal agency under both the Freedom of Information and Privacy Acts, as well as lists of contacts at each agency for matters pertaining to those laws.

Many of the materials in this book are in the public domain, and easily available to those who know where to look. Other of the material, however, particularly that pertaining to individual state governments, is less easily obtained. Even the "Short Guide to the Freedom of Information Act" was written by the federal government. On balance, then, this is a book whose limited value must be as a one-stop shop for a quick overview. Those seeking more detail, or an original viewpoint, would do well to look elsewhere.   Michael Rogers Rubin

171.   Flaherty, David H. **Protecting Privacy in Two-Way Electronic Services.** White Plains, N.Y., Knowledge Industry, 1985. 173p. index. $34.95. LC 84-15492. ISBN 0-86729-107-9.

The home television set has been jokingly referred to for many years as an electronic "eye" in all of our living rooms. Recent developments in cable television, however, have made the electronic eye less a joking matter and more a serious threat to personal privacy. This is because cable television has outgrown one-way communications, and now offers two-way electronic services like teleshopping, telebanking, and opinion polling.

These two-way services may pose a serious threat to personal privacy, since individual profiles of people that are using these systems are easily assembled. These profiles may be of interest to third parties, or even to the government. Flaherty examines the regulatory framework in place to prevent abuses of this nature, and concludes that present law is too weak to protect individual privacy. Flaherty recommends that companies incorporate privacy safeguards as part of their contractual responsibility to each of their users, and that legislation should be enacted only as a last resort. Ironically, this book had not even reached the presses before the U.S. Congress enacted the Cable Communications Privacy Act of 1984, mooting the issue of self-regulation for the industry. This is an excellent text, flawed only by the fact that its legal concerns were made obsolete before the ink had dried on its pages.

Michael Rogers Rubin

172. **Freedom of Expression and the Libraries of Canada.** By Yves de Montigny. Ottawa, Canadian Library Association, 1985. 114p. free spiralbound.

In 1984, the Canadian Library Association asked Yves de Montigny of the University of Ottawa, to investigate Canadian law regarding freedom of expression and to discuss the protection offered by the new Charter of Rights and Freedoms. The resulting document, although not an official statement of the Canadian Library Association, has been received as a resource document by the association's governing council.

In the first part of the book, de Montigny outlines the statutes related to sedition, hate literature, blasphemous and defamatory libel, offences tending to corrupt morals, and using the mails to transmit obscene matter. While this section will be helpful to librarians seeking to understand the possible impact of these laws on library practice, the reader should have access to the Criminal Code of Canada in order to follow the text. A crucial definition of the word obscenity is located in the Code, but the definition itself is not given.

Part 2 of the book contains a more general discussion of the impact of the Charter of Rights on present laws, and a suggested framework for future guidelines. While stress-

ing Canada's unique position, de Montigny refers to many legal decisions in the United States which shed light on how issues of free expression can be interpreted. In his concluding section, he writes, "I personally believe that the courts must devise something similar to the 'freedom to read' or 'freedom to acquire information' elaborated by the American Supreme Court, if freedom of expression is to have any real significance in Canada."

Canadian libraries will find this an important brief to read, and librarians in other countries may find it of value in stimulating discussion of the conceptual foundations of intellectual freedom.   Adele M. Fasick

173. Hurwitz, Leon. **Historical Dictionary of Censorship in the United States.** Westport, Conn., Greenwood Press, 1985. 584p. bibliog. index. $55.00. LC 84-15796. ISBN 0-313-23878-2.

The author is professor of political science at Cleveland State University, Ohio, and his book is compiled from a political, public policy viewpoint. Although legal terminology and concepts are present, he cautions that this work should not be considered a guide for the legal profession. The writer also points out that the text is not exhaustive, but only provides a survey of the forms of censorship in this country. Nevertheless, the book is a valuable introductory reference tool for anyone interested in gaining an understanding of the four major categories of censorship. These are political censorship in the name of national security, community censorship preserving public order and safety, censorship of speech and press when these First Amendment rights conflict with other constitutional rights, and moral censorship.

The first fifty pages describe the four major categories of censorship. The bulk of the work is alphabetically organized with each main entry standing alone. References to other main entries are noted with an asterisk. Appendices include a chronology of censorship beginning in 1644, a table of cases, and a selected bibliography. A useful index is also included after the bibliography.   James M. Murray

174. Varlejs, Jana, ed. **The Right to Information: Legal Questions and Policy Issues. Proceedings of the Twenty-first Annual Symposium....** Jefferson, N.C., McFarland, 1984. 88p. bibliog. $9.95pa. LC 83-26750. ISBN 0-89950-097-8.

Privacy and the librarian's responsibility to users in the information environment were the basic concern of this symposium. These papers do not shed any blinding light on the issues, yet they do provide some interesting perspectives not often brought out in the more "fundamentalist" approaches to intellectual freedom. Rutgers President Edward J. Bloustein brings a scholarly lawyer approach to the issues of privacy, wherein he offers little sympathy to the librarian's contention that the user has a right to expect that librarians will not reveal what access was sought in the collection. Irving Horowitz discusses the growing restrictions and marketing problems publishers are facing, particularly on the issue of who controls the social content of ideas and electronic access to them. Paul Zurkowski, the vendor's representative, promotes information as an economic resource and challenges librarians to do the same. And Shirley Echelman, ARL's chief, is the eloquent representative of the librarian, as the following will demonstrate: "The public's right to know is under threat of being officially changed to the customer's right to receive information paid for." Also valuable are the questions and answers following each presentation.

This work is a spark for discussion about some of the *real* intellectual freedom issues. However, many librarians do not want to be told that the fight for the right to information is fraught with so much responsibility and threat to professional worth. [R: C&RL, 15 Nov 85, p. 530]   Gerald R. Shields

INTERLIBRARY LOANS

175. Ford, Geoffrey, ed. **Interlibrary Lending: Practice, Politics, and Prospects. Proceedings of a Seminar of the Library and Information Research Group, London, November 1983.** London, Rossendale, 1984. 91p. £10.00pa. ISBN 0-946138-04-4.

This overview of interlibrary lending practices in the United Kingdom, one of the most effective world systems, consists of transcripts of five seminar papers in offset format: "Fundamentals of the Inter-Library Loans System," "Resources and Economic Aspects," "Quality Control in Inter-Library Loan Services," "Some User Perspectives," "Broader Issues: Interlending in the Future."

The first paper, the longest, describes the two major elements of the system: (1) The British Library Lending Division (BLLD) and the libraries, mostly university, which contribute to its Union Catalogue of Books, and (2) the ten regional library systems which provide a more decentralized service and satisfy a large percentage of public library requests. In both of these networks the borrowing library pays for the service; loan forms must be purchased to obtain books, with the BLLD charges being somewhat higher. New technology which

increases information on availability of materials raises a question as to whether use of the well-funded centralized system may decrease.

Graphs are used to show economic trends since 1974 for the price of books and periodicals, expenditure on books and periodicals, the production of new book titles, activities of the BLLD, and interlending costs.

To assess the quality of loan services, it is suggested that consideration be given not only to questions of service delivery, but also to the responsibility of the library to help users locate and request the information which will best meet their needs.

The future impact of technological developments, copyright, and commercialization are the broader issues chosen for discussion in the last paper. Several new transmission systems with a UK and European orientation (Adonis, Artemes, Apollo, Hermes) are briefly described.

This description of the British interlending system will be useful to those who have a special interest in the topic and some background knowledge of, or access to, various British reports referred to in the text and the references. [R: JAL, Mar 85, p. 54]

Esther Jane Carrier

LEARNING RESOURCE CENTERS

176. Lary, Marilyn S., ed. **Community/Junior College Libraries: National and International Aspects.** Champaign, Ill., University of Illinois, Graduate School of Library and Information Science, 1985. 1v. (various paging). index. (*Library Trends,* Vol. 33, No. 4). $8.00 pa. ISSN 0024-2594.

The last issue of *Library Trends* to deal with junior college libraries was published two decades ago in October 1965. Much more is expected of them today under their new title of learning resources centers. This change in name evolved through the "integration of library and audiovisual services, the inclusion of the production of these services, and the involvement of learning resources actively in instruction."

Topics relating to learning resources centers which are discussed in this issue include the changing organization, the trend toward centralized administration, the current status of automation, the remedial instruction function, the relationship with career resources centers, and the utilization of comprehensive learning assistance centers. In the final chapter, an attempt is made to forecast the future of community college learning resources centers with influencing external and internal factors identified. The author notes "the dominant role of computer/communications technology," and she recognizes the importance of networking for the future. An impressive variety of professional personnel contributed to this issue including four directors/librarians of learning resources centers, an associate dean of a library school, an associate dean of a community college, a computer programmer, and a college president.

This current overview of learning resources centers will be of interest to anyone involved with community colleges, but it will appeal especially to practicing librarians/researchers.

O. Gene Norman

177. Raddon, Rosemary. **Planning Learning Resource Centres in Schools and Colleges.** Brookfield, Vt., Gower Publishing, 1984. 237p. illus. bibliog. index. $33.95. ISBN 0-566-03435-2.

This book, written by an experienced British school and academic librarian, is intended to provide a framework for planning learning resource centers in a changing environment. The author discusses a general overview of the topic and enumerates the various roles of the librarian and the many change factors and patterns related to planning. In addition, the volume discusses the need to plan for resources, users, management, organization, staffing, and personal strategies. It relates ways that resources can be used for pleasure, learning, in-service training, and staff development. The book deals with evaluation of programs and services, but copyright is limited to a brief half-page. Selected lists of organizations, journals, and references follow most chapters with suggested actions one may take.

Few books are available on planning learning resource centers, and librarians with a need in this area will find many useful suggestions and illustrations in Raddon's book. American readers should be aware of the book's emphasis on the British educational system and its use of British terminology and spelling. Librarians wanting coverage of school media centers from an American viewpoint should consider John T. Gillespie's *Administering the School Media Center* (see *ARBA* 84, entry 118) or Emanuel T. Prostano and Joyce S. Prostano's *The School Library Media Center* (see *ARBA* 83, entry 159). [R: JAL, May 85, p. 110; JAL, July 85, p. 162; LJ, Dec 85, p. 74]

O. Gene Norman

LIBRARIES AND LIBRARIANS IN SOCIETY

178. Benge, R. C. **Confessions of a Lapsed Librarian.** Metuchen, N.J., Scarecrow, 1984. 223p. index. $16.00. LC 83-20405. ISBN 0-8108-1676-8.

An interesting and provocative personal essay written with the encouragement of Eric Moon, former editor of Scarecrow Press, is this excellent chronicle of the various milestones in the life of a most unusual Englishman who happened to be a librarian. Benge possesses a lively intellect and profound insight as well as a witty and charming writing style which in combination provide us with a more enlightened world view packaged in robust good humor. His personal perspectives are well defined and reveal a healthy optimism about mankind in general through the enumeration of his various experiences as a librarian, lecturer, writer, and internationalist. Benge is a retired professor of library science from Ahmadu Bello University in Nigeria, with many publications behind him (treated in part 5), still one cannot help but feel that humanistic concerns are far more important to him than are professional considerations covered in the final section, part 6, almost as an afterthought. This is true despite the fact that one of these chapters is a thoughtful and penetrating analysis of the information revolution as it affects the librarian.

Librarians with a sense of humor will enjoy part 1 which covers Benge's choice of career and in highly amusing, irreverent fashion describes the routines, the patrons, both old and young, and the eccentricities of certain professionals. His spirit seems most alive in parts 2, 3, and 4 which describe his war experiences, his colleges, and possibly most of all his Africa. Through it all he maintains a dry wit which makes understandable his decision to leave the practice of librarianship for teaching where he felt that he could give freer reign to his creative instincts. Indeed, this man has much to convey and his message should be read by all who practice the library art.

Ron Blazek

179. **Books in Our Future: A Report from the Librarian of Congress to the Congress.** Washington, D.C., Joint Committee on the Library, Congress of the United States; distr., Washington, D.C., GPO, 1984. 49p. $2.50pa. LC 84-600348. ISBN 0-8444-0490-X. S/N 052-070-05978-8.

"Ours is a Culture of the Book. Our democracy is built on books and reading. This tradition is now threatened by the twin menaces of illiteracy and aliteracy. We must enlist new technologies with cautious enthusiasm in a national commitment to keep the Culture of the Book thriving." Thus Librarian of Congress Daniel J. Boorstin introduces his program to meet a serious contemporary problem. He reviews what American citizens in families, schools, libraries, churches, prisons, publishing, and others are now doing and what more needs to be done by all concerned to combat illiteracy and aliteracy. Other brief sections outline what Congress, the executive branch, and the Library of Congress can do. In his review of new technologies he warns that effective use of the computer requires a familiarity with and a friendliness to books, while recognizing that for some purposes the newest technology can provide services superior to the traditional book — services of information, of access, and of storage, retrieval, and preservation. "We must use all our technologies to make the most of our inheritance, to move toward an American Renaissance of the Culture of the Book." The brevity and cogency of this concerned but optimistic statement recommend it to the library profession and to the public at large. [R: C&RL, Nov 85, p. 536; WLB, Feb 85, p. 417]

Frances Neel Cheney

180. Fujimoto, Patricia. **Libraries.** Chicago, Childrens Press, 1984. 47p. illus. (col.). index. $7.95. (New True Book). LC 83-26252. ISBN 0-516-01715-X.

Libraries is for readers too old for Rockwell's *I Like the Library* (E. P. Dutton, 1977) and too young for Hardendorff's *Libraries and How to Use Them* (Watts, 1979). It is part of Childrens Press's New True Book series for beginning independent readers through third grade. *Libraries* is a brief introduction to libraries, their contents, and their services. Bookmobiles and special libraries are also included. Colored photographs expand on the text and show library users engaging in a variety of activities from reading to using a computerized catalog, storytelling, and using a microfilm reader. Other photographs show library collections, book arrangement, buildings, and librarians at work. The book has a table of contents, a glossary, and an index.

This book would be useful in school or public library collections. Its weakest points are the almost oversimplification and the very rapid rate of concept introduction. Both are problems characteristic of many nonfiction books for this age reader. On the positive side, new tech-

nologies are introduced so the reader sees the library as a "now" place to be.

Carol J. Veitch

181. Harrison, Colin, and Rosemary Beenham. **The Basics of Librarianship.** 2d ed. London, Clive Bingley; distr., Hamden, Conn., Shoe String Press, 1985. 240p. index. $17.50. ISBN 0-85157-370-3.

To librarians in the United States the library profession in Great Britain is truly foreign. The "basics," however, vary little, and the functions, management, organization, and the routines of British libraries have much in common with similar practices in this country.

The Basics of Librarianship is a text aimed at the paraprofessional in British libraries. It is designed for support staff positions as prescribed by the Business Education Council of the City and Guilds of London Institute. The brief book is divided into twelve chapters, each treating a different aspect of library work. Each chapter is informative and provides an overview and concludes with sample assignments — both practical and written — about its subject. An example is found in the chapter on classification. The student is assigned to visit the local public library and locate reference works, the fiction collection, and circulating nonfiction. One of the written assignments is to list the ten main classes of the Dewey system.

The volume goes beyond its single purpose of education. It introduces British librarianship in much the same way as a standard text. It is a valuable little volume even though targeted for a limited audience.

Boyd Childress

182. Hoffmann, Frank W. **Popular Culture and Libraries.** Hamden, Conn., Library Professional Publications/Shoe String Press, 1984. 312p. index. $29.50; $18.50pa. LC 84-17165. ISBN 0-208-01981-2; 0-208-01983-9pa.

Interest in the confluence of library services and popular culture materials has increased in the last decade as the profession confronts an uncomfortable dilemma about acquiring, circulating and preserving the latter. Careful, objective efforts to answer perplexing questions are scarce; most of the existing literature falls back on literary canon forged by a high-culture elite — hardly suitable for evaluating popular culture in contemporary America. Frank Hoffmann's *Popular Culture and Libraries* avoids the high-culture approach.

After a brief introduction, "Toward a Definition of Popular Culture," Hoffmann divides his book into two parts. The first concentrates fresh attention on library services and popular culture materials, and contains essays by William Schurk on the Popular Culture Library at Bowling Green State University, and Haynes McMullen and Jay Daily on teaching popular culture in library schools. The second part addresses popular culture concepts and materials, and largely duplicates information already available in Thomas Inge's *Concise Histories of American Popular Culture* (1982). Part 2 also contains essays by Ellis Tucker on mystery and detective fiction, and Lee Shiflett on the underground press. Darryl Patrick's essay on pop art misses the mark. What he describes would hardly decorate the walls of the average American home. Scattered throughout both parts are essays by Hoffmann, apparently filling gaps between articles by invited contributors.

Popular Culture and Libraries is not the answer to the librarians' dilemma; but it is a step in the right direction. [R: JAL, Nov 85, p. 321; RQ, Summer 85, pp. 515-16; TN, Summer 85, p. 400]   Wayne A. Wiegand

183. **Joint Congressional Hearing on the Changing Information Needs of Rural America: The Role of Libraries and Information Technology.** Washington, D.C., National Commission on Libraries and Information Science, 1984. 83p. illus. free pa.

The new information technologies are increasingly pervading our daily existence. Until comparatively recent times, however, rural America, with its primarily agrarian lifestyle, had little or nothing to do with technologies such as telecommunications, databases, and computers. By July 1982, however, enough support for rural information needs had been expressed that the secretary of agriculture, the National Commission on Libraries and Information Science (NCLIS), and both houses of Congress, decided to meet to discuss the information problems of rural America, and ways in which the new electronic communications media may help to achieve their solutions.

These proceedings, which contain all of the activities of that meeting, include verbatim transcripts of oral testimony of various educators and public officials. A new term, "the electronically disenfranchised," is introduced, joining "educationally ..." and "economically ...," which are more familiar.

The general drift of these remarks is homogeneous. *Everybody* is for libraries, computer technology, and information assistance to farmers. *Everybody* is against the incumbent administration's budget cuts in this spending area. The reader is given little in the way of debate, but meets a unilateral front of advocates for funding.

Three years have elapsed since that meeting, and while certain objectives have been met, much remains on the conferees' joint agenda. This document will be shelved, no doubt, with other federal publications, which is to say it will be out of the public eye. Inessential for smaller libraries, it is nevertheless an important item for research collections.

Bruce A. Shuman

184. **The Library Association Conference Papers: Access to Published Information, Torquay 1983.** London, Library Association; distr., Phoenix, Ariz., Oryx Press, 1984. 122p. index. $21.00pa. ISBN 0-85365-876-5.

Papers in this conference address informational needs of users, with particular references to researchers, trade unionists, business people, and the general public. When taken in sum, a clearer picture emerges relative to numerous access problems pervading all currently existing formats. Notions that library resources must be advertized by publishers and promoted by libraries also surface in several papers. Other papers address problems of access and preservation of newspaper information, old and rare materials, theses, and audiovisual materials; and problems in acquisition of obscure or ephemeral publications. In expressing notions of "monitoring" and systematic acquisitions among libraries, several papers may stimulate further thought regarding acquisition policies and programs on a regional if not national scale.

In these papers, information professionals may gain additional insights, as well, regarding organizations and other cooperative efforts or arrangements promoting access or control in such areas as the sharing or furthering of bibliographic work. Readers also can reflect upon online developments and progress in technology, which will impact information-seeking behaviors and actual library resources. The proceedings effectively impart theoretical frameworks, and they also delineate needs worldwide for a sufficient provision of information in all formats.   Ray Gerke

185. Schuchat, Theodor. **The Library Book.** Seattle, Wash., Madrona Publishers, 1985. 218p. index. $18.95. LC 85-3021. ISBN 0-88089-007-X.

Newspaper columnist and self-proclaimed graduate of the Enoch Pratt Free Library of Baltimore, Theodor Schuchat has written for the general reader a lively account of how large public libraries operate. He concentrates almost entirely on the operations of his alma mater and while this produces an interesting record of a distinguished library, it does not cover the whole range of public library services. Schuchat gives due credit to Joseph Wheeler, the well-known librarian who sent books out to branchless neighborhoods by horse-drawn wagon. Also noted are Emerson Greenaway and his Greenaway Plan. The text is quite detailed, sometimes a bit too detailed for the general reader. A number of footnotes are given at the end of the volume, followed by an index, chiefly of names. Library literature is not overflowing with tributes from users, and the profession should be cheered by this enthusiastic testimonial. [R: BL, 15 Apr 85, p. 1158; WLB, Sept 85, p. 70]

Frances Neel Cheney

186. **Science, Computers, and the Information Onslaught: A Collection of Essays.** Donald M. Kerr and others, eds. Orlando, Fla., Academic Press, 1984. 276p. illus. $29.50. LC 83-15646. ISBN 0-12-404970-2.

Webster defines an "onslaught" as "an especially fierce attack," and whether the information problem can justifiably be so termed or is rather a sort of extended creeping ambush, it has been with us for a long time and is with us today. Back in June 1981, a meeting was held in Los Alamos, New Mexico, with the theme "Science and the Information Onslaught," addressing various concerns triggered by the computer revolution and related developments.

Speakers came from numerous disciplines, including mathematics, physics, linguistics, computers, national security, government, science administration (whatever that is), and libraries. All gave their estimations of the nature and extent of the onslaught, and what steps might be taken to deal with it. Some were sanguine, others were hard-nosed and pragmatic, a few seemed to despair. Ideas were rampant, however, ranging from let's-enjoy-our-Brave-New-World to why-don't-we-implant-silicon-chips-in-human-bodies-to-improve-performance? One of the speakers posited that survival, itself, depended upon understanding and harnessing our newfound information abilities into knowledge. Kind of hyperbolic stuff, this, but thoughtful, provocative reading, nonetheless.

One troublesome question remains: given the "hot topics" nature of this conference, why did Academic Press wait over three years to publish this book, and another year-and-something to get it out to reviewers? Such a time lag bespeaks a puzzling lack of interest in a subject which, by general consensus, affects all of us all of the time. In any event, this book stands up well to the passing of time, and is recommended for anyone connected with, or even worried about, alternative futuring for society.

Bruce A. Shuman

187. Tallman, Johanna E. **Check Out a Librarian.** Metuchen, N.J., Scarecrow, 1985. 180p. illus. index. $15.00. LC 85-10845. ISBN 0-8108-1823-X.

Johanna Tallman is justifiably proud of her long career as a science and technology librarian, and like many librarians she has a repertoire of stories about problem patrons, unusual reference questions, and eccentric colleagues. But however much such stories enliven library conventions and other gatherings, they don't make a very interesting book. Tallman's anecdotal autobiography includes these familiar stories and also rambles from the cataloging of partial titles to fire insurance to Brazilian taxis to her volunteer activities since retiring.

This is not a reference book in any sense, and while Tallman's pleasure in writing it is evident, Scarecrow might better have directed her to a vanity press.   Jane Pearlmutter

188. Varlejs, Jana, ed. **Communication/Information/Libraries: A New Alliance. Proceedings of the Twenty-second Annual Symposium Sponsored by the Alumni and Faculty, Library and Information, Rutgers School of Communication, Information of Library Studies 14 April 1983.** Jefferson, N.C., McFarland, 1985. 96p. bibliog. $9.95pa. LC 84-29706. ISBN 0-89950-146-X.

This text contains the proceedings of the Rutgers Twenty-second Annual Symposium sponsored by the Library and Information Alumni and Faculty—the first symposium following the merger with the School of Communication. The text is a pragmatic look at practical, ethical, and theoretical questions that can be explored from an interdisciplinary perspective.

The organization of the work features presentations in four areas: "Journalism, Mass Communication and the Convergence with Library and Information Studies," "The Impact of Information Technology and Human Communication," "Information and Communication: Some Important Links," and "The New Alliance: Prospects for Progress." Discussion excerpts follow each presentation.

The three concepts in the title are examined from the viewpoint of forging potential linkages and alliances among separate disciplines. The question of possible mergers among these disciplines as a potential response to declining enrollments and resources is explored.

This work is an excellent addition to the continuing dialogue on Whither the information profession? that so preoccupies the literature. [R: JAL, Nov 85, p. 306; LJ, Aug 85, p. 70]

Darlene E. Weingand

LIBRARY INSTRUCTION

189.   Adams, Mignon S., and Jacquelyn M. Morris. **Teaching Library Skills for Academic Credit.** Phoenix, Ariz., Oryx Press, 1985. 211p. bibliog. index. $29.50. LC 83-43238. ISBN 0-89774-138-2.

A book of practical information about credit courses in the general use of libraries as opposed to bibliographic instruction, formal or informal, with a subject emphasis.

In two parts, the first covers theory and practice; the second presents eighteen case studies of varying kinds of courses at college and university libraries. In addition to the bibliography and index, there are chapter references and an appendix: "Tricks of the Trade."

The first section opens with a description of kinds of courses and continues with the political environment, course content, materials, teaching, and evaluation of the students' and the instructor's performance.

Many of the recommendations arise from common sense and serve as a reminder-guide to the instructor, who has to think of everything, to plan as a means of avoiding crises. And much of the information is common to all teaching, but the guide addresses the librarian-instructor specifically. [R: JAL, Sept 85, p. 246; JAL, Nov 85, p. 301; LJ, 15 Oct 85, p. 56; WLB, Sept 85, p. 71]   Kathleen McCullough

190.   Coleman, Kathleen, and others, eds. **The Bibliographic Instruction Clearinghouse: A Practical Guide.** Chicago, Association of College and Research Libraries, American Library Association, 1984. 71p. illus. index. $12.00pa.; $9.00pa. (ACRL members). ISBN 0-8389-6775-2.

This book presents a review of the history, method and problems of organization, and function of established clearinghouses, followed by a how-to for organizing additional clearinghouses. The guide was prepared for librarians involved in bibliographic instruction, many of whom are functioning without alliances or other group support, or would like to expand the activities of their present clearinghouses.

The instructions cover collecting instructional materials, including kinds of materials, their classification, and their access; compiling directories of state or regional programs, including data collection, printing, and marketing; planning an instruction workshop for librarians; publishing a newsletter, assuming substance and focusing on format, with the emphasis on professional appearance ("to help the press blind itself to the uneven surfaces [of insertions], spread correction fluid as a thin caulk on the seams where you have pasted pieces");

and marketing the clearinghouse, including publicity, promotion, and public relations.

Also provided are pertinent directories, sample questionnaires, sample typefaces and layouts, and chapter bibliographies.

The book is thorough, well written, carefully prepared (the authors refrained from reducing "bibliographic instruction" to BI), and indeed practical. [R: JAL, Mar 85, p. 43]   Kathleen McCullough

191.   Fjallbrant, Nancy, and Ian Malley. **User Education in Libraries.** 2d ed. London, Clive Bingley; distr., Hamden, Conn., Shoe String Press, 1984. 251p. illus. index. $19.50. ISBN 0-85157-361-4.

Theory, philosophy, and methodology, rather than content, are the subjects of the second edition of *User Education in Libraries.* That the content of what to teach is not addressed is understandable since the treatment is international in scope, providing the development of user education in the United Kingdom, the United States, Scandinavian countries, and Australia.

A comparison of the first edition (see *ARBA* 79, entry 312) with the second reveals the addition of a chapter entitled "Education for Online Information Retrieval" which assists the reader in understanding the importance of the inclusion of this information in teaching the user. There are chapters on user education in public libraries and in schools but not in academic libraries. However, in a chapter on cooperation and coordination there is a brief discussion of ACRL activities in bibliographic instruction.

A scholarly survey with excellent bibliographies of studies, the publication would probably be most useful to those without teacher education background. Particularly so would be the chapter on goals and objectives. Chapters on case studies in the United Kingdom have been dropped from the second edition though the new edition is over seventy pages longer than the old—partially attributable to an improved format which includes larger print, more white space, and better quality paper.

Ruth E. Bauner

192.   Katz, Bill, and Ruth A. Fraley, eds. **Library Instruction and Reference Services.** New York, Haworth Press, 1984. 254p. $29.95. LC 84-505. ISBN 0-86656-288-5.

Library Instruction and Reference Services is another of Haworth Press's monographs within a journal. The journal in this case is *The Reference Librarian* (no. 10, Spring/Summer 1984). As is the case in works of this nature one of two specialists on a topic serve as editors.

Here, Bill Katz and Ruth Fraley fill this role. A number of contributors are asked to write on fairly broad topics falling within a general framework. The result is often a work of uneven quality and loose structure, and of essays that fit their topics with difficulty. Happily, these characteristics are not major detractions from this work.

Five main sections comprise this work: "Introduction" (determining the need for bibliographic instruction); "Another View" (examining the need for a BI program separate from Reference); "Techniques and Questions" (determining users' needs); "Instruction in Public Libraries" and "Instruction in Academic Libraries." Some of the information is repetitive. A few of the essays in the middle of the work would have been more useful closer to the beginning as they provide good overviews of the subject. The information is valuable wherever it falls, however, and some of it does bear repeating.

Even with a general outline provided by the editors, the essays are only loosely bonded by broad themes. Perhaps one final section summarizing the preceding ones would have given a feeling of greater unity to the work. A general index would have also been useful. Nevertheless, the essays are uniformly well written and informative. They provide the reader with a good understanding of reference and bibliographic instruction, both theoretical and practical. [R: CLJ, June 85, p. 165; C&RL, Mar 85, pp. 187-89]   Marjorie E. Bloss

193. Kirk, Thomas, and Martha White. **Teaching How to Teach Science Reference Materials: A Workshop for Librarians Who Serve the Undergraduate.** Chicago, Association of College and Research Libraries, American Library Association, 1984. 101p. illus. bibliog. (CE 205). $15.00 spiralbound; $10.00 spiralbound (ACRL members).

This publication is a compilation of handout materials from a one-day workshop designed by the authors as a continuing education course for reference librarians. The workshop format consists of a combination of lecture and problem-solving sessions which focus on search strategies and reference tools, with emphasis on periodical indexes. The indexes covered include: *Applied Science & Technology Index, Biological Abstracts, Biological and Agricultural Index, Chamical Abstracts, General Science Index, Science Citation Index, Physics Abstracts*, and *Mathematical Reviews*. The bulk of the volume consists of brief annotations and representative sections from these indexes. The remaining pages present outlines from some of the sessions and three flow diagrams of manual

search strategies. Online searching is not discussed. A six-item bibliography completes the volume.

This volume is of questionable value as a reference or teaching aid for librarians or library science educators. The book offers little beyond a few exercises for students and a brief list of sample reference questions. Furthermore, the format and print quality leave a great deal to be desired, often being totally illegible. The authors could have enhanced the usefulness of the publication by amplifying the section outlines and going beyond the workshop handouts. Judging from the contents, the workshop itself might have been worth attending. However, considering the price and quality of the volume, librarians could better spend their money on more comprehensive works such as Mary Hauer's *Books, Libraries, and Research*, 2d ed. (Kendall/Hunt, 1983).

    Andrew G. Torok

194. Taylor, Margaret T., and Ronald R. Powell. **Basic Reference Sources: A Self-Study Manual.** 3d ed. Metuchen, N.J., Scarecrow, 1985. 335p. $16.50pa. LC 84-13880. ISBN 0-8108-1721-7.

This, the third edition of a self-paced manual for the study of reference titles, had a "preliminary edition" (1971) and a first edition (1973), both authored by Taylor. The book is now in its third edition, with two authors (from the University of Michigan's School of Library Science). One congratulates the authors for the minimal changes made to the volume. The major change is, again, to bring the sources and questions up-to-date (i.e., to December 1983), and to add new sources (e.g., *Biography and Genealogy Master Index*), dropping old ones.

The book consists of 1,757 questions, with answers, carefully relating to a given list of sources. The answers are sometimes factual (e.g., "Yes, there is an alphabetical index ..."), some require more judgment. It is a nice mix. The questions are arranged in twenty-three sections the titles of which have remained virtually unchanged since 1971. Most sections reflect a type of source (e.g., yearbooks and almanacs, bibliographic sources for government publications). One section looks at search strategy in U.S. national bibliographic records. There are two sections of review questions. Within each section there is, first, a brief (longest is fifteen titles) list of sources followed by questions requiring use of those sources. The answers follow separately.

An augmented list of sources showing Sheehy numbers is at the beginning of the book. The list is noticeably heavy on U.S. sources. For example, five sections are devoted to U.S.

national bibliography, while there is one section covering all of Britain, France, and Germany. There is no mention of Canada's national bibliographic sources, which hampers use of the manual in North America. The authors have found only an inadequate answer to the challenge of electronic reference sources: they have placed a distinguishing mark beside the sources having a corresponding database.

There are small aggravations in an otherwise useful and unpretentious work. The manual does not attempt to address the broader processes of reference (the reference interview, etc.). It deals with the problem of learning reference titles. It does that admirably. It is useful in library schools as a supplement to lectures and discussions. It would serve as an invaluable guide to independent students and practitioners seeking to update their knowledge of, to review, or to begin a study of, reference sources. [R: JAL, Nov 85, p. 321; RBB, 1 June 85, p. 1376]   Elizabeth Frick

MANAGEMENT

196. Burgin, Robert, and Patsy Hansel, eds. **Library Overdues: Analysis, Strategies and Solutions to the Problem.** New York, Haworth Press, 1984. 135p. (*Library & Archival Security*, Vol. 6, Nos. 2/3). $19.95. LC 84-19736. ISBN 0-86656-376-8.

This volume comprises fifteen articles focusing on the important but rather unglamorous subject of overdues. Representative article titles include "Overdues Procedures Using a Microcomputer," "The Fines-No Fines Debate," "Dealing with Defaulters," and "More Hard Facts on Overdues" as well as an excellent reading list entitled "Overdues: A Bibliography." The articles are well written and contain many practical examples from public, academic, school, and special libraries complete with statistical data and presentations of overdues procedures. A subject index is provided.

The collection of articles presented was originally published in the volume 6, number 2, fall 1984 issue of the journal *Library & Archival Security* (see ARBA 81, entry 163). If one has this journal there would be little use in purchasing this bound reprint. However, if one did not subscribe to that particular issue, it would be worthwhile to own this copy. [R: BL, 15 Jan 85, p. 684; JAL, July 85, p. 171]

Frank Wm. Goudy

197. **Excellence in Library Management.** Charlotte Georgi and Robert Bellanti, eds. New York, Haworth Press, 1985. 71p. (*Journal of Library Administration*, Vol. 6, No. 3). $19.95. LC 85-14095. ISBN 0-86656-478-0.

This monograph reflects the published proceedings of the tenth annual Workshop on Management for Librarians sponsored by the Southern California Chapter of the Special Libraries Association. As such, the articles read like speeches, rather than like scholarly, footnoted manuscripts.

Seven papers follow a presenter-reactor format, covering the topics of managing a special library (Judy Labovitz and Meryl Swanigan), managing a public library (Carol Aronoff and Michael Cart), and managing an academic library (Gloria Werner and Glenn Brudvig). Transcribed questions and answers follow, and the work is concluded with the keynote paper, "Power and Human Relations at Work" by John J. McDonough, the only nonlibrarian on the panel.

Each of the speakers' remarks uses as a guide the eight practical points addressed in *In Search of Excellence*. Therefore, the presentations are weighted heavily on the side of practice and experience, rather than theory and research.

Many of the papers are informal, situational, broad, and anecdotal, instead of specific, insightful, thought-provoking, and analytical. They do not fully develop the topic, just gingerly pirouette around it. The best of the lot is Werner's paper which ties a case study of library innovation to the framework of the conference.

For a solid, one-volume reference of essays on the literature of library organization and management, consult *Management Strategies for Libraries: A Basic Reader* (Neal-Schuman, 1985), or *The Management Process: A Selection of Readings for Librarians* (American Library Association, 1983).   Ilene F. Rockman

198. Fraley, Ruth A., and Carol Lee Anderson. **Library Space Planning: How to Assess, Allocate, and Reorganize Collections, Resources, and Physical Facilities.** New York, Neal-Schuman, 1985. 158p. bibliog. index. $35.00pa. LC 84-18996. ISBN 0-918212-44-8.

Planning to move your library? Do you want to evaluate your collection in light of your facility? Then this may be just the guide you need. *Library Space Planning* contains many insights into the how-to of planning for library space needs. In the nine chapters the authors offer tested suggestions on issues such as measuring the collection, the financial considerations of planning, and conducting regular library operations during a move. Three appendices discuss the bid process, and a brief bibliography and index conclude the volume.

A broad range of topics is discussed in this small volume, including the development of goals and objectives, the costs involved in personnel, safety, service problems, and various shelving options. Almost any topic associated with moving a library and its collection is mentioned. Yet there are a few oddities which cause slight concern. For example, budgeting for a staff celebration following the move is emphasized more than the cost involved with moving computer equipment. With the ever-increasing importance of the computer to libraries, this is surprising. An instance such as this is more disturbing than damaging. Another minor cause for concern is the index, where topics mentioned in chapter headings (e.g., rate books) are omitted in the index. Strengths, such as the application of current management techniques, overshadow these few criticisms. This is a good, brief guide which has practical directions for a library move or relocation. [R: AL, Apr 85, p. 249; BR, Nov/Dec 85, p. 50; JAL, Nov 85, p. 299 and p. 324; LJ, Aug 85, p. 70; RQ, Winter 85, p. 277; WLB, Oct 85, p. 59]

Boyd Childress

199.   Jones, Ken. **Conflict and Change in Library Organizations: People, Power and Service.** London, Clilve Bingley; distr., Hamden, Conn., Shoe String Press, 1984. 274p. bibliog. index. (Looking Forward in Librarianship). $19.00. ISBN 0-85157-367-3.

Jones sets out to examine systematically library organizations and service in the light of different organization theories. Systematic he is and only through careful concentration can the reader follow the author's themes which are at times tortuously interwoven. The first part of the book describes the major traditional organizational theories and then goes on to discuss research on job satisfaction, leadership, groups, and interpersonal skills development.

The author then introduces his human resources/soft systems management methodology (HRSS) as an "ideal" type in the same sense as is Weber's bureaucracy or "hard systems" scientific management methodology. Jones identifies his HRSS model with the Burns and Stalker organismic style of management.

The second part of the book is devoted to moving away from a "closed" organization theory which is described as dealing with management, established authority, and not necessarily with other organization members or society at large. The author proposes a contingency model of organization, but although he draws upon specific elements of library organizations in Great Britain (and a few in North America) as illustrations, he does not reveal exactly how the model would be applied in libraries. He emphasizes the need for integration and synthesis rather than compartmentalization and closure. At the same time Jones argues

against the "dominant myth of technological omniscience" and calls for a more open and inclusive professionalism. This book adds to the growing number of works on libraries as organizations and will appeal to the serious scholar. [R: JAL, July 85, p. 185]   Helen Howard

200.   Kohl, David F. **Administration, Personnel, Buildings and Equipment: A Handbook for Library Management.** Santa Barbara, Calif., ABC-Clio, 1985. 304p. bibliog. index. (Handbooks for Library Management, Vol. 1). $35.00. LC 84-24267. ISBN 0-87436-431-0.

Library administrators require current information as an input to decision making. They often lack time to do research or to locate pertinent research findings. Kohl has reviewed thirty-four core North American journals and isolated the findings in research articles published between 1960 and 1983. Each finding has been summarized, numbered, and then listed under the appropriate subject heading category which has then been divided by type of library. The finding number identifies the article from which the finding was taken and leads to a bibliography of research articles used in the handbook.

When research in an area is segmented finding-by-finding and organized by subject, a pattern of the research being done emerges. One finds, for example, that research related to library directors appears four times more frequently than does research related to budgeting, and that in general research related to people, both users and employee, is the major component in research in library management. This mapping of research provides the profession with a picture of itself, and as the additional volumes covering other aspects of librarianship are published it will be possible to identify those areas needing research.

The handbook is useful for ready reference to locate facts concerning management concerns as diverse as copyright and job satisfaction. Often only one research article may be cited but it will be divided into several findings.

This approach to organizing our research literature has promise and is a good beginning. The handbook provides quick access to North American journal literature and when used in tandem with guides to research published in other formats (e.g., monographs and documents) is a useful reference tool. [R: AL, Apr 85, p. 220; JAL, May 85, p. 124; LJ, Aug 85, p. 71; RQ, Winter 85, p. 270; WLB, May 85, p. 618]   Ann E. Prentice

201.   **Management Strategies for Libraries: A Basic Reader.** Beverly P. Lynch, ed. New York, Neal-Schuman, 1985. 682p. index. $35.00pa. LC 85-5668. ISBN 0-918212-86-3.

Lynch has selected some of the most important writings on management, from myriad sources. Chosen from fields of business, politics, administration, and sociology, as well as librarianship, all thirty-eight articles in this compendium have been previously published in sources ranging from the *Annual Review of Sociology* to *Administrative Science Quarterly* and from *Public Administration Review* to *Harper's.* Providing a good balance among those fields, the editor has chosen about one-half of the contents from library literature. The time span incorporates "classics" in management literature written by, among others, Fredrick W. Taylor, Max Weber and A. Simon, as well as articles on current applied research and practice in the management of libraries by prolific writers such as Richard M. Dougherty and Richard De Gennaro. The editor, no stranger to management writings herself, has included three of her own writings.

The volume is arranged in three parts: "Theoretical Perspectives," "The Management Process," and "The Work of Management." Well organized with a good index—unusual in such works—the monograph is intended to "help the manager achieve success in these (management) efforts," the volume provides valuable reading for all interested in the management process—from library directors and staffs to library school faculty and students. [R: JAL, Nov 85, p. 324; LJ, Aug 85, p. 70]

Robert D. Stueart

202. Martin, Lowell A. **Organizational Structure of Libraries.** Metuchen, N.J., Scarecrow, 1984. 294p. bibliog. index. (Scarecrow Library Administration Series, No. 5). $14.50. LC 84-4859. ISBN 0-8108-1696-2.

This book is a gem. Lowell Martin, library administrator, educator, businessman, and consultant sets out to present organizational structure as a living, multidimensional body of relationships and to go beyond the visible and obvious. He succeeds admirably well.

The first part of the book is devoted to the macrocosm, or wide view of organizations: definitions, the development of a theory of organization, and contemporary concepts. The view that organization touches upon and relates to all functions of administration is well developed. This part of the volume could well serve as an introduction to the theory of administration.

The latter part of the book is devoted to the microcosm, that is, the internal organization of libraries. It begins with the organization of service as seen by the library user and then covers a library's external and internal relationships. Martin thoughtfully examines issues such as

staffing patterns, the nature of professional work, the ability of librarians to manage, and dealing with change and conflict. He describes and criticizes prevailing organization by function and urges the reader to examine the advantages of a "result-producing" structure. As an illustration of innovative structure he outlines that at the Chicago Public Library and Columbia University Libraries but does not mention Martell's proposed "client-centered" library and its implementation at the University of Illinois.

Library managers would do well to consider carefully Martin's view that organization is an environment "in which a library flourishes, drifts, or declines" and to realize that a structure need not be immutable. [R: C&RL, Sept 85, p. 443; JAL, May 85, p. 100]   Helen Howard

203. McCabe, Gerard B., and Bernard Kreissman, eds. **Advances in Library Administration and Organization: A Research Annual. Volume 4. 1985.** Greenwich, Conn., JAI Press, 1985. 235p. illus. index. $49.50. ISBN 0-89232-566-6.

As in previous volumes of this series the reader is provided with a wide variety of topics among the ten articles in this work, ranging from public library unions and academic library service to disabled students (an annotated bibliography) to satisfaction in library systems and the impacts of automation and technology. Among the twelve authors or co-authors there are five library school faculty members, five academic library administrators, and two representatives of library networks.

The articles are generally well written with useful ideas and information. The series subtitle, "A Research Annual," is not completely accurate since a number of the articles are descriptive or opinion pieces or summaries of the literature. There are valuable author and subject indexes to all of the articles.

In summary, this series continues to provide important contributions to the literature of library administration and organization but at a very high per-volume cost.

George S. Bobinski

204. Plate, Kenneth H. **Library Manager's Workbook: Problem-solving in the Supervision of Information Service Personnel.** Studio City, Calif., Pacific Information, 1985. 101p. (Professional Skills Series). $24.50. LC 85-9369. ISBN 0-913203-10-6.

Plate's workbook grew out of his experiences as a leader for library supervisor workshops. The book is actually a collection of eighty of the most common supervisory problems reported by library managers along with the author's recommendations for handling the situations. As he states in the introduction,

Plate purposely avoided personnel theory and did not rewrite a standard management text in library language; he instead encourages learning from the experiences of others.

The problems are grouped into seven chapters, each covering a very broad aspect of the supervisor's role (supervisor-employee relationship, supervisor-superior relationship, job design and performance evaluation, etc.). Within each chapter, introductory remarks, statements of problems, and recommended solutions are all meshed together into a continuous text. Because of this format, the book is most effective when read straight through—it is difficult to pick out an individual topic if seeking advice for a particular problem. No index is provided for this purpose, either. Plate aims his book at those who have had little experience as supervisors—the situations that are covered deal with very basic employee problems. The detailed discussion and examples of situational analysis will prove useful to the new supervisor, and the informal writing style and typewritten text make the problems seem less intimidating. Although some of the topics apply only to academic or public libraries, most are universal enough to be relevant in any library situation. *Library Manager's Workbook* will in no way take the place of a personnel management text, but it should provide a relatively painless way to gain some new understanding. [R: JAL, Nov 85, p. 325]   Judy Dyki

204a. Telecommunications for Library Management. By Richard W. Boss. White Plains, N.Y., Knowledge Industry, 1985. 180p. bibliog. index. $36.50; $28.50pa. LC 84-26140. ISBN 0-86729-126-5; 0-86729-125-7pa.

Boss begins with an overview of library telecommunications which may best serve to convince most neophytes that they will never totally understand the complex problems of need, technology, and economics which are discussed. The eight chapters which follow cover the specific components of a telecommunication system. Topics include aspects such as standards, suppliers, equipment, software, and procurement. The appendices include a list of suppliers, a glossary, a list of acronyms, a bibliography, and an index.

This work provides a good introductory study of telecommunications for the library administrator. It comes at a time when most administrators are dealing with decisions arising from the dramatic changes in the telecommunications system. Even though the subject matter is very similar to that in works such as Reynolds's *Introduction to Business Telecommunications* (Merrill, 1984), Boss's approach with the librarian in mind makes his work

preferable. It should be considered "must" reading.   Bill J. Corbin

205. Trumpeter, Margo C., and Richard S. Rounds. Basic Budgeting Practices for Librarians. Chicago, American Library Association, 1985. 164p. index. $25.00. LC 84-20503. ISBN 0-8389-0399-1.

From time to time ALA publishes books that are clearly intended for the small library staffed by nonprofessionals, to serve as how-to guides at the most basic level. This title, whose authors state in the preface that it is a text "designed to help teach yourself" falls into that category. The authors also see it as of use to students, aspiring administrators, and practicing administrators of public and school libraries. If this is a potential audience, it would be at the preprofessional level for individuals who have had little or no background in librarianship.

The various chapters cover different aspects of the budget process. Each is divided (step-by-step) into procedures to follow in order to project revenue, write a budget presentation, or manage the budget. Practice sections reinforce the chapter contents and the reader is told to develop a chart, or define a process or term. The selected readings following each chapter are well chosen and provide relevant basic information. The style of writing is of the look, look, see Spot run variety which, when combined with addressing the reader in the second person, can overshadow the commonsense approach to various budgeting activities.

Numerous books on budgeting and financial planning which provide guidance and understanding have been published in the past five years. The contribution that this one makes is that it is directed toward the least experienced individuals who serve in the smallest libraries. [R: AL, Apr 85, p. 222; BR, Nov/Dec 85, p. 50; JAL, May 85, p. 126; LJ, 15 Apr 85, p. 60; RQ, Winter 85, pp. 270-71; WLB, June 85, p. 699]
                                           Ann E. Prentice

206. White, Herbert S. Library Personnel Management. White Plains, N.Y., Knowledge Industry, 1985. 214p. bibliog. index. (The Professional Librarian). $36.50; $28.50pa. LC 84-26146. ISBN 0-86729-136-2; 0-86729-135-4pa.

Herbert White, dean of the University of Indiana School of Library and Information Science, has written a very readable and pragmatic book which is intended to "contribute to the manager's ability to arrive at the correct solutions to specific problematic situations as they arise." White stresses that no two institutions or individuals are alike and, therefore, generalizations are dangerous. The content of the book is an outcome of his varied experience as a manager and as an educator. He does not attempt to cover in depth the literature of personnel administration. Rather he refers to other sources for such a foundation and covers key issues in twelve chapters which provide abundant library-related examples. An underlying criticism of library managers and supervisors is that many do not know how or what to manage and thus adopt a laissez-faire attitude. White condemns this lack of leadership and courage to make decisions and believes that "we will only be rescued by the intelligence, ingenuity, sensitivity and courage of individual managers."

The text is supplemented with twelve case studies which will be useful in the classroom or as a focus for discussion of personnel problems. This volume is recommended reading for all librarians and will also be useful as a starting point in personnel administration courses in schools of library and information science.

Helen Howard

NONBOOK MATERIALS

207. Ahlsted, Phyllis Geraldine, and Paul Graham, eds. **Media Collections and Services in Academic Libraries.** Champaign, Ill., Graduate School of Library and Information Science, University of Illinois, 1985. 159p. (*Library Trends*, Vol. 34, No. 1). $8.00pa. ISSN 0024-2594.

The editors feel the value of nonprint materials in higher education is self-evident but that academic libraries have been slow to integrate them into their collections. They blame funding, unwillingness to take risks, print bias, and the inability of librarians to communicate with media specialists. To inform librarians and administrators and to encourage change, they have assembled a well-written and stimulating collection of articles that look at varied aspects of the current situation and describe emerging trends. There is a sobering article by John W. Raimo which shows that funding is indeed a major obstacle with competition for university monies strong and government and private grants — so plentiful in the past — diminished to a trickle. Other articles are encouraging. Carol L. Hardy and Judith A. Sessions describe a flourishing program at California State University Chico where the library, the media center, and the computing center have been integrated under a dean of information services. Marie P. Griffin, librarian at the Institute of Jazz Studies, Rutgers University, provides a vivid and compelling look at the use of audiovisual resources for scholarly research in the field of jazz. Mitchell Whichard offers practical and

sound advice on collection development. Beverly Teach outlines the potential for media networking by describing in detail the development and publication of the Consortium of University Film Centers' union catalog (*Educational Film Locator*, 3d ed. Bowker, 1986) and progress towards providing online access. Other articles this reviewer found especially informative were Paul Graham's report on current developments in audiovisual cataloging, Ivan R. Bender's comments on the copyright law and educational media, George L. Abbott's succinct and up-to-date overview of video based information systems, and Peter H. Wagshal's predictions about the impact of chips and interactive technologies on libraries and society.

Joseph W. Palmer

208. Murray, William A., Jr., ed. **A Guide to Basic Media Materials and Equipment Operations Training.** Aurora, Colo., Media Services-Peoria Center, Aurora Public Schools, 1985. 135p. illus. $8.53 looseleaf.

This guide has been developed by the Aurora (Colorado) Public Schools to use in training sessions for student and adult media assistants. It includes instructional modules in the operation of educational media equipment and orientation to the basic functions of media services for young people. Individual modules are included for each of the most common pieces of audiovisual equipment used in the schools as well as modules for other media assistant responsibilities such as filing catalog cards and mending books.

Each media training module states the purpose, objectives, time, and materials needed for the session, and an outline of the instructor's presentation. Handouts are included for each module where applicable. The looseleaf format of the work enables easy reproduction of the handouts and permission for reproduction is granted with purchase, if the handouts will be used in nonprofit workshops and classes. The handouts, appropriately illustrated and clearly stated in a step-by-step, operational manner, would be useful to the trainee for reference on the job.

A Guide to Basic Media Materials and Equipment Operations Training would be helpful to those individuals planning media assistant training programs and could easily be tailored to a local setting.

Thomas Wm. Downen

209. Pemberton, J. Michael. **Policies of Audiovisual Producers and Distributors: A Handbook for Acquisition Personnel.** Metuchen, N.J., Scarecrow, 1984. 330p. index. $27.50pa. LC 84-5623. ISBN 0-8108-1704-7.

This directory, which pulls together in a single alphabetic listing, information on producers and distributors of audiovisual materials, will prove very useful.

Each entry begins with the full title of the company or organization, the address, and the order contact person. At the end of the organization name is a numeric code indicating the scope of the company's activities (e.g., 1—producer with no distribution activities; 2—producer which distributes own software and no other producer's, etc.).

Other items in most entries are telephone number, special pricing information, shipping/billing policies, rush order availability, back orders policy, discounts, preview media policy, limits, return methods, details on software rental and leasing, booking cancellation deadlines, rent-to-purchase availability and stipulations on damage repair, reproduction and electronic transmission policies.

Certain specialized organizations have been omitted from the listing and the definition of "audiovisual" or "nonprint" has been narrowed to include only software in need of electronic enhancement. This means picture and map suppliers are omitted, and micropublishers are included.

In addition to the main directory, two indexes are included: the "relational" index and the state index. The relational index is an alphabetical listing of organizations and names that are related or connected to others. These include organizations that distribute for others; former, current, and popular names for organizations as well as official titles; and parent organizations and subsidiaries. The state index arranges all directory entries by state.

Policies of Audio Visual Producers and Distributors is intended to be used in conjunction with Bowker's *Audio Visual Marketplace* and Ung Chon Kim's *Policies of Publishers: A Handbook for Order Libraries*. Together these three volumes should provide the basic information needed to preview, rent, or purchase audiovisual materials.   Daniel F. Phelan

210. Saffady, William. **Micrographics.** 2d ed. Littleton, Colo., Libraries Unlimited, 1985. 254p. illus. index. (Library Science Text Series). $28.00. LC 84-28863. ISBN 0-87287-453-2.

Saffady is the leading authority on micrographics in libraries. This updated edition of his excellent 1978 text surveys the entire field of micrographics, covering topics that range from collection development to microformats, computer-output-microfilm, microform production, equipment, publishing, bibliographic control, and computer and manual retrieval systems. A final chapter looks to the future and

discusses such topics as computer-input-microfilm, microfacsimile transmission, and optical discs. The value of the text is greatly enhanced by very extensive footnoting which directs the reader to more detailed discussions of particular topics in the professional literature. Succinct but detailed, clearly written, well-organized, fully illustrated, and immensely informative, the book is unexcelled as an introduction to microform resources and technology for librarians and library school students. [R: JAL, July 85, p. 177; JAL, Sept 85, pp. 230-32; JAL, Nov 85, p. 315]

Joseph W. Palmer

211. Spreitzer, Francis, ed. **Microforms in Libraries: A Manual for Evaluation and Management.** Chicago, American Library Association, 1985. 63p. $8.95pa. LC 85-6036. ISBN 0-8389-3310-6.

The organization and management of microforms in the library and their types and technical qualities is the subject of this small basic guide.

In only forty-six pages, a step-by-step walk through the various formats, evaluations, management, equipment types and facilities, as well as the qualifications for staff and servicing of microforms and the microform collection is conducted.

A great deal of space is devoted to evaluating the quality of microforms. Everything from pre-order considerations, quality of filming and packaging and subject access is discussed.

Collection management (storage, arrangement, maintenance, etc.) is briefly covered as are the specifications for the microform reading area.

The main section of the work concludes with a discussion of the public service aspects of staffing, training, publicity, circulation and statistics.

There are three appendices: a glossary (where I learned what a "target" is), a list of standards, specifications and recommended practices, and finally a selected bibliography subdivided by sections like "Microform Librarianship," "Equipment," and "Acquisitions." A very well-produced index is also included.

Microforms in Libraries is a good, readable, simple overview of the field and is suited to both those who do not know diazo from vesicular as well as those who have some experience but would like a condensed reference guide. [R: JAL, Nov 85, p. 315; LJ, 1 Sept 85, p. 148; RQ, Winter 85, pp. 277-78; WLB, Oct 85, p. 59]

Daniel F. Phelan

PUBLIC LIBRARIES

212. Ballard, Thomas. **Knowin' All Them Things That Ain't So: Managing Today's Public Library.** Urbana, Ill., Graduate School of Library and Information Science, University of Illinois, 1985. 22p. bibliog. (Occasional Papers, No. 168). $3.00pa. ISSN 0276-1769.

There's one in every crowd. If we're lucky. Somebody inevitably comes along and challenges all the established principles of any discipline. Things that "everybody knows" are suddenly under heavy shelling, and their underpinnings, resting largely upon unproven assumptions, are suddenly shaky. The person who forces us to confront ourselves realistically is not universally applauded. Such a person is Tom Ballard. He doesn't just leap on time-honored theories: he savages them.

This time out, Ballard sets up his assault by outlining the standard reasons for multitype networking: (1) no library has everything, (2) people need more information than their local libraries can furnish, (3) technology makes networking easier (or even possible), and (4) people demand such services. Wrong, he says, and proceeds to tell us why.

Skillfully interweaving statistics with empirical observation and plenty of original thought, Ballard challenges *everything* we thought we knew about multitype cooperation, and the role of the public library in it. Beautiful buildings, long service hours, electronic wonders, central sites, emphasis on nonbook materials: the list goes on. Ballard's message is elegant in its simplicity: what people really want (and need) he says, are more books, and a convenient place to go and get them. All the rest is misdirected window-dressing. "Quality," "outreach," and the "electronic information environment" are overrated, expensive, and not working out too well.

While one might counter that the author has selected his statistical data in such a way as to stack the deck in favor of his arguments, such a contention does nothing to minimize their importance. Those contemplating the design of spacious new buildings with atria and fountains, open sixty hours or more, and seriously involved with school and academic libraries in joint ventures, might do well to read Ballard and ponder. Libraries need Tom Ballard, and this modest (and modestly-priced) pamphlet-sized offering should be purchased and read by every public library planner, and routed to the entire board. [R: JAL, Sept 85, p. 241]   Bruce A. Shuman

213. **Citizen Participation in Library Decision-making: The Toronto Experience.** John Marshall, ed. Metuchen, N.J., School of Library Service, Dalhousie University in association with Scarecrow, 1984. 392p. illus. bibliog. index. (Dalhousie University, School of Library Service, No. 1). $25.00. LC 84-10617. ISBN 0-8108-1709-8.

The first half of the 1970s was a period of reform in Toronto with community objection to planned development of highways and high rise housing resulting in the election of a reform government in 1972. Reform spread to the school system and to the library. Marshall gives us an account of the environment of social change in Toronto, the library context, and the role and shape of citizen participation.

By 1970, the library board had become far removed from the interests and concerns of the diverse communities it served. In 1974 and 1975, reform-minded trustees were appointed who commissioned studies and invited staff and community participation. In the process the library was turned around in response to the actual expressed needs of Toronto residents. Marshall's summary articles throughout this case study provide a framework within which one can observe the process of change. Articles by community participants, trustees, and planners describe the process from their unique point of view. The result is a fascinating study of how a library board of trustees initiated change, what happened, and how change was then institutionalized. It is a study in the changing of the guard, of response to social change, and of the perils of planning *for* rather than *with* a community. The contributions are very well written and thanks to Marshall's organization hang together very well. Appendices and bibliographies lead to the primary document which served as background for the decisions made during the brief (1975-1978) period of intense change. This venture in democratic action with a decidedly Canadian flavor is absorbing reading. [R: BL, 15 Apr 85, p. 1157; JAL, Mar 85, p. 49; JAL, Nov 85, p. 308; LJ, 15 May 85, p. 48; RQ, Summer 85, p. 54]   Ann E. Prentice

214. Houghton, Tony. **Bookstock Management in Public Libraries.** London, Clive Bingley; distr., Hamden, Conn., Shoe String Press, 1985. 128p. index. $16.50. ISBN 0-85157-387-8.

Libraries need techniques to help each book in the collection perform at maximum level. In this sense *Bookstock Management in Public Libraries* functions as a collection evaluation, weeding, and selection tool. Although it refers specifically to adult books, techniques and ideas are transferable to juvenile books and other library materials, for example, phonograph records. Some of the suggestions/statistical applications contained in the work would be useful to school libraries, but most would be of little interest to academic or research libraries where the number of circulations for a particular title is of less importance.

Mr. Houghton's work is divided into two parts. Chapters 2 through 6 provide a theoretical framework for applying specific techniques for measuring and analyzing library performance discussed in chapters 7 to 16. These provide the librarian with information needed to formulate and evaluate collection development policies. Chapter 17 summarizes the methodology described in chapters 7 to 16 and refers the reader back to those chapters for specifics.

The work is heavy on statistical analysis of the collection. While none of the statistical operations are particularly complex, most are time-consuming and probably not practical for small to medium-sized public libraries with small staffs. Translation from British to American becomes a problem at times especially when the reader is trying to grasp the statistical concept being discussed. The book would be most useful for large libraries or library systems which have the central office staff to carry out the procedures discussed.

Carol J. Veitch

215.   Job and Career Information Centers for Public Libraries: A Step-by-Step Manual. Chicago, American Library Association, 1985. 50p. bibliog. (The Public Library Reporter, No. 21). $5.95pa. LC 85-13519. ISBN 0-8389-3322-X.

There is a wealth of information crammed into this fifty-page booklet; it is truly a step-by-step manual. In the introduction there is discussion of the philosophy behind such centers – the need for information, the public relations benefits for the library, the options available which range from the formation of special networks to merely utilizing resources already in the collection more effectively. Throughout the booklet there are detailed outlines of steps to be taken and questions to be considered should the decision be made to set up such a center.

Pamphlets written by a committee are not easy to read and this one is no exception. Much of the information and advice is available elsewhere, of course. But be it as a reminder or as an outline of steps to be taken when setting up a job and career information center – or, for that matter, some other specialized service – the sections on factors to consider; writing a proposal; models; location, furniture, etc.; and services and programs are excellent. A pamphlet is easier to carry around when working on such a project than the many volumes on planning on which this information is based.

Suzanne K. Gray

216.   Kamin, Judith. How Older Adults Use Books and the Public Library: A Review of the Literature. Champaign, Ill., Graduate School of Library and Information Science, University of Illinois, 1984. 35p. (Occasional Papers, No. 165). $3.00pa. ISSN 0276-1769.

A useful, brief review of the literature published since 1962 on public library use patterns and reading habits of older adults, this survey reviews 68 articles and books and lists an additional 116 on related topics. The pamphlet is divided into four main themes: reading preferences, education, user/nonuser studies, and aging and life satisfaction. Under each topic, articles and books are highlighted; a summary follows each section and a conclusion completes the twenty-two pages of text.

Kamin also offers eight questions deserving future study. Some of these are addressed by a more recent publication (August 1985), the long-awaited *1983 Consumer Research Study on Reading and Book Purchasing: Focus on the Elderly* by Market Facts, Inc., for the Book Industry Study Group, Inc. This 146-page volume refutes many claims by authors Kamin reviews, and offers partial answers to others.

The major weakness of the Kamin study is its sketchy synopses of research – one study, for example, is summarized in one sentence – and its simplistic conclusion which consists of six sentences. Since she has read so much more of the literature than most of us, I wish she had told us more about it. Still, this is a useful publication for people needing guidance in what to read and willing to read it for content themselves.

Rhea Joyce Rubin

217.   Nauratil, Marcia J. Public Libraries and Nontraditional Clienteles: The Politics of Special Services. Westport, Conn., Greenwood Press, 1985. 180p. bibliog. index. (New Directions in Librarianship, No. 8). $27.95. LC 84-19342. ISBN 0-313-23818-9.

What is the service role of the public library? Should it opt for the conservative stance to serve its traditional middle class clientele or should it be an active agent for change and reach out to nontraditional clienteles? Nauratil reviews the history of the public library and incorporates the views of the revisionists who say that the library was not founded to enhance democracy but to serve as an orderly alternative to the barroom. She identifies and devotes separate chapters to nontraditional clienteles; the poor, the elderly, the illiterate, racial minorities, and those who are confined to institutions. Each is described demographically, and socio-political issues that affect that group's ability to participate in the U.S. mainstream are identified. A brief history of public library service to each group is followed by recommendations for socially responsive service. In the final chapter, the author sets forth a direction for service that demands librarians give up their reluctance to serve those who do not fit the middle class mold and reorient service and spending priorities to meet special needs.

Each chapter is an excellent synthesis of research and writing from a variety of sources. Nauratil has obviously read widely and thought carefully, and the result is writing that is concise and to-the-point. She is a socially conscious person who cares deeply and is willing to act on her concerns. Passionate social statements are rare in the 1980s. We should take heed. [R: LJ, 15 June 85, p. 46]

Ann E. Prentice

218. Nickerson, Sheila B. **Writers in the Public Library.** Hamden, Conn., Library Professional Publications/Shoe String Press, 1984. 276p. bibliog. index. $24.50. LC 83-14859. ISBN 0-208-01872-7.

Nickerson, former poet laureate of Alaska, serves as poet-in-residence to Alaska's state library system. The first part of *Writers in the Public Library* is a journal of the year she spent as an itinerant writer-in-residence in various public libraries throughout the state. Besides running adult programs in libraries, she also visited public schools and prisons. Wherever she went, people responded enthusiastically to her writing workshops. Nickerson is a firm believer in the educational role of the public library. Two-thirds of the book consists of practical advice to librarians and writers on how to set up or tap into similar programs in their states and localities. Current writer-in-residency programs nationwide are described along with writing, literacy, and arts organizations.

Appendices include sample contracts for writers-in-residence; a sample application form for the National Endowment for the Arts residence program; and suggestions on how to conduct, publicize, and organize readings and workshops.

Gary D. Barber

219. Rosenberg, Philip. **Cost Finding for Public Libraries: A Manager's Handbook.** Chicago, American Library Association, 1985. 95p. illus. index. $9.95pa. LC 85-20091. ISBN 0-8389-0442-4.

This manual is the product of the combined human and economic resources of an extensive group of people and institutions, and is the response of PLA's Cost Analysis Task Force to 1982-1983 PLA President Don Sager's challenge to come up with a method to assist "libraries of various sizes to analyze their costs of common services and operations in a consistent and efficient manner."

The manual is divided into three main sections: "Concepts and Methods," "Calculation of Costs," and "Applications of Results." Three appendices — terminology, blank worksheets and sample rules of thumb — contribute to the manual's value.

The informal writing style and numerous illustrations make considerable sense out of what many librarians may view as a chaotic activity. In spite of this apparent clarity, the ultimate test of such a manual will be the extent of its practical usefulness. Although six library managers have tested the manual and reported positive results, only time and experimentation by libraries of assorted sizes in the field will be able to affirm or deny its usefulness. However, since accountability is increasingly a mandate from funding sources and a tenet of good management, this manual is worth a try. It may well deliver much of what it promises.

Darlene E. Weingand

220. Shoham, Snunith. **Organizational Adaptation by Public Libraries.** Westport, Conn., Greenwood Press, 1984. 163p. bibliog. index. (Contributions in Librarianship and Information Science, No. 47). $29.95. LC 83-22738. ISBN 0-313-24406-5.

Libraries, like other organizations, are encountering increasingly dynamic environments. Population patterns, economic structures, political views, demographic composition, and user expectations are all undergoing significant changes. In order to retain their vitality, libraries must develop effective means of coping with these changes. This may mean taking steps to alter the environment. Or it may involve adapting to the environmental changes.

The purpose of this book is to report on an empirical study of library adaptation to environmental changes. The analysis used contemporary organizational theories to assess factors that influence how six public libraries responded to environmental demands. The research was based on case studies rather than formalized quantitive study. Some quantitive analysis was conducted, but the author considers the quantitive assessment corroborative rather than central to the study.

Attention was focused on determining how the subject libraries responded to two specific developments: changes in the population served, and reduction of financial resources resulting from Proposition 13. While many of the responses were rather predictable — modified material selection policies, reduced number of hours — the study further explores the major factors influencing the decision-making process. [R: JAL, May 85, p. 125]   P. Grady Morein

221. Statistics of Public Libraries in the United States and Canada Serving 100,000 Population or More. Fort Wayne, Ind., Allen County Public Library, 1985. 39p. $5.00pa.

Produced by the Allen County Public Library, this paper-covered list of statistics covers public library agencies (selected from the *American Library Directory*, 37th ed., 1984) which serve populations in the United States and Canada exceeding one hundred thousand.

The over three hundred libraries covered were sent a questionnaire to be answered for the calendar year or fiscal year 1984.

The data are arranged by state or province. Salary information is quoted in the appropriate U.S. or Canadian funds.

Each entry gives the name of the library, city, and state or province; the name of the library director; the number of registered borrowers; the jurisdiction population; the number of holdings; circulation figures; the number of reference transactions; aggregate salaries and benefits expended; costs for books, other costs, and a total cost figure; the salaries of the director and a typical beginning librarian; the staff turnover rate; the percentage of registration, reference questions; circulation and budget per capita; the circulation per borrower; and finally, the total budget for salaries and books by percentage.

There are also regional tables combining these figures by region.

Many other sources collect similar data both in Canada (Alberta, Ontario, and Manitoba for example) and the United States, but this brings together many aspects which have not previously been included in one source. In addition, it is also available on floppy disc.

It will be useful to libraries, library trustees, and city governments who wish to compare the various figures with their own to determine strengths and weaknesses in their systems.

Daniel F. Phelan

222. Webb, T. D. **Reorganization in the Public Library.** Phoenix, Ariz., Oryx Press, 1985. 120p. bibliog. index. $35.00. LC 82-42917. ISBN 0-89774-074-2.

This study of public library reorganization aims to "help fill the information vacuum surrounding the subtleties of library organization and reorganization." The author isolates and focuses upon five important areas of managerial behavior: goals and planning, departmentalization, intragovernmental cooperation, staff involvement, and outside consultation. Even though it is recognized that the areas overlap,

each is treated in a separate chapter written by the author, which is followed by a case study written by a library professional "involved in a reorganization project, that either illustrates or elaborates on each concept as it is presented." The case studies (drawn from large, urban public library systems) serve to illustrate how the areas interrelate in actual situations.

The individual strategies of reorganization presented in the case studies provide a useful perspective for library managers facing reorganization. The book is also important for use in library education, as well as for anyone interested in public library management and financial support. There are a short foreword by Donald Sager, city librarian, Milwaukee Public Library, and an introductory chapter, "Understanding the Problem," which provide a good summary and overview for the remainder of the book. The final chapter brings together several conclusions drawn from the cases. There are in addition a bibliography and an index.

The book is clearly written and well organized. It offers valuable insight into the complexities of public library reorganization, and is an important addition to the literature on public library management. [R: JAL, May 85, p. 108; LJ, 1 June 85, p. 104; RQ, Winter 85, p. 280]   Susan J. Freiband

PUBLIC RELATIONS

223. Franklin, Linda Campbell. **Display and Publicity Ideas for Libraries.** Jefferson, N.C., McFarland, 1985. 264p. illus. bibliog. index. $14.95pa. LC 84-43229. ISBN 0-89950-168-0.

Display and Publicity Ideas for Libraries provides both practical and creative ideas on how to merchandise library materials and services. Most of the suggestions are organized around themes, such as library services and book care, reading and learning, social issues, and sports and games. Each display idea lists the materials needed and describes the technique for assembling the display. One section suggests "Versatile Display Elements" that would involve some woodworking skills but which could be eye-catching ideas for on-going displays.

As a school librarian, I do not feel this book is particularly essential. Caroline Feller Bauer's programming books (*Celebrations*, Wilson, 1985, and *This Way to Books*, Wilson, 1983) meet my needs more effectively by incorporating display ideas into programs using specific titles. The suggestions in *Display and Publicity Ideas for Libraries* are much more general and might better serve the needs of public librarians. In all, however, this is a useful overview of suggestions for planning and producing library displays. One feature worth noting is the brief "Display and Promotion Calendar" which lists some possible events for potential displays. Another useful feature is the annotated bibliography of selected resources.

Rebecca L. Thomas

224. Kirby, John. **Creating the Library Identity: A Manual of Design.** Brookfield, Vt., Gower Publishing, 1985. 140p. illus. bibliog. index. $53.95. ISBN 0-566-03496-4.

The author has constructed this manual on the premise that its librarian/reader will have had little or no training in the development of an effective visual environment for the library's users. The purpose of the manual is to help libraries, through graphics and design, to reflect the sophisticated expectations of today's and tomorrow's society.

The contents include chapters on the library identity, setting up the program, tools and equipment, materials and processes, formats, layout and design, typography, signage within the library, guides to the collection, services and procedures, library stationery, publishing for sale, and dealing with the other professionals, such as designers, printers and photographers.

The British flavor which appears in spelling and some examples adds an international appeal to the work and is not at all distracting. The manual is extensively illustrated and should prove very easy to use.

Two added bonuses: (1) illustrations on color microfiche which show how ideas in the manual have been used in practice and (2) a folder inside the back cover containing examples of copyright-free artwork.

A useful and practical reference tool. [R: JAL, Nov 85, p. 324]   Darlene E. Weingand

PUBLIC SERVICES

225. Bloomberg, Marty. **Introduction to Public Services for Library Technicians.** 4th ed. Littleton, Colo., Libraries Unlimited, 1985. 314p. illus. index. (Library Science Text Series). $35.00; $21.50pa. LC 84-23369. ISBN 0-87287-460-5; 0-87287-461-3pa.

This text describes the full range of public services in libraries, including patron registration, circulation systems, the actual business of maintaining a collection, reference services, and interlibrary loan. Twelve chapters are devoted to annotated bibliographies of reference materials covering areas from physics and law to etiquette and travel guides. The text is liberally illustrated, many of the examples reproduced from working documents used in public or academic libraries. There is a subject index and most chapters include brief bibliographies.

Bloomberg assumes that library media technical assistants (LMTAs) will be team members in a library's public services operation, approaching their work intelligently and responsibly. His advice is sensible. There is an abundance of information in each tightly edited chapter. He accomplishes the difficult task of describing processes and procedures in a manner applicable to all types of libraries. His text could serve as a supplementary text for library school students or a useful working tool for novice professionals. [R: BL, 15 Apr 85, p. 1156; JAL, May 85, p. 110; JAL, Nov 85, p. 309; RQ, Summer 85, pp. 513-14]

Margaret McKinley

226. Peterson, Paul, comp. and ed. **Bibliographic Services and User Needs: Report of a Conference Sponsored by the Council on Library Resources Held at Linda Hall Library, Kansas City, Missouri, December 14-16, 1983.** Washington, D.C., Council on Library Resources, 1984. 116p. $10.00pa. LC 84-7679.

This book is part of the professional report literature in library and information science. It is the product of a special conference held under the auspices of the Council on Library Resources to help determine the future of that organization's Bibliographic Service Development Program (BSDP). Four "challenge or discussion" papers present ideas for discussion by four working groups at the conference. The reports of discussions offer good suggestions for action to meet the challenges of the future to insure full access to bibliographic services in response to user needs. The conference has evidently not produced any world shaking changes in the environment, but it must have been enjoyable because of its location and the quality of those in attendance. It appears, however, that the thirty-two invited participants covered old ground and appeared to be involved in convincing the convinced that something ought to be done. They were selected to provide input from "a wide range of services and users — and 32 different perspectives on how bibliographic services ought to be improved." They included the four invited speakers, research library administrators, foundation officers, network and computer center administrators, library/communications school faculty, and CLR-connected persons. A complete list of them is given in an appendix, as is the schedule of activities. There is value to the bibliography, but the book is recommended only for library science collections. [R: CLJ, Feb 85, p. 40]

Edward P. Miller

REFERENCE SERVICES

227. Katz, Bill, and Ruth A. Fraley, eds. **Evaluation of Reference Services.** New York, Haworth Press, 1984. 334p. (The Reference Librarian, No. 11). $29.95. LC 84-12898. ISBN 0-86656-377-6.

This monograph, also published as *The Reference Librarian*, Number 11, fall/winter 1984, consists of twenty-five essays. The thirty knowledgeable contributors (five essays are co-authored)—including fourteen library educators (U.S., Canadian, Australian), eight academic librarians, and three library consultants—seem to agree that more evaluation is needed in order to provide "better reference librarians, better use of reference materials (including online services), and certainly better results for the library users" (p. 4). The following sampling illustrates the diversity of topics addressed: the need to evaluate reference services, evaluating reference personnel (especially their question-answering abilities), the need for accreditation of reference services, patron-centered reference service evaluation, performance standards, evaluation of reference sources, reference collection development policies. References are appended to each essay, but there is no index to the volume. [R: BL, 15 Apr 85, p. 1157; JAL, Nov 85, p. 309; RQ, Summer 85, p. 512; WLB, May 85, p. 619]   Wiley J. Williams

228. Slavens, Thomas P., ed. **Reference Interviews, Questions, and Materials.** 2d ed. Metuchen, N.J., Scarecrow, 1985. 144p. $15.00. LC 85-1968. ISBN 0-8108-1797-7.

Reference books come in all shapes and sizes, and this tiny volume provides a perfect example of that maxim. The book is designed to expose students or library staff to the types of questions they can expect in a reference setting. The volume is divided into ten chapters, each representing one type of reference (e.g., statistical sources, handbooks, or directories). The chapters include several examples of actual reference interviews, a comprehensive listing of reference questions, and a number of sources where answers can be found.

This second edition mirrors the first (see *ARBA* 79, entry 298) in all ways but one—the list of reference sources which concludes each section. The chapters, reference settings, and questions vary little between the two editions. The 1985 edition, for example, includes only one reference interview situation not found in the first edition. There are only two such examples from the earlier edition which are not in the second. The one significant change is the additional listing of reference sources. These are merely titles lists; no bibliographic information is given.

Considering the similarities between the two editions, it is questionable if a second edition is warranted. Since the volume has a stated limited audience, this new edition seems unnecessary.   Boyd Childress

RESEARCH METHODS

229. Lynch, Mary Jo, ed. **Research in Librarianship.** Champaign, Ill., Graduate School of Library and Information Science, University of Illinois, 1984. 1v. (various paging). (*Library Trends*, Vol. 32, No. 4). $6.00pa. ISSN 0024-2594.

Two previous issues of *Library Trends* (October 1957; July 1964) dealt with research in librarianship, and, not a moment too soon, this spring 1984 issue tackles the process of research. Readers expecting a review of research studies will generally be disappointed for, although various studies are remarked upon (and one author interjects his pertinent miniresearch into his article), the emphasis is on theories and techniques. Mary Jo Lynch, director of ALA's Office for Research, introduces research—with its confusing connotations of scientific activity, scholarly pursuit, or historical perspective—as having an "uneasy connection" with the library world. This connection is explored through several essays by persons identified with librarianship but who each here bring another field (history, operations research, organizational theory, political science, public administration, psychology of information use, sociology) to bear on library problems. Comment on the contribution of these other disciplines to librarianship is the unifying premise for this collection, along with the use of method or principles from these other disciplines, and their potential for future development of library research. Articles also cover research on the economics of libraries, funding, and publishing. One essay queries whether the cycle of academics and practitioners unevenly and indifferently perpetuating undistinguished research products can be broken for a more constructive interaction between these groups.

The essays stem from an informative premise and an interesting topic. But cover-to-cover reading is heavy going, and therefore readers are presumably well enough served if they concentrate on those articles with personal appeal. [R: JAL, Mar 85, p. 45]

Claire England

230. Powell, Ronald R. **Basic Research Methods for Librarians.** Norwood, N.J., Ablex

Publishing, 1985. 188p. bibliog. index. (Libraries and Information Science Series). $29.50. LC 84-18401. ISBN 0-89391-154-2.

The author's preface states that the book is aimed at "the practicing librarian who needs to conduct research and publish," and also at those who must read and evaluate published research reports. He continues by saying that research has no single definition but adds that his reading indicates that at least two types exist. He will, he says, concern himself with "basic research methods" rather than "applied research methods," which he consigns to a five-page appendix at the end of the work. Basic research, he says, is "also referred to as pure, theoretical or scientific research," and he then equates applied research with action research. One would urge a more rigorous approach to the formulation of the definitions and concepts he employs in the book. He is, however, correct in saying that most research attempted and/or reported as library-related has been applied research.

The first three chapters of the book examine the situation now existing concerning "research and librarianship," indicate how the research study should be developed, and discuss the importance and the manner of writing of the research proposal. Chapters 4 through 7 discuss three research methodologies—survey research, including a chapter on data collection; experimental research; and historical research. The last is very weak, in part due to the fact that no investigation appears to have been made into what historians have written about how historical research is done. He does cite one or two library historians, and they are the names one would expect to find, but no work on historiography is cited, nor listed in the bibliography at the end of the book.

The chapter on experimental research is much better in terms of presentation and content. With his insistence on sticking to basic research, and avoiding applied research it is interesting to see so much space devoted to survey research. This is descriptive research, and, although certainly requiring rigor, and scientific validity, is most often used as a means of gathering data for problem solving or decision making. Operations research, systems analysis, and bibliometrics, each of which gets no more than five or six lines in the appendix, present as many opportunities to be "pure, theoretical or scientific" as does survey research. The three types of research Powell has listed are certainly valid ones for librarians to consider, but they are not more "basic," by his definition than the other three. Chapters 8 and 9, the final chapters in the book, deal with analysis of the data and writing the research report respectively and provide reasonable introductions to both facets of

research. The chapter on analysis is not overly heavy on statistical methodologies, which many librarians tend to shy away from, but it does seem to refrain from offering the suggestion that one could hire a statistician to handle the mathematical mechanics.

As an introductory work this book has some merit, but it would need to be used in conjunction with both another monograph dealing with library related research, such as Busha and Harter, *Research Methods in Librarianship: Techniques and Interpretations* (Academic Press, 1980), and with one or two of the works on social science research which Powell lists in his bibliography. [R: WLB, Sept 85, p. 71]

Margaret Anderson

SCHOOL LIBRARY MEDIA CENTERS

General Works

231. Anderson, Pauline H. **Library Media Leadership in Academic Secondary Schools,.** Hamden, Conn., Library Professional Publications/Shoe String Press, 1985. 260p. index. $26.00; $16.50pa. LC 84-28896. ISBN 0-208-02048-9; 0-208-02049-7pa.

The stated purpose of this book is to interpret the role of the library media center program within an academically oriented secondary school and to provide a starting point for discussion of media program development. In this context Anderson brings to the forefront many important recent works, for example, *A Nation at Risk: The Imperative for Educational Reform* and *Academic Preparation for College: What Students Need to Know and Be Able to Do.*

Written in a cogent, fluid style, the book contains many examples of library media programs, sample documents, and selected procedural operations, primarily from the private school sector. Difficult to find but included in this work are sections on disaster policies, conservation and preservation of library media center resources, and archives in the school library.

This work would be most useful to communicate facets of the media program to the layperson; to practitioners it would serve as a reminder or a review of what we are all about. Although the author states in the preface that the book is directed toward the media program in secondary schools committed to strong, demanding academic programs, the book is directed to all who are concerned with the role of the media program in the education of today's youth. As Theodore Sizer states in the foreword: "The techniques [Anderson] values apply to all schools.... The specifics and emphases will differ in each school, but the goals will be the same" (pp. ix-x). This reviewer can only agree. [R: AL, Apr 85, pp. 248-49]

Thomas Wm. Downen

232. Kulleseid, Eleanor R. **Beyond Survival to Power for School Library Media Professionals.** Hamden, Conn., Shoe String Press/Library Professional Publications, 1985. 173p. index. $20.00; $14.50pa. LC 85-10411. ISBN 0-208-02031-4; 0-208-02032-2pa.

In a forceful and convincing manner, the author explains why some elementary school library media programs survive and even thrive despite pressures and financial cutbacks, while others succumb to the losses of material allocations and professional staff. By extrapolating from a small sample of library media centers operating in the public schools of New York City, Kulleseid is able to offer realistic strategies that "will ensure professional and economic survival in a field which offers few opportunities for expanding or even continuing work" (p. 3). This well-conceived book includes chapters on the contexts for survival; power as formal authority; professional competencies in pedagogy and librarianship; the power of informal influence and communication; as well as the author's succinct conclusions and recommendations which "may well make the difference between mere professional survival and the measurable enhanced visibility and vitality of a thriving library media program" (p. 57).

This is an assertive guide for school library media professionals who may wish to explore new routes to professional excellence and fulfillment.

Isabel Schon

233. Michaels, Carolyn Leopold. **Library Literacy Means Lifelong Learning.** Metuchen, N.J., Scarecrow, 1985. 365p. illus. bibliog. index. $27.50. LC 84-10705. ISBN 0-8108-1719-5.

This book is an expanded revision of the author's earlier work *School Libraries Worth Their Keep.* Perhaps this work should have been classified as an autobiography written in a stream-of-consciousness style; it lacks a coherent organization and is most confusing to the reader. Useful information related to lifelong learning skills is hidden among much trivia and difficult to find for the non-persistent reader. Chapter headings tend to be misleading since all information within is totally unorganized. The definition "library literacy means lifelong learning" spread over three pages leaves the reader more confused than ever.

The two most useful items in the book are the introduction by Lawrence C. Powell and Elizabeth Stone and an extensive bibliography.

Not recommended. [R: JAL, July 85, pp. 172-73; WLB, June 85, p. 699]

Hannelore B. Rader

234. **School Library Media Annual 1985.** Volume Three. Shirley L. Aaron and Pat R. Scales, eds. Littleton, Colo., Libraries Unlimited, 1985. 525p. index. $40.00. ISBN 0-87287-475-3; ISSN 0739-7712.

Volume three of the *School Library Media Annual* maintains the structure of the first two volumes. Part 1 deals with events and issues; part 2 deals with programs and collections; part 3 deals with research and development; and part 4 deals with trends and forecasts. Some changes have been made in this edition. For example, the subsection in part 1 formerly entitled "Intellectual Freedom" has been renamed "Access to Information" in order to reflect a broader approach to the topics related to this area and now includes such topics as copyright.

This annual contains articles written by nationally known practitioners in the field with a wide variety of backgrounds. These articles covering topics of continuing interest to school library media professionals are interspersed with lists of award-winning materials, state-level school media staffs, library school faculty members, and addresses of organizations related to all aspects of the profession. Of particular interest in the edition are the examination of copyright, a survey of the struggle surrounding censorship and intellectual freedom, a review of trends in vocational education programming and library media service to gifted young adults, and an examination of the uses of microcomputers, interactive video, and telecommunications in school library media programs. This volume continues to meet the editors' stated purpose of "helping library media professionals at all levels to examine important events, issues, practices, and trends relevant to the field." [R: WLB, Oct 85, p. 76]

Donald C. Adcock

235. **Students and the School Library.** Compiled by the editors of *The Book Report.* Columbus, Ohio, Linworth Publishing, 1984. 50p. $15.00pa. ISBN 0-88244-281-3.

Students and the School Library, compiled by the editors of *The Book Report,* is a fifty-page booklet containing twenty-two reprinted articles focusing on school library media services to students. The booklet is divided into five parts: "Working with Students" (nine articles), "The Librarian as Teacher" (nine articles), "Reading Motivation" (two articles), "Discipline" (five articles) and "Library Aides and Clubs" (two articles). Written by a variety of practicing school library media specialists, the articles are uneven in quality, and the format is cluttered and unattractive. Many of the articles read like testimonies of bad experiences and appear rather negative in approach (e.g., "Did you ever have one of those days when nothing goes right?").

Since the articles are available in original format and since they offer few new and innovative ideas, this booklet is of little value to a building-level professional collection. Fifteen dollars seems extremely expensive for such a poorly compiled work.   Pat R. Scales

236. Turner, Philip M. **Helping Teachers Teach: A School Library Media Specialist's Role.** Littleton, Colo., Libraries Unlimited, 1985. 259p. index. $18.50pa. LC 85-19855. ISBN 0-87287-456-7.

In this overview of instructional design for school librarians, Turner identifies instructional design as that function which enables librarians to help teachers to teach more effectively. After three introductory chapters which provide a rationale for instructional design as the most important role of the librarian, Turner concentrates on step-by-step strategies, with plenty of specific examples, explaining how librarians and teachers can form instructional teams. Each of the eight steps in the process (needs assessment, performance objectives identification, learner analysis, test design, materials selection, activities development, implementation, and evaluation), is covered in its own chapter and is divided into three levels of progressive involvement (passive participation, reaction, and action/education).

Most of this information has been available in the professional literature during the past decade, and anyone who has kept abreast will not find what is presented here new. What Turner does, however, is to summarize and synthesize the process clearly and logically and to present realistic examples which relate directly to the librarian/teacher team. Because his emphasis is always on employing the process to provide better service, librarians will find it easy to accept and to implement. Almost every chapter includes relatively current references and additional readings as well as "thought provokers," with possible responses listed in appendix A. Of the eight appendices, the most useful is a sample unit.

While the reader may tire of the chatty voice as well as the somewhat condescending tone (e.g., "... there is a good chance that you are feeling overwhelmed ..." [p. 200]), overall, the book will be most helpful for the preservice and continuing education of school librarians.
Mary K. Biagini

Collections

237. Gillespie, John T. **The Elementary School Paperback Collection.** Chicago, American Library Association, 1985. 306p. index. $17.50pa. LC 85-11215. ISBN 0-8389-0419-X.

School and public librarians searching for additional paperback titles for elementary-age children will be interested in the publication of this bibliography. Gillespie lists more than three thousand books recommended for children. The listing is divided into two age groupings — grades 1 to 3 and grades 4 to 6. Within those sections, the selections are further broken down under headings such as "Imaginary Stories" and "Science" with each of these topics further subdivided. Access by author and title is given through an index. The cutoff date for entries was September 1984, and information given represents availability and price at that date.

The bibliographic entry for each item is brief and not very informative. The author, title, paperback publisher, and price are given along with an annotation five to fifteen words in length. The illustrators, even of the picture books, are seldom mentioned. Eight individual tales by Hans Christian Andersen are listed, but most librarians would like to know the illustrator of each before choosing among them. And anyone selecting from among the many editions of Grimm's tales would like to know that Sendak illustrated *The Juniper Tree.* Another missing bit of information is the publication date of the book, so that *Sue Barton: Student Nurse* and *The Against Taffy Sinclair Club* both appear under "Personal Problems" with no indication of the different perspectives resulting from the forty years which separate their original publication dates. Book selectors using this list will have to check the current prices and availability and will probably want to locate longer annotations of books with which they are unfamiliar. The relatively high price of this paperback guide makes it an unnecessary expense for most school libraries. Adele M. Fasick

238. Gillespie, John T. **The Junior High School Paperback Collection.** Chicago, American Library Association, 1985. 238p. index. $17.50pa. LC 85-11248. ISBN 0-8389-0420-3.

One of four titles in an ALA series to aid in the selection of books for different school levels, this recommends 2,833 books (including 427 additional titles which are part of series, sequels, or continuations of the main title). The titles are arranged in broad categories for most effective use, and each title is described in a single, short sentence. Copyright date is omitted. Titles are first divided into fiction/nonfiction, then into broad subject categories (e.g.,

LYMAN BEECHER BROOKS LIBRARY
NORFOLK, VIRGINIA

"Reaching Maturity," "Computers and Calculators") or into genres (e.g., "Science Fiction," "Historical Fiction"); both fiction and nonfiction sections must be checked for related books on a topic. More than half of the main titles included are fiction.

Most titles are young adult, with a fair representation of elementary titles and a sprinkling of adult titles, mainly classics like *Robinson Crusoe* and *The Light That Failed.* Series such as Nancy Drew and the Hardy Boys are excluded, as are books of cartoons, reference titles, and texts. Some romance series (e.g., Sweet Dreams and Two by Two) and science fiction series are represented. Although each item is numbered, the author/title index lists page numbers. Both publishers' catalogs and standard current and retrospective selection sources were consulted; the most helpful were *Voice of Youth Advocates* and the *Kliatt Paperback Guide.* The omission of copyright dates is most missed in the sciences and personal development, guidance and health sections. Although many titles are familiar, the copyright date would be useful in making selections. The major problem with this bibliography is that so many new titles have become and will become available following its cutoff date of September 1984.   Mary K. Biagini

239. **Junior High School Library Catalog.** 5th ed. Richard H. Isaacson, ed. New York, H. W. Wilson, 1985. 835p. index. (Standard Catalog Series). $80.00. LC 85-17934. ISBN 0-8242-0720-3.

The *Junior High School Library Catalog* was begun twenty years ago in order to provide a selective bibliography in the field of adolescent literature. The *Catalog* primarily covers books for the seventh, eighth, and ninth grades, but it includes levels appropriate for both elementary grades and senior high—to accommodate slower and more advanced students. This edition includes 3,192 titles and 5,380 analytical entries considered to be a basic collection, with the understanding that libraries serving large systems will need to supplement this list.

The *Catalog* is divided into three parts: Part 1, the "Classified Catalog," is arranged according to the abridged Dewey Decimal classification, and complete bibliographical information is given. Part 2 is an author, title, subject, and analytical index and serves as a comprehensive key to part 1. Analytical entries are an important feature of the *Catalog.* Part 3 is a directory of the publishers and distributors.

The *Catalog* is published through the cooperative efforts of publishers and the library community, including an advisory committee and consultants. The present edition states that

it includes a representative number of books on some of the main preoccupations of youth in the 1980s. The topics covered include computers, careers, sex, and drug abuse. While not neglecting personal concerns such as emotional development, the present edition looks outward to the world beyond the self. This edition features books that discuss the stresses of family life brought about by separation, divorce, remarriage, and adoption. Adolescents also seek to understand the problems posed by hazardous wastes, air and water pollution (including acid rain), and the nuclear threat. The presence of titles covering suicide, alcohol abuse, anorexia nervosa, and bulimia are an indication of the challenges teenagers face in dealing with both the inner and outer worlds.

In this edition, the fiction section of the *Catalog* has been expanded and an abundance of new titles reflects the current intense interest in sports. Four annual supplements are planned.

Librarians will find the following useful: listing of ALA publications, Newbery Award winners, periodicals (for articles and reviews), cataloging and classification tools, reference books, bibliographies, as well as guidelines on the management and operation of instructional materials centers.   Margaret E. Chisholm

240. Van Orden, Phyllis J. **The Collection Program in High Schools: Concepts, Practices, and Information Sources.** Littleton, Colo., Libraries Unlimited, 1985. 289p. bibliog. index. (Library Science Text Series). $23.50. LC 84-28872. ISBN 0-87287-483-4.

This text considers the collection in secondary library media centers from three points of view: the educational setting and principles of collection development, the practical considerations of selection, and the administrative concerns of collection development and management. It is well documented with references to much of the best recent source material in the area. It presents a well-organized and thorough discussion of important issues and explanation of exemplary practices. The author's well-informed, broad perspective and sound judgment on suggested practices are evident throughout. Graphic illustrations and chapter summaries help to focus the main ideas.

Unfortunately the index is incomplete in coverage and in many instances refers the reader to a bibliographic entry in an appendix, which refers to discussion of the title in some chapter for which no page reference is given. The index should include all relevant page numbers. Furthermore, bibliographies at the end of chapters do not always give citations for all titles mentioned in the body of the text. However, the list of bibliographic and selection tools in appendix

2 is extensive and provides a short, useful annotation for each.

The book will be a good source for school library media specialists and library science students. [R: BL, July 85, p. 1545]

JoAnn V. Rogers

Management

241. Hart, Thomas L., ed. **Behavior Management in the School Library Media Center.** Chicago, American Library Association, 1985. 166p. bibliog. $15.00pa. LC 85-11206. ISBN 0-8389-0429-7.

The editor has divided this volume into two parts. Part 1 consists of reprints of articles previously published in professional journals whose purpose is to provide an understanding of the theory and practice of behavior modification. It also includes selections that apply behavior modification to general education situations. Part 2 is a compilation of nine papers written by practicing school library media specialists outlining successful discipline practices in school library media centers and four articles which have previously appeared in professional journals. Part 2 is subdivided into sections dealing with high school, middle school, and elementary school library media centers and concludes with brief examples of specific problems that arise in school library media centers.

The major weakness of this work is its exclusive reliance on behavior modification as the technique to manage behavior in the school library media center. The one section dealing with critics of this technique does not provide adequate discussion of alternative methods. A second weakness is that the articles reprinted here are at least ten years old. It should also be noted that only one of the papers presented by the practitioners utilizes behavior modification as a method to manage behavior. School library media professionals may find the examples provided by the practitioners helpful but will have to look elsewhere for help in managing behavior in the library media center. [R: WLB, Dec 85, p. 56]

Donald C. Adcock

242. **Public Relations for the School Library.** Compiled by the editors of *The Book Report.* Columbus, Ohio, Linworth Publishing, 1984. 44p. $15.00pa. ISBN 0-88244-280-5.

Public Relations for the School Library is a forty-four page booklet compiled by the editors of *The Book Report* for the purpose of providing in one volume practical hints in the area of public relations for the practicing school library media specialist. The twenty-four articles are reprints from the May/June issues of *The Book Report* and "range from discussions of the good reasons for establishing a public relations program to how-to-tips on winning friends for the library." The booklet is divided into four parts: "Planning for Public Relations," "Increasing Your Visibility: Events, Contests, Special Observances," "Bookmarks, Displays and Bulletin Boards," and "Winning Friends for the Library."

The articles are written by building-level elementary, middle and high school library media specialists, district coordinators, and a professional public relations agent. The articles are not scholarly, but offer quick and easy tips for launching some type of public relations program at the local school level. In the back of the booklet is a calendar for making or mapping a public relations plan. The price is a bit too expensive for the material presented. Since the articles are reprints, this booklet's usefulness to a professional collection can be questioned.

Pat R. Scales

243. Thomason, Nevada Wallis. **Circulation Systems for School Library Media Centers: Manual to Microcomputer.** Littleton, Colo., Libraries Unlimited, 1985. 169p. illus. bibliog. index. $23.50. LC 84-29704. ISBN 0-87287-370-6.

Thomason has provided an examination of a variety of systems for circulating materials in school library media centers. Beginning with a brief but fascinating historical perspective on "charging" systems, the author then describes specific systems currently in use in many media centers. Chapters are devoted to manual, semi-automatic (including Gaylord, Sysdac, Brodac, and Demco), and microcomputer-based circulation systems. Procedures for cirulating print and nonprint materials and audiovisual equipment are presented. The description of the microcomputer based circulation systems includes some beginning information about microcomputer terminology (*bits, bytes, K, ROM, RAM,* etc.), and discusses what kinds of procedures are needed in the circulation process. Some commercially available software packages are described in an appendix as are some helpful publications. Another appendix lists manufacturers and suppliers for computer-related materials.

Basically this book provides a survey of circulation systems. The author describes each system but makes few evaluative remarks regarding a system. Throughout the book, however, the author poses questions which would aid the reader in selecting a system to meet specific needs. The questions in the microcomputer section are particularly useful. Two sample circulation policies — one for an elementary school and one for a middle school — are included and provide a helpful overview of the circulation process in specific settings. [R: BL, July 85, p. 1545]

Rebecca L. Thomas

Media Skills and Programs

244.   Bell, Irene Wood, and Jeanne E. Wieckert. **Basic Media Skills through Games. Volume I.** 2d ed. Littleton, Colo., Libraries Unlimited, 1985. 389p. illus. bibliog. $28.50. LC 84-25058. ISBN 0-87287-438-9.

Basic Media Skills through Games (see *ARBA* 80, entry 664) was published in 1979. The format of the second edition is essentially the same as that of the first edition except that a chapter on computer games has been added. In all, 112 games – card, puzzle, board, hands-on, and so forth – are included. Topics include introducing the IMC, the card catalog, the Dewey Decimal system, reference books and their use, and functions and applications of audiovisual hardware and computers. Progression in each section of the book is from primary grade (introductory concepts) through sixth grade (advanced concepts or reinforcement of basic skills). Some of the games are for individuals, others for class groups, and some can be adapted for either use. Game information includes purpose, grade level, playing time, number of players, materials needed, and game procedures. Sample game boards and questions are provided as needed. An appendix provides a sequence for introducing and reinforcing IMC skills.

All games were tested in the authors' schools, and some skill test results are reported in the preface. This is a useful work for any elementary school librarian/media specialist who wants some creative ideas for skills instruction.   Carol J. Veitch

245.   Bell, Irene Wood, and Jeanne E. Wieckert. **Basic Media Skills through Games. Volume II.** 2d ed. Littleton, Colo., Libraries Unlimited, 1985. 386p. illus. index. $23.50. LC 84-25058. ISBN 0-87287-470-2.

Through a game approach, the authors present 142 games grouped in five categories to teach alphabetizing; understanding and using dictionaries; using encyclopedias and reference sources; applying the use of maps, globes, and atlases; and enjoying literature. In each of the sections on a skill, games are arranged in grade-level sequence with games for introducing skills preceding advanced concepts and reinforcement activities. A wide variety of game types are included. The card games, dice games, board games, identification/matching games, location games, hands-on games, and puzzles are developed using inexpensive resources. An excellent introduction develops the concept of gaming strategies, game construction, game awards, and reasons for using this strategy. Library media specialists will appreciate the bibliographic suggestions at the beginning of each section. The materials suggested may be used to introduce the content. For each game, the authors provide the purpose, grade level, time, number of players, method of checking, materials, and procedures. Diagrams are provided in many cases. Games are indexed by title, method of checking, number of students, and type of game. This volume will be much used by elementary and middle/junior high library media specialists who want to use the strategy of teaching with games.   Paula Montgomery

246.   Bodart, Joni. **Booktalk! 2: Booktalking for All Ages and Audiences.** 2d ed. New York, H. W. Wilson, 1985. 388p. index. $20.00pa. LC 85-14223. ISBN 0-8242-0716-5.

In this expanded version of her well-received 1980 *Booktalk!*, Bodart offers reassurance to beginners and stimulation to experienced booktalkers, be they public or school librarians.

The first portion maintains the pattern of practical advice on the when, why, how, what, and for whom of booktalking. Aids, such as the teacher's evaluation form found in the earlier work are reproduced here. Two new chapters by outside contributors address school libraries: Larry Rakow for high schools and Elizabeth Rowland Overmyer for elementary schools.

The scope of the booktalks, pages 139-352, has been expanded to include titles appropriate for first grade through adult audiences. Appendix A lists these works by audience groups. The reader benefits from cases where more than one booktalk is provided for the same title. Owners of the first edition will want to retain their copies as the booktalks do not duplicate titles.

Appendix B, a new feature, is the "Bibliography by Theme and Genre." The "List of Publishers" is appendix C. Two more new features are appendices D and E: "Short Films Suitable for Use in Programs for All Ages" and "Handouts on Booktalking and School Visiting." The earlier listing of "Books Someone Thought Were Easy to Booktalk" (1st ed., p. 235) is not repeated.

The index refers to the main text and to authors, titles, and booktalkers in the "Booktalks" section.

As an earlier reviewer wrote "It's comprehensive in its approach and grabbingly informal and candid in its style" (Jane Manthorne, *School Library Journal* 27, no. 4 [December 1980]: 34).

A source mentioned on page 77 as Children's Services Division of the ALA is the Association for Library Service to Children, ALA.   Phyllis J. Van Orden

247. Canoles, Marian L. **The Creative Copy-cat II.** Littleton, Colo., Libraries Unlimited, 1985. 188p. illus. bibliog. index. $18.50. LC 84-29994. ISBN 0-87287-436-2.

This title is designed to supplement the ideas presented in *The Creative Copycat* (Libraries Unlimited, 1982). The focus here is on bulletin board ideas for major American holidays, the four seasons, and a few selected celebrations (e.g., Children's Book Week and National Library Week). The suggestions are arranged by seasons and then subdivided into specific observances. Each suggestion includes a drawing or photograph of the finished bulletin board and information about the background material, lettering techniques, and method of assembly. Appendices include some general advice on constructing bulletin boards, a list of Newbery and Caldecott Award winners (through 1984), and the dates of some major holidays and celebrations. An annotated bibliography is included as is a subject index.

Many of the ideas in this book seem complicated to prepare and involve advance planning to gather the suggested materials. Some of the suggestions are marked as "easy" in the table of contents, but this is not repeated on the specific page to alert the reader who is skimming through the book. The holiday ideas are not particularly original — flags for Flag Day, witches and bats for Halloween, etc. Also, in many of the displays, little emphasis is placed on highlighting library materials, thus, a valuable promotional opportunity is overlooked. Librarians and teachers who need very basic suggestions might find this a useful beginning resource, but most experienced librarians and teachers will be aware of these ideas already. [R: BL, July 85, p. 1544 and pp. 1563-64; BR, Sept/Oct 85, pp. 53-54]

Rebecca L. Thomas

248. Champlin, Connie, and Nancy Renfro. **Storytelling with Puppets.** Chicago, American Library Association, 1985. 293p. illus. bibliog. index. $19.95pa. LC 84-18406. ISBN 0-8389-0421-1.

Storytelling with Puppets is a valuable resource book on incorporating puppets into classroom and library story programs. The authors present practical information about using puppets from selecting appropriate stories to puppet-making to theater design. The book is clearly organized into six sections. Section 1, "Before the Story," discusses why puppets could enhance a story program and gives some suggestions for when and how to use puppets. The next section, "The Puppets," presents basic information on puppet-making, but also includes a descriptive list of puppet manufacturers and

dealers. Some strategies for creating characterization through voice and movement are also included. "Host puppets" and "lead puppets" are discussed in the third section, and the authors present detailed information about the uses of each type. Section 4 deals with "Participatory Storytelling" and suggests ways to involve students in the storytelling experience. The authors suggest specific stories that use sound and action and that would have opportunities for audience participation. In section 5, "Presentation Formats," various types of theaters are discussed, as are other techniques for presenting puppets, like a storytelling apron. The final section, "After the Story," provides information about follow-up activities and displays that will build on the storytelling experience.

Both authors have been involved with puppetry, and their expertise is evident in this book. Their suggestions are clear and easy-to-follow and show an awareness of the concerns of the novice while also suggesting strategies for more experienced tellers. Especially helpful are the many lists of stories to use, the excellent bibliographies on puppetry and storytelling, and the selection of photographs and diagrams to illustrate the text. This book would be a useful resource for librarians and teachers wishing to develop their skills in this area. [R: SLMQ, Summer 85, p. 224]

Rebecca L. Thomas

249. Hackman, Mary H. **Library Media Skills and the Senior High School English Program.** Littleton, Colo., Libraries Unlimited, 1985. 120p. illus. index. (Teaching Library Media Research and Information Skills Series). $23.50. LC 84-28895. ISBN 0-87287-419-2.

Library Media Skills and the Senior High School English Program is a rather specialized book that should be useful to high school library media specialists who are trying to *integrate* (not simply *relate*) the teaching of library skills with the English curriculum. The latest of the Teaching Library Media Research and Information Skills series books edited by Paula Kay Montgomery, this work is a welcome addition to the relatively small, but growing, collection of materials dealing specifically with the teaching of library skills to high school (as opposed to elementary or junior high school) students.

The material is divided into nine chapters of varying lengths and covers the following topics: the role of the senior high school library/media specialist, the historical relationship between the teaching of English and the role of the library/media center, public relations aspects relevant to this kind of program, the evaluation and development of programs and curricula, the scope and sequence of skills, the integration of skills at both the school and district levels, and how to integrate library skills into the English curriculum with Shakespeare as an example. The work concludes with an index and two appendices—one listing relevant library skills materials, the other professional associations. References are given at the end of each chapter and a number of examples of handouts and assignments are included.

Although limited to a specific discipline, this concise volume contains basics which apply to all subject areas. As a result, while this source should be most helpful to those library/media specialists who are attempting to integrate the teaching of library skills with the *English* curriculum, those who are interested in expanding into other subject areas will find much information that either relates directly or can be adapted to suit specific needs. [R: BL, July 85, p. 1544; BR, Nov/Dec 85, p. 50]

Kristin Ramsdell

250. Hart, Thomas L. **Instruction in School Library Media Center Use (K-12).** 2d ed. Chicago, American Library Association, 1985. 431p. bibliog. $12.50pa. LC 84-18405. ISBN 0-8389-0418-1.

This resource updates the 1978 title and serves as an index to instructional materials and activities for library/media skills programs. The author has prepared an overview of the current attitudes and practices in library/media instruction including the presentation of a sample scope and sequence chart (from the Leon District Schools in Tallahassee, Florida). Following this are brief articles from a variety of individuals examining many different instructional approaches: individualized, tutorial, programmed, computer-assisted, and others. These brief articles provide a variety of perspectives on library/media skills instruction.

The majority of the book is devoted to an index of materials for library/media skills instruction. Areas covered include library orientation, citizenship, parts of a book, location and arrangement of materials, classification, card catalog, methods of research, reference tools, and equipment operation. Within each section, the author lists sources which contain activities for instruction. For example, when presenting information about the card catalog to first graders, Hart includes a brief "success story" article and a reference to a library skills manual with spirit duplicating masters. Another area might include filmstrips, pamphlets, and cassette tapes. The sources that Hart cites are usually annotated, with a more general annotation included in the bibliography.

Librarians who are interested in updating their materials for library/media skills instruction will find this a very useful compilation. Hart includes a variety of types of materials and gives enough information about each one to allow for readers to decide about its usefulness. The bibliography is especially helpful since it divides the materials into types (i.e., books, microcomputer software, motion pictures, etc.). [R: BR, Sept/Oct 85, p. 54]

Rebecca L. Thomas

251. **Instruction in Library Media Skills: Supplement to a Guide to School Library Media Programs.** Hartford, Conn., Connecticut State Department of Education, 1984. 121p. illus. bibliog. free pa.

Produced jointly by the Connecticut Educational Media Association's Library Media Skills Committee and the staff of the Connecticut State Department of Education's Learning Resources and Technology Unit this volume is an attempt to provide school library media specialists and teachers with suggestions for integrating instruction in library media skills into the total school curriculum.

Specific competencies and skills for grades K-12 are identified followed by sample units for each level and each competency. Samples include objectives, activities, resources, and evaluation with careful assignment of specific objectives and activities to either the library media specialist or the classroom teacher. It is regrettable that not all the objectives in the sample units are stated in behavioral terms.

A very complete bibliography is found at the end of the volume.

Units and lessons can be utilized exactly as they are presented, or they can be adapted to local needs and conditions. Furthermore, they can serve to stimulate the development of additional units integrated with other subjects in individual schools.

Many good suggestions are found in this very useful volume.   Sara R. Mack

252. Leonard, Phyllis B. **Choose, Use, Enjoy, Share: Library Media Skills for the Gifted Child.** Littleton, Colo., Libraries Unlimited, 1985. 153p. illus. index. (Teaching Library Media Research and Information Skills Series). $23.50. LC 85-4532. ISBN 0-87287-417-6.

Leonard has written a thoughtful book about the many possibilities for meeting the needs of a gifted child through using the library media center and its personnel. She suggests that the services of the library media center are ideal for a gifted child, offering a wide variety of materials and topics for exploration. She stresses the need for teachers and library media professionals to cooperate in the development of challenging projects for gifted students. She has developed a clear rationale for having the library serve as the focus for activities for gifted students.

Leonard describes many kinds of giftedness and discusses how the library program can extend student experiences on many levels. She emphasizes the options that are available in a well-organized, well-staffed library media center. Her choose, use, enjoy, share (C.U.E.S.) approach incorporates many library materials into student projects and she especially recommends the use of picture books and easy readers with students of all ages.

Leonard has not written a cookbook on library media skills. Many of her suggestions are presented in an anecdotal format and display her own solid knowledge of children's literature. Each suggestion is not described in minute detail. Instead, Leonard recognizes the intelligence and experiences of her readers and allows them to expand her suggestions to meet their own needs. The activities which are described in more detail are clear and would be easy to adapt to other situations. When visuals are presented (i.e., sample activity sheets), they are very helpful.

Choose, Use, Enjoy, Share stresses flexibility and spontaneity in the development of projects for gifted children. Librarians will find Leonard's ideas refreshing and supportive not just as suggestions for services to the gifted, but also as a statement on the far-reaching impact of a quality school library media program. [R: BL, 1 Oct 85, p. 276]

Rebecca L. Thomas

253. Polette, Nancy. **The Research Book for Gifted Programs.** O'Fallon, Mo., Book Lures; distr., Metuchen, N.J., Scarecrow, 1984. 170p. illus. $14.95pa. ISBN 0-913839-28-0.

This book outlines a very complete research program of independent study for gifted children that may be used by a school librarian/media specialist or classroom teacher. The book is organized extremely well with an easy-to-understand overview of characteristics of gifted children related to research strategies, thinking, and research skills. Each critical thinking, critical reading, and communication skill is presented with a thorough definition/explanation and warm-up activities. This is followed by a taxonomy of research skills that are included in most library/media programs. Each skill in this section plus the following three, which divide research activities by levels (grades 1-3, 4-6, 7-8), includes student activities on blackline masters which may be reproduced (thirty copies during one school year.)

The book is easy to read and easy to use. Not only is it very complete and useful with exciting but practical activities, it is also attractive with many drawings and graphics. It would be an excellent addition to any elementary or middle school library/media center or gifted classroom.

Marie Zuk

254. Toor, Ruth, and Hilda K. Weisburg. **Media Skills Puzzlers.** Berkeley Heights, N.J., Library Learning Resources, 1984. 126p. illus. $17.00 spiralbound. ISBN 0-931315-00-X.

Children enjoy working puzzles so media skill puzzles can be a great teaching tool. *Media Skills Puzzlers* is geared for students from elementary school through senior high school with some puzzles simple enough for second or third graders and others difficult enough to challenge a high school student. Most of the puzzles have a language arts or social studies tie-in.

The book is divided into five sections and includes a variety of media center skills ranging from the use of the card catalog and basic reference tools to the use of more sophisticated reference tools and techniques. The "Reference Questions" section contains twenty-nine puzzles which give students practice in using a variety of reference techniques. The nine "Hidden Words" puzzles are geared to people and terms the students should know. Only the first two puzzles in this section have lists of the hidden words; students must develop their own lists for the remaining puzzles. Card catalog skills are stressed in "Missing Words" (eight puzzles) and "Crossword Puzzles" (fourteen puzzles). The last section "Double Treats" are two puzzles in one. Part 1 is a research skills puzzle. Answers from this puzzle are the words in the seek-a-word part of the "double treat." Titles of puzzles are intriguing and will create interest in the puzzles. Answers for all puzzles are provided in a section at the back of the book.

Media Skills Puzzlers is a spiralbound softback, 8½-by-11 inches in size, ready for quick copying. Reproduction rights are granted for individual libraries, but not entire school systems. This work would be a useful adjunct for any school media center with a strong emphasis on teaching media skills. Thirty-three of the sixty-six puzzles included have, however, been previously published in *The School Librarian's Workshop* (Learning Resources, 1980-1984) which would make this volume less useful to schools subscribing to the newsletter. [R: SLJ, Apr 85, p. 44]

Carol J. Veitch

Microcomputer Use

255. Microcomputer Information for School Media Centers. Nevada Thomason, ed. Metuchen, N.J., Scarecrow, 1985. 316p. bibliog. index. $25.00. LC 84-23566. ISBN 0-8108-1769-1.

If the work has a fault, it's simply that it wasn't published six or seven years ago at a time when school library/media specialists were struggling with the emergence of microcomputers. Groping then for guidelines, school library/media specialists would have benefitted greatly from this compilation of excellent, practical articles. The book carries a misleading 1985 copyright date, since the articles are selected from journals published in the early 1980s; consequently, much of the information is dated and in some cases obsolete. The reader should note the caution in the preface that there is difficulty in trying to define a state of the art "during a period of dynamic activity such as microcomputers have experienced during the past decade." That dynamic activity has already dated the information, and in some instances the advances predicted in the book are history. Technical notations about printers, perhaps no longer valid, serve as an excellent example; references to specific microcomputer models and brands which have been replaced by newer, better accepted models is another.

However, the book has great value in that it seeks to bring together in one place some of the basic information about microcomputers. Divided into five sections, the book presents a series of articles from various periodicals which early on provided readers with information on microcomputer use. Included are articles presenting an overview of the microcomputer's role in education, a feeling for the language of the computer world, and a look at the computer's usefulness in teaching and media administration. Perhaps in that sense the book does present a starting point from which a novice may proceed into more recently published books and journals. The appendices are useful, especially the bibliography which appears to have been updated through 1984. [R: BL, July 85, pp. 1544-45; EL, Nov/Dec 85, p. 32; JAL, July 85, pp. 169-70]

Anthony C. Schulzetenberg

256. Putting the Microcomputer to Full Use in the School Library. Compiled by the editors of *The Book Report*. Columbus, Ohio, Linworth Publishing, 1984. 55p. illus. $15.00pa. ISBN 0-88244-297-1.

This chatty collection of about twenty-five one- or two-page articles, most reprinted from *The Book Report*, will reveal what each of the author-practitioners knows about the use of microcomputers in school libraries, based on his/her own experiences. It will not prepare you to do as the title indicates unless the "full use" which you intend in your media center is the same as one of the authors'. Several articles discuss a method and process used to select hardware and software which can be generalized to some extent. But there is no mention of interface with bibliographic utilities or computer networking in a local area network. In sum, this collection lacks an overview of the application of technology in libraries. School librarians should strive to be conversant with what is happening in other types of libraries but would be better advised to consult sources such as *Library Technology Reports* and general monographs on the topic.

JoAnn V. Rogers

SERVICE TO DISABLED USERS

257. Clark, Leslie L., with Dina N. Bedi and John M. Gill, eds. **A Guide to Developing Braille and Talking Book Services.** Munich, New York, K. G. Saur, 1984. 108p. (IFLA Publications 30). ISBN 3-598-20395-0.

This book, a collaborative effort sponsored by several organizations and approved for publication by the IFLA section of Libraries for the Blind, has drawn heavily for its content from an international survey of producers of braille and talking books. The survey revealed the current levels of production, methods of distribution, data on devices used to read talking books, some idea of the use of available information on demand and its influence on the contents of books, the capability of presses to meet increasing demand, and some idea of the social context within which a particular press or facility was established.

It is clearly written in nontechnical language for "a planner and developer of new talking book and braille book production facilities in an area or country or nation in which no such services were available before." It advises on methods of obtaining information about the population served and on the creation of both talking book and braille book facilities.

The book's stated purposes are fulfilled: to provide an overview of current practice in braille and talking book production; to describe some typical methods for producing reading materials; to give guidance to those wishing to establish new, or to update old, facilities for producing reading materials. It is highly recommended for those facing this task. [R: RQ, Winter 85, pp. 273-74]

Jean Weihs

258. Dalton, Phyllis I. **Library Service to the Deaf and Hearing Impaired.** Phoenix, Ariz., Oryx Press, 1985. 371p. illus. bibliog. index. $39.50. LC 83-43242. ISBN 0-89774-135-8.

Library services for the deaf and hearing impaired are not so fully developed as library services to other disabled people. Perhaps the major reason for this is the widespread misunderstanding of the reading problems of many deaf people; most librarians incorrectly assume that deafness has no effect on reading ability. The lack of a federal program, such as the National Library Service for the Blind and Physically Handicapped, to serve a leadership role has also been an obstacle. And a third problem has been the lack of a good, comprehensive guide to the provision of such services.

Although recent books on the handicapped have included chapters on the deaf, this is the first book in a decade to focus totally on this subject. A wide range of topics, from history of legislation in the area to sample library promotion pieces, is covered in this valuable work. Dalton outlines the services and materials necessary for a good program and stresses the need for cooperative planning, implementation, and evaluation. To that end, she provides sections on other professional organizations, consumer associations, and community involvement. She discusses the environmental requirements for a suitable facility, the current technology available to assist us, the need for personnel training, and the economics of providing services. The book also contains much background information—definitions, statistics, and tables—to help the newcomer understand the hearing-impaired population. [R: LJ, Dec 85, p. 74; RQ, Winter 85, p. 276; WLB, June 85, p. 699]

Rhea Joyce Rubin

SERVICES FOR THE AGING

259. Bewley, Lois M., and Sylvia Crooks. **Urban Public Library Service for the Aging in Canada.** Halifax, School of Library Service, Dalhousie University, 1984. 123p. bibliog. (Occasional Papers Series, No. 34). $11.50pa. ISBN 0-7703-0181-9.

The aging of the North American population is an increasingly recognized phenomenon. Although librarianship has not been slow over the past few decades to articulate a responsibility to senior citizens, public libraries have generally been somewhat slower in following through with policy, programs, and collections for seniors. The literature on these aspects has been growing, and this volume extends the literature for Canada by providing a Canadian dimension to the applicable reading from American librarianship. Easily read in an evening, this work has a very useful chapter on Canada's demographics.

Reference to theories of social gerontology and to the myths and realities of aging also create a background to remarks on a 1982 survey of libraries. Bewley surveyed the thirty-one members of Canada's Council of Administrators of Large Urban Public Libraries and, from her thirty returned questionnaires, compiled some findings about staff, budgets, activities, etc., in this area of service to seniors. She concluded that "library services for the aging in Canada has been and still is inextricably part of the general library programs and services designed for adults." Accordingly, she says, "Service specifically ... for the elderly ... is not clearly differentiated by these library systems, although every library offers something of use and value to them." Not a surprising or dramatic finding, but the paper's summary conclusions and recommendations do point to a need to be more definite about service to seniors. Papers like this one are indicative; they generate implications for future development and remind libraries of their evolving role in the community.

Claire England

260. Casey, Genevieve M. **Library Services for the Aging.** Hamden, Conn., Library Professional Publications/Shoe String Press, 1984. 168p. bibliog. index. $18.50; $13.50pa. LC 83-16218. ISBN 0-208-01946-4; 0-208-01947-2pa.

The author, for many years a staunch advocate for appropriate library services for the aging, has presented a readable, well-organized treatment of various aspects of library services to the aging. Introductory chapters cover the demography of aging and the intellectual capabilities of older adults. Many who are unfamiliar with the situation of the aging in today's world will find in these chapters some demythologizing, for example, the fact that the vast majority of older people are not in nursing homes. Furthermore, there are some straight facts, based on research (e.g., sensory perception declines in both quantity and quality with advancing age). Chapters on education, trends in public library service to the aging, and services to those in nursing homes are also based on research studies and give a number of examples of successful programs. These are followed by chapters on resources both for the aging and for those doing research in gerontology, on education for librarians serving the aging, on planning public library services for the aging and, finally, on the meaning of aging. Each chapter is followed by a brief list of readings, many of which are also found in the selected annotated bibliography in the appendix. Many of the references are from the mid-seventies – only a small number were published in the 1980s – and perhaps this is due to the idiosyncracies of publishing, but it is hoped that a second edition might bring the references more up-to-date. Nevertheless, Casey has brought together a great deal of very useful information on the topic which should be valuable to those in the field and also those in library education.

Lucille Whalen

SPECIAL LIBRARIES AND COLLECTIONS

General Works

261. **Archives, Libraries, Museums, and Documentation Centres.** Munich, New York, K. G. Saur, 1984. 118p. index. (International Council on Archives, Vol. 30). $28.00. ISBN 3-598-21230-5.

The computer revolution is enticing fields such as archival management, library science, museology, and documentation centers management, to clarify their concerns, jurisdictions, and boundaries, and explain their methodologies. Implied in this challenge is the need to identify professional relationships in order to foster cooperation between the fields. In the present issue of this well-known French-English international publication, recognized authorities discuss their professional concerns and outline the major problems that impede field cooperation. B. C. Bloomfield, keeper of the Department of Oriental Printed Books and Manuscripts of the British Library, identifies such common denominators as preservation, conservation, and the policies regarding automated data processing. The other contributors are Oscar Gauye, director of the Swiss Federal Archives; Patrick J. Boylan, director, Leiscestershire County Council's Museums, Art Galleries and Record Services; and M. J. Dreese, advisor in documentary information, Zoetermeer, The Netherlands. All articles have abstracts in English, French, German, and Spanish. The second part of the periodical consists of title, subject, and country indexes to articles in the thirty volumes of *Archivum* published thus far.

This issue is intended for archivists, librarians, museologists, and documentalists, though the second part contains essential information for all subscribers to the journal.

Antonio Rodriguez-Buckingham

262. **Federal Library Resources: A User's Guide to Research Collections.** 2d ed. New York, Science Associates/International, 1984. 103p. index. $37.50pa. LC 83-51497. ISBN 0-87837-019-6.

The second edition of *Federal Library Resources* was published in 1984, to replace the first edition, which appeared in 1973. Its 103 pages contain information about three hundred U.S. federal government libraries: name, address, name of librarian, agency affiliation, hours, telephone, services, and resources.

The size of the holdings of the libraries surveyed vary from one hundred volumes to the 19.5 million volumes of the Library of Congress. Also included in resources are periodical subscriptions, photographs, films, microforms, and videotapes.

By consulting this directory, the user is able to locate the address of federal libraries specializing in a certain subject or belonging to a specific agency. The user can also find out whether it is possible to visit the library in person, and whether borrowing on the spot is permitted. The entries also indicate whether interlibrary loan requests are accepted, whether ALA/ILC forms must be used, and whether requests may be forwarded by means of the OCLC online network.

The entries are clear, concise, and easy to read. There are usually three or four entries to a page, arranged in double columns. Indexes provide access by subject, by name of library and affiliation, and by geographical location.

This directory is recommended for those who deal frequently with federal government libraries or who handle a large number of interlibrary loan requests. Other users may be satisfied with the larger, more comprehensive library directories. [R: LJ, Aug 85, p. 71]

Barbara E. Brown

263. Neway, Julie M. **Information Specialist as Team Player in the Research Process.** Westport, Conn., Greenwood Press, 1985. 194p. bibliog. index. (New Directions in Librarianship, No. 9). $29.95. LC 85-5488. ISBN 0-313-24508-8.

Neway, head of information services at a major research institute, set out to write a monograph for information specialists. She presents the history of proactive reference service and describes examples in the academic, business, clinical, community, and scientific research setting. Chapter 1 reviews the extensive body of literature but deals with the various settings separately and therefore does not provide a synthesis of the history or a clear definition of her concept: integration of the information specialist into research groups. The history inadequately deals with special library librarians who have often been on the cutting edge of the development of information services.

The next four chapters discuss specific examples of the team concept. Each chapter begins with an all-too-brief discussion of the information habits of patrons in a setting. The examples are brief descriptions of projects which have received attention in the literature. A final section discusses how to become a team member and the future of the concept.

The volume lacks focus because the concept has not been well defined and too much tangential material is included. The volume would be much stronger if the information habits sections were omitted and the number of examples significantly reduced so that more space could be devoted to exploring the team member concept more fully. The excellent bibliography provides access to the literature on proactive reference service for beginning information specialists or library and information science students but it will likely not be helpful to the experienced information specialist.

Thomas G. Kirk

264.   **Subject Directory of Special Libraries and Information Centers.** 9th ed. Brigitte T. Darnay and John Nimchuk, eds. Detroit, Gale, 1985. 5v. index. $625.00/set. LC 85-645199. ISBN 0-8103-1890-3.

Intended as a companion volume to the ninth edition of Gale's *Directory of Special Libraries and Information Centers* (1982), this volume provides information on over 17,500 special libraries and similar resources in the United States and Canada. Although the same information is found in the *Directory of Special Libraries and Information Centers*, it is the arrangement of this material — in five subject-oriented volumes — that continues to make the *Subject Directory* so helpful to special librarians, researchers, interlibrary loan departments, and large reference departments.

Twenty-seven subject areas are included in the five volumes. Business (1,242 entries), law (1,429), military (311), and transportation (205) libraries are included in volume 1; audiovisual (329), educational (657), information science (298), publishing (349), rare book (98), and recreational (179) libraries are identified in volume 2; volume 3 is devoted entirely to health science libraries (2,912); volume 4 lists area/ethnic (469), art (609), geography/map (133), history (1,950), humanities (416), music (305), religion/theology (945), social science (1,093), theater (62), and urban/regional planning (285) libraries; volume 5 covers agriculture (255), computer science (300) (appearing for the first time as a separate section), energy (428), environment and conservation (383), food sciences

(131), and science and technology (3,234) libraries. A typical entry includes, when available, the library's official name, name of sponsoring organization or institution, address with zip, name and title of person in charge, names and titles of other professional personnel, collection statistics, description of the subjects with which the library or collection is concerned, policies regarding use of the collection, services provided, publications, and telephone number with area code. In addition to a subject index, each volume contains an alternative name index that provides cross-references from variant names for libraries.

Although major academic and large public libraries may wish to acquire the entire five-volume set, it is probable that many special libraries will wish to purchase only those volumes applicable to their area of endeavor.

G. Kim Dority

265.   **Who's Who in Special Libraries 1985-86.** Washington, D.C., Special Libraries Association, 1985. 196p. index. $25.00pa. ISSN 0278-842X.

The always useful directory of the members of the Special Libraries Association (SLA) — the preeminent body of special librarians in North America — was apparently a partial victim of the move of SLA's headquarters from New York to Washington, D.C. This work is less complete than last year's. Furthermore, the paper seems to be newsprint quality.

However, a plus is the reversion from last year's experimental main listing by subject divisions with alphabetical index of members names and a chapter approach. This year there is an alphabetical main (and only) listing of member's names.

Statistically, it is noted that SLA's current membership of 11,775 is concentrated with 1,386 members in the New York chapter, 856 in the Washington, D.C., chapter, and in Illinois, 657. The South Carolina provisional chapter is smallest at 23 members. The SLA divisions are subject-based and are important for program emphasis. "Business and Finance" leads with 2,366 members; "Information Technology" has 2,005; "Library Management" has 1,541; and "Science-Technology" has 1,496. Trailing is "Physics-Mathematics Astronomy Division" as the smallest at 142 members.

The usual strategy when searching for a special librarian is to look first in whichever is newer: this work or the "Personnel Index" to Gale Research's *Directory of Special Libraries and Information Centers*. This year they are about equal with the Gale being distributed in October and SLA's in December. Gale does have more librarians in the subspecialties, such as law, medicine, and music. Gale's ninth edition lists 28,875 names from 17,476 institutions.

E. B. Jackson

Archival Collections

266. Evans, Frank B., François-J. Himly, and Peter Walne, comps. **Dictionary of Archival Terminology: English and French with Equivalents in Dutch, German, Italian, Russian and Spanish. Dictionnaire de terminologie archivistique....** Munich, New York, K. G. Saur, 1984. 226p. (ICA Handbooks Series, Vol. 3). $27.00. ISBN 3-598-20275-X.

The *Dictionary* was compiled as a result of deliberations of the International Council on Archives established in 1977. The present work is intended to supersede the *Lexicon of Archival Terminology* (Elsevier, 1964), being the first attempt on an international scale to draw up a glossary of terms in use principally in European countries. It was produced when microforms were in their infancy, when records management was not yet fully developed, and when computer techniques were still a dream.

This new work attempts to assemble about five hundred definitions of terms in common use throughout the archival profession today. It makes no attempt at completeness in every field of archival work nor in either of the two working languages, as the archivist has traditionally borrowed terms from other disciplines, due to variations in legal and administrative traditions.

The text is arranged by English language in alphabetical order, with definitions in English, followed by the French equivalent and definition. The equivalent terms are included in Dutch, German, Italian, Russian, and Spanish, without definition. Indexes are included for each of the six foreign languages.

The *Dictionary* is highly recommended to archivists and librarians dealing with records management.

Carol Willsey Bell

267. Hedstrom, Margaret L. **Archives & Manuscripts: Machine-Readable Records.** Chicago, Society of American Archivists, 1984. 75p. illus. bibliog. (SAA Basic Manual Series). $8.00pa. LC 84-51383. ISBN 0-931828-60-0.

This volume is another fine product of the Society of American Archivists' Basic Manual series. The "archives of the future"—computerized records—are the subject here, and this manual provides a brief introduction to both computers and the storage of data in computerized media. The bulk of the volume, however, is devoted to how archivists should deal with machine-readable records (MRR). The author accurately points out that many archival principles and practices still hold with these types of records, but that their unique nature demands that archivists concern themselves with both the informational value of data and how that data was created and stored. Much of the discussion centers on how archivists should establish archival control over MRR and systems in their institutions. Procedures are discussed for surveying automated record-keeping systems and deciding which data files and related textual records are best kept permanently. Processing and preservation are outlined as well as how one describes or catalogs machine-readable data files and how public service levels are to be defined. The manual concludes by briefly alerting readers to looming challenges such as the explosion of floppy diskette storage media and the promise of disk technology for more compact and longer-lasting storage of data.

Above all, however, this is a practical manual, with a good glossary and bibliography and useful illustrations. Not many archives are now acquiring MRR, but all will face it sooner or later. Libraries, too, are addressing the questions of acquiring, cataloging, and servicing computerized database storage media and computer software. This manual is directed more towards "unpublished" material, if that term means anything with computerized data, but it, nevertheless, is one of the few basic, but very useful, tools available today for comprehending this topic. [R: C&RL, July 85, pp. 367-68]

Leon J. Stout

268. **A Modern Archives Reader: Basic Readings on Archival Theory and Practice.** Maygene F. Daniels and Timothy Walch, eds. Washington, D.C., published for the National Archives and Records Service by the National Archives Trust Fund Board, 1984. 357p. bibliog. index. $14.00; $12.00pa. LC 84-8327. ISBN 0-911333-11-8; 0-911333-12-6pa.

This is both a significant contribution to the literature of the archival profession and a disappointment in terms of scope and content.

A Modern Archives Reader is intended to be a "collection of basic essays" for students studying archival administration, growing out of the Modern Archives Institute that has trained many archivists since its inception in 1945. This book will become a foundation volume for introductory archives courses with readings on the European archival tradition, pre-archival functions (records management), records appraisal, archival acquisition, arrangement, description, reference, public programs, establishing priorities, and appendices on archival terminology, and suggested further readings. This is a good introduction to the range and breadth of archival writings.

A Modern Archives Reader is also disappointing for what it does not include. The editors note that they did not include essays on technical subjects (such as preservation or microfilming) or concepts still evolving such as sampling records. As a result the volume seems somewhat dated and, lacking any introduction on issues that are controversial or debated within the profession, the *Reader* makes the archival profession seem rather static, which is not the case. Moreover, there are other notably absent topics such as the history of American archives and archival training and education.

Still, this effort is a noteworthy one since it heralds a new beginning for the National Archives as a publisher of archival literature and gives archival administrators and educators another basic volume to use in training archivists.   Richard J. Cox

Art Libraries

269. **Current Issues in Fine Arts Collection Development.** Tucson, Ariz., Art Libraries Society of North America, 1984. 36p. $7.50pa. ISBN 0-942740-03-3; ISSN 0730-7160.

This occasional paper published by ARLIS/NA, the largest professionally oriented organization of art librarians in the United States and Canada, includes five papers on the general topic of developing collections of visual arts books and materials. Four of the papers were presented at the society's annual conference in Philadelphia in 1983. Susan Davi of the University of Delaware was invited to contribute a fifth report, "Automatic Acquisition Plans," to round out the project with some highly practical information to those concerned with developing art library collections. As the sponsors came from the academic field, many of the comments are of primary value to college and university art librarians. However, some of the methods, charts, and concepts have substantial merit for all art libraries. The final paper is a lively account of the methods by which the Portland School of Art developed its art book collection from a start of twenty-two hundred volumes to ten thousand volumes in eighteen months primarily to satisfy accreditation standards. It is an upbeat, positive account of how to reach a library goal with ingenuity, intelligence, and dedication. This thirty-six-page pamphlet has current value to those in the specialized discipline of art librarianship.

William J. Dane

270. Pacey, Philip, ed. **A Reader in Art Librarianship.** Munich, New York, K. G. Saur, 1985. 199p. (IFLA Publications, No. 34). $20.00. ISBN 3-598-20398-5.

Pacey's collection brings together some of the best essays on art librarianship written in the last seventy years, drawn from professional journals, newsletters, and conference papers. Pacey, having served as editor of both the *ARLIS Newsletter* and *Art Libraries Journal* and as chairman of ARLIS(UK) and the IFLA Section of Art Libraries, chose to focus on the unique character and role of the art librarian rather than concentrate on art library materials (already discussed in his excellent *Art Library Manual* [Bowker, 1977]).

The essays are grouped into four general sections: "The Art Librarian," addressing the personal, professional, and educational qualifications desirable in the art librarian; "Whom We Serve," discussing the individual needs and methods of various groups of art library users, including art historians and curators, artists and art students, designers, and the general public; "The Challenge of Art and the Visual Dimension," analyzing the special considerations which result from the nature of art itself; and "Cooperation and Association," detailing the national and international developments toward art library associations. Contributors to the volume include some of the best-known spokespersons for art librarianship: Trevor Fawcett, Guy A. Marco, Wolfgang Freitag, Clive Phillpot, and of course Pacey himself. Although most of the essays reflect modern perspectives, Pacey chose to include a few historical writings, from as early as 1908, to show that the essentials of art librarianship resist change. Because of the dated philosophy, ideas, and writing style, however, these essays add little of real value to the volume. The remaining writings, as in any collection, vary in quality, but most provide valuable insights into this highly specialized field.

Judy Dyki

Business Libraries

271. Johnson, H. Webster, Anthony J. Faria, and Ernest L. Maier. **How to Use the Business Library: With Sources of Business Information.** Cincinnati, Ohio, South-Western Publishing, 1984. 267p. illus. $7.45pa. LC 83-60484. ISBN 0-538-05750-5.

This unique and inexpensive volume does a credible job of accomplishing two goals simultaneously. While the authors tout its "textbook" insights into library research methods, they also manage to list a surprising breadth of useful business publications. After a concise first chapter on how to use the library, a number of vital research concepts are highlighted throughout the book. Oft-overlooked topics such as interlibrary loan and the "volume indexes" found in periodicals are described, as well as database searching, federal depository libraries, and even computer output microfilm.

While such explanations are indeed useful to business students and researchers, the numerous annotations of business information sources will interest librarians and instructors as well. Unfortunately, many annotations do not include publication date or frequency, and both redundancies and overlooked titles can be spotted. In addition, this volume's format consists of run-together source lists which lack precise subject arrangement. On the plus side, however, a number of associations and databases are described, although frequent revisions will be required to keep entries up-to-date. Particularly interesting chapters feature aids to small business, business report writing, audiovisual materials, and international information sources.

Although inconsistencies in organization and the lack of an index limit this volume's usefulness as a reference work, it remains a unique instructional and collection development tool. Overall, the sheer number of important information sources described makes this inexpensive compendium a worthwhile investment.

Mary Ardeth Gaylord

Government Publications Collections

272. **Committee on the Records of Government Report.** Washington, D.C., [Council on Library Resources], 1985. 191p. index. free pa.

This report, dated March 1985, sets out to explain why "the United States is in danger of losing its memory." The scope of the problem is vividly described and clearly stated: government, at all levels, has lost control of paper records. Technological advances have served to exacerbate, rather than resolve the problem. Electronic record keeping has certainly solved the space problem, but improper identification of documents is widespread. The fear is that an "indiscriminate disappearance" of documents may repeatedly occur.

The Committee on the Records of Government was created to address this monumental problem, and to propose a course of action for the federal government. The committee was co-sponsored by the Council on Library Resources, the American Council of Learned Societies, and the Social Science Research Council. Chaired by Ernest R. May (the Charles Warren Professor of History at Harvard), the committee contained several experienced public servants (e.g., Joseph A. Califano, Jr., Edward H. Levi, and Richard W. Bolling).

The committee's final report fills only thirty-five pages of this volume; the remainder of the text consists of various background reports and supplementary material (such as a historical overview of programs to manage government records, a report on conservation problems, the "Technology Assessment Report" of the National Archives and Records Service, a chronology of relevant legislation, surveys, guidelines, and a retention/disposition schedule for federal records).

Three major recommendations emerge from the report. First, "responsibility for managing records must rest within the individual government agencies"; lines of authority, standards, and procedures need to be clarified. Second, the Archivist of the United States is directed to establish a bold and creative new role for the National Archives (provide active leadership on preservation and retrieval methods, improve reference service to government records). Third, the President should issue an Executive Order on government records, which would establish a Records Management Policy Council. An extensive draft of such an order is attached to make things easier for the staff of the executive office.

This report is compulsory reading for heads of government agencies, archivists, documents librarians, librarians in general, and the informed public-at-large. Pressure for reform can only come about when the problem is identified, and this report admirably fulfills that function.

Thomas A. Karel

273. Hernon, Peter, and Charles R. McClure. **Public Access to Government Information: Issues, Trends, and Strategies.** Norwood, N.J., Ablex Publishing, 1984. 457p. illus. bibliog. index. (Libraries and Information Science Series). $49.50; $25.00pa. LC 83-27597. ISBN 0-89391-100-3; 0-89391-252-2pa.

This landmark work in government documents librarianship is the first issue-oriented book in the field which addresses trends and strategies relating to public access to government information. It analyzes current and needed research and attempts to establish a theoretical base in the field.

The literature of documents librarianship has been dominated by practice, rather than by theory and research, and has dealt mainly with bibliographies of government publications, and various procedures and techniques for organizing and servicing documents collections. The focus of the work is on the federal depository library system and the publications printed by or under contract to the Government Printing Office (GPO) and distributed or sold by the Superintendent of Documents. But, it takes a much broader approach, not only with respect to government information but also documents librarianship. It analyzes issues related to the broader spectrum of federal government information policies including non-GPO publications, technical report literature, nonprint formats, electronic databases, and other new or emerging technologies. It considers the total field of government information, including local and state governments and international governmental organizations. It examines documents librarianship and documents collections within the broader context of a library's total collections and services. The authors advocate greater integration of government publications, both bibliographically and physically to bring them into the mainstream of a library's services and collections. Separate chapters are devoted to public access, bibliographic control, collection development, exploiting new technologies, reference and referral services, microforms, administrative considerations, physical facilities and space management, planning and evaluation of services, processing, cooperation and resource sharing, education and professional development, and restructuring the GPO depository program. The authors critically assess current practices and traditional assumptions within the broad context of librarianship and information policy; evaluate current and needed research; and offer solutions and practical recommendations by which government information policy and services can be made more effective. LeRoy C. Schwarzkopf

274. **Provision of Federal Government Publications in Electronic Format to Depository Libraries: Report of the Ad Hoc Committee on Depository Library Access to Federal Automated Data Bases to the Joint Committee on Printing, United States Congress.** Washington, D.C., Joint Committee on Printing, United States Congress; distr., Washington, D.C., GPO, 1984. 126p. index. (Committee Print S.Prt. 98-260. 98th Congress, 2d Session). $5.50pa. S/N 052-070-05970-2.

This is the final report of the Ad Hoc Committee on Depository Library Access to Federal Automated Data Bases which was established by the Joint Committee on Printing (JCP) in May 1983, and chaired by JCP staff member Bernadine Hoduski. Its fifteen other members included six representatives from professional library and information industry associations; five from the executive branch; and four from the legislative branch. Its charge was to evaluate the feasibility and desirability of providing access to federal government information in electronic format. The committee concluded that such information should be provided; that it was

technologically feasible; and that the economic feasibility should be investigated through pilot projects. The report itself is short (fourteen pages), and asks more questions than it answers, but in doing so raises the key policy issues which must be addressed by the pilot studies or further investigation. Most of the publication consists of twelve appendices. Among them is a schedule and summary of twenty-five presentations made at the two-day monthly meetings held by the committee during the remainder of 1983, and summaries of eight presentations made at a workshop conducted for the committee by the Congressional Office of Technology Assessment. The most useful appendix is the text and summary report of a comprehensive survey of depository libraries regarding their capability for handling information in electronic format, and types of databases desired. The report was submitted in December 1984 to the Joint Committee on Printing, which took no action on it during 1985. However, this is a landmark document in depository library history since it is the first attempt by the federal government to raise an important issue which must ultimately be addressed in this electronic age.

LeRoy C. Schwarzkopf

Law Libraries

275. Banks, Margaret A. **Using a Law Library: A Guide for Students and Lawyers in the Common Law Provinces of Canada.** 4th ed. Toronto, Carswell, 1985. 249p. index. $39.00. ISBN 0-459-37610-1.

Last revised in 1980, this new edition of a standard guide to Canadian legal publications is important because it includes the Constitution Act of 1982. A special section on the new act has been added to the chapter on statutes.

Other chapters are "Law Reports," "Legal Encyclopedias and Digests," "Reference Books, Treatises, and Periodicals," and "Automated Legal Research." Both Canadian and English sources of Canadian law are discussed in all parts. Sample pages from many of the titles under review are used to illustrate the text. There are detailed notes on how to use the books as well as general tips on how to find Canadian law. Appendices include listings of periodical abbreviations, preferred citation forms for law reports, and other Canadian legal research guides.

The text is directed primarily at beginning law students, but previous editions have been used as texts in library schools as well. The book identifies the sources of statutes, cases, and discussions of the law, and it tells readers how to find and use the materials in law libraries.

Berniece M. Owen

276.   Dyer, Susan K. **Manual of Procedures for Private Law Libraries. 1984 Supplement.** Littleton, Colo., published for the American Association of Law Libraries by Fred B. Rothman, 1984. 130p. index. (AALL Publications Series, No. 21). $18.50. LC 84-11589. ISBN 0-8377-0119-8.

This is an important supplement to a major work on private law librarianship. Anyone faced with responsibilities involving private law librarianship will benefit by using this book as either an introductory resource tool or as a quick reference guide. The supplement, however, must be used with the original work, since topics are not thoroughly covered in the updated text. The supplement regularly refers to specific pages of the original text when significant revisions and additions have been made.

In addition to updating the 1966 publication, the supplement also adds five new chapters covering major changes in the field during the last eighteen years: appraisal of collections, branch libraries, interlibrary loans/networking, micrographics, and managing computer-assisted research. A final chapter has also been added, offering "tidbits," or rather, insights to common problems and questions. Appendix 1 adds to bibliographic material published since the main work was issued. Appendix 2 provides an updated and detailed seven-point directory of publishers and dealers of interest to private law librarians.   James M. Murray

Medical Libraries

277.   **Cost Analysis, Cost Recovery, Marketing, and Fee-based Services: A Guide for the Health Sciences Librarian.** M. Sandra Wood, ed. New York, Haworth Press, 1985. 268p. bibliog. index. $29.95. LC 85-888. ISBN 0-86656-353-9.

Produced as a monographic supplement to the journal *Medical Reference Service Quarterly* (vol. 4, Spring 1985), this volume provides a good introduction to the increasingly important field of cost analysis, cost recovery, and marketing of library services. Prompted in part by the elimination of subsidies from the National Library of Medicine and the demands for stringent cost controls in hospitals, health science libraries have been forced to provide realistic accounting of library services with the goal of becoming self-supporting departments within their institutions. Major sections in the volume are devoted to cost analysis, cost recovery, marketing of reference services, and fee-for-service; a comprehensive annotated bibliography completes the volume.

Each section includes a survey article about the topic followed by shorter papers describing actual case studies. The survey papers are sufficiently broad to explain the technical concepts involved; the examples show varied applications of these concepts. The programs described are frequently performed for several institutions or separate departments within an institution; there is thus a need to apportion costs. The case studies include online search services, photocopy services, systems for charging for a share of total library service as well as a price structure for an information brokerage firm. Most of the examples are from the medical/hospital library environment; the methods described are equally applicable to other academic or special library situations.

Suzanne K. Gray

278.   **Directory of Mental Health Libraries and Information Centers.** Barbara A. Epstein and Ellen Gay Detlefsen, eds. Washington, D.C., American Psychiatric Press, 1984. 297p. index. $20.00. LC 84-21582. ISBN 0-88048-047-5.

The stated justification for compiling this directory is a distinct need by mental health librarians to identify library collections in the United States and Canada. The directory is based on a 1984 survey sent to over eighteen hundred mental health facilities. To be included in the directory the library had to match the following criteria: a collection profile in mental health or the behavioral sciences, membership in AMHL or MLA's Mental Health section, current subscriptions to a minimum of twenty-five journals, and management by a professional librarian. The directory includes 274 library collections that match the above profile.

Arranged alphabetically by state, the entries provide library name, address and phone number, institutional affiliation and funding, staffing, collection description, specialized services, hours of operation, access policies, and publications. After the five Canadian entries there are personnel, institutional, and subject indexes.

The directory is produced from a computer database that yields easy-to-read and complete entries. This reference work promises to be an outstanding informational and referral tool. When compared with the *American Library Directory*, it does a much better job of locating and describing collections in mental health. [R: JAL, Sept 85, p. 244]   Tom Smith

Music Libraries

279.   Bryant, E. T., with Guy A. Marco. **Music Librarianship: A Practical Guide.** 2d ed. Metuchen, N.J., Scarecrow, 1985. 449p. bibliog. index. $32.50. LC 84-27731. ISBN 0-8108-1785-3.

First published in 1959, this is a thoroughly revised edition of E. T. Bryant's *Music Librarianship.* Intended primarily for British public libraries, but with less British emphasis thanks to Guy Marco's assistance, this guide is quite useful for U.S. public libraries and for music departments of academic libraries. The book is divided into five chapters which cover the subjects of music library administration, reference materials and service, cataloging, classification, and sound recordings. It is well organized, very informative, and readable.

It is unfortunate that the reference materials section was not updated to include the 1983 *New Oxford Companion to Music* and the 1984 edition of *Baker's Biographical Dictionary of Musicians.* The index is idiosyncratic and quite inadequate. This type of book calls for a real subject index.

Public and academic librarians as well as library school students will want to have this guide in their library collections.

Natalia Sonevytsky

National Libraries

280. **Library of Congress Acquisitions, Manuscript Division, 1982.** Washington, D.C., Manuscript Division, Library of Congress, 1984. 53p. illus. free pa. ISSN 0275-9616.

281. **Library of Congress Acquisitions, Manuscript Division, 1983.** Washington, D.C., Manuscript Division, Library of Congress, 1984. 55p. illus. free pa. ISSN 0275-9616.
The Annual Report of the Librarian of Congress was a basic part of library literature since the early Putnam days. The vast collections and the accelerated acquisitions have long since outgrown the confines of a monolithic annual report, and reports of various units are more practical, certainly more useful to scholars in specialized fields. The great majority of the collections in the Manuscript Division relate to American history, although the scope is worldwide. The two reports at hand contain well-written, judiciously illustrated narrative descriptions of major collections by divers hands, and a list of other new acquisitions showing source and extent. There is a broad range, from sixteenth century Mexican manuscripts to papers of contemporaries, from Mrs. Franklin Pierce to Margaret Mead, from Civil War generals to modern psychiatrists. The plethora of peripheral figures (e.g., Lana Turner, Ezra Pound) mentioned in these reports suggests the utility of an index. Over the years these reports will amount to an indispensable guide to the

most important of all collections of source material on U.S. history.

Lawrence S. Thompson

282. **The Library of Congress 1983: A Brief Summary of the Major Activities for the Fiscal Year Ending September 30, 1983.** Washington, D.C., Library of Congress, 1984. 43p. illus. free pa. ISSN 0162-6426.
Intended as an annual review of activities and services, the work is divided into nine sections: "Introduction," "Collections," "Additions to Collections," "Housing the Library's Collections and Programs," "Preserving the Collections," "Accessing the Collections," "Serving the Congress," "Automated Information Services," "Serving the Public"—with subsections on outreach, special visitors, copyright and publishing activities, and staffing. Each section briefly reviews highlights, major developments, and accomplishments of the previous year.

Events and activities summarized include the move of the Motion Picture, Broadcasting, and Recorded Sound Division to the James Madison Memorial Building; congressional authorization for the Librarian of Congress to initiate a study of the changing role of the book in the future; the completion of the first voice-indexed dictionary, accomplished by the national Library Service for the Blind and Physically Handicapped; continuing inventories of collections; revision and initiation of new acquisitions policies for materials in "Fine and Applied Arts" and "Photography"; expansion of reference collections in the Performing Arts Reading Room and the European Reading Room; developments in photo-duplication and cataloging; major acquisitions and resource sharing efforts; and physical space priorities and rearrangements.   Edmund F. SantaVicca

283. **National Library of Canada Annual Report. Bibliotheque Nationale du Canada rapport annuel 1984-1985.** Ottawa, National Library of Canada, 1985. 71p. free pa. ISBN 0-662-53824-2.
The annual report of the National Library of Canada for 1984-1985 is the first to be issued by Marianne Scott, who assumed the post of national librarian in April 1984. She is the third to hold this position.

She has introduced several changes in the appearance of the annual report. It now contains the English and French texts in parallel columns, instead of tête-bêche. The cover has a satellite picture of the Earth, with Canada outlined and projected in green, with a background in black. There is also a title change: *Annual Report, National Library of*

Canada, instead of *Annual Report of the National Librarian* (in French, *Rapport annuel, Bibliothèque Nationale du Canada*, instead of *Rapport annuel du Directeur Général de la Bibliothèque Nationale du Canada*).

The first half of the report covers the various services offered by the Library and the work of the different divisions. This includes reference services, interlibrary loan requests and document delivery service, collections and collection management, Canadian theses on microfiche service, bibliographic services such as CanMARC, CONSER and DOBIS, and publications such as *Canadiana*, the national bibliography. It also establishes standards for Canadian libraries and publishes guides for catalogers and for public library service. Each section is introduced by a brief summary of the purpose of the division under discussion. This is followed by the events and statistics for the year, and a pie or bar chart (colored this year for the first time) illustrating the statistics.

The second half of the report contains appendices listing the staffs of the various Library divisions, boards and committees, along with others containing statistics, a list of publications, and an organization chart. Only the total budget figure for the year is given; the details are found in the annual volumes of the Department of Finance entitled *Estimates and Public Accounts*. Because the National Library of Canada is a federal government body, this is the procedure that is followed.

On the whole, this is a well prepared, well presented, and good looking annual report, which contains all the information expected.

Barbara E. Brown

Rare Books

284. Laurenti, Joseph L. **A Catalog of Spanish Rare Books (1701-1974) in the Library of the University of Illinois and in Selected North American Libraries.** New York, Peter Lang, 1984. 210p. bibliog. index. (American University Studies. Series II: Romance Language and Literature, Vol. 12). $23.40pa. LC 84-47693. ISBN 0-8204-0129-3; ISSN 0740-9257.

This is a continuation of Laurenti's *The Spanish Golden Age (1472-1700). A Catalog of Rare Books Held in the Library of the University of Illinois* (1979). It includes all Spanish rare books in the University of Illinois Library, the locations of copies of these books in other libraries of the United States, as well as references to and descriptions of them found in other catalogs and bibliographies. Laurenti locates more than two dozen copies for some of the works included. For others only the University of Illinois Library is listed as having a copy.

Pages 1-138 compose the catalog; pages 139-91, "Hispanic Bibliography," are divided into general, regional, and topical. There is a name index.

It is a pity that there is no good definition of "rare" as it is used to describe books.

The University of Illinois Library has one of the finest collections in the world of material by H. G. Wells. The Spanish translations of his works are listed, but a note does not always indicate the original English title.

Typographical errors would appear to be almost nonexistent.

Students of Spanish literature for this period will find this catalog to be quite useful. All libraries with an interest in Spanish culture should purchase it.   Hensley C. Woodbridge

285. **The Lilly Library: The First Quarter Century 1960-1985.** Carla DeFord, ed. Bloomington, Ind., Lilly Library, Indiana University, 1985. 157p. illus. (part col.). $15.00pa.

A story is told by Joseph Duveen, the brilliant art collector of this century, on Henry Ford. Duveen attempted to woo Ford out of some of his millions for the art world. He had gone to the trouble of lavishly producing a book displaying some original paintings hoping to entice Ford to part with even a small bundle of his great wealth. Ford did not fall for the ruse and, when it became apparent to Duveen that no other way was possible, he dropped the charade and told Ford the books had been made up so that Ford would buy the originals. Ford replied, "But why would I want to buy the originals when the pictures here in these books are so beautiful?"

Lucky for bibliophiles, not all philanthropists are as bohemian as Ford. One philanthropist, Josiah Kirby Lilly, Jr., was not content to see a copy of a manuscript in a picture book. And, luckily, Indiana University had on hand one of the world's most knowledgeable rare bookmen, David A. Randall, when Mr. Lilly decided to unload his chest of drawers. Nearly overnight Indiana University library passed from one more large building holding lots of books, to one of the world's most important repositories of rare books, rivaling, in some ways, even the Huntington and the Folger.

The coffee table production before us recalls the first twenty-five years of the Lilly endowment purchases. If the next twenty-five years or even the next fifty, are only half as productive as this first quarter, the Lilly Library will be virtually unmatched in its holdings of bookish *rara-avis*. Perhaps more impressive than any one single volume in the Lilly is its variety, its girth of appetite. Mr. Lilly collected rare tomes in medieval literature, early printing,

United States and Indiana history, British and Russian history, American and British literature, medicine, cookery, and even children's literature. In the case of the latter, the Elizabeth W. Ball collection, presented to Lilly curators in 1983 may in fact be the single most important collection in that genre anywhere in the world.

The Lilly Library may be of dubious reference value to scholars, save for the mere fact of identifying for them the types of materials within the Lilly walls. But more important than this, the volume opens up to librarians and scholars alike the love, the beauty, and the *sine qua non* nature of book collecting. Indeed, as D'Israeli aptly pointed out, there is an art to everything, and this book evinces for bibliophiles everywhere the art of one of the world's oldest and best joys. Produced in beautiful color and fully illustrated, *The Lilly Library* is a pleasure to gaze on. Librarians wanting to splurge a bit and offer their patrons, however few in number they may be, a chance to revel in a Tiranogue of books, this volume may be the starship to get them here.

When asked what he wanted to be remembered for, G. K. Chesterton replied that he wanted to be recalled as one who had aided "the Divine Gift of language and letters to outlive us all." "The Divine Gift." That says it best, for thumbing through this remarkable little memoir, one cannot help but feel he is in the presence of something quite miraculous.

Mark Y. Herring

286. Nixon, Howard M., comp. **Catalogue of the Pepys Library at Magdalene College, Cambridge. Volume VI: Bindings.** Suffolk, England, D. S. Brewer/Boydell & Brewer, and Totowa, N.J., Rowman & Littlefield, 1984. 1v. (various paging). illus. (part col.). $140.00. ISBN 0-85991-145-4.

This is the fourth of a projected nine-volume catalog of the remarkable library of the seventeenth-century diarist Samuel Pepys. It is also the final work of the outstanding authority on early English bookbinding, Howard M. Nixon, who died shortly before its completion.

Nixon's intensive investigation of Pepys's three thousand books has enabled him to date nearly all of the bindings, at least to within a decade. The bindings are classified by style into ten major groups, with a number of subgroupings. The excellent introduction to the *Catalogue* defines these groups in detail, examines the problems of identifying Pepys's binders, and provides information about the "fine" bindings in the library.

The *Catalogue* itself identifies each of the three thousand books with a short title and its binding group designation; those bindings

which do not belong to a group are briefly described. There follow thirty-six full-page plates of standard bindings, fifteen plates (including five tipped-in color plates) of "fine" bindings, and a number of photographs of rubbings to illustrate binder's tools attributed to John Berresford. There are numerous cross-references between the plates and the page numbers on which the bindings are discussed in the introduction. There is a separate table of measurements of each of the books in the plates.

This is obviously a specialist's book, but, as with studies of almost any aspect of Pepys, its introductory essay also has much to say about the culture of late seventeenth-century England.

Philip R. Rider

287. Schreyer, Alice D., ed. **Rare Books 1983-84: Trends, Collections, Sources.** New York, R. R. Bowker, 1984. 582p. index. $39.95. ISBN 0-8352-1756-6.

The title (of this first issue of a projected series of annual volumes) is indicative of its contents. The editor is a rare books librarian, with prestigious credentials, who is with LC's Center for the Book. The contributors are all well-respected rare books and manuscripts professionals and include Terry Belanger, John Y. Cole, Joan M. Friedman, Katherine and Daniel Leab, G. Thomas Tanselle, and others. The book is divided into five parts. Part 1, "Reports from the Rare Book and Manuscript Field," contains seven survey articles on the trade in books and manuscripts, auction highlights, and the state of collecting and collections in the United States, Canada, and Great Britain. Part 2, "Review of Bibliographical Scholarship and Publishing," contains three first-rate bibliographical essays by Tanselle, Daniel Traister, and Peter M. Van Wingen. Part 3, "Issues and Programs in the News," contains nine essay reports including explications of importance such as Belanger's on Columbia University's "Rare Book School, 1983," Hall and Hench on "The Program in the History of the Book in American Culture at the American Antiquarian Society," and Cole on "The Center for the Book ...".

Part 4, "Educational Opportunities," lists fellowships and lectures and has a five-page list of programs and courses which is essentially a list of accredited library schools of the United States and Canada, similar to the *Bowker Annual* listing. Part 5, "Directory of Collections and Sources," makes up more than half of the book and may, or may not, be a useful feature. This part includes directory lists of associations, auctioneers, appraisers, rare book and manuscript libraries, and book dealers. This would not really be a reference of first resort since familiar volumes such as the *American Book Trade Directory, A. B. Bookman's Yearbook, American Library Directory*, and *Subject Collections* are readily available. It may be that the directory information was included because of its availability in Bowker's computer databases. However, the review material is welcome and should be useful to teachers, students, and professionals working in the rare books field. [R: Choice, Nov 85, p. 428; C&RL, May 85, pp. 272-74; JAL, Jan 85, p. 359; RBB, 1 June 85, p. 1384]

Frank J. Anderson

288.   Tannen, Jack. **How to Identify and Collect American First Editions: A Guide Book.** 2d ed., rev. New York, Arco Publishing, 1985. 142p. bibliog. index. $14.95. LC 85-18507. ISBN 0-668-06526-5.

This revised and updated edition helps book collectors in two ways: it lists (alphabetically) the methods used by some 392 American publishers to identify their first editions and it lists in eight chapters some of the best reference works devoted to ten areas of book collecting including Americana, children's books, mystery, and science fiction. Unfortunately, these ten chapters sometimes list old editions (the chapter on Americana, for example, lists the 1966 rather than the revised 1974 edition of *The Harvard Guide to American History*) and sometimes omit important reference works (the chapter on science fiction, for example, omits L. W. Currey's 1979 *Science Fiction and Fantasy Authors: A Bibliography of First Printings*, the best work of its type on this genre). In addition, some of the chapters (such as the four-page one on science fiction) are simply too brief and rudimentary.

Tannen's book is more up-to-date but less comprehensive than E. Zempel and L. Verkler's *First Editions* (Spoon River Press, 1984) which covers over one thousand American and British publishers. It would be useful if future editions of this work covered twentieth-century British publishers and added discussions of such emerging areas of collecting as photography books, science and medical books, old paperbacks, and ephemera. In addition, future editions should expand the list of specialized bookdealers (currently limited to sixty-two dealers), should place the names of these dealers at the end of the appropriate chapter (rather than grouping them together as in this edition) and should provide a separate chapter on buying at the major auction houses.

Joseph H. Cataio

Science and Technology Libraries and Collections

289.   Lambert, Jill. **Scientific and Technical Journals.** London, Clive Bingley; distr., Hamden, Conn., Shoe String Press, 1985. 191p. index. $19.00. ISBN 0-85157-375-4.

According to the introduction, Lambert directs this work primarily to students of librarianship/information, "although it is hoped that the chapters covering electronic journals and electronic document delivery will also be of interest to practitioners." This statement follows the author's indicating three principal reasons for the increased attention given in the last two decades or so to science/technology journal literature: journals are expensive to acquire and budgets are extremely tight; journals are inadequate communication tools; and there is new technology which offers new communication forms—including electronic journals.

After a brief review of the origins and development of science/technology journals, the author discusses (1) the types of journals—primary and secondary—and their publishers (learned societies and professional bodies; commercial publishers; nonprofit organizations; educational, government, and research institutions; industrial and commercial organizations) and (2) problems of journal publication (publication delays, proliferation and specialization, economic factors—number of subscribers, inflation rates, publishers' profits, photocopying and copyright, etc.). The stage is thus set for the remaining two-thirds of the text to discuss, successively, alternative methods of publication, electronic journals, electronic document delivery systems, citation studies of journals, and identification and location of journals through systems like CODEN and the International Standard Serial Number, serials directories, union lists, etc. Each of the eight chapters concludes with a selective bibliography of English-language articles and books and/or research reports mostly prior to 1983. (The reviewer spotted, say twenty-five references to 1983 titles and only three or four to 1984 ones.) The text likewise contains few 1983 or 1984 references. As to post-1982 information, it is not clear why if a 1984 page charge for certain journals can be included (p. 52), the change of name (January 1984) of *The Bell System Technical Journal* (p. 36) to *A T & T Bell Laboratories Technical Journal* is not given. And there is no mention of the CONSER Abstracting and Indexing Coverage Project (commencing late 1983) to enrich the CONSER database with information about title coverage by abstracting and indexing services.

These points notwithstanding, *Scientific and Technical Journals* should be of considerable value and interest to both librarians/ information scientists and publishers. [R: JAL, July 85, p. 184; JAL, Sept 85, p. 234; JAL, Nov 85, p. 322]   Wiley J. Williams

290. Mount, Ellis, ed. **Data Manipulation in Sci-Tech Libraries.** New York, Haworth Press, 1985. 131p. $19.95. LC 85-5569. ISBN 0-86656-441-1.

In the past decade the use of computers in libraries and information centers has grown by leaps and bounds. Ellis Mount is editor of *Science & Technology Libraries*, and this volume is essentially the bound version of volume 5, number 4 of that journal. Mount has selected some excellent papers. The first two are devoted to an academic setting. These are the Georgetown University Medical Center and the Indiana University Chemical Information Center. Special libraries are well documented by Maryde F. King who is the manager of the General Electric Company Corporate Research and Development Center Technical Library. In her paper she places specific emphasis on the downloading of the CA Condensates. Downloading, according to King, is relatively easy to accomplish but the user may encounter higher costs if there is no compatibility with in-house computer equipment. Lawrence G. Mondschein of Jannsen Pharmaceutica, has documented the applications of a Wang-Advanced Functional List Processing and Visual Memory to test animals in a vitro database. Estelle Brodman of the World Health Organization describes medical library services in the Pacific. Doris B. Ottaviano, Head Reference Librarian of the U.S. Naval War College Library, has prepared a bibliography on modern weapon systems, including online databases such as DIALOG and DISSERTATION ABSTRACTS. This volume is worthwhile for libraries considering automation. Major drawback is the editor has failed to provide an index.   Larry Chasen

291. Mount, Ellis, ed. **Fee-based Services in Sci-Tech Libraries.** New York, Haworth Press, 1984. 105p. (*Science & Technology Libraries*, Vol. 5, No. 2). $19.95. LC 84-19186. ISBN 0-86656-326-1.

This collection of articles discusses the changing role of sci-tech libraries regarding user fees brought about by conditions whereby traditional methods of financing have been reduced or eliminated. Selected papers show how fee-based services have been implemented in academic, public, and corporate libraries for such services as online searching, interlibrary lending, visual reproductions, borrowing of materials from outside users, and so on.

These articles were originally published in the volume 5, number 2, winter 1984 issue of the journal *Science & Technology Libraries* (see *ARBA* 82, entry 216). Therefore, if you have that publication there is no need to purchase this bound reprint. Although the articles contained in this title are of sufficient quality, there needed to be a much greater depth of coverage on this important and timely topic in order to justify its being sold as a monograph.

Frank Wm. Goudy

292. Mount, Ellis, ed. **Management of Sci-Tech Libraries.** New York, Haworth Press, 1984. 169p. $27.95; $9.95pa. LC 84-6615. ISBN 0-86656-280-X; 0-86656-284-2pa.

This monograph was also published as volume 4, numbers 3 and 4 of *Science & Technology Libraries*, Spring/Summer 1984. It contains two kinds of papers, the first dealing with the management of certain types of libraries, such as the academic scientific, federal scientific, and branch corporate library, the corporate information center, and the public library technology department. The other papers are concerned with management topics of interest to all scientific/technical libraries, such as budgeting, staffing, the education of librarians, and the structure of libraries.

The introductory article, by the editor, points out the relationship between the quality of management and the success of library operations. The final paper shows how statistical analysis relates to library management. Following the papers some regular features of the series are presented. These are (1) an annotated list of new reference works in science and technology, (2) "Sci-Tech Online," which presents database news and a short list of related publications and search aids, and (3) reviews of a few recent scientific journal articles.

The papers of this monograph focus on the most crucial current (and, in some cases, perpetual) problems of sci-tech libraries. For the most part they are addressed quite well.

Theodora Andrews

293. Mount, Ellis, ed. **Role of Maps in Sci-Tech Libraries.** New York, Haworth Press, 1985. 122p. illus. (*Science & Technology Libraries*, Vol. 5, No. 3). $17.95. LC 84-27919. ISBN 0-86656-395-4.

This republication of volume 5, number 3 of *Science & Technology Libraries* (February 1985) is intended as a general introduction to maps for sci-tech librarians. Of the half of its pages that is devoted to maps (the other half being composed of standard columns of the periodical, plus a most helpful survey of information sources on artificial intelligence), three of the articles are concerned with specific map collections — Branner Earth Science Library, Stanford; NYPL's Map Division; and Defense Mapping Agency (DMA) libraries — while the remaining two articles deal with the National Cartographic Information Center and with the storage of maps on nontraditional media, such as optical discs.

Overall, the tone is relaxed, with the NYPL article close to jocular. The last-mentioned article is a bibliographic survey of reference works and maps most useful in the NYPL collection; the Stanford article is more in the nature of a survey of what that library does and has, with some bibliographical information included; while the DMA article is a brief description of the collection, services, and facilities, including two black-and-white photographs, one of the map stacks (seven cases high) and one of the book stacks (ten shelves high). The National Cartographic Information Center article provides a good introduction to that agency's services; while the article on maps in nontraditional format performs the same service for its topic. This is an appropriate volume for sci-tech librarians; it is also suitable for map collections whose new patrons may require a brief introduction to maps in the sciences.

Mary Larsgaard

294. Mount, Ellis. **University Science and Engineering Libraries.** 2d ed. Westport, Conn., Greenwood Press, 1985. 303p. bibliog. index. (Contributions in Librarianship and Information Science, No. 49). $35.00. LC 84-6530. ISBN 0-313-23949-5.

This book is intended for librarians employed in college and university sci-tech libraries as well as library science students and other librarians interested in these types of libraries. As in the earlier edition, health science libraries are not included. The volume is divided into six sections. The first section, consisting of one chapter, describes the general nature of academic sci-tech libraries. These are compared and contrasted with their public and special library counterparts. The second section, containing seven chapters, deals with management issues such as planning and budgeting, staff supervision, marketing, evaluation, and so on. The third and fourth sections deal with technical and user services respectively. The fifth section discusses collection development, and the sixth section addresses facilities and library equipment. These sections amount to an additional ten chapters. An appendix presents the survey instrument and results of interviews on sixteen campuses in 1983, which formed the basis for

much of the information presented in this volume. Included among the seven illustrations are library layouts for Swarthmore College, the University of California at Berkeley, and Harvard University. A bibliography and index complete the volume.

This edition devotes more space to computer applications and networking, and omits much of the guide to literature found in the first volume. The work is a welcome addition to the growing publications about special libraries. [R: LJ, 1 May 85, p. 42; WLB, June 85, p. 699]

Andrew G. Torok

295. Scott, Catherine D., ed. **Aeronautics and Space Flight Collections.** New York, Haworth Press, 1985. 229p. (*Special Collections*, Vol. 3, Nos. 1/2). $29.95. LC 84-15725. ISBN 0-86656-251-6.

This volume describes a few notable collections of materials relating to aeronautics and space flight. In addition to those described, a number of other important collections are mentioned. All aspects of the aeronautical record are considered, from dime novels to the latest satellite imagery.

The chapter on *Aerospace Bibliographic Control* by Buchan and Eckert will be of particular interest to technical librarians, since the bibliography of the field, especially technical reports, is difficult to trace.

Although many other collections in this field are listed in Lee Ash's *Subject Collections*, Gale's *Directory of Special Libraries and Information Centers*, and similar guides, the present volume concentrates on a relative few especially important collections.

Although a considerable amount of bibliography is included, this book should not be mistaken for a general guide to the literature of the field.

This book will be a required purchase for all libraries with substantial interests in any aspect of aeronautics and space science, including public, academic, and special libraries. Even those libraries holding the journal *Special Collections*, of which this is an issue, will probably buy the book for their reference shelves.

Edwin D. Posey

Serials

296. Bowman, Mary Ann, comp. **Library and Information Science Journals and Serials: An Analytical Guide.** Westport, Conn., Greenwood Press, 1985. 140p. index. (Annotated Bibliographies of Series: A Subject Approach, No. 1). $29.95. LC 84-15787. ISBN 0-313-23807-3.

In the past few years, the bibliographic control of the library science literature has enjoyed a vogue in the profession. Purcell and Schlachter brought together the library science reference literature in their 1984 effort *Reference Sources in Library and Information Services* (ABC-Clio). Wynar and Cameron's *Library Science Annual*, begun in 1985, seeks to cover comprehensively the monographic literature. And now Bowman, building on the Stevenses' 1982 compilation *Author's Guide to Journals in Library & Information Science* (Haworth), has produced this guide to library and information science journals and serials.

Whereas the Stevenses' work purported to aid would-be authors in placing their manuscripts with suitable journal publishers and was therefore selective, Bowman's compilation is intended to assist in the serials selection process and seeks to be comprehensive within specific parameters: all English-language library science serials with at least an annual frequency published in the United States and abroad, excluding staff newsletters, statistical compilations, and annual reports, are included. In addition, serials in fields related to library science, such as educational technology or children's literature are selectively listed.

Arranged alphabetically by title, each entry consists of a full bibliographic description with purchasing information as well as a brief evaluative annotation. Cross-references from former titles to current ones are included. There are a geographical index, an index of publishers, and a classified list of titles.

Unfortunately, the author has fallen short of her goal of comprehensiveness. Among the missing library science journals are *The Reviewing Librarian* (Ontario Library Association, 1974-), *Microcomputers for Information Management* (Ablex, 1981-), and *Small Computers in Libraries* (Meckler, 1981-). A related field, educational technology, is represented by five titles, but two of the most important serials are missing: *Educational Media and Technology Yearbook*, 1985- (formerly *Educational Media Yearbook,* 1973-) and *Tech Trends*, 1985- (formerly *Instructional Innovator*). Also absent is *Quill & Quire*, the national periodical for Canada's book trade which devotes considerable space in each issue to library matters.

The annotations, while somewhat evaluative, are in most cases too brief to serve as the basis for a purchasing decision. The acquisitions information, however, appears to be complete and will no doubt be useful once the decision to subscribe has been made. [R: JAL, May 85, p. 119; JAL, Sept 85, pp. 229-30; JAL, Nov 85, p. 304; LJ, 15 Nov 85, p. 42; RQ, Summer 85, pp. 500-501; WLB, May 85, p. 618]

Heather Cameron

297. Melin, Nancy Jean, ed. **Library Serials Standards: Development, Implementation, Impact. Proceedings of the Third Annual Serials Conference.** Westport, Conn., Meckler Publishing, 1984. 164p. $35.00. LC 84-3789. ISBN 0-88736-008-4.

Papers delivered at this conference by librarians, publishers, vendors, and standards guardians themselves form a potpourri of information about and attitudes towards standards. There are discussions of locally and regionally developed standards, staff performance standards, and national standards for publishers and librarians and a look at the impact of standards on libraries. Charlotta Hensley's directory of official international and national standards for serials will be an especially valuable reference source for those concerned with published standards. Hensley also contributed an extensive annotated bibliography of recent literature related to serials standards. About half of the presentations are limited in scope to standards for serials publications or records, the remainder discuss the topic of serials standards only incidentally. The papers included have been carefully edited. Many are thought-provoking. All are sensible and practical with a good measure of humor. [R: LJ, 15 May 85, p. 48]

Margaret McKinley

Social Science Collections

298. **The Library of the Hoover Institution on War, Revolution and Peace.** Peter Duignan, ed. Stanford, Calif., Hoover Institution Press, 1985. 163p. illus. bibliog. $22.95; $14.95pa. LC 85-838. ISBN 0-8179-8161-6; 0-8179-8162-4pa.

A guide to the rich resources of one of the "world's leading research libraries for advanced study of the problems of political, social, and economic change in the twentieth century" (p. 12), this slender but oversized and well illustrated volume describes the development of the Hoover Institution, its library and archives, and its dozen or more major area study collections and units. Founded in 1919 through the wartime interests of Herbert Hoover, the library has become a repository of unique materials from all over the globe, consisting in 1984 of "some 1.5 million volumes, 42,000 reels of microfilm, 25,000 serial titles with subscriptions to over 3,000 current newspapers and journals," and "an archival depository having over 3,700 collections" (p. 13). Written by the heads of the units they oversee, the first three chapters (part 1) deal with the general history and description of the library and archival resources and procedures for their use. The next seven chapters (part 2) treat in turn collections specializing in Russia, the Soviet Union, and East Europe;

Central and Western Europe; East Asia; Africa; the Middle East and North Africa; Latin America; North America; and international affairs. Chapters on the archives and bibliographical research conclude the text and precede a brief bibliography used in preparation of the guide and a directory of the Hoover Institution's staff. The work is unusually adept at providing details of coverage and specific items in the collections, as well as photographs and brief anecdotes and notes of human interest in the wide margins. Although perhaps not quite as systematic in detail as the *Guide to the Research Collections of the New York Public Library* (Chicago: American Library Association, 1975), with which it invites comparison, this first general descriptive introduction to the library will be valuable not only to researchers themselves, but to library historians who chart the progress of collecting in this century. [R: JAL, Nov 85, p. 319]   Donald G. Davis, Jr.

State Libraries

299.   Shavit, David. **Federal Aid and State Library Agencies: Federal Policy Implementation.** Westport, Conn., Greenwood Press, 1985. 146p. bibliog. index. (Contributions in Librarianship and Information Science, No. 52). $27.95. LC 84-21233. ISBN 0-313-24610-6.

The Library Services Act of 1956 was Congress's first serious attempt to upgrade library service throughout the states. In 1964, the Library Services and Construction Act (LSCA) provided for buildings, consultants, services, and materials for all libraries, rural and urban, and attempted to upgrade and strengthen state library agencies, as well. An amended version, dated 1970, went farther towards strengthening state agencies.

Shavit's work is essentially an implementation analysis, asking whether the funds and efforts of that 1970 amended law made a significant difference in states' library networks, and whether the difference was positive. Using five states (all midwestern) as case studies, and supporting data from a handful more, Shavit performs intense critical analysis of results, using data supplied by the federal government, the state libraries, and unstructured interview material with a number of state library officials who administered LSCA funds.

Finally, the author makes some sound, logical recommendations for state library funding in the future (assuming that state library programs have a future) and alternative strategies for coaxing a cost-conscious Congress to continue funding state library programs. If the work reads like a reworked dissertation, it wouldn't be the first time, but there is value in

the case histories and a lesson to be learned from the analysis of success and failure in the book's final chapters. Recommended for those who deal with state funding of libraries and for policy-makers in general. [R: JAL, Sept 85, p. 245; JAL, Nov 85, p. 310; WLB, Dec 85, p. 57]
Bruce A. Shuman

Theological Collections and Church and Synagogue Libraries

300.   Anderson, Jacqulyn, comp. **How to Administer and Promote a Church Media Library.** Nashville, Tenn., Broadman Press, 1984. 80p. $5.95 spiralbound. LC 84-21452. ISBN 0-8054-3711-8.

The major purpose of this spiralbound manual is to instruct church members, who are not librarians or media center specialists, in effective management and administration of church media centers. So central is this purpose, that course credit is actually available upon completion of questions contained within the manual. Credit is offered by the Sunday School Board of the Southern Baptist Church, located in Nashville, Tennessee.

A brief foreword outlining the purpose of the manual is followed by a table of contents. The manual is divided into four lessons, the first lesson addressing the organization of the library media staff (hiring, assigning responsibilities, training of personnel). The second lesson discusses methods of operating an effective church media library, while the third and fourth lessons concern the selection of media, collection maintenance, and promotion of the media center. The table of contents is preceded by suggestions for the teacher, an explanation of the church study course, and a list of questions to be completed for course credit. The manual is heavily illustrated with black-and-white photographs, sketches, and diagrams, and important points are highlighted in red type throughout the manual.

Use of this manual will most probably be of an in-house nature, due to the specificity of the material and the church affiliation. Purchase, therefore, is recommended for some church libraries, but not public, academic, or research libraries. Of more use in a public library and in church and synagogue libraries is *Church and Synagogue Libraries* (Scarecrow, 1980) edited by John F. Harvey. Although not so instructional as the manual, it does give an overview of library and media center management and traces the history of Jewish, Catholic, Protestant, and other Christian libraries, in addition to including information about religious library associations.   Barbara Sproat

301. Kohl, Rachel, and Dorothy Rodda. **Church and Synagogue Library Resources.** 4th ed. Bryn Mawr, Pa., Church and Synagogue Library Association, c1975, 1984 (4th ed.). 20p. (A CSLA Bibliography). $3.00pa. LC 75-1178. ISBN 0-915324-08-3.

In a short twenty pages, this annotated bibliography manages to include general works on organizing and operating a small library, specific works dealing with forming church and synagogue libraries, a listing of names and addresses of library suppliers including religious suppliers, materials on acquisitions, periodicals (some religious, others with a more general librarianship scope), items dealing with other media from making audiovisuals to processing nonprint media for a library, technical aids (how to process materials, how to catalog and classify), promotion, dealing with archives, a list of church and synagogue library associations, audiovisual resources, and a list of publishers' names and addresses.

For a trained or volunteer librarian who is trying to form or run a church or synagogue library, this could be a valuable reference. It not only lists a lot of basic informational materials, but lists their cost and where to write for them. While not the sort of publication to receive a wide readership, it could lead to a wider readership of library materials in religious libraries through helping librarians acquire materials that would in turn result in better organization and availability.

Recommended to church and synagogue libraries, though of little or no use to public or academic libraries.

Judith E. H. Odiorne

302. McMichael, Betty. **The Church Librarian's Handbook: A Complete Guide for the Library and Resource Center in Christian Education.** Grand Rapids, Mich., Baker Book House, 1984. 277p. illus. bibliog. index. $9.95pa. LC 77-6722. ISBN 0-8010-6166-0.

Saint Paul has written, "that some should be apostles, some prophets, some evangelists, some pastors and teachers" in his letter to the Ephesians (Eph. 4:11) — and to that, some might add the call to minister through making available the writings of others. This book was written with that in mind: anybody who feels called to start and continue a church library could use this book as a guide, even without having had academic training in librarianship.

McMichael begins at the beginning, assuming that one must overcome inertia, find a location, and go through all the necessary boards and committees to receive church approval. She also deals with fund-raising and acquisitions, nonprint media, public relations and promotion, basic cataloging and classification and how to process books and media for use, and even how to prepare a library policy and find staff to help keep the library running smoothly.

Photographs of various church libraries are included to provide an idea of the wide range of possibilities. There are also illustrations showing everything from practical ways to mark library property to kinds of shelves, racks, cabinets, and other materials available through the various library suppliers. A list of such suppliers is included, along with a bibliography.

Highly recommended to any and all churches as a means of additional outreach.

Judith E. H. Odiorne

303. Slavens, Thomas P. **Theological Libraries at Oxford.** Munich, New York, K. G. Saur, 1984. 197p. illus. bibliog. $32.50. ISBN 3-598-10563-0.

The purpose of this work, as stated in the preface, is to investigate the development of the theological library collections at the University of Oxford. The first chapter, mistitled "Theology in Medieval Oxford," addresses, via an overabundance of quotations and gossipy tidbits excerpted from secondary sources, the origins of the University rather than the study of theology per se during those early years. The focus of chapters 2 and 3 is on the historical development and present operation of the renowned Bodleian Library. The remaining three chapters provide snippets of information regarding the collections of two major "faculty libraries" (i.e., history and theology), of five theological colleges and halls, and twenty-six affiliated colleges and halls which are primarily secular but which contain significant theological materials. The length of these latter chapters is in inverse relationship to the significance of the type of library discussed. Thirty-nine mostly full-page, but sometimes too dark, halftone illustrations are included.

The work is generally tedious, uninspiring, and sometimes repetitive. The reader familiar with the British educational system will learn little from the author's cursory treatment of the subject, whereas the noninitiated reader will look for, but not find, definitions and explanations. The text as such is poorly written (convoluted, run-on, badly written sentences abound) and badly typed (typing errors and/or inconsistencies were noted on thirteen of the twenty-one pages of chapter 1 alone); it was photoreproduced from typescript. Chapter 3 is titled but not numbered. Several footnote reference numbers are missing from the text in two chapters, and the notes for chapter 4 are missing altogether. Stylistic errors and incomplete footnote entries were noted elsewhere as well. The work also lacks an index.

Glenn R. Wittig

TECHNICAL SERVICES

304. Bloomberg, Marty, and G. Edward Evans. **Introduction to Technical Services for Library Technicians.** 5th ed. Littleton, Colo., Libraries Unlimited, 1985. 397p. illus. bibliog. index. (Library Science Text Series). $30.00; $20.00pa. LC 85-10332. ISBN 0-87287-486-9; 0-87287-497-4pa.

Because library technicians are specialists in library routines, texts written for their use must stress practice rather than theory. This is an impossible task for a one-volume textbook dealing with a large topic such as technical services which must cover the details of both manual and automated cataloging, classification, authority control, cataloging sources, acquisitions, bookkeeping, filing, serials control, and binding. This book is, and can only be, a starting point for both teachers and students. The authors state, for example, that the chapters dealing with cataloging must be used in conjunction with the *Anglo-American Cataloguing Rules*, second edition (*AACR2*).

Three charts outline the authors' perceptions of the tasks presently undertaken, rather than those ideally undertaken, in different sections of a technical services department by librarians, library technicians, clerks, and student help. Each chapter is complemented by review questions and has appropriate illustrations.

There are two caveats to the use of this helpful textbook. Library technician programs outside the United States should note that this text has been written for the U.S. market and includes only a few British sources and brief information on Canadian utilities, some of it out-of-date, e.g., UNICAT/TELECAT was dissolved in June 1980 (p. 34). The authors have also ignored some of the corrections and revisions to *AACR2*, for example, the incorrect punctuation in describing the dimensions of kits and the incorrect playing speed of sound cassettes which were corrected in the March 1984 reprinting of *AACR2* are not reflected (pp. 199, 206) nor is the 1982 rule revision which adds another category to entry under corporate body (p. 217).

This book is recommended for classes where the teacher is knowledgeable and can expand the content. [R: JAL, Nov 85, p. 316]

Jean Weihs

305. Godden, Irene P., ed. **Library Technical Services: Operations and Management.** Orlando, Fla., Academic Press, 1984. 272p. index. (Library and Information Science). $32.00. LC 83-15645. ISBN 0-12-287040-9.

This slim volume with six chapters is supposed to update Tauber's classic *Technical Services in Libraries* (1954), published over thirty years ago. As is well known, Tauber's work originated in connection with his teaching responsibilities at Columbia; one of the messages it conveyed was the "unity" of technical services, which this well-known author clearly advocated throughout his life, not only in this work but in many articles he wrote since 1954. What is offered by this new work, edited by Irene Godden? Six essays ("Technical Services Administration," by L. A. Manning; "Automation: The Context and the Potential," by K. L. Horny; "Acquisitions," by M. T. Reid; "Bibliographic Control," by B. G. Bengtson; "Preservation and Materials Processing," by A. D. Larsen; and "Circulation Functions," by L. A. Manning) plus an introduction by the editor, provide readers with a refresher course on topics that are discussed with varying skill.

As was noted by a review in *College & Research Libraries*, the publication of Tauber's work heralded the arrival of a new organizational structure, or even identity, for the technical services unit. This compilation appears at a time when that identity no longer exists or, at the least, is undergoing serious rethinking. What is new in this book, or rather in this series of essays? Very little. It provides a good, or shall we say an adequate, overview of the functioning of several departments but no new concept crystalizes. Some of the material is even poorly edited or written, especially a chapter on bibliographic control (fifty pages) that purports to cover cataloging and classification. The chapter on circulation functions, appropriate for Tauber's book, is out of place here, thirty years later.

Library Technical Services will probably be compared with Bloomberg and Evans's *Introduction to Technical Services for Library Technicians*, a new edition of which was published in 1985. Personally, I prefer Bloomberg and Evans. The material is clearly presented and it offers more information for the uninitiated. [R: C&RL, Mar 85, pp. 184-86; WLB, Jan 85, pp. 350-51]

Bohdan S. Wynar

Part III
REVIEWS OF PERIODICALS

Reviews of Periodicals

NATIONAL

306. **Canadian Library Journal**, Vol. 26- , No. 1- . Ottawa, Canadian Library Association, 1969- . bimonthly. $30.00/yr.; $25.00/yr. (Canada); $35.00/yr. (others). ISSN 0008-4352.

The *Canadian Library Journal* began life in 1944 as the *Bulletin* of the recently formed Canadian Library Council (CLC), a coalition of librarians seeking to enhance the visibility of Canadian librarians within the American Library Association and those seeking to form a national association. Since then, through several name changes, it has remained the chief periodical of the national association of anglophone Canadian librarians, now called the Canadian Library Association (CLA). Through those years the publication has mirrored the changes in that association and in the profession in Canada.

When the CLC was formed the *Bulletin* was a small, newsy publication with regular reports from regional and provincial associations. Today, CLA is a national association with stature in the international world of librarianship, and the *Canadian Library Journal* (*CLJ*) reflects the broader scholarly interests of the association's membership.

The publication has had three different names: from its birth in 1944 through January 1960 it was the *Bulletin*. It was called *Canadian Library* from March 1960 until the end of 1968, but with volume 26, no. 1 of 1969, it became the *Canadian Library Journal*. The name signalled a desire to confirm its credibility as a serious national publication contributing to the world's literature on librarianship.

In 1944 the *Bulletin* was published bimonthly from October to June and a subscription was an astonishing fifty cents. When in 1946 the *CLJ* was formed, a subscription became free to members. The frequency of publication varied slightly until 1948, when it settled back to six issues annually. Today it is a bimonthly publication.

Throughout the early period, many of the major names of Canadian library history appeared in the *Bulletin*: Nora Bateson, Marie Tremaine, W. Kaye Lamb, to name a few.

The *Bulletin* had at its inception what every fledgling publication needs: a strong hand at the wheel. Elizabeth Homer Morton, the secretary of the CLC and first executive director of CLA, was editor of the *Bulletin*. She retired in 1968 leaving a publication that had established itself in the professional life of the country.

A readership survey published in the *Canadian Library Journal* in June 1982, and conducted by the Centre for Research in Librarianship in Toronto, made clear that the contents of the journal answer a majority of the needs of its readers. In all, 68.6 percent of the sample rated the general quality of the journal as, at least, "good."

No stated purpose for the publication was given in 1944. Now a masthead statement states that the *Canadian Library Journal* is designed as a professional journal providing "a forum for the discussion, analysis and evaluation" of issues in librarianship and information science. The purpose, at least as exemplified by the material printed, has changed considerably since the early days. In 1944, the material was primarily news and brief articles (under ten thousand words) on subjects of professional interest. With the change of format in 1946, the content changed too. There were now more articles (still short, between three hundred and one thousand words), and considerably fewer news notes. In 1956 a new CLA publication, *Feliciter*, still in publication today, took over the news function from the old *Bulletin*.

The format of the *Bulletin* was fairly standard: a main article of perhaps a page and a half in length, a calendar of professional events, short news items, longer news or reports of conferences, and a list of publications for librarians. There were items of national interest (e.g., "Tentative Constitution and By-Laws of the Proposed Canadian Library Association"), as well as items of more particular concern (e.g., "Edmonton's Street Car Library").

The October 1946 issue of the *Bulletin* was the first to be issued by the CLA and the Christmas issue of that year showed readers a new, more artistic, less "newsletter-like" format. Small, attractive drawings and prints were added for the first time, paper stock showed improved quality, and a new typeface was used. By the following issue, the *Bulletin* was accepting commercial advertisements.

The content of the *Bulletin*, and, later, of *Canadian Library*, continued to evolve until the late 1960s when it began to resemble what it is today. Today the *Canadian Library Journal* has six to ten articles of between twenty-five hundred and seventy-five hundred words, all more or less scholarly, an editorial, a number of signed book reviews, a list of books received, advertisements (comprising some 30 to 40 percent of the publication), and an index to advertisers. There is no classified advertising, only commercial advertisements from publishers, distributors, and manufacturers. The content is, for a great part, focused on the Canadian experience with frequent looks at international developments. The layout is clean and spacious, giving the same feeling of airy modernity as that given by *The Journal of Academic Librarianship*.

Those who have contributed to the journal over the years have been a varied lot: librarians, politicians, British writer Walter de la Mare (1954), and Canadian writers Claude Ryan (1964) and Pierre Berton (1974). A study of authors reported by Carol Steer in June 1982 showed that the majority of articles are written by practicing librarians (close to 64 percent in the ten years studied) with library science faculty a strong second (14.5 percent). This is a pattern similar to that of comparable library journals in the United States as reported by the Olsgaard and Olsgaard study in *College & Research Libraries* in 1980.

The *Canadian Library Journal* announced in 1983 an innovative Student Article Contest, sponsored by the editorial board. Each year the three winning papers are considered for publication in one issue of *CLJ*.

Never noteworthy for their imagination, the covers of current issues lack panache, though they are clean and consistent. Briefly, with the new format in 1946, the covers showed a dignified charm which sat well with the content. Then, again briefly, under the design editorship of Diane Nemiroff in the late 1960s and Edith Pahlke in the mid-1970s, the covers were truly beautiful. Since then, the covers have been, with occasional exceptions, rather bland.

The journal is refereed: the regular articles are evaluated by an editor and by a member of the board or an outside reader before being accepted for publication.

Canadian Library Journal is indexed in *Library Literature, The Canadian Periodical Index (CPI), Library and Information Science Abstracts (LISA), The International Index to Multi-Media Information* and in *Current Index to Journals in Education (CIJE)*. CLA published an index to volumes 1 through 6 in 1950.

One final aspect of the journal — the language in which it is published — is worth noting both in light of Canada's official policy of bilingualism, and the fact that this is the official publication of the CLA. In its early years CLA had a bilingual name (the Canadian Library Association/Association canadienne des bibliothèques), a name which remained until, with the September/October 1968 issue, and for reasons which the journal never seems to have explained to its readers, the French portion of the association's name was dropped. In the mid-1950s, the Association canadienne de bibliothécaires de langue française, now the Association pour l'avancement des sciences et des techniques de la documentation (ASTED), was formed, and published its own periodical. The journal meantime was publishing fewer and fewer articles in French. Today the *Canadian Library Journal* publishes only in English.

Elizabeth Frick

307. **Catholic Library World**, Vol. 1, No. 1- . Haverford, Pa., Catholic Library Association, 1929- . bimonthly. $35.00/yr.; $40.00/yr. (foreign); $3.00 (single issue). ISSN 0008-820X.

As the official journal of the Catholic Library Association, the *Catholic Library World* is sent to over twenty-five hundred librarians in secular and Catholic libraries in the United States, Canada, and throughout the world. From its inception as a mimeographed, ten-page publication in 1929, concerned primarily with the news of the association, the *CLW* has evolved to a forty-eight-page national journal which is indexed in *Book Review Index, Library Literature, Library Science Abstracts, Reference Book Review, Cerdic-Universite des*

Sciences Humaines de Strasbourg, Current Index to Journals in Education (ERIC), and the Catholic Library Association's own *Catholic Periodical and Literature Index.*

Published in its early years by the chairperson of the association or its secretary/treasurer, the *CLW* has had a distinguished roster of editors. Among those who held this dual position of association executive and editor were Francis E. Fitzgerald, John M. O'Loughlin, Eugene P. Wilging, Alphonse F. Trezza, Jeannette Murphy Lynn, and Matthew R. Wilt. In 1963 Jane F. Hindman became the full-time editor of the journal, followed in 1973 by John T. Corrigan, CFX, the present editor.

Throughout most of its fifty-six-year history the journal has contained columns on the news of the association, reviews of recent publications, positions available lists, and the Conference Proceedings of the CLA. But true to its title, the journal has also interpreted Catholic in its universal application. Volume 3, no. 3 contains an interesting article by Leonard Feeney on the complexity of using the Bodleian Library in Oxford. In the sixth issue of that volume Jeannette Murphy is the author of a long, scholarly, and critical article on the shortcomings of the Schedule on Religion of the Library of Congress. Of interest to school librarians is the article by William A. Fitzgerald on the "Secondary School Library and Librarian Standards," which was published in volume 10, no. 4.

Another interesting article "Franciscans and the Art of Printing" by Irenaeus Herscher traces a connection between Gutenberg's invention of printing and the Franciscans he worked with in his early years (vol. 11, no. 7). In issue number 4 of that same volume we find an article on "Public Education, Books and Libraries in Colonial South America" by David Rubio, the curator of the Hispanic Foundation of the Library of Congress. Concern with Latin America is continued in the article "Early Printing in Latin America" by John M. Lenhart (vol. 12, nos. 5 and 6).

Not all articles have been concerned with library history. An article on "Bibliotherapy" by Thomas Verner Moore explores the therapeutic effects of guided reading (vol. 15, no. 1). In issue number 7 of the next volume we find an article on "Guiding the Teen Age Reader in the Public Library" by the acknowledged expert in that subject, Margaret C. Scoggin of the New York Public Library. In 1947 Charles F. Hoban wrote on "Audio-Visual Materials and the Library" before this became a popular topic in the late sixties (vol. 18, no. 6). In that same year we find a first-hand account of the devastation to libraries and book collections in war-ravaged

Europe by Oliver L. Kapsner, who was a chaplain to American soldiers in World War II (vol. 18, no. 8).

Another very useful feature found in the *CLW* during the forties and fifties was the series on "Contemporary Catholic Authors." These comprehensive bibliographic essays were not only on famous authors such as Paul Claudel (vol. 12, no. 2) and Graham Greene (vol. 16, no. 3); but gave equal treatment to less well-known authors such as Karl Adam (vol. 16, no. 4) and Eileen Duggan (vol. 16, no. 7).

In volume 28, the newly appointed executive director of the CLA, Alphonse F. Trezza, in his position as editor of the journal, began an interesting series of histories of companies publishing Catholic books. One of the highlights of his term as editor was the article "The Library: Foundation of the University" by Nathan M. Pusey, president of Harvard (vol. 31, no. 5).

Under the leadership of Matthew R. Wilt, who became editor in 1962, the *Catholic Library World* continued its universal vision of librarianship with articles by Padraic Colum, the Irish poet and story teller (vol. 33, no. 1); Harry La Plante on the Vatican Microfilm Library (vol. 33, no. 4); and a perceptive article on the importance of MEDLARS for hospital libraries by Helan Yast (vol. 34, no. 9).

With the appointment of Jane F. Hindman, who was its first full-time editor, the *Catholic Library World* increased the number of issues in volume 35 (1963-1964) from eight to nine; began to feature illustrated covers; and attracted such writers as Emerson Greenaway who wrote on "Library Public Relations" (vol. 37, no. 3), and Louis Shores who explored the expanded image of librarianship in "Our Quiet Force: The Changing Role of the Librarian" (vol. 38, no. 9).

In 1973, John T. Corrigan, CFX, the present editor, assumed direction of the *CLW*. He increased the issues in each volume to ten (monthly except for July/August and May/-June). A significant new feature of his editorship was the single-theme issue. Volume 45, no. 9 was devoted entirely to library service for the handicapped. Library service to the disadvantaged was the theme of volume 52, no. 4; and no. 9 of that same volume treated the theme of bilingual library service. Other innovations of his editorship included a "Washington Notebook" on the latest legislative information from the Capital; "Comment On," an opinion column, where librarians respond to advanced copies of an essay on a controversial subject by one of their colleagues; and a special reviewing section called "Religious Resources," which featured a brief article of interest to religious education teachers and reviews of books and media useful for their work.

Some of the significant articles of the last few years have included "The Future of the Librarian Lies outside the Library," a provocative look at the paperless, electronic information society by F. Wilfrid Lancaster (vol. 51, no. 9); Toni Carbo Bearman's report on NCLIS's current activities and its future plans (vol. 53, no. 5); and the delightful acceptance speeches of the Regina Medal winners at each annual conference. The Regina Medal, which is awarded by the Catholic Library Association for "continued, distinguished contribution to children's literature," inspired Tomie de Paola (vol. 55, no. 1) and Jean Fritz (vol. 57, no. 1) to share the youthful, very personal experiences which influenced their books.

With volume 57, no. 1 (July/August 1985) the *CLW* began a new publication schedule. Instead of ten issues a year, it will be published bimonthly. The *CLA Handbook and Membership Directory*, which was formerly published as the January issue, will be a separate publication appearing in late January. The July/August issue of the *CLW* contains the proceedings of the CLA annual convention and the November/December issue contains the preliminary schedule for the forthcoming Easter Week Convention. The format of the journal is 8½ by 11 inches, printed with illustrations on glossy stock. Each issue contains advertising from publishers and library service companies.

The editorial content of the *CLW* is not parochial in its interests, but, as we noted, covers a wide range of areas of concern to the library professional. Each issue has five or six articles on a selected theme, news of persons and activities in the Catholic Library Association and the library profession in general, news of recent advances in technologies helpful to the profession, a calendar of continuing education opportunities, commentary on and selected readers' responses to a topic of current concern to librarianship, columns from interest sections and roundtables of the CLA, and an extensive reviewing section for print and audiovisual media. Specialized bibliographies frequently appear in the journal.

The writing and editorial organization of the *Catholic Library World* has remained of a consistently high quality throughout its history.

In connection with this article, we examined other religious library association publications. *Church and Synagogue Libraries* is primarily a bimonthly newsletter with short articles. *Lutheran Libraries* is a quarterly of modest size (twenty pages) with conference planning, chapter news, and reviews of religious books. *Christian Librarian* is a conservative

journal reflecting the concerns of its membership. The only journal which is similar in scope and scholarship to the *CLW* is the new, biannual *Judaica Librarianship*, which superseded the *Association of Jewish Libraries Bulletin* in 1983.

As the journal of an association which counts among its members elementary, high school, and college and university librarians; directors of great research libraries and parish librarians; medical and other special librarians; the *Catholic Library World* serves the Catholic Library Association and the library profession with a catholic range of scholarly and practical information.   Emmett Corry, OSF

308. College and Research Libraries, Vol. 1- , No. 1- . Chicago, Association of College and Research Libraries, American Library Association, 1939- . bimonthly. $35.00/yr. ISSN 0010-0870.

Barely a year had gone by when the newly formed division of the American Library Association, College and Research Libraries, introduced their quarterly journal. It was a severe looking, plain-covered emulation of the scholarly journal of the period. It has survived and today has a cover that speaks of serious, slick academic sophistication. Gloria S. Cline wrote her doctoral dissertation on the evolution of this journal and she claimed that its continued success has been based upon a consistent purpose as outlined by the premier editor.[1] William A. Katz has for a decade consistently listed it as "an important journal for the professional collections of many large public and special as well as academic libraries."[2] And Lucy Heckman writing in *Serials Review* spoke highly of the book reviews in *CRL* although she did not make any comparisons as to quality and quantity with the other review media.[3]

It would seem that *CRL* is accepted as a major journal that belongs in the hands of academic librarians. Little comparison was found in the literature with its only other rival *Journal of Academic Librarianship* founded by a former editor of *CRL*, Richard M. Dougherty. Evidently there is room for two journals devoted to the academic library scene. However, there are some considerations that should be taken into account that may not dim the reputation of *CRL* but should provide additional evaluative insight for new or potential users of the journal.

It has been from its inception a membership journal. It was the major communication format available to the ACRL member. It provided a dissemination service for many of the papers delivered at annual conferences. It was an outlet for articles from leaders in the field providing a forum for the development of consensus. It functioned as a newsletter, a book review service and, somewhat secondarily, as a stimulant to research and experimentation. It is interesting to note that in surveying the commentary on *CRL* and on reading its masthead instruction to authors one finds no mention of peer review of materials submitted for publication. It can be assumed that the special editors whose names appeared on the masthead until recently functioned as some sort of screening device but it is doubtful that review was either exacting nor rigorous.

Katz and others refer to the editorship of *CRL* as being professional. The editors over the past forty-six years have been distinguished but they have all been working librarians or library education faculty: A. F. Kaufman, 1939-1941; Carl M. White, 1941-1948; Maurice F. Tauber, 1948-1962; Richard B. Harwell, 1962-1963; David Kaser, 1963-1969; Richard M. Dougherty, 1969-1974; Richard D. Johnson, 1974-1980; C. James Schmidt, 1980-1984, and Charles R. Martell, 1984 to date. They have not been exclusive, full-time editors as has become the tradition with say, *American Libraries* or *Library Journal.* Many society and professional scholarly journals draw from the working profession for their editors who function as overseers on editorial and policy matters while leaving matters of design, layout, and logistics to others.

In 1956 *CRL* became a bimonthly and in March of 1966 it shed its news and association activity reporting role by introducing a spin-off called *ACRL News* at first but later shifted to *College and Research Libraries News* to insure an understanding of its relationship to *CRL.*

Cline's study is enlightening for one main reason. It clearly shows the slow but almost unerring push by the academic library administrators for the trappings and appearance of a scholarly image. It reflects the development of the drive for status and rank within higher education institutions as well as a growing concern for cost-effective systems design. The journal has had a steady decline in the number of articles published to an average of about 6.5 per issue by 1979. A spot check since that time indicates the average seems to be holding at that level. The length of the average article grew from about 3 to about 8 pages where it has settled into constancy. In the early days it was quite common to publish articles without documentation, footnotes, or citations appended. Cline says about 45 percent of the early journals featured that type of article. But by 1979 that average had fallen to 9 percent and a random sampling of recent issues would indicate that figure has softened ever further. It can be noted

in Cline's paper that the sharpest decline in articles without citations occurred about the time that librarians began to win some recognition for their claim to status and rank on their campus in the late 1960s and early 1970s.

It should surprise no one familiar with the membership of the Association of College and Research Libraries that the journal articles heavily emphasize administrative and library-organization matters. General survey articles and articles on technical services seem to be tied for second. Cline further indicates an increase in quality and scholarly content of the articles published. Certainly the creation of the *News* was a factor in helping to enforce a more serious and purposeful goal for the journal. Soon D. Kim and Mary T. Kim in a smaller study of the *CRL* articles supported the apparent shift toward a more discipline-oriented journal; they also cited the emergence of research articles from regular teaching faculty in the academic institutions. The Kims seemed to view the latter as a back-handed compliment in that librarianship was beginning to be viewed as a good area for research while at the same time librarians were not so interested in research. They feared that the more sophisticated researchers might crowd out the librarians. They write, "Academic librarians have performed well to date, conducting the descriptive studies which lay the ground work for future research. Their role for the future is clearly to expand their efforts in experimental and casual research."[4] Clearly there are those who feel that academic librarians have not progressed far enough in their search for acceptance of their practice as a scholarly discipline. Charles R. McClure and Alan R. Samuels recently took out after the administration of academic libraries insisting that they ignore many types of information sources that could improve the quality of their decision making. They accuse librarians of having little respect or understanding for empirical data and original research.[5]

When the current editor of the *CRL* took over he felt compelled to write about his goals for the content of the journal. He said that "we should be able to look to our professional literature for guidance, for hints, and for thought-provoking judgement so that we can cope ... more effectively. I have become wary, even tired, of research that fails to meet the simple criterion of 'so what.' I read too many articles that offer data but not synthesis, information but not understanding."[6]

CRL, therefore, will be only as effective as its profession. In reviewing its publishing history it became clear how closely tied in with the personal evaluation of professional worth and the future of its readers the journal has become. If the journal is to continue to occupy that unique spot as the best of the journals for large research-oriented information services and collections, the practitioners and writers for the journal are going to have to arrive at a better understanding of the role of research in the cumulative process of developing a disciplinary literature. Katz is right, this is an important journal and as Cline points out there is a measurable growth over its first forty years, yet, in this reviewer's evaluation, the process has leveled off in the past five years. This leaves room for the *Journal of Academic Librarianship* to move into the leadership role, if it is so motivated.

Notes

[1]Gloria S. Cline, "CRL: Its First Forty Years," *College and Research Libraries* 43 (May 1982): 208-32.

[2]William A. Katz and Linda Sternberg Katz, *Magazines for Libraries*, 4th ed. (New York, R. R. Bowker, 1982), 562.

[3]Lucy Heckman, "College and Research Libraries," *Serials Review* 5 (January 1979): 66-67.

[4]Soon D. Kim and Mary T. Kim, "Academic Library Research: A Twenty Year Perspective," in *New Horizons for Academic Libraries* (New York, K. G. Saur, 1979), 382.

[5]Charles R. McClure and Alan R. Samuels, "Factors Affecting the Use of Information for Academic Library Decision Making," *College and Research Libraries* 46 (November 1985): 495.

[6]Charles R. Martell, Editorial, *College and Research Libraries* 45 (March 1984): 247.

Gerald R. Shields

309. **The Journal of Academic Librarianship**, Vol. 1- , No. 1- . Ann Arbor, Mich., Mountainside Publishing, 1975- . bimonthly. $22.00/yr.; $38.00/yr. (institutions); $22.00/yr. (elementary and high school libraries/media centers); (foreign add $4.00); $6.34 (single issue). ISSN 0099-1333.

Ten years ago Richard M. Dougherty and his cohort Bill Webb took "one giant step" for academic librarianship by introducing a new journal, a feat that many said was risky and some said couldn't be done successfully. In the editorial of that first issue Dougherty postulated that "for a significant number of librarians the status quo is less important than the asking of questions. And academic librarianship has

matured to the point where significantly increased dialog between professionals through scholarly exchange is both necessary and inevitable." Started as a journal that could complement rather than compete with *College and Research Libraries*, the editors believed that "academic librarianship would benefit if they had a medium, independent of a professional organization, in which to air points of view and debate issues." Over the years this belief has proven accurate with the success of this journal and its role complementary to *CRL*.

In 1975 the new journal came kicking and screaming onto the cusp of the last quarter of this century's academic library world which was facing many significant problems, not the least of which was a shrinking or stable budget picture, which almost precluded purchasing new titles, let alone investing capital to start a new journal. Immediately the journal made its presence known with a tight editing style, a concentration on major issues, publication of research findings as well as opinion pieces, and a cadre of writers and editorial board members from the academic librarianship world, which reads like a "who's who" spanning the decade from the old guard to the young turks. From the beginning its purpose has been to report the results of research and new ideas; and to identify trends, relate events, and share the views of opinion makers. But the primary goal which has been achieved is the publication of a journal that is attractive and interesting to read as well as informative.

The journal has reached new levels of quality as it has matured. Its adolescent years are approaching with a spirit of innovation and imagination. The style is captivating, almost forcing the reader to explore the content from cover to cover. Most articles are refereed by a dozen-member editorial board, with occasional input from other experts. Others are solicited to address specific issues on which the author would have some expertise.

The 8½-by-11-inch format has remained consistent over the years, with a series of typescripts and blocked-out phrases presenting a welcome variety. Photographs, present on the covers of the first two volumes, soon gave way to a highlighted "content" on the bold-colored cover. The logo used throughout the issues to identify new sections and articles, and on the cover, has become recognizable throughout the world. This reviewer has seen it displayed in libraries on four continents.

Although the issues addressed relate primarily to academic libraries and librarianship in the United States, the scope is much broader, encompassing issues faced by librarianship in general and by all types of libraries on this side of the oceans and on the other sides. Basically the content is presented in three major sections: articles, features, and book reviews.

Since articles are refereed by more than one person, a standard of quality checks has been built into the publication process. The half dozen or so articles in each issue are occasionally supplemented by a special "symposium" format. Over the years this "symposium" format has been used to introduce important issues facing the profession. Such a forum provides commentary and an exchange of views by knowledgeable individuals who speak to the issue at hand from a variety of perspectives. The most recent one, for example, is on "The Ownership of Bibliographic Data—OCLC's Experience" which includes comments by seven experts, among them the president of OCLC, the director of RLIN, and the executive director of a major regional network.

One of the best features has remained the book review section which includes in-depth reviews of between six and twelve recent contributions to the library and information science literature.

In addition, "The JAL Guide to the Professional Literature" is a unique feature, summarizing reviews which have recently appeared in selected library and higher education journals. Each entry includes a full bibliographic citation, statement of the book's purpose, and the reviewer's recommendation. It is the one source where librarians, administrators, and library school students can get a good overview of the current monographic literature. Arranged into over two dozen subject categories, this section usually contains about 150 reviews. A handy "Index to the JAL Guide" immediately following is arranged by author.

Other features are an editorial page and a classified advertisement section. Periodically a short "Little Lessons from Library History" article, which describes little-known facts in library history, is also published. Several pages of advertisement do not detract because they are at the beginning, the end, and interspersed between the major sections.

All organizations and individuals who are concerned with or committed to academic librarianship will find this an invaluable addition to their library's professional collection or to their own personal collection.

Robert D. Stueart

310. **SLJ/School Library Journal**, Vol. 1- , No. 1- . New York: R. R. Bowker, 1961- . monthly (June and July, bimonthly). $51.00/yr.; $69.00/yr. (foreign); $5.25 (single issue). ISSN 0362-8930.

The evolution of *SLJ*'s title, format, distribution, and scope reflects changes in and increasing attention to library work for children and young adults over the past century. The subject was within the original scope of *Library Journal* (*LJ*) (1876-), a publication designed to address the entire field of librarianship. However, by 1948, *LJ* included a monthly column entitled School Libraries by Frances Henne and Ruth Ersted. In 1954 *Junior Libraries: The Journal of Library Work with Children & Young People* appeared as a separate publication, as well as a monthly section of *LJ*. The present title, *SLJ/School Library Journal: The Magazine of Children's, Young Adult, & School Librarians*, was adopted in 1961. An ever-increasing bulky-sized *LJ*, a growing list of subscribers for the independently issued *SLJ*, and changes in editorial patterns of responsibilities were among the factors that led to *SLJ* becoming a completely separate publication in January 1975. This date also marked the separate publication of *Previews*, which for the previous two years had been a part of *LJ* and *SLJ*. When *Previews* ceased in 1980, *SLJ* again picked up the appropriate reviewing responsibilities.

In their September 1974 editorials, both Lillian N. Gerhardt[1] and John Berry[2] expressed their combined but separate commitment to continue, through communication and cooperation, carrying out the long established (1876) purpose of *LJ* to cover the entire field of library and bibliographic interests. The 1980s reader would recognize familiar features in these mid-1970s issues. The book review section was well established, the annual book review policy statement started in 1967 appeared each September, and the In the YA Corner column appeared monthly.

The magazine has, according to Katz, "gained a deserved reputation for publishing material, both from librarians and staffers, that leads rather than follows the movements in the library field."[3] One of these staffers is Lillian N. Gerhardt, quoted above, who was appointed to the newly created position of editor-in-chief in September 1971 and who continues to serve in that capacity. Her editorials stimulate thinking and Kaye perceives them as "the most consistently provocative feature of the journal ... often controversial, occasionally biting, but never dull ... remarks [that] appear to be designed to elicit feedback and arguments."[4] The validity of this assessment can be found in SLJ/-Letters, in activities and in discussions taking place in the field in reaction to an SLJ editorial or article.

The articles and monthly features regularly offer the reader thoughtful, stimulating issue-oriented pieces as well as practical advice and news of the field. As one example, the lead article in the 15 September 1954 *Junior Libraries* was Thomas Zimmerman's "What to Do about Comics." The abstract states "some practical suggestions for dealing with a complicated contemporary problem, for which there is no pat solution." Indeed, the role of comics in the library is still debated and was addressed in two articles in the 1970s: "Spider-man," the August 1981 issue cover feature, introduced Larry Dorrell and Ed Carroll's "Spider-man at the Library" article which generated discussion from readers published in the October and November 1981 issues. This is only one example of why this reviewer agrees with Kaye that "*SLJ* has done a remarkable job of maintaining a series of continuing dialogues among librarians."[5]

The *SLJ* reader can quickly turn to regularly scheduled articles or monthly features of interest. Topics handled as articles on an annual basis include: "Expenditures for Resources in School Library Media Centers" (first appearing in 1983); "Reference Books Roundup" (a May feature); and "Best Books of ..." (a December feature). Other types of regular features are the "Audiovisual Forecasts" and the spring/fall Children's Book Announcements with their index to advertisers. Regularly covered conferences include those of AECT (Association for Educational Communications and Technology) and ALA's (American Library Association) annual and midwinter conferences. Such features and articles provide information not otherwise readily available to librarians serving children and young adults.

This stimulation and practical information is also found in the monthly columns, which include Up for Discussion started in 1973; Practically Speaking (1973), In the YA Corner (1974), and Video Watch (1981). These columns provide further opportunity for readers to present their views or engage in dialogues with others.

The informative departments include "Editorial," "Letters," "Calendar," "News," "People," "Classified," and "Checklist." The latter is a timely service alerting the reader to pamphlets and other inexpensive publications of interest. "Media Tie-Ins," started in 1979, is another handy service.

A major contribution of *SLJ* and its forerunners has been the reviewing service. Here again, the coverage offered has been timely in terms of the needs of the field, whether the subject is professional reading or materials in the newest format. For example, a feature article in the September 1984 issue on computer software became the monthly "Computer Software Review" section in the October 1984 issue.

For many years, librarians have turned to *LJ* and its related magazines for reviews of books and audiovisual materials. To aid the reader in interpreting the reviews, *SLJ* began in 1974 the practice of annually publishing the book selection policy. This practice has been applied since 1981 to the policy for selection of audiovisual materials.

The reviews, especially those for books, have been the subject of a number of studies (see References at the end of this review). Without going into an in-depth analysis of the review coverage or comparing the quality of reviews with other sources', this reviewer will limit the current discussion to some of the advantages and disadvantages of the *SLJ* approach: The *SLJ* reader knows the name and position of each reviewer; this information can provide clues to the experience and biases of the reviewer. Librarians, in the field, who write the reviews can query children and young adults about their reactions to the material under review (although using field-based reviewers may increase the time lag between publication of a work and publication of a review). *SLJ*'s record of reviewing the largest portion of juvenile titles published within a year has been consistently documented. *SLJ*'s reviews generally include comparisons with works similar to the one being reviewed. Finally, *SLJ* does provide an annual policy statement, and an opportunity for the reader to challenge or raise questions regarding a specific review or the reviewing process itself.

SLJ is indexed in *Library Literature, ACCESS, Book Review Digest,* and *Library Science Abstract.*

Notes

[1]Lillian N. Gerhardt, "SLJ from LJ," *School Library Journal* 20 (1974): 7.

[2]John Berry, "SLJ to Go It Alone," *Library Journal* 99 (1974): 2111.

[3]Bill Katz and Linda Sternberg Katz, *Magazines for Libraries*, 4th ed. (New York: R. R. Bowker, 1982), 573.

[4]Marilyn Kaye, "School Library Journal," *Serials Review* 15 (1979): 20.

[5]Ibid.

References

Carter, Betty, and Karen Harris. "The Children and the Critics: How Do Their Book Selections Compare?" *School Library Media Quarterly* 10 (1981): 54-58.

Craver, Kathleen. "Book Reviewers: An Empirical Portrait." *School Library Media Quarterly* 12 (1984): 383-409.

Lee, Joel. "Library Periodicals in Review." *Serials Review* 5 (1979): 7-39.

Mott, Frank Luther. *A History of American Magazines: 1865-1885*. Cambridge, Mass.: Harvard University Press, 1938.

Silver, Linda R. "Criticism, Reviewing, and the Library Review Media." *Top of the News* 35 (1979): 123-30.

Spalding, Helen H. "SLJ, School Library Journal." *Serials Review* 3 (1977): 20-21.

Weber, Rosemary. "The Reviewing of Children's and Young Adult Books in 1977." *Top of the News* 35 (1979): 131-37.

Witucke, Virginia. "A Comparative Analysis of Juvenile Book Review Media." *School Media Quarterly* 8 (1980): 153-60.

Phyllis J. Van Order

311. **Wilson Library Bulletin**, Vol. 1- , No. 1- . New York, H. W. Wilson, 1914- . monthly (July and August, bimonthly). $30.00/yr. (incl. Canada); $35.00/yr. (all other foreign); $4.00 (single issue incl. Canada); $4.50 (single issue all other foreign). ISSN 0043-5651.

Perhaps no better historical reason for *Wilson Library Bulletin*'s existence can be cited than Pope's famous line, "What dire offenses from am'rous causes springs/What mighty causes rise from trivial things." *WLB*, begun as an in-house publication in 1914, rose comet-like to spectacular heights. Moreover, not unlike the comet, it dazzled (and dazzles) with visual (not to mention, intellectual) luminosity. The publication's history is extraordinary on two counts: longevity and quality. *WLB* won over its loyal readership by persevering with saint-like devotion to quality, intellectual content, literary accomplishment, and timeliness—all of which have endured more than seventy years.

Until recently, the journal's face had not changed significantly during its long life. Moreover, some of the finer points of magazine production, often overlooked by journals both in and out of the profession, have been followed with meticulous care by *WLB*'s editors. Whether these finer points resulted in a change to cleaner, more readable typefaces, or were simply a matter of style (such as placing the news section of the magazine in the middle, where most periodicals naturally fall open, instead of the front), *WLB* has kept a careful and vigilant eye out for changes that will appeal to and attract readers.

From its first editor, Edith Phelps, to its seventh and present one, Milo Nelson, *WLB* has been blessed with highly talented editors. These editors have evinced an uncanny knack for initiating new columns and then finding the only living column editors capable of successfully pulling those columns off. The name Frances Neel Cheney, for example, comes quickly to mind. From the moment she took the column Current Reference Books in hand in 1942, to her last written word for that column in 1972, Cheney brought to her column style, wit, and a professional suavity that has made her and her work a legend. Although all of *WLB*'s editors contributed to the rich legacy that is the magazine's, the turning point in its meteoric rise to success began under editor Kathleen Moltz (1963-1968) and continued under editor William R. Eshelman (1969-1979). The stimulating variety of topics and the increased readership attest to this claim.

Moltz began to reshape the face of *WLB* in 1963 by giving the magazine a brighter look, both visually and intellectually. Articles by E. J. Josey ("In Defense of Academic Freedom," October 1965) and Susan Sontag ("The Avant-Garde and Contemporary Literature," June 1966) alerted librarians that something distinctively different was taking shape. The continuation of Cheney's column coupled with Jesse Shera's Without Reserve (a thought-provoking column that allowed readers to sample the vast array of ideas in the field of librarianship) capped off a bright, new beginning. Under Eshelman, the excellence continued.

Although Cheney's tenure ended during Eshelman's reign, *WLB* was not without its celestial lights under his direction. Charles Bunge took over Cheney's column. Barbara Dill, editor of the *Children's Catalog* (H. W. Wilson, 1976) added her expert touch to the column, Picturely Books for Children. Cine-Opsis, that well-known column meant to supply librarians at small and medium-sized libraries with a collection development scheme for films, also began in the seventies (June 1974), before such a thing became *de rigueur*. Also added during this time were the columns Book Trucking (a column very reminiscent of *The New Yorker*'s Talk of the Town; an irreverent piece that educated as often as it enraged readers) and

Library Front Liners (a column which "high-lighted outstanding personalities at the front lines of library service"). Both Moltz and Eshelman farmed out the covers of *WLB* to a talented array of artists: Roger Duvoisin; Icelander Louisa Mattiasdottir; Henry Evans; the famed sixties flower child, Peter Max; and Caryl Di Paoli, to name a few.

The latest *WLB* editor, Milo Nelson, continues the tradition of experienced editors. Nelson brings to his post a rich and varied background as a well-known library analyst, and editor of the state publication *The Idaho Librarian*. With Nelson has come the inevitable itch for change. But has that change been justified?

Recent issues of *WLB* examined for this review leave one short of encomia and ambivalent in feeling. Apart from the unnecessary change in size of the publication (from 25 cm to 27½ cm), Nelson and his staff have changed the typeface, layout, and coverage of the *Wilson Library Bulletin*. Upfront News has replaced the once famous Month in Review. It is similar to *Library Journal's* and *American Libraries'* short-take approach to the news. Cine-Opsis has given way to Front Row Center. Murder in Print, Kathleen Maio's delightful new column on detective novels, seems, nevertheless, an inordinate amount of space to devote to a fascinating but minor genre of literature.

Book Trucking has gone the way of all flesh. In its place are yet more "snap shot" reviews, much like those found in *Choice* and *Library Journal*. Although probably viewed by hundreds of public librarians as a godsend, one still cannot help pitying Bruce Pollock's lot in magazine life: reviewing, from month to month, the world's popular music. Evidence that progress leaves no stone unturned appears in the column on software available for use in libraries. James Rettig's assumption of that old stand-by, Current Reference Books, however, proves once again that everything changes while remaining the same.

The new version of *Wilson Library Bulletin* offers many new features that will undoubtedly please librarians and augment the magazine's attractiveness. From Dateline-Washington, a very brief piece on news in the nation's capital affecting librarians, to Online Update, *WLB's* answer to both *RQ's* Sources: Databases and *Library Journal's* Online Databases, librarians of all covers will find something new under this sun to improve their daily work. One cannot, however, look through the old issues and come to the new ones without feeling a sense of loss. Does one charge the new *WLB* with trendiness and newness for their sakes alone, or does one charge one's own

feelings with *laudator temporis acti*, with praising old things simply because they are old? It is difficult to tell at this early stage and so I will leave it to time, that fury who is both old and brazen enough to eventually and mercilessly reveal everything.

Wilson Library Bulletin is indexed in *Education Index, Library Literature* and *Popular Periodical Index*, and abstracted in *Library & Information Science Abstracts, Historical Abstracts* and *America: History and Life*. Book reviews are indexed in *Book Review Index*.

Mark Y. Herring

SUBJECT-ORIENTED

312. **Collection Building**, Vol. 1- , No. 1- . New York, Neal-Schuman, 1978- . quarterly. $55.00/yr. ISSN 0160-4953.

As happens occasionally, several new journals covering the same topic start publication at almost the same time. *Collection Building* (Neal-Schuman), *Library Acquisitions: Practice and Theory* (Pergamon Press) and *Collection Management* (Haworth Press) all began in the mid- to late 1970s to meet what was perceived to be a need for a journal that addressed the issues of collection development and acquisitions. Given the fact that all three are still being published almost ten years later, there must be enough reader interest to sustain publication, even if the profit margin may be narrow.

Collection Building tends to emphasize the selection aspects of collection development, whereas *Collection Management* tends to emphasize policy issues, budgeting, evaluation, and weeding with few articles addressing selection. Over the past five years, *Collection Building* has published articles by many of the top people in the field in the United States and Canada. Several very well-known and knowledgeable individuals have regular columns—Bill Katz's Perspective, Sandy Berman's Alternatives, Audrey Eaglen's Library-Publishing Connection, Rhea Joyce Rubin's Stress Points, Kathleen Weibel's Genres, Marilyn Moody's Government Documents, and Ilse Moon's Free and Inexpensive Materials. Articles range from four to ten pages in length and are of the applications variety. Many articles are reviews-of-current-practices or guides to selecting classes of material. Fortunately, there are only occasional how-we-do-it-good articles and even the few that do creep in have a few paragraphs that attempt to provide a more general application. Quality of editing is sound and editorial standards are good.

Although the journal is distributed internationally, there are very few articles contributed from outside the United States. Perhaps the editors could put together an international issue every two or three years to inform North American librarians about developments elsewhere. Certainly in the last ten years there has been a marked increase among European librarians in thinking and writing about the areas of collection development and materials selection.

The journal is well worth reading if you are involved in collection development or public services. Unfortunately, the subscription price puts the journal beyond most individuals and all too few libraries seem willing to spend very much money on materials to keep the staff in touch with current developments in the field.

G. Edward Evans

313. Data Base Informer: The Newsletter of Information USA's Computer Data Service, Vol. 1- , No. 1- . Chevy Chase, Md., Information USA, 1984- . monthly. $78.00/yr.

This newsletter, the first three issues (March-May 1984) of which were titled *Computer Data Report*, is "designed to show decision makers where to find external data and how it can be used for computerized decision making" (back cover of each issue). It aims to identify data, especially unique free or low-cost databases, and to provide information on how to format the data or construct and manage databases. It fulfills the first aim better than the latter. The 1984 volume (ten issues) has been reprinted in soft cover with a table of contents organized into such categories as free databases; money saving tips for using online vendors; comparison buyer's guide to popular database subjects; sources of free and low-cost offline database searches; sources of data tapes, files, and diskettes; information sources and research tips; and free books, directories, newsletters, and conferences on the database industry. Most issues of the newsletter are twelve pages, but some issues contain long tables that make the issue run to eighteen or twenty pages; for example, the July 1985 issue published "Searching Databases by SIC Codes," which lists sixty-nine databases available from some ten different vendors.

There is a plethora of newsletters in the online industry. This one's niche is very general in subject matter with an emphasis on free and low-cost services of interest to the user of data in business, government, research, and other organizations. It is wider-ranging in subjects and sources, has more directly practical tips for its audience, and covers less online industry news not directly related to actual use of the data than *Database Alert* (Knowledge Industry), *Database Update* (DB Newsletter Associates),

Information Today (Learned Information), or the new *Database End-User* (Meckler Publishing). Joyce Duncan Falk

314. Emergency Librarian, Vol. 1- , No. 1- . Vancouver, British Columbia, Dyad Services, 1973- . bimonthly (October-June). $35.00/yr. ISSN 0315-8888.

Emergency Librarian (*EL*) was founded as a newsletter by Sherrill Cheda and Phyllis Yaffe, who served as co-editors, to provide an alternative channel for addressing youth-service-related library issues not presented in other Canadian journals. In 1979, Carol-Ann and Ken Haycock became joint editors, and in their first issue the Haycocks vowed to continue the tradition of forthrightness and speaking out on issues with the "sole purpose of improving library service for young people with a view to assisting them to realize their potential." Although the concentration on women's and social issues of the early years has disappeared, *EL* continues as "a professional journal for teachers and librarians working with children and young adults in school and public libraries addressing contemporary concerns of the field."

Typically, each issue of *EL* presents between three and five articles to develop a special theme. Recent themes have included library program advocacy and power, youth and the law, research and its implications, children's reading, and information skills in the curriculum. The editors have noted that they wish to strike a balance "between theory that provides a foundation for what we do and the practice that gives us the strategies and tools to do it." They have managed to do just that consistently and well. Articles, aimed at the practicing librarian are well written, well edited, and timely. Writers are encouraged to make their point, even if that point breaks with commonly held assumptions and practices.

A review of the past five years of *EL* reveals that columns have come and gone as ideas have been presented and developed and then have given way to new ideas. Presently, review columns deal with magazines, recordings, and paperbacks for children and young adults and professional materials for librarians and educators. "Noteworthy" provides short descriptions of newer professional resources. Each issue is further supported by five special departments including ongoing discussion of microcomputers in libraries; reports of research studies; and news notes about conferences, workshops, learning resources, and developments in professional associations. A special popular feature that appears with great regularity is a poster suitable for removal and use. Many articles are refereed and all articles and reviews are signed.

In the past few years there have been efforts to internationalize the journal by adding non-Canadians to the advisory board and by publishing material from writers in Ireland, Great Britain, Australia, and the United States. In spite of these efforts, plus the inclusion of United States library news and events and many references to materials published in the States, the thrust of the journal is Canadian. No matter, for the concerns, issues, and trends reported and discussed are universal.

EL is a pleasure to read. The 8½-by-11-inch forty-eight-paged journal is well designed with illustrations, original and reprinted, including cartoons, line-drawings, and whimsey that bring a smile of appreciation for the editors' sense of humor. The content is always pertinent and thought-provoking. Librarians who appreciate *VOYA* will appreciate *EL* for the same type of dynamism, openness, and no-nonsense approach which guides the editors.

Patricia Feehan and Marilyn L. Miller

315. Information Technology and Libraries, Vol. 1- , No. 1- . Chicago, American Library Association, 1982- . quarterly. $25.00/yr.; $12.50/yr. (with membership); $7.50 (single issue). ISSN 0730-9295.

Beginning with volume 1 in 1982, *Information Technology and Libraries* continues the *Journal of Library Automation*, which had a fourteen-volume run from 1968 (volume 1) to 1981 (volume 14). In January 1973, it also absorbed the *JOLA Technical Communications*. It is the official publication of the Library and Information Technology Association (LITA), a division of the American Library Association, but publication of materials in the journal does not constitute official endorsement by either association. Thus, the scope covers all aspects of library and information technology, including such topics as automated bibliographic control, audiovisual techniques, communications technology, cable systems, computerized information processing, data management, facsimile applications, file organization, legal and regulatory matters, library networks, storage and retrieval systems, systems analysis, and video technology. The intended audience is the LITA membership and others interested in the technical applications of technology in libraries.

Typically, each issue contains between four and six refereed feature articles which offer original research, state-of-the-art reviews, or comprehensive and in-depth analyses; a "special section" of descriptive papers on a related topic; brief research reports, technical findings, and application notes; short "reports and working papers"; news and announcements; assigned reviews and lists of recent publications; letters to the editor; and an index to advertisers. The journal's format emphasizes a compact presentation of information with short abstracts for feature articles, section headings, few illustrations, occasional tables, and often extensive citations. The four to six book reviews in each issue are substantive, in-depth, and critically evaluative.

The writing is typically highly technical, thoroughly researched, extensively documented, and clear. The ambitious stated scope of the journal has been met over the years, providing the profession an excellent place to keep up with current technological developments and applications easily.

Danuta A. Nitecki

316. Journal of Education for Library and Information Science, Vol. 1- , No. 1- . State College, Pa., Association for Library and Information Science Education, 1960- . 5 issues/yr. $30.00/yr.; $6.00 (single issue). ISSN 0748-5786.

Celebrating its twenty-fifth anniversary in 1985, *JELIS* (pronounced "jealous") was derived from three earlier publications of the Association for Library and Information Science Education (formerly the Association of American Library Schools): *Report of Meeting, Directory,* and *Newsletter.* Its first editor was Harold Lancour (1960-1964) followed by William A. Katz (1964-1971), Norman Horrocks (1971-1976), Lucille M. Wert (1976-1980), and Charles D. Patterson, the current editor. Throughout the history of the journal Janet Phillips, presently also the executive secretary of the association, has served as its assistant editor.

When first developed by Lancour and other members of the association's Publications Committee (Thelma Eaton and Howard W. Winger), the journal was titled *Journal of Education for Librarianship*, a title it held for its first twenty-five years. *JELIS* continues today as a refereed journal publishing predominantly scholarly papers relevant to library and information science education: papers with quantitative evaluation of teaching methods, state-of-the-art reviews in the field, reports of studies highlighting results and implications, and reports with supporting data on such topics as personnel, student admissions, and retention, placement, and continuing education.

In addition to scholarly papers, the journal includes a section devoted to association activities as well as columns focusing on a variety of areas: Research Record, Teaching Methods (titled "The Visible College"), Continuing Education, and International Library Education.

The journal's fifth issue each year (since 1970) is published as a directory issue. The directory lists all institutional members of the association—listing for each its name, address, and phone number, with date of establishment. All faculty members, including part-time and summer-session faculty are listed giving for each up to five subject areas in which the faculty member holds major interest. The issue also includes a list of faculty members qualified to teach in a foreign language, the present year officers of the association, its bylaws, and its present goal, objectives, and priorities. The directory is available separately for the single copy price of six dollars.

Only one other journal covers the same area as *JELIS: Education for Information*, an international journal on education and training in library and information science. Published by Elsevier Science Publishers B.V. (North Holland), *Education for Information* was first issued in March 1983. This journal is also published quarterly and includes book reviews, a feature not present in *JELIS*. Based upon an analysis of the nine issues available, the journal publishes many of the same authors as does *JELIS*, but has considerably more contributions from non-U.S. and Canadian authors. It remains to be seen whether the publication of this journal will impact the number of articles submitted to *JELIS* each year and subsequently those published in the journal. Informal observations by library and information science educators also indicate that other journals not specifically oriented to education have shown an increasing interest in publishing articles with education themes; e.g., *Special Libraries* or the *Journal of Academic Librarianship*, may be publishing an increasing number of articles specifically oriented to education in their areas. If this is indeed happening, this trend could also affect the nature and perhaps quality of what is published in *JELIS*.

In most studies which attempt to rate journals in library and information science,[1] educators rate *JELIS* as the fifth in terms of importance and prestige. In a field, not known for its outstanding scholarly publications, *JELIS* is one of the most significant of the established scholarly refereed publications in the field.

Notes

[1]For citations to many recent studies, see Charles D. Patterson, "An Assessment of the Status of the Journal," *Journal of Education*

for Library and Information Science 25 (Spring 1985): 301-12.

Jane Robbins-Carter

317. **Library Resources & Technical Services**, Vol. 1- , No. 1- . Chicago, American Library Association, 1957- . bimonthly. $30.00/yr.; $15.00/yr. (Resources & Technical Services Division members); $7.50 (single issue). ISSN 0024-2527.

From its beginning in 1957, *Library Resources & Technical Services* has been more than a house organ for its sponsor the ALA Resources and Technical Services Division. It is a window on the problems and issues facing all aspects of what has traditionally been called "technical services" in libraries. In the first issue a statement appeared that still governs its editorial policy and serves as a concise description of the nature and purpose of the journal. It said, "... the pages will be open to papers and discussions of all topics pertinent to the interests of the Division and its sections, both those general and inclusive in scope and those of specific questions or considerations" (1, no. 1 [1957], 4). *Library Resources & Technical Services* (*LRTS*) was formed from the merger of *Serial Slants* (1950-1957) and the *Journal of Cataloging and Classification* (1948-1957), formerly *News Notes* (1944-1948).

During its almost three decades of service only five editors have been appointed, a fact that can account for its consistent quality and reliability. Esther J. Piercy served from 1957 until her death in 1967. She was followed by Paul Dunkin (1967-1971), Robert Wedgeworth (1971-1973), Wesley Simonton (1973-1979), and the present editor, Elizabeth Tate.

The journal's content varies but mainly consists of articles submitted for editorial consideration dealing with problems or trends in the areas of cataloging and classification, copying and micrography, serials, and acquisitions and collection development. Occasionally a theme issue, designed by the editor, will appear. Besides this, news of the profession and book reviews make up a typical number. There are several noteworthy features, however. One is the annual or biennial reviews of literature in the principal areas covered by the journal. These reviews are not only useful for current practitioners who wish to keep up with the literature and current developments, but also serve as a source for the history of developments in these areas over the past thirty years. Another is the annual reports of the Resources and Technical Services Division and its individual sections—

serials, acquisitions, cataloging and classification, and copying and micrographics. Finally, the text for each conferring of the Margaret Mann Citation and the Esther J. Piercy Award, as well as the recipients' remarks, are presented.

The quality of articles appearing in *LRTS* is high. The type of article ranges from the discursive to the quantitative, but rarely will esoterica or the flamboyant and showy piece be found in the pages of the journal. Criticisms of current practices and trends are also well documented and responsibly written.

Items for the journal are indexed in *Library Literature, Library and Information Science Abstracts, Current Index to Journals in Education, Science Citation Index*, and *Hospital Literature Index*. Its book reviews are recorded in *Book Review Digest, Book Review Index* and *Review of Reviews*. An index to the contents of *LRTS*, volumes 1-25 (1957-1981), prepared by Edward Swanson, was published in volume 25, no. 4 (October/December 1981), pages 411-74.

LRTS has consistently served the profession as a conduit for new ideas, new developments, reflection on the state of the art and quality comment on the issues facing this area of librarianship. In spite of the increase of the number of periodicals published in this subject area over the past ten years, it still remains the best and most comprehensive.

Robert H. Burger

318. **Link-Up: Online and Videotex for Business, Personal, and Educational Use**, Vol. 1- , No. 1- . Medford, N.J., Learned Information, 1984- . monthly. $22.00/yr. (U.S., Canada, and Mexico); $48.00/yr. (other foreign countries).

This relatively new newspaper, initially published by On-Line Communications, is found to have a diverse group of readers. Perusal of two most recent issues reveals articles suited to a variety of needs and tastes. Human interest stories abound and no doubt will offer further insights to readers, from trained intermediary searchers of online systems to consumers investigating the potential of these systems, videotex services, or online information sources of any sort. Among the diverse topics addressed are online searching applications such as looking for the right college or university, microcomputer software packages available to investors, use of bulletin board systems by psychologists, and search services that provide information gathering for investigative purposes. The tabloid also provides current microcomputer product information available on disks, new hardware and software products, new online services, and book, software, and database reviews.

Particularly engrossing to this reader were several articles on "gateway" systems which enable access to a multitude of databases offered by online vendors. One of these, EasyNet, is a relatively new service. The tabloid style lends itself well to browsing, for example in checking illustrations of sample EasyNet searchers. In serving a diverse readership, the newspaper is appropriate to academic, public, and special library collections.

Ray Gerke

319. **Media & Methods**, Vol. 1- , No. 1- . Philadelphia, American Society of Educators, 1965- . bimonthly (September-June). $27.00/yr.; $36.00/yr. (foreign). ISSN 0025-6897.

Media & Methods, aptly subtitled "America's Magazine of the Teaching Technologies," provides practical information and suggests instructional strategies for using all types of media, including books, in the classroom and media center. Each issue contains articles; media reviews; new product information that describes product capabilities and their uses; columns about free materials, funding sources, and successful partnerships between public schools and corporations, universities, and foundations; a calendar of conferences; and sources for educational media and equipment. One issue includes a yearly buyers' guide and directory for media and equipment. Other issues have a guide with directory that focuses on one type of media, such as film, computers, or outstanding educational products. Materials and producers who have made a significant contribution to excellence in education also are identified. Finally, new or changing directions in educational media are covered in special sections or by reports from publishers and producers.

The articles, columns, buyers' guides, and reviews are consistently well written and very useful. The three to five feature articles focus on innovative ways to use media, successful class or student media projects, management of media centers, interviews with authors and other media-related people, and discussions of media issues. Written in an informal style by teachers and media specialists, the articles often tell the reader how to implement a similar project. They also provide helpful charts, checklists, guidelines, and sources of information. The Short Takes column describes current educational media ranging from books and laserdiscs to reports and surveys about media uses. Age and grade levels as well as ordering information are included. Other columns report changes in equipment, services, materials, publishers, and academic programs.

Each issue contains from ten to twenty signed reviews of media including film, video, filmstrips, recordings, books, and software. Ordering information is provided. The reviews are written by teachers, library media specialists, and other experts in the media being reviewed. Reviewers summarize the content, indicate the audience, describe uses for the media, comment on the technical quality, and state an overall evaluation. Between four and seven books for students are reviewed. An introduction to the reviews summarizes the themes or explains the purpose of the books. Occasionally, books for educators also are reviewed. The reviews of computer software list required equipment.

Begun in 1965, *Media & Methods* continues to emphasize new and innovative ways teachers, librarians, and media specialists from elementary through high school level can use audiovisual materials, books, and other media. The journal has maintained a high level of quality and usefulness, adding sections and changing focus in response to teacher needs. Although similar to *A V Guide* and *TechTrends, Media & Methods* is still the basic resource for those who want to know more about media and changing directions and about how to use media in the classroom, and want reliable reviews of all types of media.　　　Mary Lou Mosley

320. Microcomputers for Information Management: An International Journal for Library and Information Services, Vol. 1- , No. 1- . Norwood, N.J., Ablex Publishing, 1984- . quarterly. $28.50/yr.; $59.50/yr. (institutions); (add $8.50 for foreign orders). ISSN 0742-2342.

This journal is an excellent addition to the limited number of quality resources available to the library and information science professional. It covers a variety of topics related to microcomputer applications in the United States and abroad.

Each issue usually contains the abstracts and texts of five major articles on topics involving microcomputers and communications, database systems, online search, management, networks, etc., for library and information system specialists. In addition to the main articles, there is an introductory editorial by Ching-chih Chen, the editor; a section called "Microwatch" which provides information on new developments; and a biographical section about contributing authors. Guidelines for contributors, a table of contents, and notices of forthcoming books in the field are also included.

This journal will be of great use to professionals who desire to stay abreast of new and current developments dealing with micro-

computer technology in the library and information services areas.　　　Bill J. Corbin

321. Small Computers in Libraries, Vol. 1- , No. 1- . Westport, Conn., Meckler Publishing, 1981- . monthly (July/August, bimonthly). $20.00/yr.; $24.00/yr. (institutions). ISSN 0275-6722.

SCIL is a small (ten-to-twelve-page), newsletter-style publication aimed at the librarian interested in practical applications of microcomputers to library management and service situations. Originally (through 1984) edited by Allan Pratt and published at the Graduate Library School, University of Arizona, *SCIL* remains the same in format and focus. Issues contain mostly short news items on applications in particular settings, developments and availability of hardware/software, and sources of information relating to microcomputers and the library field. In addition, each issue usually includes one in-depth article, frequently written by a practitioner, explaining a specific implementation (e.g., a microcomputer in a microsized library, microcomputer aids for the visually handicapped, new technology for library micros).

Similar information can be gained from more general library or computer periodicals (e.g., *Library Journal, Personal Computing*), as well as from more extensive tools dealing with the use of computers in library and information settings (e.g., *Microcomputers for Information Management* and Meckler's own *Library Software Review*). *M300 and PC Report* (also published by Meckler) is similar to *SCIL* in approach, audience, and price. Since its area of concern (the specific use of the IBM PC and OCLC M300 workstation) is also of interest to *SCIL* readers, the two publications could easily be combined.

Although *SCIL* does offer a quick look at current developments, it is not recommended as the sole source of information for the librarian interested in the topic.

　　　Michael B. Eisenberg

REGIONAL

322. Minnesota Libraries, Vol. 1- , No. 1- . St. Paul, Minn., Office of Library Development and Services, Department of Education, 1904- . quarterly. free. ISSN 0026-5551.

The first volume of this journal was published in December 1904 as *Library Notes and News*; the title changed to *Minnesota Libraries* in volume 13, no. 1, March 1940.

The journal is offered free to all Minnesota libraries and on exchange to out-of-state and out-of-nation libraries. As the official state library journal, it contains articles of interest, state mandates, and legislative summaries for all types of libraries. Its major focus, however, is public libraries; it produces articles of general interest to the library profession. Items appearing annually are the "Minnesota Plan for Long Range Services," "Minnesota Public Library Statistics," and the "Directory of Public Libraries in Minnesota."

While published for Minnesota library personnel, it has excellent articles, often reprints of speeches, that have significance for other areas of the country as well. Its inclusion of information on special libraries, such as the Hill Monastic Manuscript Library and the James J. Hill Library, are noteworthy. The statistical and planning information can be extremely useful for comparison purposes and for use in planning. The articles have current interest and are well written.

Minnesota Libraries is indexed in *Library Literature* and *Library and Information Science Abstracts*; it also has its own index in the last issue of each volume or in early issues of following volumes.　　　　　Wesley Simonton

323. **OLA Bulletin**, Vol. 1- , No. 1- . Columbus, Ohio, Ohio Library Association, 1932- . 3 issues/yr. free (with OLA membership); $10.00/yr. (students, retired and lay members). ISSN 0029-7135.

OLA Bulletin, edited by Martha S. Alt, is the official publication of the Ohio Library Association. Its first issue was published in May 1932 under the title *Ohio Library Association News Bulletin* which was changed in spring of 1984 to *OLA Bulletin* (*OLAB*). Prior to 1950, each OLA president was responsible for editing this bulletin. The major objective of the *OLA Bulletin* is to provide information on OLA activities as well as on various professional issues facing libraries and librarians in Ohio. Sometimes separate issues of *OLAB* are devoted to special topics (e.g., "Building on Our Heritage" [vol. 46, no. 4, 1976], "Total Communication for the Handicapped" [vol. 49, no. 5, 1979], "Libraries: Learning for Life" [vol. 55, no. 1, 1985]).

A typical issue begins with an editorial focused on some timely library issue. It is followed by a number of rather short articles (average size between two and three pages) pertaining to OLA activities and/or various library topics (recent examples include "Video for Small Libraries," "Conservation of Library Materials," "Your Automated System: What to Do When It Dies," "A Brief Look at Turnover in Public Libraries"). *OLAB* issues include black-and-white photographs and/or other graphic materials, as well as publishers' announcements.

OLA Bulletin is not a research-oriented periodical—in this respect it is similar to other serials published by various state library associations. The quality of articles varies: some are documented (although the source base and references to professional literature usually are limited); some are not. In general, the articles are descriptive, brief, and informative.

The format and physical features of the bulletin are very good and appealing to the general reader. In 1982 a cumulative index (*OLA Bulletin Fifty Years Index*) was published covering the years 1931 to 1980 and providing author and subject access to fifty volumes of the bulletin. In the future, the editor of this serial may wish to take into consideration the following suggestions: upgrading the articles so that they are more research oriented; and introducing separate review and bibliographic "OHIOANA" sections, which would increase the professional respectability of this official OLA serial. Since OLA publishes the *Ohio Libraries Newsletter* (vol. 1- . 1970-), some materials from *OLAB* pertaining to the association's activity may be published in this newsletter. Thus, *OLA Bulletin* may gain some space for expanding its content and scope. *OLA Bulletin* is indexed in *Library Literature*.

Lubomyr R. Wynar

324. **Texas Library Journal**, Vol. 1- , No. 1- . Austin, Tex., Texas Library Association, 1924- . quarterly. $12.00/yr.; $4.00/yr. (members); $4.00 (single issue). ISSN 0040-4446.

Beginning as a four-page, single-fold news bulletin, the official organ of the Texas Library Association (TLA) has evolved with the profession within the state into a professional journal that maintains its unique identification with the needs of Texas librarians. From 1924 through 1931 the periodical focused on news and other material of interest primarily to public and school librarians and was edited by the TLA president usually drawn from these ranks. An editorial board oversaw *News Notes* from 1932 through 1949 and the content came to include more substantive articles and a greater number of academic library contributors. Assuming its present name in 1950, the *Texas Library Journal* began a period of more scholarly interest and the leadership shifted to an appointed editor, now usually affiliated with a university library or library school. The editor with the longest tenure during this period was Mary Pound (1965-1975) who was associated with the University of Texas at Austin General Libraries. After 1975, a succession of editors experimented with the form and content until mid-1982 when Jay Martin Poole, then of Texas A & M University Library, restyled the periodical and set it on its current course, a course that continues, following his departure in 1985. A new editor will be named in spring 1986.

The current format has returned to the commentary mode, without the news orientation, of an earlier era, but with sophistication and flair derived from the present. The 6-by-9-inch, thirty-six-to-forty-page, double-columned format is handsomely styled and each volume reproduces on the cover and throughout line-drawings from illustrations of notable Texas books. Besides the editorial, commentary, and letters sections, there are currently a dozen or so regular columns, each between two and four pages in length and each planned (if not actually written) by a contributing editor. These cover association news, automation, books and publishing, collections, grants, information/reference, intellectual freedom, legislation, management, oral history, public relations, and user education. Occasional feature articles and new columns allow for some development. Not trying to compete with material appearing in the proliferated professional literature of general and specialized journals, these brief essays and reports cut across type of library lines and provide a variety of contributions that have stimulated professional writing throughout the state. The straightforward arrangement avoids lengthy and documented articles, book reviews per se, or news items (aside from those of major import to the association). Some have felt that the format has been too rigid and that column editors are forced to fill space at times. Others lament the lack of complete coverage of TLA business, news, and information—though much of that now appears in the monthly news sheet *TLA/CAST* and the *TLA Membership Directory*. Nevertheless, the experiment has resulted in some lively writing on a breadth of topics by a diverse group of contributors. *TLJ* is clearly aimed at delivery of information to the widest cross-section of Texas librarians and appears to be succeeding reasonably well for its four thousand subscribers. A special sesquicentennial issue, to be produced in March 1986, will focus on the influence of libraries on the cultural life of Texas. What modifications the new editor will make are not known.

Donald G. Davis, Jr.

325. **Wisconsin Library Bulletin**, Vol. 1- , No. 1- . Madison, Wis., Division for Library Services, Department of Public Instruction, 1905- . quarterly. free. ISSN 0043-6526.

Designed to be a periodical containing issues of statewide concern, this *Wisconsin Library Bulletin* (*WLB*) has a history of presenting both collections of articles under the umbrella of a central theme, and informative topics such as the Wisconsin Long-Range Plan for Library Services.

A sampling of theme issues over the years includes "Rural Wisconsin and Education" (1946), "Library Education and Training, Library Buildings and Facilities" (1967), "New Concepts in Audiovisual Services" (1972), "Larger Units of Service, Legislation: Boon or Blow" (1974), and "Alternative Funds" (1980). *WLB* has also included Wisconsin Library Association (WLA) news and conference reports.

The *WLB* appeared bimonthly until 1980. In 1981, beginning with volume 77, the *Bulletin* became a quarterly, and the previous subscription rate of $7.50 was dropped. In 1981, the size changed from 5-by-8-inches to the present 8½-by-11-inches. The *Bulletin* was originally published by the Wisconsin Free Library Commission. For many years, the *Bulletin* was part of the membership package of the Wisconsin Library Association, but this connection was severed in the 1970s.

Since the Wisconsin Library Association is now beginning to produce its own journal, the Division for Library Services decided to discontinue that forum. The Division is also encouraging the WLA journal effort because the tightening of federal funds has mandated that the Division set priorities as to how LSCA monies are to be allocated. The result is that the Division has felt it appropriate to bow out of the journal business and defer to the fledgling *WLA Journal*.

WLB has been an integral communication link in the Wisconsin library community for many years. It was intended for the professional audience and the writing has been thorough and competent. The recent format has been visually pleasing and the typeface easy to read. *WLB* has been a well-respected periodical and, to many members of the profession, will be a significant loss when it ceases publication with the next issue.

Darlene E. Weingand

DATABASES

326. **Library & Information Science Abstracts (LISA).** Vendor: Dialog ($75.00/connect hr.; $0.25/full record); SDC ($75.00/connect hr.; $0.25/full record). Coverage: 1969 to present. updated monthly. 71,000 records as of October 1985.

The LISA database corresponds to two printed indexes published by the Library Association: *Library & Information Science Abstracts* (*LISA*), and *Current Research in Library & Information Science*. The records in the *LISA* portion of the database date back to

1969 while those from *Current Research* go back to 1981. About 500 *LISA* records are added to the database every month and about 350 *Current Research* records are added quarterly.

Dialog and SDC offer the same version of the database and charge the same for connect time and for offline prints. Searchers can order a database chapter from either vendor and a user manual from Learned Information (P.O. Box 8, Abingdon, Oxford OX13 6EG, England).

The major part of the database consists of references on library and information science while a smaller part includes material on related fields such as publishing, bookselling, printing, and writing. The citations in the database are primarily to journal articles but books, conference proceedings, theses, research projects, and technical reports account for about 18 percent of the file. LISA is international in scope drawing material from about 60 countries in 34 different languages. About 550 journals are scanned (not indexed) for relevant articles for inclusion in the database.

A nice feature of the database, as well as the printed index, is that regardless of the language of the original document, titles and abstracts are in English. This is not true of all databases. The *MLA Bibliography*, for example, does not translate titles making free text searching difficult.

Records in the database are assigned anywhere from two to eighteen descriptors. The policy of assigning such a large number of subject headings to one citation can sometimes cause problems for the searcher. For example, a four-page article that appeared in *College & Research Libraries* in 1978 was assigned sixteen subject headings. The article described a study in which citation analysis was applied by a university library to its masters' theses in engineering. The study led to the library's decision to reduce the number of its journal subscriptions in favor of purchasing more books. Probably three or four descriptors are all that are necessary to access this reference. More than this leads the searcher to irrelevant results. The usefulness of some of the assigned descriptors—"Funds," "Finance," "Budgets," "Purchasing"—are questionable.

Searching LISA via the computer is not only faster than looking through the printed indexes but often identifies more references on the same topic. A search for material on the Canada Institute for Scientific and Technical Information (CISTI) produced nineteen references through the computer but only fifteen references in the printed indexes. The four references that were not found in the print version were not listed under "Canada Institute

for Scientific and Technical Information" or under "CISTI" in the name or subject indexes. The computer retrieved them because "CISTI" appeared in the abstract of each of the four records. Abstracts, by the way, are included in all LISA records back to 1976. Some other ways the database can be searched, making it superior to the print version in producing more relevant and precise results, are by journal name, corporate source, and language. Citations from the *Current Research* portion of the database are tagged and can be isolated (or eliminated) when searching the database.

Some mention should be made of *Library Literature*, which recently became available on WilsonLine. Although *LISA* and *Library Literature* index many of the same journals, the former indexes (or at least scans) quite a few more. LISA has two advantages over *Library Literature* at this time. LISA has abstracts and is retrospective to 1969. The *Library Literature* database only goes back to October 1984. Search results, consequently, tend to be quite small because of the limited time coverage. In several years the *Library Literature* database will be a lot more useful.

LISA is a worthwhile database that is recommended to all librarians interested in their profession.   Brenda Coven

327. **Library Literature (LIB)**. H. W. Wilson. Vendor: H. W. Wilson WILSONLINE. ($45.00 -$20.00/hr., depending on subscription). Coverage: October 1984 to present. updated biweekly. 11,000 records as of November 1985.

Since Wilson has decided to make its online databases available only on its proprietary WILSONLINE retrieval system, a review of *Library Literature* online must also incorporate review of the system.

Document coverage is identical to that of the printed version which includes 185 "key" periodicals in library and information science, plus relevant articles covered in other Wilson indexes, plus books, pamphlets, microforms, library school theses, and government publications. Although language coverage is primarily English, other major European languages are present, with language of original noted, and an English translation of the title provided.

Type of material covered is especially broad, excluding only announcements of meetings, advertisements, microforms also available in print, and article abstracts where the full article is covered in another Wilson index. In addition to being provided for journal articles, full monographs, analytics, and book reviews, indexing is provided for charts and graphs, "significant" letters to the editor, obituaries, appointment notices, and similar material. Thanks to the design of WILSON-LINE, each of these items is directly retrievable, a most useful feature, at least when the database grows.

Entries follow the expected format of the printed index, with the addition of subject and format descriptors and similar special features, such as language. A potentially useful feature is the indication, and indexing, of such features as portraits, bibliographies, maps, floor plans, and the like. Thus, it is theoretically possible to search for architectural plans which illustrate the location of online public access catalogs. As the file grows, this ability will become more important.

Subject and name indexing are based on Wilson's own authority list, consisting of terms from the literature, other Wilson indexes, and LC subject headings. Unfortunately, the index is available only online at this time, forcing the user either to spend extra money online, or have access to the printed *Library Literature*. Given the amount of planning which went into the system, this lack is rather surprising.

Use of the online authority list, fortunately, is quite easy. All terms (except a small stopword list) appear both in the "basic index" and in the appropriately tagged indexes. By use of the **neighbor** command, the user may either see a particular index, or all occurrences of the term, as desired. Subject terms can be expanded to their related terms either directly, or from the "neighbor" display. Relations include use of the term as a subheading.

Another useful feature is the presence of cross-references in the system. If the term has been added, a user can search on the invalid term, and receive both a message giving the correct term, and the postings under that term. Were the list of invalid terms larger, this could be a most useful feature, not present on most systems.

Use of the **expand** command, of course, can be confusing to one used to other systems, such as DIALOG. This problem is partly overcome with WILSONLINE's **Rename**, which, unfortunately, must be re-done with each logon.

One last subject feature of the system worth noting is the presence of full pre-coordinated subject heading strings (e.g., "Catalogs,online—user education—congresses"). In theory, one can use this full string to limit searching to quite specific topics. Whether this is more effective than "anding" subject headings remains to be seen, especially in view of the need to type rather long strings in order to use this feature.

Since WILSONLINE is a new system, evaluation of training and support must be tentative. At present, the firm has provided a number of training sessions on the system, but relatively little for specific databases. Printed aids include a "Quick Reference Guide" and a "Tutorial" as well as a large system manual. Specific aids for *Library Literature*, as for the other databases, include only a few pages in the general system manual. (As of the date of this review, these pages were not available to the public, and were seen by the reviewer in draft form only.) In general, such aids are reasonably well done, but some errors are still to be found. Fortunately, the toll-free help service works well.

Output can be tailored to one's specific desires, both on- and off-line, a very useful feature. The searcher can choose both the elements to appear, and the order of their appearance. Unfortunately, printing from this file is also the biggest frustration of the system: The print qualifiers are not the same as the search qualifiers (e.g., "SU" to search a subject, but "SUB" to print the term), a needless complication. And, regardless of what the command states, the system prints out only a few online records at a time, then pauses to ask if the user really meant the command. This feature forces continued close attention to the terminal, to avoid running up high online bills, a truly pointless waste of time.

One very useful feature is the ability to search several WILSONLINE files at the same time, with one search strategy. This permits one to save entry time, and obtain the results all at once.

The major competitor, of course, is LISA (*Library and Information Science Abstracts*), available on Dialog and SDC. LISA begins coverage in 1969, includes abstracts from 1976, and has better non-North American coverage, as well as the advantage of being available on the larger database vendor systems. However, *Library Literature* is not only updated faster, with more records, but has much greater depth of coverage for the items indexed, as well as greater depth of retrieval. At the present, LISA definitely has the size/date coverage advantage. Over time, especially if Wilson changes its policy on allowing "outside" vendors to carry *Library Literature*, it will become a most useful tool, particularly for the library, as opposed to information science, community.

James H. Sweetland

Part IV
ABSTRACTS OF LIBRARY SCIENCE
DISSERTATIONS

Abstracts of Library Science
Dissertations by Gail A. Schlachter

INTRODUCTION

Unlike the commercially produced monographs, reference books, and journals described elsewhere in this edition of *Library Science Annual*, doctoral dissertations are cloaked by fragmented and sluggish bibliographic announcements and distribution channels. While it is possible to contact library schools at the end of each year to identify dissertations completed there during that year, the only way to learn about dissertations dealing with library and library-related topics that were prepared outside of library schools is to wait until they are listed in *Dissertation Abstracts International* (*DAI*). However, dissertations completed in the third and fourth quarter of one year are frequently not included in *DAI* until the third or fourth quarter of the next year. As a result, it was impossible to review dissertations completed in 1985 and meet the manuscript submission date for this edition of *Library Science Annual*. Thus, this volume provides a review of the 1984 dissertations and, similarly, each subsequent volume will cover dissertations completed in a previous year.

To date, 120 library and library-related dissertations completed in 1984 have been identified. To place those doctoral studies in perspective, the following quantitative profile is modeled after the statistical analysis provided in Schlachter and Thomison's *Library Science Dissertations, 1925-1972: An Annotated Bibliography* (Libraries Unlimited, 1974) and *Library Science Dissertations, 1973-1981: An Annotated Bibliography* (Libraries Unlimited, 1982).

Completion Data

On the average, 14 dissertations were completed each year between 1925 and 1972. From 1973 through 1981, the yearly average increased 800 percent, to 111 dissertations per year. The number of dissertations completed in 1984 (120) was up from the 1972 to 1981 yearly average, and more than the 1983 total of 102 reported in volume 1 of *LSA*.

Sponsoring Schools

The 120 dissertations reviewed for this edition of the *Annual* were completed at 45 private and public institutions of higher learning in the United States and Canada, about one-third the number of schools involved in the total production of library and library-related dissertations between 1973 and 1981. The six "top" producing universities, responsible for nearly 40 percent of the doctoral studies reviewed for 1984, are University of Illinois (9 percent), Case Western Reserve University (8 percent), University of Pittsburgh (6 percent), University of Michigan (6 percent), Drexel University (5 percent), and Rutgers University (5 percent). Only Case Western Reserve University, University of Pittsburgh, and Rutgers University were also listed as top producers in this section of the *Library Science Annual* analysis last year.

Degrees Received

Following the pattern set between 1925 and 1981, the Ph.D. remained the most commonly earned degree (83 percent) in 1984, followed by the Ed.D. (14 percent), and the D.L.S. (3 percent). Although in past years other degrees (e.g., D.L.A., D.Ed., D.B.A.) were also represented in the dissertations reviewed, to date none of these have been reported for studies completed in 1984.

Methodology Employed

As in the analyses reported by Schlachter and Thomison in the two volumes of *Library Science Dissertations*, each of the 120 dissertations completed in 1984 was placed into one of seven research categories: citation/content analysis, experimental design, theoretical treatment, operations research (systems analysis and all forms of information storage and retrieval), survey research (case studies, mailed questionnaires, interviews), historical analysis (including biographies and bibliographies), and other (including those dissertations for which insufficient information was available to determine methodology employed). The ranking of research methodologies employed in the 120 dissertations completed during 1984, from most to least used, is survey research (58 percent), operations research (13 percent), citation/content analysis (10 percent), historical analysis (7 percent), experimental design (7 percent), theoretical treatment (4 percent), and other (1 percent). This ranking of methodologies differs somewhat from the rankings reported in this section of *Library Science Annual* last year. While survey research continued to be the most commonly applied methodology in 1984, more attention was paid to operations research and slightly less to citation/content analysis, historical analysis, and experimental design.

Sex

Although women have consistently constituted the majority of practicing librarians, they authored only a minority of library and library-related dissertations from 1925 to 1979. It was not until 1980 (and again in 1981) that women were responsible for over half of the dissertations completed. This situation was reversed, however, in 1983 and 1984, when only 45 percent and 46 percent of the dissertations reviewed for those years, respectively, were written by women.

Summary

Using the results of this quantitative analysis, it is possible to develop a profile of the library science dissertation completed in 1984. As in the preceding 50-year period, the typical dissertation continued to be written for the Ph.D. degree by a male using survey research methods at one of a handful of major universities in the United States.

Because of space limitations, it is not possible to describe each of the 120 dissertations covering library and library-related topics that was completed in 1984. Instead, 50 of these dissertations — chosen because of their quality, interest, relevance, or representativeness — are abstracted below.

ABSTRACTS

328. Aguilar, William (Ph.D., University of Illinois at Urbana-Champaign, 1984). **Relationship between Classes of Books Circulated and Classes of Books Requested on Interlibrary Loan.** 156p. Order no. DA8409739.

PURPOSE: This study examined the relationships among subject classes, relative use, and interlibrary loan by testing the hypothesis that libraries are least likely to borrow materials in underused classes and most likely to borrow in overused classes.

PROCEDURE: Aguilar examined nearly two million monographic circulation transactions (including over eighty-five thousand interlibrary loans) at eighteen Illinois Library Computer System (LCS) libraries between July 1980 and December 1981. He divided the holdings of each participating library into thirty-three subject categories and reviewed over five hundred subject classes. Relationships in the data collected were studied by using five statistical tests: Chi-square, t-test, Kendall's Tau, Spearman's rank correlation, and Pearson's product moment correlation.

FINDINGS: Underused subject classes placed less demand on interlibrary loan than "normal use" or overused classes. The converse was also documented.

CONCLUSIONS: The purchase of materials in overused subject classes is justified, but the acquisition of additional materials in underused areas is questionable.

329. Alire, Camila Ann (Ed.D., University of Northern Colorado, 1984). **A Nationwide Survey of Education Doctoral Students' Attitudes Regarding the Importance of the Library and the Need for Bibliographic Instruction.** 159p. Order no. DA8411459.

PURPOSE: In this dissertation, Alire focused on four aspects: (1) education doctoral students' attitudes toward the library, (2) their views on the importance of library use and knowledge, (3) their assessment of their own ability to use the library and its resources for extensive literature searches, and (4) their knowledge of library research methodology and their interest in making bibliographic instruction an elective or required course on the graduate level.

PROCEDURE: Questionnaires were sent to a proportional stratified sample of education doctoral students.

FINDINGS: The majority of students surveyed thought that knowledge of the library and its resources was important to academic success, that library usage was important to academic success, that they were deficient in their knowledge of library research methodology, that bibliographic instruction was needed, that such a course should be required on the graduate level, and that they would take such a course even as an elective.

330. Badran, Odette Maroun (Ph.D., Case Western Reserve University, 1984). **A Probabilistic Approach to Information Retrieval.** 238p. Order no. DA8414067.

PURPOSE: In an attempt to identify techniques that could filter irrelevant references from the output of Boolean searches, Badran examined Disjoint Inter-Communication Classes, Communication Chains (both based on the Indirect Method developed by William G. Goffman), and Normalized Symmetric Difference (a special case of the Indirect Method suggested by C. J. Van Rijsbergen).

PROCEDURE: An experimental approach was used to test the effectiveness of the three filter techniques and the effectiveness of three modes of content representation: bibliographic coupling, co-citation, and title keywords. These techniques and modes were evaluated on the basis of recall, precision, and a composite measure of effectiveness.

FINDINGS: Badran found that co-citation and Disjoint Inter-Communication Classes produced the best results; when used in conjunction with Boolean searching, they improved output by reducing the retrieval of irrelevant references.

331. Banks, Julia Ann (Ph.D., North Texas State University, 1984). **The Effects of Extended Loan Period, Released Time, and Incentive Pay on Increasing Shelving and Shelf-Reading Productivity of Student Assistants in Academic Libraries.** 204p. Order no. DA8414084.

PURPOSE: The purpose of this study was to determine if the productivity of student assistants in the circulation departments of academic libraries could be affected by the following three factors: extended loan period, released time, or incentive pay.

PROCEDURE: Banks used two questionnaires to collect data for this study. One was sent to forty private university libraries throughout Texas to identify libraries effectively using similar motivational techniques. The other was sent to forty-nine student assistants working in the circulation departments of Abilene Christian University (the control group), Bishop College, Dallas Baptist College, Southwestern Baptist Theological Seminary, and Texas Christian University, to poll their feelings about shelving, shelf reading, and the motivational techniques covered in this study. In addition, two quasi-experimental studies were conducted: the first to determine the motivational value of loan, time, and pay given across the board; the second to measure the motivational effect of pay tied to productivity for student assistants (the study group was taken from the Texas Christian University's circulation department).

FINDINGS: While motivators did not produce greater shelving productivity at Bishop College or at Texas Christian University, extended loan and pay given across the board proved to be effective at Southwestern Baptist Theological Seminary. Pay was an effective motivator for shelf reading at Texas Christian University (the only institution in the study that had completed enough data on this topic for interpretation). The motivators most liked by student assistants did not necessarily correlate with productivity but they did with job satisfaction.

CONCLUSIONS: Pay tied to productivity, which influenced shelving but not shelf-reading behaviors, proved to be the most effective motivator.

332. Baughman, Steven Alan (Ph.D., Florida State University, 1984). **The Role of Academic Library Administrators in Academic Library Consortia: A Study of Perceptions.** 142p. Order no. DA8505284.

PURPOSE: This study was conducted to describe the role of academic library directors in academic library consortia and to assess the impact their participation had on their work setting and their own work.

PROCEDURE: Academic library directors participating in academic library consortia formed the population for this study. Data were collected on such dependent variables as participation benefits, participation problems and costs, and effects of budget constraints. Among the independent variables studied were consortium governance, consortium administration, sizes and types of institutions participating, and control status of the institutions.

FINDINGS: Library administrators tended to be responsible for consortium governance, a responsibility they did not view as burdensome. Areas benefiting from consortium participation included interlibrary loan (the major area), circulation, and reference. The costs associated with consortium participation were not viewed as heavy. While funding was sometimes mentioned as an area of concern, no major problem areas were identified by the library administrators studied. Participants agreed that communication skills were an important asset in a consortium setting.

333.   Blue, Richard Irving (Ph.D., University of Illinois at Urbana-Champaign, 1984). **Content Duplication among Documents on Specific Subjects.** 247p. Order no. DA8409749.

PURPOSE: This study was conducted to determine how the duplication of textual content in medical documents varied over time.

PROCEDURE: Sets of documents on the same specific medical subjects were selected through MEDLINE searches and formed the study group in this investigation. Blue performed text analysis on these documents (duplication of sentence segments was used to indicate duplication of content between two documents) and used the results to compare two measures of document overlap: sentence segment duplication and interdocument duplication of index terms (described earlier by Cleverdon and Kidd).

FINDINGS: Current documents were more likely to contain duplicated sentence segments than were older documents. More variability was found in the text overlap measure than in the duplication of index terms measure.

CONCLUSIONS: In many ways, the results of this study were inconclusive. However, it appeared that textual content duplication was more discerning than interdocument duplication of index terms.

334.   Cameron, Ulysses (Ed.D., Virginia Polytechnic Institute and State University, 1984). **The Application of Human Resources Planning to the University of the District of Columbia Library.** 269p. Order no. DA8500904.

PURPOSE: This study represents one of the first doctoral attempts to apply human resources planning to libraries; in it, Cameron uses various processes to calculate the human resources needed at a medium-sized multimedia library.

PROCEDURE: Using the library at the University of the District of Columbia as the test site, Cameron employed William Castetter's human resource planning process to forecast the human resources needed during the next five years.

FINDINGS: Models similar to Castetter's will need to be modified to be used systematically to conduct human resources planning in academic libraries.

CONCLUSIONS: Human resources planning is most effective when done on a continuous basis and updated frequently.

335.   Casserly, Mary Frances (Ph.D., Rutgers University, 1984). **Self-Study and Planned Change in Academic Libraries: A Case Study Analysis of Regional Accreditation Self-Study Experiences.** 249p. Order no. DA8411555.

PURPOSE: This study was designed (1) to examine planned change processes in academic libraries (focusing on the self-study technique) and (2) to prepare recommendations for their improvement.

PROCEDURE: Data were collected through questionnaires and interview schedules based on Kells's Desired Attributes of Self-Study and Lindquist's Adaptive Development Model of planned change. In addition, document analysis was used to study the regional accreditation-related self-studies conducted at four academic libraries.

FINDINGS: Casserly found that successful self-study processes utilized activity factors (participation openness, focus on goals and effectiveness, and use of client and expert opinion), organizational factors (past experiences with self-study and planning processes, timing, and group self-perception), and approach factors (commitment, leaders, design, and motivation). Further, she determined that successful sites involved users and/or experts in the preparation of needed reports. Successful self-study was not found to relate to classes of evaluation addressed; specific resources, capabilities, products, or services addressed; number of assessment measures included; or extent to which the accrediting association standards were addressed. Self-studies tended to be descriptive and to focus on library processes. For quantitative assessments of library activities, annual reports proved to be a richer source.

CONCLUSIONS: Successful self-studies in academic libraries can be described in terms of changes, improvements, organizational benefits, and personal benefits. Many of the outcomes proposed in the Kells and Lindquist models were not realized at the sites studied.

RECOMMENDATIONS: Approach and planning factors, user and/or expert opinion, organizational factors, evaluation team training, and accreditation standards providing guidance in assessing effectiveness should be emphasized. There is a need for the development of a useful general theory of planned change.

336. Christovao, Heloisa Tardin (Ph.D., Drexel University, 1984). **The Aging of the Literature of Biomedical Sciences in Developed and Underdeveloped Countries.** 161p. Order no. DA8404023.

PURPOSE: The purpose of this study was to determine if differences existed between developed and underdeveloped countries in terms of the communication patterns and the time it takes to evaluate the scientific literature.

PROCEDURE: To conduct the investigation, Christovao developed a method of displaying patterns of communication among regions and changes over time in the use made of scientific literature. The method, based on the identification of documents published by developed and underdeveloped countries and the analysis of references contained in them, involved the selection of samples from *Cumulated Index Medicus, 1979* for each of three different biomedical sciences topics: DNA, arrhythmia, and schistosomiasis. The sampled documents and their references were analyzed on the basis of language, date of publication, place of publication, level of collaboration, and subheadings.

FINDINGS: The literature of "international" areas of science aged similarly in developed and underdeveloped nations. "Local" areas of the literature aged slower in underdeveloped countries than in developed countries. Underdeveloped nations cited the literature of developed nations more than their own literature. The center-periphery model applied to communication patterns among regions, at least as measured by publication level.

CONCLUSIONS: Underdeveloped nations are scientifically peripheral to developed nations, have unique problems in local informal and formal communication, should develop their own science policy studies, and should emphasize research relating to their own scientific communication systems. Further research should be conducted to determine the role of journals published by underdeveloped countries and the manner in which they participate in the integrative and evaluative processes of science.

337. Connors, Maureen (Ed.D., Boston University, 1984). **The Superintendent's Perception of the School Library Media Center.** 220p. Order no. DA8414682.

PURPOSE: This study was designed to identify Massachusetts superintendents' attitudes toward their school library media centers and the way in which these attitudes fostered or inhibited media center growth in their systems.

PROCEDURE: The study utilized both questionnaires (sent to 238 Massachusetts superintendents) and interviews (of eighteen randomly selected library media specialists).

FINDINGS: Many superintendents viewed library media specialists as absolutely necessary, although one-quarter of the respondents saw media specialists as a luxury. The majority (75 percent) believed teachers would notice if the media center closed and would have to change their teaching approach. The cuts reported of media center specialists were not so great as anticipated; the greatest cuts occurred in the middle schools (17 percent reduction).

CONCLUSIONS: The overall school library media center picture in Massachusetts looked encouraging. The superintendents' attitudes towards media centers were generally positive. The greatest area of concern centered around the impact media specialists could make on the instructional program. It may be that the media specialist's background is too general or limited to make the necessary impact.

338. Davis, Hiram Logan (Ph.D., University of Michigan, 1984). **An Analysis of the Relationship between Actual and Preferred Library Goals Based on the Perceptions of Academic Librarians.** 264p. Order no. DA8502790.

PURPOSE: Using the theory employed by Gross and Grambusch in their study of university goals, Davis examined the relationship between actual and preferred goals as perceived by academic librarians.

PROCEDURE: Davis sent a questionnaire consisting of thirty-five goals (sixteen output goals and nineteen support goals) to 336 academic librarians at twenty-six Ph.D. degree-granting universities (70 percent response rate).

FINDINGS: Academic librarians perceived that output goals were being pursued over support goals. Perceptions of actual and preferred goals differed on the basis of librarian position and responsibility. The librarians studied preferred traditional goals (i.e., library mission/service related output goals) less than management or other support-related goals. Librarians' perceptions of actual and preferred goals were not influenced by type of academic library, years of experience, or physical characteristics.

CONCLUSIONS: Davis developed a theoretical model to assist academic librarians in identifying goals related to service requirements, library resource development, educational objectives, technological change, and other areas.

339. DeCoster, Barbara Lou (Ph.D., University of Texas at Austin, 1984). **A Comparative Study of OCLC, Inc. and the Washington Library Network in Twenty-Nine Pacific Northwest Academic Libraries.** 421p. Order no. DA8513207.

PURPOSE: This study was conducted to compare OCLC and the Washington Library Network (WLN) on the basis of perceived usefulness and user satisfaction.

PROCEDURE: Questionnaires were sent to 202 academic librarians at twenty-nine libraries in the Pacific Northwest that were members of either OCLC or WLN (77 percent response rate). As part of the survey, participants were asked to use a five-point Likert-type scale to indicate their satisfaction with twenty-one aspects of their bibliographic databases and their views on the usefulness of twenty-four database capabilities (regardless of whether or not they were available on their bibliographic database).

FINDINGS: WLN librarians were more satisfied with their bibliographic database than were OCLC librarians. When asked about usefulness, WLN librarians valued the abilities to order materials online from vendors and to perform title keyword searches while OCLC librarians valued the abilities to perform interlibrary loan transactions online and to limit searches by date or format. The ratings differed by employment categories, however. Administrative librarians were most satisfied with the use of personnel and system trouble shooting; technical services librarians were most satisfied with update training and the input and edit of Library of Congress records. Both OCLC and WLN librarians indicated that the most important factors considered in the process of deciding which database to join were improved technical services and quality of the chosen database.

CONCLUSIONS: There are some substantive differences in the opinions of academic librarians using WLN and OCLC.

340. Diener, Richard A. V. (Ph.D., Rutgers University, 1984). **A Longitudinal Study of the Informational Dynamics of Journal Article Titles: A Treatise on the Science of Information.** 102p. Order no. DA8411558.

PURPOSE: In this exploratory investigation, Diener examined journal articles to determine if the information content of their titles had increased over time.

PROCEDURE: Diener reviewed thirty annual samples of journal article titles taken from four journals, noting the number of words, keywords, and relations in each title. Linear regression techniques were used to determine the patterns of change over time.

FINDINGS: Of the thirty-six regression analyses performed, thirteen yielded statistically significant results. However, while the number of words and keywords in each title has been increasing over the years, the rate of change has been negligible. Similarly, Diener found no discernible patterns in the number of relations per title over time.

CONCLUSIONS: Neither the quantity of information nor the amount of structure in titles (which aids meaning) has increased substantively over the years.

341. Dunn, Kathleen Elisabeth Kelpien (Ph.D., University of Southern California, 1984). **Psychological Needs and Source Linkages in Undergraduate Information-Seeking Behavior: A Factor Analytic and Multiple Correlation Study.** (Copies available exclusively from: Micrographics Department, Doheny Library, University of Southern California, Los Angeles, CA 90069).

PURPOSE: Because little research has been conducted to determine the underlying psychological variables that contribute to information-seeking behavior, Dunn investigated the internally perceived needs that motivate undergraduate students to seek needed information for their classes.

PROCEDURE: After collecting data from two sets of interviews, Dunn sent a pretested questionnaire to a stratified random sample of undergraduate students at Loma Linda University in Riverside, California. The responses were analyzed using factor analysis and canonical correlation analysis techniques.

FINDINGS: Six need categories were identified as motivators for information seeking: for success in a chosen profession, for self-approval, for self-extension, for a successful college experience, for other approval, and for intellectual stimulation. Five sources were found to satisfy those needs: personal materials, experts, libraries, family, and friends. Friends and family were chosen as sources of information by undergraduates with strong needs for other approval. Libraries and experts were used by undergraduates with strong needs for professional success and intellectual stimulation.

CONCLUSIONS: The variables identified in this study can contribute to our understanding of the psychology of information-seeking behavior.

342. Freedman, Janet (Ed.D., Boston University, 1984). **Empowering Librarians: A Study of the Women's Movement on the Careers, Work Modes, and Leadership Styles of Feminist Librarians.** 192p. Order no. DA8406745.

PURPOSE: Using feminist research methods, Freedman explored the career paths, work modes, and leadership styles of professional librarians who viewed themselves as feminists.

PROCEDURE: The design of the study was based on methods used by Oakley, Spender, Stanley, Wise, Blumer, and Denzin. Freedman interviewed twenty feminist librarians chosen from respondents to a questionnaire mailed to the members of two feminist librarians organizations. She used analytic induction to extract thematic material from the in-depth interviews.

FINDINGS: The interviewed librarians fit the typology of radical feminists. Feminism influenced not only their work but their lives outside of the workplace.

CONCLUSIONS: Feminist librarians have made substantive contributions to the creation of new styles of leadership and work modes within the profession.

343. Fuller, Sherrilynne Shirley (Ph.D., University of Southern California, 1984). **Schema Theory in the Representation and Analysis of Text.** (Copies available exclusively from: Micrographics Department, Doheny Library, University of Southern California, Los Angeles, CA 90069).

PURPOSE: In this dissertation, Fuller used the schema theory (that texts have an inherent structure which is used by individuals both to understand texts and to produce texts) to examine published reports of clinical trials. The study was conducted in an attempt to better understand how stored items can be indexed to facilitate later retrieval.

PROCEDURE: Fuller developed a trial schema, consisting of essential trial elements, by conducting a review of the literature. She searched the MEDLINE database to select a random sample of trial reports. These reports were stratified by disease category (e.g., respiratory, nervous system, digestive system, virus) and then submitted to chi-square analysis.

FINDINGS: In general, trial reports reflected clinical trials as envisioned by the experts (taken from the literature review). However, chi-square analysis revealed that this replication varied by disease classification.

CONCLUSIONS: Schema theory may provide a paradigm for indexing that permits the capture of both inter-document relations (i.e., data on groups of documents) and intra-document relations (i.e., holistic structure of the document).

344. Gregor, Margaret Anne Norville (Ed.D., University of Virginia, 1984). **The Provision of Learning Resources Center Services to Off-Campus Community College Students.** 365p. Order no. DA8424874.

PURPOSE: This dissertation assesses the role that five factors play in the provision of learning resources center (LRC) services to off-campus community college students: the institutional emphasis placed on the delivery of off-campus instruction, the LRC's role within the instructional decision-making process, the LRC budget appropriation, the LRC's organizational structure, and the provision of LRC services off campus.

PROCEDURE: Questionnaires were sent to LRC chief administrators at public two-year institutions belonging to the Southern Association in 1981 (63 percent response rate).

FINDINGS: According to the chief administrators, a relationship existed between the provision of LRC services off campus and the emphasis placed by the institution on the delivery of off-campus instruction. No relationship was found between the amount of the LRC budget and LRC's role in the instructional decision-making process or LRC's organizational structure.

345. Greiner, Joy Marilyn (Ph.D., Florida State University, 1984). **A Comparative Study of the Career Development Patterns of Male and Female Library Administrators in Large Public Libraries.** 245p. Order no. DA8503167.

PURPOSE: Greiner examined the relationship among three facets of career development (career progression, salary, and library support levels) and the following independent variables: professional experience, education, and personal and family characteristics.

PROCEDURE: Using the thirty-fifth edition of the *American Library Directory*, Greiner identified 420 public library agencies serving populations of 100,000 or more and sent questionnaires to their directors; 321 questionnaires were returned from the directors (76 percent response rate): 189 from males and 132 from females. The collected data were submitted to chi-square analysis.

FINDINGS: Male directors received higher salaries than women, regardless of their initial aspirations or number of career interruptions. Males also tended to work at libraries with higher support levels, that is, at libraries with larger operating budgets, more professional workers, and higher entry-level salaries for professionals. There did not appear to be a relationship between sex and size of the materials collections. Sex was also not a factor in the salaries received by single directors or by directors with master's degrees in both a subject area and librarianship. Male directors were more likely to have worked in a number of libraries at progressively more responsible positions while the female directors were more likely to have been promoted from within an institution.

346.   Hafter, Ruth Anne (Ph.D., University of California, Berkeley, 1984). **Computers in the Library: How Bibliographic Networks Affect the Organization, Quality, and Visibility of Professional Work.** 244p. Order no. DA8512841.

PURPOSE: The focus of this study is on the effects (both intended and unintended) of database creation on the organization, quality, visibility, and work of professional catalogers.

PROCEDURE: To collect data for this study, Hafter interviewed academic library catalogers, academic library administrators, and network quality control personnel.

FINDINGS: Hafter found that increased dependence on online bibliographic networks has resulted in increased deprofessionalization of cataloging work; that cataloging quality control policies have not yet been fully developed as "instruments for the social control of the work of catalogers" (to date, networks have used error rates and the identification of master catalogers to serve as mentors or network advisory committee members); that master catalogers receive enhanced status and assignments as a result of network membership; and that competing standards and definitions of quality control are being developed by catalogers, administrators, and network personnel (catalogers are favoring detailed and complex quality controls standards, administrators are supporting more flexible standards based on patron responses to online catalogs, and network personnel are taking a middle position.

347.   Harrington, Jan Lee (Ph.D., Drexel University, 1984). **The Effect of Error Messages on Learning Computer Programming by Individuals without Prior Programming Experience.** 188p. DA8408713.

PURPOSE: In this experimental study, Harrington examined the effect that various levels of error messages had on the ability of novices to learn how to do computer programming.

PROCEDURE: The thirty-nine naive programmers participating in the experiment first completed standardized tests for programmer aptitude and received a four-hour tutorial covering Applesoft BASIC. The subjects were then divided into three groups, with each group to receive increasingly more specific error messages in the experiment. The subjects participated in two experimental sessions, one involving debugging and the other original programming. Data were collected on number of errors, average number of attempts to correct errors, success on the task, and latency between the printing of an error and an attempt to correct it; the data were submitted to multivariate analysis of covariance.

FINDINGS: The expected relationship between task success and increasing specificity in error reporting did not materialize. Significant relationships were discovered, however, between aptitude and task success.

CONCLUSIONS: Aptitude is a more important factor in determining success at computer programming than is merely increasing the specificity of error message texts.

348.   Holton, Edwin Lee (Ph.D., Florida State University, 1984). **An Investigation of the Use, Cost, Perceived Value and Social Context of Telecommunications Tools in Two-Year College Libraries in the Southeastern United States.** 285p. Order no. DA8416707.

PURPOSE: In this descriptive study of the use, cost, perceived value, and social context of telecommunications tools in two-year colleges, Holton had a three-fold purpose: (1) to determine the use and cost of telecommunications tools, (2) to assess the perceived value of those tools, and (3) to envision the social context of the use/nonuse of those tools.

PROCEDURE: First, Holton sent a questionnaire to 269 two-year colleges in the southeast (77 percent response rate) to determine organizational patterns and to identify library managers. Next, he sent a questionnaire to 175 libraries (59 percent response rate) to determine their use and perceived value of telecommunications tools. Finally, he attempted to collect data from 48 libraries which had used five or more telecommunications tools (66 percent response rate). Using these data, Holton constructed a social model to describe the use of telecommunications tools.

FINDINGS: Only a few libraries in the southeast used telecommunications tools to any extent, primarily because such tools are expensive and budgets are limited. However, when telecommunications tools were employed, the usage was extensive (although generally by only a few students). Video technology was more commonly employed than computer technology. Librarians were generally positively inclined toward telecommunications tools, but they tended to perceive that price inhibited use. Approximately one-quarter of the surveyed librarians supported the application of user fees for telecommunications tools.

CONCLUSIONS: When Holton applied his social model, he concluded that the use of telecommunications tools will result in a major social, technical, and procedural change for librarians. This change, he suggests, will affect the distribution of knowledge and alter role expectations among information professionals. From his point of view, dialectical procedures will serve as a "useful choice for affecting stability in library related information roles."

349. Ivy, Barbara Anne (Ph.D., University of Pittsburgh, 1984). **Academic Library Administration: Power as a Factor in Hiring and Promotion within a Feminized Profession.** 120p. Order no. DA8421296.

PURPOSE: This study examined the following five factors to assess their importance in the hiring and promotion process within a feminized profession: characteristics of the candidate's current employer, the candidate's position, power in the candidate's current position, power available within the library profession, and power-consolidating behavior.

PROCEDURE: Ivy asked a national sample of library directors from academic institutions to evaluate the importance of various credentials that a candidate might present when applying for the position of library director at a similar institution.

FINDINGS: The variable viewed most important by the surveyed library directors was power within the current position, followed in ranked order by power within the profession, power-consolidating behavior, the candidate's background, and the candidate's current employer. Ivy found that the larger the institution, the more important power within the profession became in the hiring process; in fact, at institutions with more than ten thousand students, this variable was listed as the most important consideration.

CONCLUSIONS: Power was viewed as the most important factor in the hiring process for an academic library director. The importance placed on power correlated positively with the size of the hiring institution. Perhaps the reason there were fewer women library administrators at major academic institutions is because they placed less value on this variable.

350. Johnson, Lora Lee (Ph.D., Brown University, 1984). **The Hellenistic and Roman Library: Studies Pertaining to Their Architectural Form.** 298p. Order no. DA8422440.

PURPOSE: Unlike the earlier architectural studies of Callmer, Wendel, Tonsberg, Makowiecka, and Strocka, this dissertation provides a critical discussion of the architectural features of Hellenistic and Roman libraries, including steps, insulation corridors, podiums, and rectangular niches.

PROCEDURE: The study involves an examination of the features of buildings identified as libraries during Greek and Roman times: the Celsus Library at Ephesus, the Library of Pantainos at Athens, the Rogatinus Library at Timgad, the Library in the Forum at Philippi, the Hellenistic Library at Pergamon, the Serapeum Library at Alexandria, the Library at Nysa, the Library in the Ptolemeion at Athens, the Library of Hadrian at Athens, the Militine Library at Pergamon, the Palatine Library, the Library in the Portico of Octavia, the Library in the Templum Pacis, the Ulpian Library, the Library in the Baths of Trajan, and the Library in the Baths of Caracalla.

CONCLUSIONS: Johnson questioned the interpretation that steps, insulation corridors, podiums, or rectangular niches served a library function (i.e., provided protection for the books, storage space, or limited access).

351. Kania-Schicchi, Antoinette (Ed.D., Rutgers University, 1984). **The Development of a Model Set of Regional Accreditation Standards for Academic Libraries.** 248p. Order no. DA8424049.

PURPOSE: The purpose of this dissertation was to develop a model set of regional accreditation standards for academic libraries that would contain (1) quantitative performance measures for local use and (2) qualitative standards for self-evaluation.

PROCEDURE: First, Kania-Schicchi used content analysis to identify a core of library standards (taken from the standards of seven regional accreditation commissions of higher education in 1982). Next, she asked sixty-five library and accreditation leaders to review the core of standards and indicate their perception of the level of adherence that should be required for each of the standards. After a second draft instrument reflecting the reformatted standards was submitted to the sixty-five leaders, Kania-Schicchi sent a third instrument (which included corresponding performance standards) to sixteen experts for their review.

FINDINGS: The regional accreditation commissions of higher education agreed on only half of the major topics mentioned in their standards, included less than half of the fifty-seven subtopics in any one of the commission's standards, and generally omitted output measures from either the topics or subtopics covered in the standards. Only one-third of the standards were viewed as "musts" by the sixty-five library and accreditation leaders who looked at the first instrument, but they increased the output orientation of the instrument to 18 percent. In the second instrument (which became the model set), the relative output orientation was increased to 25 percent and the overall acceptability was rated at better than 90 percent. The third research instrument yielded twenty-four performance measures that the experts assessed as applicable and reasonably practical to replicate.

CONCLUSIONS: As a result of this process, Kania-Schicchi developed a new set of library standards that incorporated performance measures.

352. Kerby, Ramona Nolen (Ph.D., Texas Woman's University, 1984). **The Effects of Library Skill Instruction on the Academic Achievement, Knowledge of Library Skills, and Attitudes toward Reading of Sixth Grade Students.** 113p. DA8502654.

PURPOSE: To assess the effect of bibliographic instruction on elementary school students, Kerby compared the attitudes toward reading, academic achievement, and knowledge of library skills of two groups of sixth grade students: those who did not participate in a library instruction program and those who did participate.

PROCEDURE: In the randomized control-group posttest only design used in this study, the experimental group consisted of 410 sixth grade students from five elementary schools with library instruction programs and the control group consisted of 330 sixth grade students from five elementary schools without library instruction programs. To measure the participants' attitudes toward reading, academic achievement, and knowledge of library skills, Kerby used the Estes Reading Attitude Scale, the California Achievement Tests (CAT), and the Ohio School Library/Media Test respectively. A three-factor analysis of variance was used to measure the data collected.

FINDINGS: The mean scores of the control and experimental groups were not significantly different in the areas of academic achievement, knowledge of library skills, or attitudes toward reading.

353. Lin, James Jihming (Ph.D., Southern Illinois University at Carbondale, 1984). **Acquisition Programs in Selected Community College Learning Resource Centers in the United States.** 132p. Order no. DA8425131.

PURPOSE: Concerned with the processes used to build collections of print and nonprint materials in community college learning resource centers (LRCs), Lin focused on the following four questions in his doctoral dissertation: (1) How are acquisitions policy statements formulated? (2) How are available funds allocated? (3) How are the various selection methods applied? (4) How are the various order procedures handled?

PROCEDURE: A four-section questionnaire was sent to 531 community college LRCs in the United States. The data collected were analyzed using percentage and frequency distributions.

FINDINGS: Most LRCs did not have a written acquisitions policy. LRC/library administrators had the primary responsibility for the allocation of the materials budget. Balance and pragmatism were reflected in the distribution of the materials budget. While faculty, LRC/library administrators, and LRC/library professional staff shared responsibility for book and journal selection, Lin discovered that the smaller the college, the greater the role of faculty in selecting these materials. Whatever the size of the library, faculty had primary responsibility for the selection of audiovisual materials. After reviewing the data submitted, Lin found it difficult to determine the relationship of the materials budget to the colleges' total budget.

354. Lowe, Joy Lambert (Ph.D., North Texas State University, 1984). **A Comparative Analysis of Reading Habits and Abilities of Students in Selected Elementary Schools in North Louisiana with and without Centralized Libraries.** 174p. Order no. DA8423876.

PURPOSE: The issue considered in this dissertation was whether or not the provision of centralized school library services related to elementary school children's reading abilities and habits.

PROCEDURE: Data were collected from three sources: (1) the reading records of 763 students in third through fifth grade classrooms in four Lincoln Parish (Louisiana) elementary schools, (2) the reading achievement test scores of those students, as measured by the Science Research Associates standardized test in the areas of comprehension, vocabulary, and overall reading ability, and (3) questionnaires sent to the surveyed students and their parents and teachers. Two of the schools in the study had centralized libraries and two did not.

FINDINGS: Students read more books (both for school work and for general information) and more students liked to read for recreation in schools with centralized libraries than in schools without centralized libraries. However, no relationship was found between the students' overall reading abilities and the provision of centralized school library services.

RECOMMENDATIONS: When further studies are conducted, longitudinal and cross-sectional designs should be used with other subjects and in other settings, and additional control variables should be introduced, including professional qualifications of library staff and accreditation status of schools.

355. Mason, Florence Margaret (Ph.D., University of Southern California, 1984). **The Emergent Information Manager: A Structured Observation Study of the Nature of the Information Manager's World.** (Copies available exclusively from: Micrographics Department, Doheny Library, University of Southern California, Los Angeles, CA 90069).
PURPOSE: The purpose of this study was to assess the work activities and work patterns of information managers (IMs) in the public and private sectors.

PROCEDURE: Mason used a structured observation methodology in this study to assess the work performance of five information managers employed in one government agency and four private companies. The data collected were analyzed using both qualitative and quantitative techniques.

FINDINGS: The work activities of IMs fall into five roles; in ranked order these are: General Manager, Information Manager, Strategist, Information Handler, and Professional. IMs' activity patterns resemble general managers' work patterns.

CONCLUSIONS: While IM positions used to be characterized as expert jobs (limited responsibilities and specialized work), they are increasingly becoming managerial jobs (broader responsibilities and less specialized work).

356. Morris, Betty J. (Ph.D., University of Alabama, 1984). **Student Assistants in Academic Libraries: A Study of Training Practices.** 201p. Order no. DA8513570.
PURPOSE: In studying the training of student assistants in libraries, Morris focused on two aspects: (1) the materials and methods most commonly used to train student assistants and (2) library administrators' perceptions of the effectiveness of these materials and methods.

PROCEDURE: Questionnaires were sent to 159 randomly selected academic library directors throughout the United States (114 responses).

FINDINGS: Morris identified fifteen tasks routinely performed by student assistants. In general, these tasks occurred most frequently in the acquisitions, reference, and audiovisual departments. Student assistants were beginning to conduct literature searches (previously viewed as a professional task). There was a larger number of effective methods and materials used in training student assistants than expected. Demonstrations proved more effective than orientations. Both tapes and computers were underutilized as training methods.

RECOMMENDATIONS: The recommendations offered by Morris at the conclusion of her study included the following: The total library training program should be evaluated in academic libraries, not just the program for student assistants; in evaluating the student assistant training program, input should be solicited from the student employees; librarians should study the possibility of expanding the range of tasks assigned to student assistants; graduate library administration courses should cover the problems of training and supervising student assistants; and more use should be made of computers and tapes in the training of student assistants.

357. Mudge, Charlotte Regula (Ph.D., University of Toronto, 1984). **Bargaining Unit Composition and Negotiation Outcomes: A Study of Academic and Public Library Personnel in Ontario.**
PURPOSE: This dissertation attempts to determine if the type of collective bargaining unit—homogeneous or heterogeneous—affects what the group achieved (as theorized by Archie Kleingartner).

PROCEDURE: The bargaining units representing academic and public library personnel in Ontario were divided into three groups (librarians only; support staff only; and mixed) and then collapsed into homogeneous and heterogeneous units. Questionnaires were sent to each bargaining unit. Mudge analyzed the content of each unit's first and latest collective agreement, to determine the working conditions first experienced and those later achieved.

FINDINGS: Mudge found that the following variables related to the bargaining unit's success in obtaining professional-type working conditions: type of library (academic libraries were more successful than public libraries), age distribution of bargaqining unit members, size of unit, number of librarians who were union officers, and specific union involved.

CONCLUSIONS: As Kleingartner had predicted, the type of collective bargaining unit affected the goals achieved. Homogeneous units were more successful in acquiring professional-type working conditions than heterogeneous units. However, heterogeneous units do have some advantages for librarians: they place librarians in a larger bargaining unit and they may promote more harmonious working relationships with support staff.

358.   Mullins, James Lee (Ph.D., Indiana University, 1984). **A Study of Selected Factors Affecting Growth Rates in American Law School Libraries, 1932-1976.** 100p. Order no. DA8424874.

PURPOSE: This is the first quantitative research study to examine the organizational factors that affected the growth rate of American law school libraries between 1932 and 1976.

PROCEDURE: Mullins reviewed all the quantitative data available on the seventy-five law libraries approved by the American Bar Association that were members of the Association of American Law Schools in 1932 and were still in existence in 1976.

FINDINGS: No significant difference was found between the growth rate of law libraries that were autonomous (administered as part of the law school) and those that were integrated (administered as part of the university library system). Similarly, no significant difference was found between publicly and privately supported institutions or between university and law library growth rates. However, growth rate did significantly relate to the influence of the dean, law librarian, and director of university libraries. Because there were not enough data, no conclusion could be drawn about the roles of new buildings or government depository designations.

359.   Namlah, Ali Ibrahim (Ph.D., Case Western Reserve, 1984). **Infrastructure of Information Needs and Resources in the Country of Saudi Arabia: An Assessment.** 293p. Order no. DA8425571.

PURPOSE: In an attempt to provide a framework for the formulation of a national information policy for Saudi Arabia, Namlah examined the information situation and its relationship to other development sectors in that country.

PROCEDURE: Using a modification of the Index of Information Utilization Potential, which is based on 230 variables placed in twenty-one structural and seventeen functional groupings, Namlah chose 171 variables to match the corresponding variables employed in the technique. In addition, eleven previously studied cases, relating to other countries, were included in the study. The data were analyzed using linear regression and factor analysis techniques.

FINDINGS: Saudi Arabia, well equipped in the background conditions, was found to be lacking in the information needs, uses, activities, and services.

CONCLUSIONS: Based on the strength of the potential users, Namlah concluded that Saudi Arabia's infrastructure of information needs and resources can move in a positive direction, provided that the other components in the infrastructure (e.g., information policies) can be met. Namlah stressed the need for the country to further redefine, reorganize, and restructure the information infrastructure componets, including the information technologies, information users and uses, and information institutions.

360.   Nichol, William Thomas, II (Ph.D., University of Minnesota, 1984). **Catholic Subject Headings: Investigation of Use in Catholic College and University Libraries and Comparison to Library of Congress Subject Headings.** 305p. Order no. DA8413809.

PURPOSE: This study represents the first attempt to critically examine *Catholic Subject Headings* (*CSH*) since its publication in 1942.

PROCEDURE: Nichol sent questionnaires to all Catholic college and university libraries; 191 librarians responded (81 percent response rate).

FINDINGS: Of the 191 respondents, half (96 librarians) had never used *CSH*, 37 were currently using the list; and 85 formerly had used the list. Almost all (95 percent) of the *CSH* users also used *Library of Congress Subject Headings*. When Nichol examined the two subject headings lists, he found that 59 percent of the 3,010 headings in the fifth edition of *CSH* were basically identical to the headings in the ninth edition of *LCSH*. Of the 1,212 headings unique to *CSH*, the variations were based on form, specificity, terminology, or proper nouns covered. Over the last thirty years, there has been a steady decline in the use of *CSH*, primarily because of the acceptance of *LCSH*, the use of OCLC, the problems inherent in trying to use two lists, and the interest in simplifying cataloging procedures.

CONCLUSIONS: The *CSH* thesaurus should be restructured to minimize variations from *LCSH*.

361.   Olaisen, Johan Leif (Ph.D., University of California, Berkeley, 1984). **Toward a Theory of Information Seeking Behavior among**

Scientists and Scholars. 356p. Order no. DA 8512944.

PURPOSE: The focus of this dissertation is on the information-seeking behavior of scientists and scholars, particularly in a decentralized Norwegian college system.

PROCEDURE: Olaisen sent questionnaires to all faculty members of a decentralized Norwegian college system that was established in the 1970s (84 percent response rate), held interviews, conducted field research (participation and observation), and reviewed the research literature to collect data for this study.

FINDINGS: Important sources of information for the surveyed faculty included journals, bookstores, personal recommendations, and personal informal contacts during a research project. Of little importance to the respondents were bibliographic tools, library catalogs, and the library staff. Few of the faculty ever visited other academic libraries, although more of them went to public libraries. A wide variation in the importance of conferences was reported. A relatively small proportion of the faculty (11 percent) were responsible for the largest number of publications (three or more works each in 1980-1981).

362.   Olsgaard, John Newman (Ph.D., University of Illinois at Urbana-Champaign, 1984). **The Relationship between Administrative Style and the Use of Computer-Based Systems: An Attitudinal Study of Academic Library Professionals.** 230p. Order no. DA8409822.

PURPOSE: Using survey research techniques, Olsgaard investigated academic library professionals' attitudes on (1) the level of participative management used by immediate supervisors and (2) computer-based systems.

PROCEDURE: Questionnaires were sent to two groups: a 100 percent sample of academic librarians working in thirteen libraries in the midwest (70 percent response rate) and a stratified random sample of personal members of American Library Association's Association of College and Research Libraries (70 percent response rate).

FINDINGS: Olsgaard found statistically significant nonlinear relationships among the variables studied.

CONCLUSIONS: Based on the relationships discovered, Olsgaard constructed and tested a model to explain variations in academic librarians' attitudes toward computer-based systems. The model developed explained over 80 percent of the variance.

363.   Ostendorf, Paul John (Ph.D., University of Minnesota, 1984). **The History of the Public Library Movement in Minnesota from 1849 to 1916.** 599p. Order no. DA8413812.

PURPOSE: In this historical study, Ostendorf examined the public library movement in the United States, focusing on its protean character, particularly in Minnesota.

PROCEDURE: To collect data for this study, the author examined all available primary documents, reviewed relevant secondary sources, and visited forty-six communities in the state.

FINDINGS: From the beginning, Minnesota libraries supported the twin goals of education and social service. Although a law was passed in 1879 that permitted the support of libraries by taxpayers, growth in the state was slow. By 1900, only thirty communities had established public libraries. Between 1899 and 1908, the number of libraries in the state increased substantially, due primarily to the efforts of Clara Baldwin, Gratia A. Countryman, and the Minnesota Federation of Women's Clubs. Also affecting this growth period were the Carnegie grants, the right of women to vote on library issues, the creation of a traveling library system, and the establishment of the Minnesota Library Commission (which was responsible for regional/state cooperation, national prestige, professional library training, increased taxation for libraries, and an official journal). Not all the developments during this period were positive; there were also numerous ill-advised laws and inadequately financed facilities.

CONCLUSIONS: The development of public libraries in Minnesota paralleled the growth of libraries in other parts of the country. Among the important stimuli for library growth in the state were the arrival of educated immigrants (mainly Germans and Scandinavians), the educational leadership of women, the Carnegie grants (although some facilities were inadequately financed), and the sense of socialization, service, and altruism that characterized library development throughout the United States.

364.   Phelan, Jo Ann Keach (Ph.D., Texas Woman's University, 1984). **A Study of the Utilization of Fees for Services in Tax-Supported Medium-sized Public Libraries in the United States.** 191p. Order no. DA8509234.

PURPOSE: This study focuses on medium-sized public libraries and attempts to identify and evaluate selected characteristics of those libraries charging fees for services (e.g., community size and location, library budget size, collection size, librarians' philosophy of user fees, patrons' reactions to fees, relationship between user fee and library use).

PROCEDURE: Phelan collected data from more than 200 librarians working in medium-sized public libraries throughout the nation. These data were analyzed by using such statistical measures as frequency and percentage distributions, Pearson product moment correlation, chi-square, and analysis of variance. For the purposes of this study, "medium-sized public library" was defined as a library serving communities of 50,000 to 200,000 population and "user fee" was defined as a "non-refundable patron-specific charge for a service." Fines for overdue materials and charges for damaged or lost materials were specifically excluded from the study.

FINDINGS: Phelan found that most of the respondents charged fees for at least one service, had increased fees since 1975, felt that fees were inappropriate but often necessary, collected cost data to determine the amount of a specific fee, charged the highest fee for auditorium/meeting room rental, and believed that overhead, materials, and new technology costs had the greatest impact on increased fees.

365. Sibai, Mohamed Makki (Ph.D., Indiana University, 1984). **An Historical Investigation of Mosque Libraries in Islamic Life and Culture.** 447p. Order no. DA8417184.

PURPOSE: This study represents the first historical account (in either English or Arabic) of the mosque libraries and their close connection to Muslim scholarship.

PROCEDURE: The author utilized archival material and secondary sources in researching this study.

FINDINGS: Mosques were the first places where books were found in Muslim society. It was a Muslim custom to bequeath copies of the Quran to favorite mosques. Furthermore, there was widespread acceptance and active utilization of the mosque as a principal place of learning. A number of the mosque collections eventually grew into libraries. Those libraries had a more diverse and dynamic life than has been recognized previously. They were not merely reading rooms or storehouses but working libraries that reached high stages of development and social prominence.

366. Stam, Deirdre Corcoran (D.L.S., Columbia University, 1984). **The Information-Seeking Practices of Art Historians in Museums and Colleges in the United States, 1982-1983.** 254p. Order no. DA8427477.

PURPOSE: This dissertation deals with the information-seeking behavior of art historians

working in museums or colleges in the United States.

PROCEDURE: Stam used questionnaires and interviews to collect the data for this study.

FINDINGS: The information-seeking behavior of the surveyed art historians varied with both location and the nature of the employing institution. Respondents in New York City made much higher use of informal channels of communication than did respondents outside the city. Similarly, art historians in museums made higher use of informal channels than did those on college faculties. Whatever the kind of institution or location, respondents indicated they had only weak ties to "invisible colleges." Instead, their "gatekeepers" tended to be directors in their museums or colleagues and deans in their academic institutions. Art historians relied more on slides and personal collections than on any film medium or computer program (except for the use of RLIN and OCLC in non-New York City colleges). When pursuing authoritative information, they most frequently began with colleagues and experts, then consulted footnotes and bibliographies in familiar monographs and, as a last step, turned to bibliographic tools and librarians. Librarians were viewed more as "gatekeepers" than as members of the "invisible college" and were more accepted as colleagues by art historians in museums than those in colleges.

367. Struminger, Leny (Ph.D., Rutgers University, 1984). **Methodology for Evaluating Related Databases and a Computerized Algorithm for Merging Their Output.** 128p. Order no. DA 8424163.

PURPOSE: Struminger pursued a dual purpose in this dissertation: (1) to develop a methodology for evaluating related bibliographic databases and (2) to develop a programmable computer algorithm to identify duplicate citations among related databases.

PROCEDURE: Using a sample of 331 articles (from twenty-two randomly selected medical journals) indexed in both the EXCERPTA MEDICA database and MEDLINE, Struminger analyzed the file content and record content of each of these two databases.

FINDINGS: The author field after editing was found to be in agreement in 97 percent of the cases and the pagination field was found to be correct and in agreement in 99 percent of the cases.

CONCLUSIONS: Struminger developed a computer algorithm to identify duplicate citations among related databases that can be used to analyze other computerized databases. The resulting programs can be used to edit the output from cross-database searching to provide the user with a more practical bibliography.

RECOMMENDATIONS: Based on the patterns observed in the treatment of authors, titles, volume, issue, pagination, abstracts, and journal, Struminger made recommendations for record standardization.

368. Todaro, Julie Beth (D.L.S., Columbia University, 1984). **Competencies of Children's Librarians: An Attitudinal Assessment.** 337p. Order no. DA8511561.

PURPOSE: This study was conducted to determine the competencies of children's librarians as measured by selected professionals who have knowledge about and interest in children's librarianship.

PROCEDURE: An attitudinal survey (based on forty-five competencies selected from the literature from 1960 through mid-1981) was given to selected children's librarians, public library directors, personnel officers, library school deans, library educators, and state library children's consultants working either in library systems that serve populations of at least 100,000 or in ALA-accredited library schools. The attitudes measured involved three types of competencies (skills/abilities, knowledge, and attitudes) and seven subject area clusters (administrative, materials, programmatic, audience/child, community, institutional, and professional). A five-point Likert scale was used to measure the participants' attitudes and nonparametric regressional analysis (Multiple Classification Analysis Regression) was employed to analyze the data.

FINDINGS: Todaro examined several factors (including the attitudes of public library directors toward administrative competencies and the attitudes of children's librarians and library educators toward types of competencies); analyzed the relationship between demographic/personal variables (such as age) and attitudes toward competency; and compiled lists of expected competencies, subject area clusters, and competency types for children's librarians.

369. Welmaker, Roland Bernard (Ph.D., University of Michigan, 1984). **The Relationships of Perceived Management Systems and Job Satisfaction of Public Librarians.** 149p. Order no. DA8502950.

PURPOSE: In this dissertation, Welmaker examined various relationships that might exist between job satisfaction and prevailing man-

agement systems in public library settings.

PROCEDURE: Questionnaires measuring job satisfaction (using the "Job Descriptive Index" developed by Smith, Hulin, and Kindall) and identifying managerial systems (using a short form of Likert's "Profile of Organizational Characteristics") were sent to librarians working in nine large public libraries located in southeastern states.

FINDINGS: A positive relationship was found between the extent of job satisfaction and perceived managerial systems. Librarians in systems viewed as less participative experienced significantly less job satisfaction than librarians in settings viewed as participative. Similarly, librarians in lower-level positions were significantly less satisfied with their salaries and assignments than librarians in higher-level positions. No relationship was found, however, between level of position and satisfaction with promotions, colleagues, or supervision. Likewise, no relationship was found between levels of job satisfaction and age, sex, or education. Tenure and governance were found to correlate: librarians with more tenure perceived their management systems as significantly more participative in the areas of communications, leadership, and motivation than did librarians with less tenure. Paralleling this, librarians with more work experience perceived goal setting, decision making, and control as more participative than did librarians with less work experience.

370. White, Cecil R. (Ph.D., North Texas State University, 1984). **The Extensive Subject File: A Study of User Expectations in a Theological Library.** 104p. Order no. DA 8423908.

PURPOSE: The purpose of this study is three-fold: (1) to assess the problem of long subject files in theological library catalogs, (2) to identify the most important elements on the catalog card for selecting materials from the subject files, and (3) to establish a process for converting these elements into access points in a computerized catalog system.

PROCEDURE: The Graduate Theological Union Library in Berkeley, California, was the setting for this study. White first identified subject headings with long files in the card catalog there and then interviewed library patrons.

FINDINGS: The majority of users interviewed (80 percent) reported they used at least all of the information from the main body of the card to select entries from the file. Prior to the interviews, it was anticipated that the objective elements used to select records from the file would rank: complete title, language of the title, publication data. The interviews revealed that the actual ranking was: complete title, publication data, and language of the title. It was further anticipated, prior to the interviews, that the useful subjective elements would rank: author recognition, publisher's reputation, patron's previous knowledge of the work, and recognition of items in the tracings. Instead, the interviewees reported the following order: author recognition, previous knowledge of the work, publisher's reputation, and patron's recognition of items in the tracings.

CONCLUSIONS: The objective and subjective elements that patrons used most frequently should be built into a pattern of search keys for accessing subject entries in a computerized catalog system.

371. White, G. Travis (Ph.D., University of Denver, 1984). **Factors Associated with Successful Adaptation to Environmental Change in College and University Libraries.** 482p. Order no. DA8429974.

PURPOSE: The purpose of this study was to identify factors associated with successful adaptation to environmental change in academic libraries.

PROCEDURE: A qualitative method of analysis (open-ended questionnaires and interview schedules) was used in this study. Data were collected from librarians working in twelve libraries perceived as having been successful in adapting to environmental change (Group I) and in twelve libraries perceived as having been unsuccessful (Group II) between 1971 and 1981.

FINDINGS: Several factors emerged as characterizing libraries that had successfully adapted to environmental change; these included large budgets, perceived strong leadership, more automation, less centralized organization, strong support from campus leaders, and an institutional environment that was conducive to change. Of all the factors considered, leadership appeared to be one of the most important (72 percent of Group I respondents identified leadership as a key factor compared to 16 percent for Group II respondents). Group I respondents described leaders as being aggressive, risk-oriented, charismatic, and basically democratic in management style. The factors most commonly associated with unsuccessful adaptation in the study included: library staff resistance, unforeseen delays, inadequate communication, and inadequate planning.

372. Williams, Lauren Sapp (Ph.D., Florida State University, 1984). **The Service Orientation of Government Documents Librarians in Academic Libraries of the Southeastern United States.** 184p. Order no. DA8501844.

PURPOSE: For the purposes of this dissertation, the service orientation of government documents librarians in academic libraries was measured on four scales: actual, ideal, user, and resource.

PROCEDURE: Williams sent questionnaires to 298 documents librarians at 151 academic federal depository libraries in the southeast (76 percent response rate). The data collected were analyzed using factor analysis, mean scores, percentages, Pearson product moment correlation, and t-test.

FINDINGS: Williams found that the user scale correlated with educational background, size of collection, bibliographic access, percent of FTE time spent working with government documents, percent of FTE, classification scheme, publicity, and circulation policy; the ideal scale correlated with sex, educational background, professional activities, prior occupational activities, size of collection, percentage of FTE time spent working with government documents, classification scheme used, and publicity; the actual scale correlated with age, educational background, size of collection, bibliographic access, percent of FTE time spent working with government documents, and percentage of FTE; the resource scale correlated with bibliographic access, classification scheme used, and circulation policy. More personal and environmental characteristics correlated with the user service orientation scale than any of the other three scales.

CONCLUSIONS: The user's delivery system was more interesting to documents librarians than the resource base of service. Government documents librarians have a positive perception of service.

373. Wittig, Glenn Russell (Ph.D., University of Michigan, 1984). **Bibliographic Control in Selected Abstracting and Indexing Services for Religion: A Comparative Analysis.** 419p. Order no. DA8502958.

PURPOSE: The purposes of this study were (1) to compare selected indexing and abstracting services covering the serial literature of religion and (2) to evaluate these services (singly and as a group) on the basis of scope of the service, structure of the subjects, and demographic factors.

PROCEDURE: First, twelve subject literatures, six sub-discipline literatures, and the literature as a whole were analyzed bibliometrically to determine structural characteristics. Using 1976 as the base year, bibliographies were compiled for each literature from a population of 9,798 source documents. The serial titles identified in this process were rank ordered and divided into three productivity zones; these were then compared against the title lists supplied by each of nine general and special abstracting and indexing services for religion.

FINDINGS: The amount of material covered by the abstracting and indexing services differed by demographic factors but not by structure of the subjects or intended scope of the service. In general, the coverage of the literature provided by any one of the secondary services was poor. Control over the literature improved when several services were used in combination but still was deficient. Of the services studied, *Bulletin Signalétique 527* and *Index to Religious Periodical Literature* (now *Religion Index One*) provided the most comprehensive coverage.

374. Woelfl, Nancy Newman (Ph.D., Case Western Reserve University, 1984). **Individual Differences in Online Search Behavior: The Effect of Learning Styles and Cognitive Abilities on Process and Outcome.** 180p. Order no. DA8503614.

PURPOSE: This experimental study was conducted to determine if cognitive ability affected online search behavior.

PROCEDURE: Woelfl studied the conduct and outcome of 176 MEDLINE searches performed by forty-four subjects working on the same four questions. She collected data on two measures of search results (precision and recall) and five measures of searching (descriptors keyed, commands used, cycles completed, references printed, and connect time). These measures were correlated with eight variables derived from the following three tests of human cognition: Symbolic Reasoning Test, Learning Style Inventory, and Remote Associates Test.

FINDINGS: Woelfl found an indirect effect between search outcome and two facets of learning modes: reflection and action. Highly reflective searchers tended to conduct extended searches and print numerous references; highly active searchers, on the other hand, tended to conduct brief searches. She found a direct effect only between search behavior/search results and deductive ability. Searchers who scored high on the Symbolic Reasoning Test tended to use less connect time, fewer commands, fewer descriptors, and more focused strategies than searchers who did not score as well. Subjects who described themselves as concrete in learning style used multicycle strategies to complete their searches while subjects who described themselves as abstract completed their searches in one (very integrated) cycle. Subjects describing themselves as active invested less effort in their searches than subjects who described themselves as reflective.

CONCLUSIONS: Some variability in searching behavior results from cognitive differences among online bibliographic searchers.

375. Wright, Arthuree Rosemille McLaughlin (Ph.D., University of Maryland, 1984). **Access to Publication Channels in Urban Education: An Assessment of Authorship and Citation Patterns.** 268p. Order no. DA8510473.

PURPOSE: In this exploratory study, Wright investigated the relationship between race and journal publication in the area of urban education. Specifically examined were the methods chosen by authors, the journals chosen by authors, and the patterns of citation among journals.

PROCEDURE: Using the 1969, 1974, and 1979 volumes of *Current Index to Journals in Education* as a base, Wright selected a sample of 178 articles from thirty journals that had published three or more articles on urban education. Qualitative content analysis was used to identify author-related variables (e.g., race, gender, workplace), article-related variables (e.g., primary topic, funding source, citations received, type of article, philosophical position), and journal-related variables (e.g., coverage in abstracting and indexing tools, subject classification, type of publisher).

FINDINGS: More articles in the sample studied were authored by whites (68 percent) than either blacks (24 percent) or biracial teams (8 percent). Articles by whites tended to be published in commonly indexed journals while articles by blacks tended to be in less-accessible journals. However, white authors were no more likely to be cited than black authors. Articles employing a concept deficit or cultural difference framework and articles addressing psychological processes were cited most often, regardless of the race of the author. Articles advocating system transformation were least likely to be cited.

CONCLUSIONS: An author's race had some relationship to the type of journal in which the articles were published, the type of article written, and the position espoused.

376. Yother, Larry Wayne (Ph.D., University of Connecticut, 1984). **A Study of the Extent of Automation in Small College Libraries and the Relationships of Attitudes of Library Directors toward It.** 147p. Order no. DA841082.

PURPOSE: This study was conducted to examine three areas: the extent of automation present in small college libraries (those with fewer than 100,000 volumes); small college library directors' attitudes toward automation; and the relationship between these attitudes and the extent of automation in small college libraries.

PROCEDURE: Data were collected from a national random sample of 175 college libraries with fewer than 100,000 volumes and submitted to analysis of variance and stepwise multiple regression analysis.

FINDINGS: Most directors of small academic libraries reacted favorably to the idea of automation. Their attitudes did not relate to a background in automation for either the director or a staff member. Size of collection proved to be a predictor of the extent of automation. Public college libraries were not more likely to have automated operations than private college libraries. Similarly, the presence of grant money did not seem to relate to the extent of automation (or the directors' attitudes toward automation). Library directors were not concerned about or particularly knowledgeable about computer software packages.

377. Yucht, Donald (Ed.D., New York University, 1984). **Development of a Handbook to Assist in the Evaluation of Library Services and Collections of Colleges and Universities Granting Graduate Degrees in Professional Industrial Education.** 254p. Order no. DA8505460.

PURPOSE: In this dissertation, Yucht developed the first handbook to assist faculty, staff, and members of accreditation teams who will be involved in evaluating the library services and collections of academic institutions offering graduate degrees in industrial education.

PROCEDURE: Yucht developed the handbook in three phases. In the first phase, he identified the criteria most often cited that related to library evaluation and compiled a bibliography based on repeated citations of commonly available materials. During the second phase, he attempted to validate the suggested criteria and bibliography by consulting with panels of experts. Drawing on their responses, Yucht drafted the handbook, which he submitted to another panel of experts. Their responses were incorporated into the draft and the final handbook was prepared in the third phase.

CONCLUSIONS: The completed handbook is designed to assist faculty, staff, and members of accrediting teams who are involved in evaluating library services and collections.

Author/Title Index

Unless otherwise indicated, reference is to entry number. References to authors or titles mentioned only in an annotation are identified by an *n* following the entry number (e.g., 102n). References to page number are identified by a *p* (e.g., p. 4).

Initial articles have been deleted from all titles.

Subject Index

Unless otherwise indicated, reference is to entry number. References to page number are identified by a *p* (e.g., p.4).

Initial articles have been deleted from all English titles.